The Rule of Reason
The Philosophy of Charles Sanders Peirce

Charles Sanders Peirce (1839–1914), the founder of Pragmatism, was an American philosopher, logician, physicist, and mathematician. Since the publication of his *Collected Papers* began in 1931, interest in Peirce has grown dramatically. His work has found audiences in such disciplines as philosophy, computer science, logic, film studies, semiotics, and literary criticism. While Peirce scholarship has advanced considerably since its earliest days, many controversies of interpretation persist, and several of the more obscure aspects of his work remain poorly understood.

The Rule of Reason is a collection of original essays examining Peirce's thought by some of the best-known scholars in the field. The contributors investigate outstanding issues and difficulties in his philosophy and situate his views in both their historical and their contemporary contexts. Some of the essays clarify aspects of Peirce's philosophy, some defend its contemporary significance, and some do both. The essays explore Peirce's work from various perspectives, considering the philosophical significance of his contributions to logic; the foundations of his philosophical system; his metaphysics and cosmology; his theories of inquiry and truth; and his theories of mind, agency, and selfhood.

JACQUELINE BRUNNING is an associate professor in the Department of Philosophy at the University of Toronto. PAUL FORSTER is an assistant professor in the Department of Philosophy at the University of Ottawa.

The Rule of Reason

The Philosophy of Charles Sanders Peirce

EDITED BY

Jacqueline Brunning
and Paul Forster

UNIVERSITY OF TORONTO PRESS
Toronto Buffalo London

© University of Toronto Press Incorporated 1997
Toronto Buffalo London
Printed in Canada

ISBN 0-8020-0829-1 (cloth)
ISBN 0-8020-7819-2 (paper)

Printed on acid-free paper

Toronto Studies in Philosophy
Editors: James R. Brown and Calvin Normore

Canadian Cataloguing in Publication Data

Main entry under title:

The rule of reason

(Toronto studies in philosophy)
ISBN 0-8020-0829-1 (bound)
ISBN 0-8020-7819-2 (pbk.)

1. Peirce, Charles S. (Charles Sanders), 1839–
1914 – Criticism and interpretation.   I. Brunning,
Jacqueline, 1934–   .   II. Forster, Paul, 1957–   .
III. Series.

B945.P44R85 1997   191   C96-931389-6

University of Toronto Press acknowledges the financial assistance to its
publishing program of the Canada Council and the Ontario Arts Council.

In memory of David Savan
(1916–1992)

Contents

viii   Contents

Abbreviations

The following abbreviations are used throughout this volume for citations from the various editions of Peirce's works.

(1.343, 1903)

References of this form cite passages in *The Collected Papers of Charles Sanders Peirce*, vols 1–6 edited by Charles Hartshorne and Paul Weiss (1931–5); vols 7–8 edited by Arthur Burks (1958) (Cambridge, Mass.: Belknap Press of Harvard University Press). They show the volume number, the paragraph number, and, in some cases, the year in which the passage was written. The example provided refers to volume 1, paragraph 343, written in 1903.

(W2:303, 1869)

References of this form cite passages in the chronological edition of the *Writings of Charles S. Peirce*, edited by M.H. Fisch, E.C. Moore, and C.J.W. Kloesel et al., 5 vols (Bloomington: Indiana University Press 1982–93). They indicate the volume number, the page number, and, in some cases, the year in which the passage was written. The example provided refers to volume 2, page 303, written in 1869.

(NEM3:124, 1879)

References of this form cite passages from *The New Elements of Mathematics by Charles S. Peirce*, edited by Carolyn Eisele, 4 vols (The Hague: Mouton Publishers 1976). They indicate the volume number, the page number, and, in some cases, the year in which the passage was written. The example provided refers to volume 3, page 124, written in 1879.

(HS1:34, 1856)

References of this form cite passages from *Historical Perspectives on Peirce's Logic of Science: A History of Science*, 2 vols, edited by Carolyn Eisele (Berlin: Mouton-DeGruyter 1985). They indicate the volume number, the page number, and the year in which the passage was written. The example provided refers to volume 1, page 34, written in 1856.

(RLT 123)

References of this form are to *Reasoning and the Logic of Things*, edited by Kenneth L. Ketner (Cambridge, Mass.: Harvard University Press 1992). They indicate the page number. The lectures in this volume were all written in 1898.

(MS145, 1898), (L125, 1898)

References such as these cite Peirce's unpublished manuscripts and letters, respectively. The numbers refer to those in Richard Robin's *Annotated Catalogue of the Papers of Charles S. Peirce* (Amherst: University of Massachusetts Press 1967). Additional details concerning manuscripts, where required, are provided in footnotes to these references. The examples provided refer to manuscript 145 written in 1898 and letter 125 written in 1898, respectively.

Acknowledgments

Throughout the preparation of this volume, we enjoyed the enthusiastic support of our colleagues in the University of Toronto Philosophy Department, and especially of Calvin Normore and James Brown. We are indebted to the University of Toronto Press and to Ron Schoeffel, editor-in-chief, who recognized the merit of this project, and Darlene Zeleney, editor, for her astute guidance and professional assistance. We wish especially to thank Margaret Allen, copy editor, whose intelligent reading and meticulous care greatly improved the text.

Our largest debt is to our contributors, who were unusually faithful in meeting their deadlines and invariably understanding when we failed to meet ours.

Finally, we should like to thank the Social Sciences and Humanities Research Council of Canada, and the Department of Philosophy in the University of Toronto, for the financial support of the Peirce conference held at the University of Toronto in October 1992. All the papers in this collection were either written for that conference, or solicited by the editors for inclusion in the volume.

The Rule of Reason
The Philosophy of Charles Sanders Peirce

Introduction

JACQUELINE BRUNNING AND PAUL FORSTER

Charles Peirce (1839–1914) never produced a systematic statement of his philosophy. Much of his most original philosophical work was never published or even read by his contemporaries. However, while Peirce's influence on the thought of his time was confined to a small group of philosophers and logicians, his knowledge of the intellectual scene of that period was anything but limited. Controversies of detail aside, Peirce attempted to develop and to systematize the most exciting discoveries of his day (several of which were his own) in a broad range of disciplines.

Since the publication of his *Collected Papers* began in 1931, interest in Peirce has grown dramatically. His writings have found audiences in logic, epistemology, metaphysics, philosophy of science, semiotics, computer science, literary criticism, and film studies. While Peirce scholarship has advanced considerably since its earliest days, many controversies of interpretation persist and several of the more obscure aspects of Peirce's work remain poorly understood. This volume presents a broad selection of work devoted to outstanding issues and difficulties in Peirce's philosophy. Some essays clarify aspects of Peirce's philosophy, some defend its contemporary significance, and some do both. Each is published for the first time here. All but a few are accessible even to those unfamiliar with Peirce's work. This brief introduction provides a summary of their contents.

Peirce on Logic and Philosophy

The papers that open the volume explore Peirce's contributions to logic and their significance for his broader philosophy. From the time of his introduction to the subject at the age of twelve, Peirce thought of problems in every discipline as exercises in logic. He saw logic as the key to understanding the nature of knowledge, the operation of the human mind, and even the laws that govern the universe. Peirce's many contributions to formal logic (most notably in quantification theory, the logic of relations, statistical inference, modal logic, and number theory) are significant not only in the history of that discipline but also in the development of his philosophical system.

Jaakko Hintikka discusses the place of Peirce's work in modern logical thought and situates Peirce's logical writings within the more general framework of his 'Pragmaticism' (the term Peirce coined to distinguish his version of pragmatism from that of William James, which he thought to entail relativism).

Hintikka divides modern logicians into two groups: those who view language as a universal medium, a veil that stands between subjects and the world, and those who hold a model-theoretical view of language, according to which language is a reinterpretable calculus. On this classification Russell, Frege, the Vienna Circle of the 1930s, Quine, and Heidegger are 'universalists,' while Boole, Schröder, Löwenheim, and Peirce are 'model-theoreticians.'

Hintikka contends that Peirce's failure to develop the universalist idea of a formal system of logic explains why his work in logic continues to receive less attention than that of Hilbert, Frege, Russell, and others. Yet, Hintikka argues, Peirce's model-theoretical approach to logic netted him deep insights into the nature of quantifiers and also provided a perspective from which to develop modal logic. These advantages of Peirce's approach have been ignored by the dominant universalist tradition in logic, and thus, according to Hintikka, Peirce's marginalization in the history of logic continues.

The next two papers in the volume demonstrate the importance of the logic of statistical inference for Peirce's epistemology and metaphysics. As a member of the United States Coast and Geodetic Survey for nearly thirty years, Peirce became not only well-versed in the use of statistical techniques, but also an innovator in their application in such fields as geodesy and psychology (see, for example, W5:262–74 and W5:122–35). Moreover, Peirce's philosophy was profoundly influenced by developments in, and extensions of, statistical methods in science throughout the nineteenth century.

Peirce stridently defended an objectivist conception of probability. On his view, probability claims describe the frequency of an event of a particular class (e.g., coin tosses coming up heads) in relation to a broader containing class of events (e.g., coin tosses in general). Thus, true probability claims describe objective features of reality, and not, as Laplace had argued, subjective degrees of belief. Isaac Levi shows that, despite his opposition to Laplace, Peirce was deeply concerned with the nature of credal probabilities.

Levi discusses the development of Peirce's conception of logic from the earliest formulation, according to which logic involves the analysis of forms of inference based on syllogistic argument, to Peirce's final view of logic as the study of the role of various methods (i.e., abduction, deduction, and induction) in successful inquiry. In Levi's view, this change was the result of Peirce's work on the problem of direct inference (that is, reasoning from knowledge of statistical probabilities to credal probabilities, or, judgments of the fairness of betting rates in particular cases). Specifically, Levi maintains that Peirce was prompted to make this shift as the result of his adoption of a rationale for confidence-interval estimation (similar to that later developed by Neyman and Pearson) as the basis of induction. This move was made as a result of difficulties with Peirce's early account of direct inferences. Thus, according to Levi, the problem of credal probabilities lies at the heart of one of the most significant transformations in Peirce's logical thought.

The importance of Peirce's early theory of statistical inference for the development of his metaphysics is explored in Paul Forster's essay. Largely as the result of the success of celestial mechanics, scientifically inspired intellectuals of the nineteenth century viewed determinism as the basis of scientific reasoning and thus as a condition of the intelligibility of the universe. Peirce was perhaps the first to develop a sophisticated scientific metaphysics of indeterminism, a view largely based on his doctrine of 'tychism,' the thesis that chance is an agency in the universe. Forster explores the origins of this radical innovation.

Forster argues that Peirce had developed the foundations of indeterminism by 1866, some fifteen to twenty-five years earlier than previous estimates by Peirce scholars. This means that indeterminism was not a late development in Peirce's thought but a pervasive theme throughout his career. Forster also shows how Peirce derived this theory from his early theory of statistical inference. He further argues that the conceptual revolution that Peirce's indeterminism represents was triggered, not by evolutionary theory or by statistical mechanics, as previous scholars have claimed, but by his Kantian reading of Boole's *Laws of Thought.*

The next two papers in the volume consider one of the most difficult and innovative aspects of Peirce's thought, his graphical logic. Peirce's system of logical graphs is not intended to provide a tool for facilitating inferences, but rather a diagrammatic technique for the analysis of logical structure. In 1934 W.V. Quine called Peirce's graphs cumbersome, and he questioned their usefulness as an analytical tool. Yet he added that, 'it is not inconceivable that advances in the diagrammatic method might open possibilities of analysis superior to those afforded by the algebraic method' (*Isis*, 22, no. 2 (1934):553). Subsequent work on Peirce's graphical logic has proven Quine correct. Not only have Peirce's graphs been shown to provide an elegant system for logical analysis, but extensions of this system have proven fruitful in work on semantic networks in artificial intelligence and in computational linguistics.

Peirce's system of existential graphs has three parts: alpha, beta, and gamma. The alpha graphs correspond to the propositional calculus, the beta graphs are equivalent to classical first-order calculus with identity, and the gamma graphs provide a treatment of modal logic as well as an account of the logic of abstraction.

While Peirce's beta graphs incorporate the resources of quantification theory, they make no use of free variables. Robert Burch provides a reconstruction of Peirce's beta graphs that demonstrates how a Tarski-style semantics can be applied to them. He also offers sketches for completeness and consistency proofs for this system. While departing from Peirce's own presentation, Burch claims his system is true to Peirce's intentions. The result is a reconstruction that illustrates the power of Peirce's graphical logic but in a form that is accessible to those familiar with modern symbolic logic.

Jay Zeman argues that the treatment of modalities in the gamma graphs shows that Peirce was very close to the contemporary idea of possible world semantics. As Zeman notes, states of information can be represented in Peirce's graphical logic using what Peirce calls 'selectives.' (Selectives are implicitly quantified variables, that is, they are symbols attached to 'hooks' representing the places of predicates, these predicates being represented by 'spots'.) Zeman develops Peirce's hint that knowers' states of information can be treated as values for selectives using the system of 'tinctured graphs' developed in Peirce's 'Prolegomena to an Apology for Pragmaticism' (4.530–72). In that system the modalities of various states of affairs are represented by the 'Mode of Tincture,' that is, by the colour or pattern of shading of the portion of the page on which a particular logical diagram is inscribed. Zeman shows that these tinctures can be interpreted as selectives for states of information, states of affairs, or states of things. So construed, a tincture is an implicitly quantified variable which draws its values from a domain of states of affairs, or, in other words, a domain of possible worlds. Using only the graphical capabilities of a personal computer, Zeman develops a diagrammatic system that includes the equivalent of the Lewis-modal S4. He demonstrates the power of this approach by showing how, by altering the rules for access among worlds in this system, many varieties of modal logic can be produced.

Peirce's Philosophical Orientation

Pragmatism is at once a doctrine of meaning and a philosophical method. In its most general form, pragmatism is the thesis that the significance of a philosophical dispute is to be determined by examining the different practical, or, experiential, consequences of competing positions so as to render them susceptible of experimental testing. In Peirce's case, the pragmatic method is often exploited as a means of reconciling intuitions underlying philosophical views traditionally presumed to be incompatible: realism and idealism, materialism and dualism, naturalism and transcendentalism, theism and scientism. While Peirce's dissatisfaction with these traditional philosophical dichotomies is widely acknowledged, there remains considerable disagreement about how, and in what sense, Peirce can be said to have united seemingly irreconcilable doctrines. The papers described in this section deal with some of these controversies and discuss the unity of Peirce's thought more generally.

Sandra Rosenthal's essay addresses the apparent tension between Peirce's allegiance to Kant's architectonic approach to philosophy (that is, to the project of uncovering a permanent form of knowledge through an a priori, nonnaturalistic deduction of its categorical structure) and his defence of such naturalistic themes as the fundamental importance of experimental methods to knowledge and the view that methods of knowing are the product of evolution.

While Peirce's inventory of fundamental concepts, or 'categories,' evolved, he ultimately settled on three, aptly named 'Firstness,' 'Secondness,' and 'Thirdness.' In virtually every aspect of his thought, Peirce makes much of the claims that these categories are: (i) universal, since they apply to all elements of being; (ii) irreducible, since no combinations of monads (firsts) and dyads (seconds) can constitute a genuine triad (third); and (iii) exhaustive, since everything that has being can be reduced to combinations of firsts, seconds, and thirds.

Rosenthal argues that, despite his debt to Kant, Peirce's derivation of the categories appeals not to a transcendental deduction but rather to the experimental methods with which pragmatism is more traditionally associated. Moreover, she claims that, unlike Kant, Peirce is a pluralist; that is, he does not view his list of categories as providing a unique, unrevisable, or even transcendentally necessary philosophical framework. Rosenthal thus challenges those who would drive a wedge between the naturalistic rejection of transcendental metaphysics by William James and John Dewey and Peirce's commitment to the architectonic conception of philosophy.

Richard Robin further explores the foundations of Peirce's philosophical system. Robin discusses the 'proof of the truth of pragmatism' which Peirce often claimed to have completed, but never actually produced. According to Robin, what Peirce had in mind was a demonstration of the systematic coherence of his views on logic, epistemology, and metaphysics. Robin's reconstruction of the various attempts at, and aspects of, Peirce's proof shows how Peirce's architectonic framework grounds a comprehensive, holistic world-view with pragmatism at its core.

The tension in Peirce's thought between his simultaneous allegiance to both realism and idealism is discussed by Helmut Pape. Pape outlines a view he calls 'logical idealism,' the basic tenet of which is that there is a structural isomorphism between logical and material processes. Pape argues that this view provides a framework that links what many have found to be disparate and incompatible elements of Peirce's philosophy.

According to Pape, Peirce's logical idealism is aimed at explaining the unity of thought and experience by uncovering the logical structure of mental operations. He further suggests that, for Peirce, thought is a process that establishes a triadic connection between sequences of mental processes (that is, it produces relations out of relations). The resulting unity has the form of what Pierce calls 'teridentity,' a logical relation that, according to Pape, characterizes the process whereby diverse representations become 'welded' together to yield the continuity of mind.

Pape further argues that Peirce's semiotics, his graphical logic, his categories, and his logic of relations form the basis of a more general theory of the processes by which ideas develop. This theory in turn illuminates both Peirce's account of objectivity and his enigmatic metaphysical thesis that 'matter is effete mind' (6.25).

Carl Hausman also addresses the question of realism and idealism by examining Peirce's view of experience. Hausman seeks to reconcile Peirce's insistence on the pervasiveness of interpretation in experience, a view which suggests that the mind determines or constitutes perceptual content, with Peirce's claim that there is a brute element of experience that is non-discursive or 'pre-interpretive,' a view suggesting that it is experience that determines the mind.

Hausman notes that Pierce views feeling and cognition not as distinct classes of entities, or kinds of experience, but rather as elements that pervade all experiences; elements that are ontologically inseparable, even though analytically distinct. Thus, on Hausman's reading, Peirce views perception as a continuous process of which qualitative 'percepts' and cognitive 'perceptual judgments' are merely components or phases. Yet, Hausman argues, despite this insistence on the continuity of brute presentation and interpretation, Peirce's recognition that the interpretation of percepts is constrained by what he calls 'dynamical objects' saves him from the charge of idealism. Peirce's view, according to Hausman, provides a *via media* between forms of realism that posit a realm of objects with a determinate structure that is independent of the ways it can be known or conceived, and forms of idealism that attribute the determinate structure of reality to the mind or to the conceptual schemes of a community of inquirers.

Peirce on Inquiry and Objectivity

The papers in this section consider the implications of Peirce's theory of inquiry and his view of the knowing subject for his conception of objectivity. The core of Peirce's epistemology is what has come to be known as his doubt-belief model of inquiry. According to that view, inquiry is a struggle directed at removing the felt irritation of doubts, triggered by recalcitrant experiences, through their replacement by stable beliefs. Peirce defends the objective methods of science as superior to other forms of fixing beliefs, since, he claims, they would ultimately yield permanent, rational agreement among all inquirers, however various their beliefs at the outset.

According to Peirce's pragmatic maxim, the content of any belief can be expressed in terms of conditionals of the following form: 'if act A were to occur under conditions C, result R would occur $p\%$ of the time.' True beliefs would therefore serve as reliable rules of conduct insofar as they would yield correct predictions about the consequences of various courses of action. For this reason, Peirce views the acquisition of true beliefs as a process of acquiring habits (and conversely). Moreover, since the rational assessment of beliefs in inquiry is a special case of practical deliberation about rules of conduct, logic is for Peirce a normative science that falls under the more general heading of ethics. Consequently Peirce's view of rational inquiry undermines the traditional separation of theoretical judgment and practical judgment.

Christopher Hookway explores Peirce's views of the connection between sentiment and rationality. As Hookway recognizes, Peirce does not view the cognitive, the volitional, and the aesthetic as distinct mental faculties, but rather as various aspects or elements of all experiences. Hookway notes, however, that Peirce seems to be unclear about the precise role of sentiment in rational inquiry. Sometimes Peirce denies it any role in scientific inquiry, while at other times he argues that reliance on sentiment is essential to inquiry. Similarly, there are times when Peirce seems to view sentiment as antithetical to rationality, while at other times he suggests that sentiment can be an even more reliable guide to action than reason. Hookway resolves these tensions through an examination of Peirce's view of the function of sentiment in rational self-control.

Hookway examines Peirce's view that rational inquiry requires certain ethical dispositions, chief among them a lack of selfishness and identification with a potentially unlimited community of inquirers. He also shows how these follow from Peirce's view of inquiry, which in turn is based on his logic. Hookway argues that despite his linking inquiry to practical deliberation, Peirce manages to preserve something like the traditional distinction between theory and practice, drawn now between the general epistemic interests of the inquirer and more narrow practical interests of individual agents.

Hookway further argues that, on Peirce's view, sentiments constitute immediate judgments that are not subject to rational criticism, since they are involuntary and instinctual. These form a contingently indubitable framework of inquiry. Since it is against some such framework that inquirers must assess rules and strategies for attaining their goals, sentiments function as constraints that mediate between immediate experience and more general regulative hopes. Insofar as these sentiments are *cognitive* states, reliance on them need not be a betrayal of rationality. Thus, Hookway argues, Peirce does have a consistent view that assigns sentiment a fundamental role in the pursuit of cognitive perfection.

Douglas Anderson discusses the social implications of Peirce's theory of inquiry and his distinction between theory and practice. As Anderson points out, though Peirce wrote little about ethics and politics, he was very concerned about the impact of developments in the natural sciences and logic on the human sciences and on ethical and political practice. Anderson focuses on Peirce's view about the function of science in political life and its cultural role more generally.

Anderson argues that although Peirce views scientific inquiry as a special case of practical deliberation, he also holds that present science is rational only if it would be upheld by inquiry were it to be pursued indefinitely over the totality of possible evidence. This raises a question about the relevance of current, provisional scientific results to practical concerns here and now. According to Anderson, Peirce's view rests on his distinction between theoretical matters, which are the proper domain of rational inquiry, and practical matters, which are more reliably dealt with by instinct. However, as Anderson demonstrates, Peirce maintains these distinctions while at the same time defending the continuity of theory and practice, of instinct and reason.

Finally, Anderson argues that Peirce's conception of the relation of theory and practice yields a view of the cultural role of science that departs substantially from the views of James and Dewey. This leads Peirce to a general vision of social life that rivals those of his fellow pragmatists.

The theme of the relation of theoretical and practical interests is picked up in a very different way by Susan Haack. The focus of her discussion is Peirce's 'first rule of reason': 'that in order to learn you must desire to learn, and in so desiring not be satisfied with what you already incline to think ...' (1.135).

Haack sees this rule as the basis for Peirce's conception of the disinterested scientific inquirer, that is, one motivated by what Haack calls the pure truth-seeking attitude. Haack contrasts these genuine inquirers with utility-driven inquirers (those who are interested in truth only insofar as it is useful), sham reasoners (who argue to foregone conclusions), and fake reasoners (who are interested only in promoting their own reputations). Haack argues that genuine inquirers are likely to be more productive epistemically than others, even if they do not themselves get to the truth.

While acknowledging that her typology of inquirers is simplified, Haack insists that it is not simplistic. She argues that Peirce's account of inquiry contains important morals for contemporary philosophy. In Peirce's first rule of reason she finds an antidote to the disastrous effects of the growing professionalism in philosophy and to the growth of various forms of pseudo-inquiry inspired either by scientism, current trends in literary criticism, or political agendas such as feminism.

Peirce on Agency, Selfhood, and Consciousness

The next two papers in the volume consider various aspects of Peirce's view of the self and its relationship to his broader philosophy. There is a close connection between Peirce's theory of inquiry, his semiotics, and his theory of human nature. Peirce rejected the view of the self as a permanent entity or noumenal substance that grounds the appearances of inner sense. On his view, the continuity of personal identity is just the logical continuity of thought-signs. Hence, the self is something that comes into being and evolves by means of semiotic processes that establish that continuity rather than an antecedently existing entity that grounds or explains those processes.

Vincent Colapietro argues that Peirce's conception of the knowing subject ties together his views about semiotics, pragmatism, and rational criticism. Colapietro claims that an important aspect of Peirce's pragmaticism is his reconceptualization of the notion of things-in-themselves as 'dynamical objects,' that is, objects that are knowable in principle, yet whose natures are independent of what anyone might happen to believe. Colapietro further argues that accompanying this shift is the transformation of the knowing subject from a transcendental ego into a 'situated, deliberative agent.' This in turn has important implications for Peirce's view of critical reflection.

As Colapietro explains, Peirce held that it is through error that the distinction between sign and object (appearance and reality, knower and known) arises. Once manifest, the possibility of error (and of overcoming it) becomes a phenomenon to be explained within semiotics itself. Colapietro argues that Peirce's view of the deliberative subject yields an account of self-reflection that is equally at odds with forms of historicism that deny the possibility of criticism altogether, and with forms of transcendentalism rooted in the illusion of an ahistorical God's-eye perspective on reality. The result is a fallibilistic account of the growth of critical self-awareness which, Colapietro argues, forms an integral part of Peirce's more general evolutionary cosmology.

The emergence of self-consciousness is further explained in Thomas Short's essay. Short explicates and defends Peirce's claim that knowledge of the inner world is not gained immediately through introspection, but rather is derived only by hypothetical reasoning from knowledge of external facts. As noted above, Peirce held that self-consciousness emerges with the awareness of error. Short argues that since this requires some mastery of language, language acquisition is, for Peirce, an essential precondition of self-consciousness. Moreover, since language is acquired through interaction with socialized beings in a common environment, the emergence of self-consciousness is fundamentally a social process: one not only attains self-consciousness as a member of some community, but the self of which one becomes conscious is socially formed.

To explain this process further, Short describes Peirce's notion of 'hypostatic abstraction,' an inferential process whereby abstract concepts are reified as entities or objects of reference. Short shows how Peirce uses this form of inference to explain the development of self-knowledge. Short also shows that although Peirce insists that knowledge of the mind is derived from knowledge of the external world, he is neither a behaviourist nor a physicalist.

Finally, Short argues that, for Peirce, hypostatic abstraction explains not only self-knowledge, but the very emergence and evolution of the self through critical reflection. On this account, the self is perpetually a work in progress, a dynamic network of belief-habits that is continually rediscovered, reconstructed, and refined.

As a coda to the collection, Calvin Normore traces David Savan's double philosophical lineage – Spinoza and Peirce.

In 'A Guess at the Riddle' Peirce outlined his plan for a philosophical framework 'so comprehensive that, for a long time to come, the entire work of human reason [in every discipline] shall appear as the filling up of its details.' That system proved to be more comprehensive than Peirce's own powers of expression. However, as the papers in this volume attest, that system is philosophically rich and remains well worth exploring.

The Place of C.S. Peirce in the History of Logical Theory

JAAKKO HINTIKKA

1 Logic as Language versus Logic as Calculus

Speaking of someone's 'place in history' is often a preface to eulogy. But we have come to study Peirce, not to praise him, and only incidentally to try to see that his good ideas are not interred with his bones or with his unpublished papers.

One of the difficulties in studying Peirce is his elusiveness. Peirce's writings are brim-full of perceptive and provocative ideas, but do they add up to a coherent overall view? Even though Peirce himself offers a general perspective on his own ideas, it is not clear how his specific results are supposed to be parts of a larger picture. This has been my problem when I have tried to offer specific observations on the details of Peirce's ideas in my early publications. How are they related to Peirce's general philosophical ideas?

In this paper, I shall pursue one lead as to how to make our ideas of Peirce clear. This way is to compare Peirce with certain other thinkers, including Frege, Wittgenstein, and Quine. Such comparisons will, I hope, illuminate both the general character of Peirce's thought, so to speak his position on the overall map of the history of philosophy, and also his specific intellectual relationships to other thinkers.

Consequently, the main purpose of this paper is to define and describe Peirce's *locus* in the landscape of certain important but specific traditions in the kind of philosophy he practised. I am not only going to offer scholarly observations concerning the details of Peirce's ideas. (Several of the detailed observations I shall discuss here have in fact been published in my earlier papers.) I shall try to show that these bits and pieces of ideas of Peirce's are in reality parts of a large jigsaw puzzle which can be put together. In other words, I am primarily endeavouring to present a general perspective on his thought. I expect that this perspective will help to lend direction and perhaps also a conceptual framework for more detailed studies.

The history in which I am trying to place Peirce is primarily the history of logical theory. Hence I have to discuss in some detail certain aspects of Peirce's work in logic, and to compare him with other logicians (and logically oriented philosophers). However, what I shall say has much broader implications, especially concerning the nature and the presuppositions of Peirce's pragmatism (or pragmaticism).

The main coordinate axis of the map on which I am trying to locate Peirce is provided by a distinction between two contrasting visions of language and its relations to the language user and the world. These two views have been labelled *language as the universal medium* (or *the universality of language*) and *language as calculus* (or *the model-theoretical view of language*). (See Hintikka 1988.) These terms are not self-explanatory, and have to be taken with more than one grain of salt. With a couple of interesting exceptions, the terms of this contrast are not found in the earlier literature, the main reason being that the majority of philosophers have been blissfully or banefully ignorant of the role which the contrast has played in the philosophical thought of the last hundred-odd years.

A believer in the universality of language sees language (and the conceptual system it codifies) as an indispensable intermediary between 'you' and your world (*the* world). You are virtually a prisoner of your language; you could not, for instance, step outside it and have a look at the way it is related to the world. Or, less metaphorically speaking, you cannot express in language (in 'the only language I understand,' as Wittgenstein put it) its semantic relations to the world, without committing nonsense or tautology. As either formulation shows, *semantics is ineffable* according to the doctrine of the universality of language.

As a consequence, you cannot, strictly speaking, understand another language without making it part of your own. 'A language that I don't understand is no language,' to speak with Wittgenstein again. Hence, a believer in language as the universal medium can escape linguistic relativism only by adopting a kind of linguistic solipsism. This connection between linguistic universality and linguistic relativism is one of the grains of salt needed to acquire a taste for my terminology.

Conversely, the conception of language as calculus implies that we can perform all those neat feats a universalist claims we cannot perform, for instance, to discuss the semantics of a language in that language itself. For another instance, on this view, we can vary the interpretation of our language, that is, admit other 'models' for its propositions than the actual universe. In other words (worlds?), language is like a calculus in that it can be freely assigned a new interpretation. Hence the term. However, a defender of this view does not hold that language (our very own home language) is like an *un*interpreted calculus, but only that it is *re*-interpretable as a calculus is. Nor does a model theorist hold that his or her language is a mere tool for purely formal (calculus-like) inferences. These observations provide a couple of further grains of the proverbial salt needed to understand the import of what I have called the idea of language as calculus.

Some of the further consequences of the two tenets are clear. For instance, all systematic model theory presupposes something like a belief in language as calculus, at least as applied to the specific languages (often the formal languages of a logician) whose model theory is at issue. There nevertheless is nothing incoherent in an intermediate position like Tarski's according to which we can happily develop model theories for particular formalized languages but not (just because of its universality) for our overall colloquial language.

Tarski's name reminds one of another issue that separates the calculus men from the universality boys. This issue is the definability of the central semantic concept of truth. An all-out model-theoretical philosopher would like to see the notion of truth for a language defined in this language itself, while a universalist would dismiss any such attempt as a hopeless daydream.

The thesis of the universality of language may strike you as being far more outlandish than its rival. Yet it was the dominant view in the early logical theory and the early analytic philosophy of language. The universalist position was embraced by Frege, early and middle Russell, Wittgenstein, the Vienna Circle of the early thirties, and, in a certain sense, Quine. (If you want to find an apostolic succession here, be my guest.) On the so-called continental side, the same belief in the ineffability of truth and of other semantical concepts was shared by, among others, that secret admirer of Frege, Martin Heidegger. (See Kusch 1989.) Through Heidegger's influence, the universalist tenet became a cornerstone of the hermeneutical and deconstructivist traditions.

Against such powerful (though often unacknowledged) allies, the early tradition of language as calculus might at first look like a trickle even in the history of logical theory (cf Sluga 1987). This tradition includes people such as Boole, Schröder, and Löwenheim who are scarcely household names even in philosophical families. Only later, through the work of Tarski, Gödel, and Carnap the born-again semanticist, did the model-theoretical tradition gradually gain the upper hand among logicians, though to a much lower degree among philosophers.

Moreover, at the early stages of the tradition of language (and its logic) as calculus, only a minuscule part of the totality of model-theoretical tools was brought to bear on logic, that is to say only such algebraic techniques as could facilitate the drawing of logical inferences.

2 Peirce's Own Testimony

One of the main theses of this paper is that Peirce was an integral member of the model-theoretical tradition (i.e., the tradition of language as calculus). A further thesis I shall argue for is that this observation throws into a sharper relief a large number of aspects of Peirce's many-faceted thought and even opens new ways of understanding them. The import of these claims will become clearer as the paper proceeds, and so will the contrast between language as calculus and language as the universal medium.

Peirce's membership in the model-theoretical tradition is not controversial. Peirce himself identifies with perfect clarity the 'very serious purpose' of his language of graphs, by saying that 'this system is not intended to serve as a universal language for mathematicians or other reasoners like that of Peano' (4.424). This disassociates him completely from the universalists.

Peirce continues: 'Third, this system is not intended as calculus, or apparatus by which conclusions can be reached and problems solved with greater facility than by more familiar systems of expression ... But in my algebras and graphs, far from anything of that sort being attempted, the whole effort has been to dissect the operations of inference into as many distinct steps as possible' (4.424; I am grateful to Susan Haack for first drawing my attention to this passage).

In spite of the verbal disagreement, this statement shows that Peirce was dealing with interpreted logic, not merely formal inferences. In other words, Peirce was unmistakably taking a model-theoretical or 'calculus' view of his formal language. In fact, he says in 4.423 that he will only later move on to see what purely formal rules might correspond to the initial interpreted inferences: 'Part II will develop formal "rules", or permissions, by which one graph may be transformed into another without danger of passing from truth to falsity and without referring to any interpretation of the graphs ...'

3 Peirce versus Frege

One subject we can appreciate better from the vantage point of the contrast I have sketched is precisely what Peirce's places is in history. To begin with a relatively superficial aspect of this location task, Peirce's membership in the model-theoretical tradition will already explain something about his posthumous stature. It is usually said that the founder of contemporary logic is Frege. (Compare here van Heijenoort 1967.) Why not Peirce? Admittedly, Frege was the first to publish a treatment of the basic part of logic that is variously known as quantification theory, lower predicate calculus, or first-order logic. But Peirce and his associates developed a logic of quantifiers completely independently of Frege. What is a couple of years' publication priority among friends?

It is a historical fact that Peirce not only independently discovered the importance of quantifiers and developed a notation for them, but that he also discussed their nature in a most perceptive way. In particular, Peirce showed much keener awareness than Frege of the nature of dependent (nested) quantifiers and their importance for logical reasoning. For instance, in 4.483 Peirce says that 'when a proposition contains a number of *anys* and *somes*, it is a delicate matter to alter the form of statement while preserving the exact meaning.' These insights of Peirce's are not trifling; related ideas have since played a crucial role among other developments in Hilbert's metamathematical thought and in game-theoretical semantics. I shall soon return to this subject in greater detail.

Unlike Frege, Peirce also outlined or foreshadowed several subsequent developments in logic, especially in modal logics. In general, the bag of logical tools we find in Peirce's writings is much richer than what we find in Frege.

Peirce's failure to have much of his best work in logic published explains some of the modesty of his later reputation. But Frege, too, was little known in his own day. Hence Peirce's failure to publish does not fully explain why his reputation should have languished in comparison with Frege's.

The fate of Peirce's logical work is to a considerable extent due to the fact that he happened to be a member of a less dominant tradition than Frege. Both Frege and his discoverer, the early Russell, were firmly in the universalist tradition, and so in a way is W.V. Quine, who has probably more than anybody else helped to turn Frege into the major saint in the calendar of modern logicians that he is by now, in the majority view (cf Hintikka 1990). Admittedly, from the vantage point of the universalist tradition, Frege's claims to fame are exceedingly well-founded. For instance, he created the conception of a formal system of logic which has remained paradigmatic for a century (cf van Heijenoort 1967).

Frege's universalist stance helped to make his work look impressive. Frege presented first-order logic as the central part of a relatively simple universal language which was calculated to capture faithfully the world of our concepts. (This is the point of Frege's calling his formal language a *Begriffsschrift*.) For Peirce, the self-same quantification theory was only one kind of logical system among many. Characteristically, Frege did not see any need of explaining or analysing its ingredients, such as quantifiers, any further. He probably would have agreed with one of his latter-day followers who has said that if he does not understand first-order logic, he does not understand anything at all in logic. In contrast, far from taking any set of accustomed logical principles for granted, Peirce was constantly trying to give them a deeper foundation or extending their range.

Now to say that the graphical procedure is more analytical than another is to say that it demonstrates what the other virtually assumes without proof. (NEM4: 319)

The one universally valid method is that of mathematical demonstration; and this is the only one which is commonly avoided by logicians as fallacious. (NEM4:21.)

As a consequence of this constant presence of interpretational ideas in his work on the formal rules of logic, Peirce did not feel the need of making a hard-and-fast distinction between, on the one hand, the formal axioms of logic and its formal inference rules, and, on the other hand, its derived truths. They all had to be justified by means of semantic considerations, which could be evoked at any stage of the proceedings. Thus, to the detriment of his later reputation, Peirce, unlike Frege, never came to develop explicitly the idea of a formal system (axiomatization) of logic.

4 Peirce as a Modal Logician

Several aspects of these remarks need to be explained further. First, Peirce's pioneering work in modal logic reflects deep philosophical assumptions which are closely related to his model-theoretical conception of logic. A universalist like Frege could never have developed a modal logic. Why not? The answer is obvious. If language (our actual language or any alternative that can do an appreciable part of the same job it does) cannot be re-interpreted, it can be used only to speak of one and the same world, what is to say, our actual world. No serious alternatives are possible, and hence the notions of possibility and necessity lose their natural Leibnizian sense. Consequently, modal notions have either to be abandoned as meaningless, as Quine urges, or to be suitably re-interpreted, as in Russell's proposal to define necessity as universality. In particular, for a universalist logical truths are not truths about all possible worlds. Rather, as Russell once put it, for a universalist thinker like himself logic deals with the actual world quite as much as zoology, albeit with its more abstract denizens. The main alternative open to a universalist who does not want to consider logical truths as truths about our world is to declare logical truths to be tautologies, as Wittgenstein did.

Thus the predominance of the tradition of language as the universal medium explains why modal logic failed to catch the attention of most philosophers until the late fifties. And in so far as it enjoyed a modest earlier flowering, as in C.I. Lewis's hands, it did so outside the mainstream tradition in logical theory.

Indeed, anyone who takes modalities and modal logic seriously must countenance some version of the view of language as calculus. Here we are obviously approaching Peirce again. Unfortunately, this is not the place to offer an exhaustive study of Peirce's theory of modality. The main facts can nevertheless be registered. They show once again Peirce's firm place in the tradition of language and logic as calculus.

1 At least in his mature thought, Peirce understood modalities realistically in a straightforward metaphysical sense, without trying to explain them away, for example, epistemically.

2 In his actual work in logic, Peirce developed ways of studying modal logics. In his logical theory in general Peirce used freely ideas that presuppose a multiplicity of possible worlds (or other possibilia).

3 Peirce influenced the subsequent development of explicit systems of modal logic. In particular, he was greatly admired by C.I. Lewis.

4 The philosophically deep point here is that Peirce showed a much keener awareness of the crucial distinction between truth (truth *simpliciter*) and the ill-named concept of 'logical truth' than the members of the universalist tradition.

In the light of these observations, we can see why, for a universalist like Quine, Peirce's anticipations of modal logics were scarcely a recommendation. And by the time the tide had turned and modal logics and algebra-oriented and model-theoretical approaches had again become important, the actual detailed methods of theorizing in logic had surpassed what Peirce could offer.

Thus, to ask Quine to be the main speaker when Peirce's logical work is being discussed is a little bit like asking Cardinal Manning to deliver a eulogy on John Henry Newman.

5 Peirce as a Game-Theoretical Semanticist

Furthermore, Peirce's interest in the deeper nature of quantifiers turns out to lend him a remarkable place in the entire model-theoretical tradition. Since I have dealt with this matter at some length in other recent papers, I can be quite brief.

What do quantifiers mean, anyway? What is their logical status? A one-world universalist like Frege is likely to try to get away with saying merely that quantifiers are second-order predicates of a special kind. For instance, the existential quantifier $(\exists x)$ in the sentence $(\exists x)$ S[x] is a second-order predicate (predicate of predicates) which says that the (possibly complex) first-order predicate S[x] is not empty. But Frege never gives any explanation of what is special about such second-order predicates. His explanation does not work without a great deal of hand-waving for nested (dependent) quantifiers. And a model theorist will ask in any case for further explanations. What makes a second-order predicate an existential quantifier is not its extension in the actual world, but the way this extension is determined in any old (or new) world. And this 'way of being determined' is never explained by Frege.

Inevitably, when our present-day conception of a quantifier was first conceived of by the likes of Skolem and Hilbert, it was related to the idea of a choice function (Skolem function). A sentence containing a dependent existential quantifier, for instance

(1) $(\forall x)(\exists y) S[x,y]$

in effect asserts the existence of a choice function. For instance, (1) is equivalent with

(2) $(\exists f)(\forall x) S[x, f(x)]$

Now the remarkable thing here is that Peirce had this way of looking at quantifiers down pat. He felt called upon to explain the logical behaviour of the quantifier words *some* and *any* in a way which goes beyond the mere formulation of the rules of inference in which they play a part. 'Every *some*, as we have seen, means that under stated conditions, an individual could be specified of which that which is predicated of the *some* is [true], while every *any* means that what is predicated is true of no matter what [specified] individual; and the specifications of individuals must be made in a certain order, or the meaning of the proposition will be changed' (4.483).

As Risto Hilpinen has shown, Peirce spells out quite explicitly the game-theoretical meaning of quantifiers. If I am right, something like this meaning is the only model-theoretically natural way of dealing with quantifiers. Here Peirce's comments on quantifiers offer further evidence of his model-theoretical stance.

Peirce's comments may be more than an anticipation of the idea of quantifiers as being based on choice functions. The notion of Skolem function (choice function connected with a quantifier) was foreshadowed by Löwenheim's use of double indexing, which he inherited from Schröder. Now Peirce, who in his semiotic theory had the idea of quantifiers as asserting the possibility of choices or 'specifications' of a certain kind, is known to have influenced Schröder's logic significantly. Is it therefore likely that Peirce not only anticipated the idea of quantifiers as choice functions, but in a sense started it? Further historical research is needed before a convincing answer can be given to this question.

It is considerably easier to tell why Peirce, Schröder, and Löwenheim never managed to implement this idea in a way that would have enabled them to put it to use in their logical theory. They had not reached Skolem's idea of codifying the relevant choices in an explicitly mentioned function (Skolem function). Now what is the game-theoretical meaning of such a function? It is a partial codification of a verifier's *strategy*. Before the general game-theoretical concept of strategy was formulated by von Neumann (or at least before the special case of this concept in the form of a Skolem function was available), there simply was no obvious model for a full-fledged development of Peirce's game-theoretical interpretation of quantifiers.

6 Peirce and Metalogic

One particular consequence of the universalist position is that our language and its logic can be neither self-applied as a whole, nor discussed in its entirety in a separate metalanguage (except for its purely formal features, of course). This consequence, which was noted by van Heijenoort in his pioneering paper (1967), offers some of the most useful tests of actual historical membership in the two traditions. If there were any lingering doubts about Peirce's allegiance to the model-theoretical tradition, they would hence be quickly dispelled by his willingness to discuss logic by means of logic. A case in point is offered by Peirce's theory of existential graphs. For instance, in 4.527 he writes:

> I will now pass to another quite indispensable department of the gamma graphs. Namely, it is necessary that we should be able to reason in graphs about graphs. The reason is that reasoning about graphs will necessarily consist in showing that something is true of every possible graph of a certain general description. But we cannot scribe every possible graph of any general description and therefore if we are to reason in graphs we must have a graph which is a general description of the kind of graph to which the reasoning is to relate.

And Peirce goes on to develop in some detail a notation for 'gamma expressions of beta graphs,' which is precisely a logic applied to logic.

One has to be careful here, however. For a universalist, too, has to apply logic to itself, just because it is universal and hence has to apply to everything. What distinguishes the two is (among other things) that a believer in the 'logic as calculus' conception feels free to develop a separate new technique, even a new language (a metalanguage, perhaps) if need be, for the purpose.

That this is what Peirce was in effect doing is clear from his writings, indeed clear from the examples already given.

7 The Very Idea of Formalization

One particularly important and particularly subtle set of consequences of the two contrasting approaches concerns the idea of formalism in logic and mathematics. What is subtle here is that the attitude of both the universalists and the model theorists to the idea of formalism is bound to be ambivalent. Take first a believer in logic as calculus. As the very term highlights, such a theorist is likely to emphasize the usefulness of calculus-like systems in the study of logic. Indeed, this tradition was at an early stage of its development known as the tradition of the algebra of logic. The idea was to find quasi-algebraic laws by means of which logical formulas could be manipulated in the same (or a similar) way in which algebraic equations were manipulated.

Here we can in fact see one of the many symptoms which show that Peirce was fully and firmly a member of the model-theoretical ('logic as calculus') tradition. As every student of Peirce knows, most of his work in logic belongs historically speaking to the 'algebra of logic' movement. At first sight, the use of the techniques of old-fashioned elementary algebra might seem indicative of a concentration of interest on formal matters rather than interpretational ones. But it is crucial to realize that, but for the believers in the model-theoretical conception, formalism was a servant, not the master. As was found in section 2 above, Peirce in any case distinguished his interests from those of the logical algebraists. They were merely looking for rules to facilitate the drawing of actual logical inferences; Peirce was deeply concerned with the model-theoretical basis of such inferences, especially with analysing them into the shortest and most obvious steps.

In general, like all believers in logic as calculus, Peirce was not only ready to provide an interpretation for their calculi at the drop of a symbol. He could – or thought they could – discuss such changes systematically in an explicit language. The very freedom of choosing a formalism differently on different occasions was sometimes a consequence of their belief that it is the underlying representational realities that really matter, not the formalism. In some typical and important cases, one can see how a formalism and even a temporary adoption of a formalistic attitude in reality served substantive interpretational purposes.

The interplay between formalism and interpretation can be further illustrated by considering Hilbert's often-misunderstood program. Hilbert the axiomatist conceived of his axioms as interpretable systems. They served a purpose as soon as they had one realization, one interpretation which made all the axioms true. But how can we be sure that a given axiom system has such an interpretation? If we have available to us, as Hilbert thought, a complete and completely formal system of logic, then it would suffice to study the axiom system purely formally to answer the question. If it can be shown that one can never derive a contradiction from the axioms in a purely formal way, then the axiom system is consistent also in the interpretability sense, granted of course the completeness of one's formalized logic. What concerns us here is merely the fact that Hilbert's formalism was in this important sense merely a means of reaching interpretational (semantic) results. He was trying to prove the semantic consistency of axiom systems by proving their syntactical consistency, one might say.

Peirce, too, found it useful in his logical work to give a 'pure mathematical definition of existential graphs, regardless of their interpretation' (4.414). As with Hilbert, this does not mark any lapse from model-theoretical virtue.

Likewise, a believer in the universality of logic and in the ineffability of semantics is also likely to care for the basic interpretational meaning of his or her interpreted *Begriffsschrift*. But that meaning cannot be discussed in language. Consequently it cannot be theorized about or studied in a systematic fashion. It has to be taken for granted. It is presupposed, not discussed. It can be studied only in so far as it manifests itself in the purely formal behaviour of one's logic and language. Hence a universalist's belief in the ineffability of semantics easily leads him or her, too, to a formalist practice. It is for this reason that Frege the universalist created our current paradigm of a formal system of logic and that Wittgenstein the lifelong believer in the ineffability of semantics became the fountainhead of the idea of a 'logical syntax of language,' in spite of the fact that both had many strong views about the relation of language and the world.

Of course, different philosophers' ideas about formalism are likely to have their mirror image in the same philosophers' ideas about the non-formal aspects of language, that is, about the representative function of language and its logic. One might perhaps expect that an emphasis on calculation in logic might divert a philosopher's attention from the intuitive picture-like representativeness of language. Yet the contrary is usually the case. The free re-interpretability of language according to the calculus conception is apt to focus one's attention on the interpretation and the representative functions of language.

8 The Iconicity of Logic

Here I am obviously touching on one of the most characteristic features of Peirce's ideas about language and logic, namely, the role of what he called icons and iconicity.

My readers are all undoubtedly familiar with Peirce's distinction between an *index*, an *icon*, and a *symbol*. I am interested here in the second of these three vehicles of linguistic representation. An icon, Peirce says, represents whatever it represents by resembling it. Moreover, this resemblance need not mean looking alike in a vulgar sense of the expression. The similarity is essentially a *structural* similarity. The parts or elements of an icon are related to one another in a way analogous to the way the corresponding ingredients of what it represents are related to each other.

What is instructive here is that Peirce's model-theoretical attitude is revealed by his emphasis on the role of icons in logic, reasoning, and thinking in general. The point is not difficult to appreciate. Another way of expressing the iconic relation of a sign to what it represents is to say that the sign is a model of what it stands for in a sense not completely different from logicians' use of the term. One way of illustrating this iconicity is by reference to the technique (which goes back at least to Henkin) of using suitable sets of formulas (e.g., model sets, or maximal consistent sets) literally as their own models. Hence Peirce's willingness to theorize about icons and to use them in his actual work in logic is but another facet of his model-theoretical approach to language and logic.

By and large, Peirce's model-theoretical attitude, in contrast to Frege's universalist stance, shows up in his actual work on (and with) formal rules of inference in the following way: Both logicians obviously rely on tacit interpretational ideas to set up the basic rules of inference. But Frege is suspicious of such semantic ideas, undoubtedly because they apparently cannot be expressed in a correct *Begriffsschrift* and apparently hence cannot be subject to the same standards of argumentative rigour and clarity as that which can be so expressed, including (Frege thought) mathematical concepts.

Moreover, Peirce's idea of the iconicity of logic highlights still another difference between Frege and Peirce. For Frege, finding the right principles of logic is a matter of thought, not of intuition. By the same token, when we proceed from logical axioms to logical theorems, we cannot expect any bottom-line help from intuition, and we should not trust other interpretational ideas very much, either. Hence, all told, for Frege there is only a limited role for interpretational considerations in pure logic, and properly speaking no real role for intuitions at all. They are at best dispensable auxiliary aids to logical thought.

Thus, Frege writes in *Foundations of Arithmetic* (section 60): 'Time and again we are led by our thought beyond the scope of our imagination, without thereby forfeiting the support we need for our inferences.'

In contrast, Peirce's characteristic logical techniques are iconic and graphic, and in that sense involve intuition (in the general sense in which sense-perception is a species of intuition). Sometimes he even denies that 'demonstrative reasoning is something altogether unlike observation' (3.641). And the foundation of this claim is precisely the iconic element in reasoning: 'The intricate forms of inference of relative logic call for such studied scrutiny of the representations of facts, which representations are of an *iconic* kind, that they represent relations in the fact by analogous relations in the representation, that we cannot fail to remark that it is by *observation* of diagrams that the reasoning proceeds in such cases' (3.641).

Peirce's iconic methods did not, as far as I can see, anticipate the specific ideas which subsequently guided the model-theoretically oriented axiomatizations of logic, such as the Beth-Hintikka idea of construing a (first-order) logical proof as a frustrated attempt to construct a counter-example. Such later ideas are closer to the spirit of Peirce's philosophy than to its letter. This spiritual kinship is nevertheless unmistakable. One of its many symptoms is Peirce's comment on the usefulness of icons: 'The Icon does not stand unequivocally for this or that existing thing, as the Index does ... But there is one assurance that the Icon does afford in the highest degree. Namely, that which is displayed before the mind's gaze – the Form of the Icon, which is also its object – must be *logically possible*' (4.531). This is essentially just the other side of the interpretational coin minted by Beth and Hintikka. If proofs are frustrated attempts to construct a counter-example, then a completed construction will *ipso facto* show that a counter-example is indeed logically possible. (Such uses of the techniques of logical argumentation are still being neglected by philosophers.)

The Beth-Hintikka idea is precisely to interpret a logical proof as an attempt to construct an iconic counter-example to the putative conclusion. What the logician who carries out this construction hopes is that this attempted construction is seen to fail inevitably, whereby the result to be proved is shown to be logically necessary.

9 Theorematic versus Corollarial Inferences

In some specific respects, however, Peirce did anticipate later semantics-friendly conceptualizations in logic.

Indeed, an excellent case study of the role of iconic thinking in Peirce is offered by a distinction to which he himself attached considerable importance. It is a distinction between what Peirce called corollarial and theorematic reasoning in logic. (See Hintikka 1983.) The paradigm case is geometrical reasoning, which of course is often overtly iconic, relying on geometrical figures as an aid to reasoning. In elementary geometry, familiar to many readers from their school-days, some theorems can be proved by considering simply the configuration of geometrical objects mentioned in the statement of the theorem. Such proofs Peirce calls *corollarial*. But in other cases, a proof is possible only by reference to other geometrical objects not mentioned in the original statement. In the traditional jargon of elementary geometry, we need 'auxiliary constructions' in order to be able to carry out the proof. Such proofs Peirce calls *theorematic*. Peirce's choice of terms is in fact very much in keeping with traditional geometrical terminology.

A distinction of this kind can be drawn only on the basis of some sort of iconic representation of reasoning, which in the case of geometry is provided by the familiar geometrical figures. When geometrical reasoning was 'formalized' in the sense of being considered as strictly logical reasoning, many philosophers, for instance Bertrand Russell, thought that any conceptualization that is made by reference to figures is dispensable and off the mark in rigorous geometry. They were wrong because they overlooked the potential iconicity of all logical reasoning.

Indeed, Peirce's brilliant insight was that all logical reasoning is at bottom iconic. This is the basic reason why the contract between corollarial and theorematic reasoning can be applied to *all* logical reasoning. For since all such reasoning is iconic, it involves representatives of the entities involved in the reasoning, either representatives of some particular individuals or else of suitable sample individuals the reasoner is considering. Hence we can always distinguish such (theorematic) reasoning as requires more complex configurations of entities than are mentioned in the result to be proved (or in the premises one has available) from such (corollarial) reasoning as merely involves reshuffling an iconic configuration that has already been given. Obviously, a general distinction of this kind is possible only if one can consider all logical reasoning as an iconic or model-theoretical process.

A long time ago (cf Hintikka 1973), I came independently upon the same distinction in my work in the philosophy of logic, only to discover that the same insight had been reached by Peirce.

Peirce's place in the history of logical theory is vividly illustrated by the incomprehension with which his distinction between corollarial and theorematic reasoning was met. This incomprehension was undoubtedly due to the prevalence of the universalist tradition at the time. As was indicated, this rejection of ideas like Peirce's distinction was based on the formalization of all mathematical reasoning as a sequence of purely logical conclusions. Since, this tradition maintained, all reasoning in theories like elementary axiomatic geometry can (and must) be capable of being represented in the form of strictly logical inferences codifiable in terms of a completely formalized logical system, conceptualizations like Peirce's which rely on geometrical constructions (or on other iconic representations) are irrelevant.

Russell is a representative example of thinkers adhering to this line of thought. Unfortunately for them, they miss what in reality is Peirce's deep insight, to wit, that even the kind of apparently purely symbolic reasoning we carry out in formal logic is in the last analysis iconic. This is the same insight as is expressed in a different way by the Beth-Hintikka idea of considering all first-order logical arguments as frustrated counter-model constructions. As soon as we realize this iconicity of logical reasoning, we can make the Peircean distinction, which therefore is a telling example of his way of thinking in general.

Ironically, my unwitting reconstruction of Peirce's distinction has met with precisely the same misunderstanding as that which led the vast majority of logicians and philosophers to overlook the significance of Peirce's discovery. For instance, Hookway (1985: 199–200) considers this reconstruction of Peirce's distinction merely as a way of 'developing Peircean themes' in specialized contemporary logical theory and rejects it as not being able to 'help us to get to the heart' of Peirce's thought. Yet the evidence Hookway himself marshals tells eloquently against his judgment rather than for it. He mentions several wider issues in Peirce to which my reconstruction is alleged to be irrelevant. They include 'the use of abstract reference as crucial to the most important and widespread forms of theorematic reasoning' (ibid. 200). In reality it is the introduction of new objects by existential instantiation that creates the most interesting problem of abstract reference, namely, the problem of the status of the 'arbitrary objects' or 'witness individuals' that are apparently referred to by the 'dummy names' introduced in existential instantiation. And this problem, far from being neglected in my reconstruction, is thrust into prominence by it. Moreover, I have pointed out that the problem of understanding existential instantiation is a time-honoured one, going back to the interpretation of the logical and mathematical notion of *ekthesis* in Aristotle and Euclid (Hintikka 1974).

Again, Hookway places considerable emphasis on the connection between Peirce's distinction and questions of decidability. This connection is nevertheless a mere corollary to my interpretation and hence tells in its favour. Not only is it the case that corollarial reasoning is mechanizable and decidable. On my reconstruction, the decidability of a theory becomes simply the problem of telling which 'auxiliary constructions' to carry out – or even merely how many of them will be needed for a proof. Predicting this number is equivalent to the decision problem of the theory in question.

Even Peirce's at first somewhat surprising speculation that 'the need for theorematic reasoning reflects the current state of mathematical ignorance' turns out to have an interesting point. For if the mathematical theory we are dealing with happens to be (deductively) complete, decidability follows from axiomatizability. Hence Peirce's conjecture might simply reflect a (mistaken but natural) surmise that decidability (completeness) entails the possibility of corollarial reasoning.

Hence, far from forcing us to ignore such Peircean claims and conjectures, my reconstruction offers an excellent framework for discussing and even evaluating them. In reality, it is Hookway who fails to 'get to the heart of' Peirce's thought, which in this case is the iconicity of even purely formal inferences of symbolic logic.

In emphasizing the importance of diagrams, graphs, and icons in reasoning, Peirce is not primarily talking about some new fancy forms of reasoning different from the traditional modes of reasoning in geometry or other kinds of mathematics or from the modes of logical reasoning developed since Peirce. To allege this is to miss completely his deeper point. His point is that all these different modes of reasoning are at bottom iconic and diagrammatic. This result may have striking philosophical consequences – as, for example, Kettner maintains – but they are not tied to any particular method of doing logic. To claim that they are is comparable to accepting a logical argument only as long as it is expressed in French, but not in English translation. The philosophical consequences in question must be capable of being argued for in terms of any method of logical systematization. To try to connect them to Peirce's idiosyncratic and quaint techniques in logic is to misunderstand completely Peirce's point and to block the path of inquiry in logical theory.

Peirce's idea of the iconic character of logic can be illustrated by a different comparison. It is an index of the subtly ambiguous relations between formalism and representation that a universalist thinker like the early Wittgenstein could also maintain the iconicity of language under the guise of his ill-named 'picture theory of language.' Thus an emphasis on iconicity does not *per se* put Peirce in the model-theoretical camp. The true differences between the two traditions are revealed by more elusive clues. But even though elusive, these clues are real. Not only does the pictorial character of language *apud* the Wittgenstein of the *Tractatus* belong to what can only be shown but cannot be said, which for Wittgenstein implies that we cannot speak about the iconicity of our language in the language itself. Wittgenstein's sometime picture conception of language is completely static, completely timeless. It serves only to account for the way sentences (both atomic and complex sentences) represent the world. In contrast, in Peirce, iconicity is the key to logic and logical inference. 'Icons are specially requisite for reasoning,' he wrote (4.531).

10 The Role of Human Action in the Constitution of Meaning

The role of game-theoretical concepts in the model-theoretical tradition is but a special case of a wider phenomenon. On the universalist conception, the representative relations have to be there before any one particular use of language. One can use them, but one cannot change or generate them – or at least one cannot systematically discuss in one's own language such changes and generations nor theorize about them. Hence, particular concrete human actions cannot be a constitutive element in such semantic relationships. Consequently, for a believer in the universality of language there is likely to exist a sharp contrast between the study of the semantics of language (in so far as it is possible) and the study of the use of language. This distinction is of course the one generally known as the contrast between the semantics and the pragmatics of a language. As a matter of historical fact, a belief in the inexpressibility of the semantics of language (as maintained by the Viennese positivists) was the background of Morris's creation of the semantics versus pragmatics contrast (Morris 1938, 1946). What is remarkable about the distinction is not just the postulation of some sort of boundary between two theoretical enterprises, but the idea that pragmatics inevitably involves the peculiarities of the language users in question and hence inevitably belongs to the psychology and sociology of language rather than its logical and philosophical study.

Hence, the received distinction between semantics and pragmatics is not only inspired by a universalist vision of language, but loses its *raison d'être* if the universalist paradigm is given up. Of course, such a violation of the semantics versus pragmatics distinction takes place in game-theoretical semantics, once again showing its inseparable ties with the model-theoretical tradition.

Peirce is quite explicit about the role of certain interpersonal activities in the semantic interpretation of uttered propositions in general, not just in the case of quantifier sentences. He is also aware of the game-like nature of those interpersonal activities. 'The utterer is essentially a defender of his own proposition, and wishes to interpret it so that it will be defensible. The interpreter, not being so interested, and being unable to interpret it fully without considering to what extreme it may reach, is *relatively* in a hostile attitude, and looks for the interpretation least defensible' (MS9: 3–4).

This passage has been quoted earlier by Risto Hilpinen (1983:267), who adds: 'Peirce occasionally calls the interpreter of a proposition its "opponent" (e.g. in MS515). Thus the language-game played by the utterer and the interpreter with respect to an indeterminate proposition is, according to Peirce, a zero-sum game.' It is of a particular interest to us here to see how according to Peirce an interpretation of an utterance, far from being fixed ahead of time, comes about during the 'language-game' between the utterer and the interpreter.

This shows vividly once again the closeness of Peirce's ideas to those codified in game-theoretical semantics. At the same time it can be seen how Peirce's game-theoretical interpretation of quantifiers that was discussed in section 5 above is merely a special application of more general ideas connected with his pragmatism.

Moreover, Peirce practises in his actual work in logic what he preaches in his semiotic theory. His entire theory of existential graphs is, as the very name suggests, an exercise in iconic representation. Peirce's semiotic ideas, such as his distinction between icons, indices, and symbols, sometimes occur in the midst of his purely logical work and are made use of there (cf, e.g., 4.447).

Here we are obviously touching on some of the most characteristic general features of Peirce's theories of language and meaning.

11 The Model-Theoretical Attitude as a Presupposition of Pragmatism

To put the general point even more bluntly, Peirce's pragmatism (or pragmaticism, if you prefer) is predicated on a denial of any absolute separation of semantics and pragmatics and hence predicated on some version of what I have called the calculus conception. For without it, the use of a word or a sentence either is irrelevant to its meaning in any theoretically interesting sense or else cannot be discussed in language.

A comparison with Wittgenstein might be instructive here. Like Peirce, Wittgenstein believed that the use of language is constitutive of its meaning. And like Peirce, Wittgenstein does not mean by 'use' a mere verbal use, that is, a 'game' whose moves are language-acts. Both are emphasizing the use pragmatically in the sense of its language utilization. (Witness, for instance, how Wittgenstein compares language to a box of tools.) But there the similarities end. As a universalist, Wittgenstein could not officially say anything about language-games in general or even develop a real theory of any particular kind of language-games, in complete contradistinction to Peirce. What is even more striking, as far as their semantic role is concerned, is that Wittgensteinian language-games were essentially static. Their role was to constitute the network of meaning relations that connects language with the world. Paradoxically, they do not help very much to understand how we humans actually use those relations. For all his fame as a theorist of logic, Wittgenstein never had anything interesting to say about logical *inference*, which was precisely one of Peirce's long suits. For Wittgenstein, logic has to be considered as a mere calculus, without any references to a semantic foundation that could be discussed in language.

These observations throw some ironic light on Peirce's place in history – or perhaps on the way his place in history is conceived of by later philosophers. Much of the recent resurgence of interest in Peirce and in particular in his theory of language has been in the context of traditions which emphasize pragmatics and, more generally, the roots of language and meaning in the language community, in its customs, rules, and practices. Such an emphasis is apt to lead to many valid insights into Peirce's thought. However, in so far as this tradition presupposes a contrast between semantic approaches to language, including explicit formal semantics, and use-oriented approaches, it is in one important respect foreign to Peirce's thought and likely to distort it. For Peirce, there cannot be any impenetrable boundary between pragmatics and a formal study of language, or between semiotics and logic. As his own words show (e.g., in the application to the Carnegie Foundation in 1902), logic was for Peirce formal semiotics. It is not just that according to Peirce we have to study the pragmatics of language over and above its syntax and formal semantics. A rightly understood semantics, even the most formal one, *is* part of pragmatics, and even the most purely syntactical (formal) rules of logical inference are anchored in the semantics and even pragmatics of the symbols involved in it. Conversely, if there ever was an idea that Peirce would have found foreign, it is the idea that we could study semiotics without sooner or later needing the help of symbolic logic. Peirce's ideas about the need of an interpretant or about the game character of quantifiers are not calculated to replace a logical and formal study of language, but to show what such a study is supposed to capture. In a later jargon, Peirce is not maintaining a contrast between pragmatics and semantics (including logical semantics), but is pointing to their ultimate unity. In this respect, too, Peirce's place in history can be defined more sharply than has been done in the earlier literature.

This point is not disproved by the often striking similarities between Peirce and the later Wittgenstein. Wittgenstein made certain rule-governed activities, his 'language-games,' the basis of all meaning. The result was a denial of the presence of any sharp logic in our actual language. But if so, how could Peirce find a foundation for his exact logic in essentially the same human activities? The answer is that those *prima facie* similarities are in some cases only skin deep. Admittedly, there are genuine kinships between the two, such as the role of human activity in linguistic meaning and anti-scepticism, manifesting itself as a reliance on truths which are indubitable because they are not doubted. Similarities between Peirce and the later Wittgenstein can be used as evidence against the unity of logic and semiotics only if Wittgensteinian language-games are conceived as social games of using language in the sense of speech-acts and other language-acts. Only then can these language-games be contrasted to logic and logical theory. This is, however, a rank misinterpretation of Wittgenstein, as I have shown elsewhere (cf Hintikka and Hintikka 1986).

But another question arises here. How can Wittgenstein, unlike Peirce, maintain the ineffability of semantics if that semantics is based on rule-governed human activities? Surely we can talk about such activities, including their rules, all the time in our language! The answer lies in Wittgenstein's peculiar holism. In his mature view, entire language-games are conceptually primary in relation to their rules. We do not understand a language-game by guessing its rules, according to Wittgenstein. We can only grasp the rules of the game by learning to master the entire game. And that game as a whole is ineffable. In Peirce, in contrast, there is no assumption of irreducible holism.

Once again Peirce and Wittgenstein turn out to be at one and the same time very close to each other and yet worlds apart.

12 Placing Peirce in History

So what *is* Peirce's place in the history of logical theory? He was a working member of a tradition which was largely suppressed in his own time and in the next couple of decades. Because of this suppression, few if any of his most interesting ideas were developed by others. By the time the model-theoretical tradition was revitalized again among logicians and philosophers, some of Peirce's problems and ideas had been superseded and even forgotten. Others were found to be brilliant anticipations of ideas that were later rediscovered independently. Undoubtedly there may be further ideas in Peirce that still deserve to be taken up and developed further. (For instance, it is turning out that Peirce's graphical notation is well suited for the purpose of avoiding a certain important trap into which Frege fell in developing his notation.) A genuinely interesting and important interpretation of Peirce has to be able to sort out his ideas into these categories. And that can be done only on the basis of a solid knowledge of the subsequent history of the ideas Peirce had and of the substantive issues involved in his work. At the same time, the forays into the details of Peirce's logical and philosophical views that I have reported in this paper (see especially sections 5 and 9) provide examples of how interesting and important Peirce's ideas are even from a contemporary perspective.

References

Peirce is quoted in the standard editions, unless otherwise indicated, plus Carolyn Eisele, ed., *The New Elements of Mathematics by Charles S. Peirce*, 4 vols (The Hague: Mouton 1976). Abbreviations are as given at the beginning of this volume.

Freeman, Eugene, ed. 1983. *The Relevance of Charles Peirce*. La Salle, Ill.: The Hegeler Institute.
Hilpinen, Risto. 1983 'On C.S. Peirce's Theory of the Proposition: Peirce as a Precursor of Game-Theoretical Semantics.' In *The Relevance of Charles Peirce*, 264–70. See Freeman for full citation.
Hintikka, Jaakko. 1973. *Logic, Language-Games and Information*, Oxford: Clarendon Press.
– 1983. 'C.S. Peirce's "First Real Discovery" and Its Contemporary Relevance.' In *The Relevance of Charles Peirce*, 107–18. See Freeman for full citation.
– 1988. 'On the Development of the Model-theoretical Viewpoint in Logical Theory.' *Synthese* 77: 1–36.
– 1990. 'Quine as a Member of the Tradition of the Universality of Language.' In *Perspectives on Quine*, edited by R. Barrett and R. Gibson, 159–75. Oxford: Basil Blackwell.

Hintikka, Merrill, and Jaakko Hintikka. 1986. *Investigating Wittgenstein*. Oxford: Basil Blackwell.

Hookway, Christopher. 1985. *Peirce (The Arguments of the Philosophers)*. London: Routledge and Kegan Paul.

Kusch, Martin. 1989. *Language as the Universal Medium vs. Language as Calculus. A Study of Husserl, Heidegger and Gadamer*. Dordrecht: Kluwer Academic.

Morris, Charles. 1938. *Foundations of the Theory of Signs*. International Encyclopedia of Unified Science, vol. 1, no. 2. Chicago: University of Chicago Press.

– 1946. *Signs, Language and Behavior*. New York: Prentice-Hall.

Sluga, Hans. 1987. 'Frege against the Booleans.' *Notre Dame Journal of Formal Logic* 28: 80–98.

van Heijenoort, Jean. 1967. 'Logic as Language and Logic as Calculus.' *Synthese* 17: 324–30.

Inference and Logic According to Peirce

ISAAC LEVI

1 Introduction

In his *Minute Logic* of 1902, Peirce wrote:

> Logic is the science of the general necessary laws of Signs and especially of Symbols. As such, it has three departments. Obsistent logic, logic in the narrow sense, or *Critical Logic*, is the theory of the general conditions of the reference of Symbols and other Signs to their professed Objects, that is, it is the theory of the conditions of truth. Originalian logic, or *Speculative Grammar*, is the doctrine of the general conditions of symbols and other signs having the significant character. Transuasional logic, which I term *Speculative Rhetoric*, is substantially what goes by the name of methodology, or better, of *methodeutic*. It is the doctrine of the general conditions of the reference of Symbols and other Signs to the Interpretants which they aim to determine ... (2.93)

Peirce's identification of three main branches of logic includes one branch, critical logic, which he calls 'logic in the narrow sense.' In his first Harvard Lecture of 1865, Peirce claimed that symbols must satisfy 'three distinct systems of formal law.' Failure of a putative symbol to satisfy any one of these three codes converts it to nonsense bearing 'a certain resemblance to a symbol without being a symbol' (W1:174). The three systems of formal law are laws of 'Universal Grammar,' 'Logic,' and 'Universal Rhetoric,' respectively (ibid. 175). Substitute 'Speculative' for 'Universal' and one obtains two of the three branches of what is considered logic in 1902. What is called 'logic' in 1865 corresponds to 'Critical Logic' or 'logic in the narrow sense' in 1902. There are no doubt some differences between the disciplines identified in 1865 and in 1902. For example, in 1865 the trichotomy is restricted to the study of symbols. In

1902, it is extended to cover the cases of indices and icons. Even so, in both 1865 and 1902, speculative or universal grammar concerns syntactical features of representations, critical logic is concerned with semantic features, and speculative or universal rhetoric or methodology is concerned with conditions for legitimate inference. What appears to be different in 1865 and in 1902 is Peirce's characterization of logic. Logic in the 1865 sense is a species of logic (to wit, 'critical logic') in 1902.

The question I wish to consider is this: What, if anything, is the substantive change in Peirce's view that induced this change in terminology?

The answer cannot be that Peirce was uninterested in methodology in his earlier work and became more engaged with it in later life. The range of interests revealed in the Harvard Lectures of 1865 seems to have remained with him in later life. Moreover, the 1865 lectures are full of methodological reflections. My conjecture is that the shift in terminology is prompted by difficulties with Peirce's early views concerning direct inference and induction combined with his abiding insistence that the domain of logic includes not only deductive inference but inductive and hypothetic or abductive inference as well. Direct inference is reasoning from knowledge of statistical probability or chances to judgments about subjective or credal probabilities – that is, judgments of the fairness of betting rates in the single case. Peirce's initial efforts to offer an account of inductive reasoning focused on reaching conclusions about chances from experimental data. His insightful and original resolution in the 1870s and 1880s of the difficulties with his views in the 1860s concerning direct inference and induction prompted a dialectic in his thinking that led to his abandoning his efforts to provide a semantic account of the validity of inductive and abductive inference of the sort he sought in the 1860s in favour of understanding the conditions of legitimacy of deductions, inductions, and abductions in terms of their efficacy in performing the tasks of inquiry. In order to include investigation of these normative questions within the domain of logic, Peirce extended his conception of logic to include methodological questions.

2 Unpsychologistic Logic

The ostensible purpose of Peirce's Harvard Lectures of 1865 and the Lowell Lectures of 1866 was to argue that inductive and hypothetic reasoning were properly included in the subject matter of logic.

In the first Harvard Lecture of 1865, Peirce attributed to Kant the definition of logic as 'the science of the necessary laws of the Understanding and Reason – or what is the same thing – the science of the sheer Form of thought in general' (W1:164). Although Peirce preferred Kant's conception to Mill's, it remained, none the less, too psychologistic. It suggested that the forms of interest to logicians are realized only in thought. Peirce contended that such forms are realized in any symbol whether it is a psychological event, linguistic expression, or other bit of behaviour or physical process. Peirce conceded that symbols need to be understandable by agents and that this requires psychological processing; but, in contrast to the more psychologistically inclined logicians, Peirce did not require that symbols be understood in order to qualify as symbols as long as they were capable of being understood (ibid. 165–6).

Peirce emphasized that one of the advantages of his 'unpsychologistic' view of logic is its elimination of the Millian view of logic as concerned with explaining and predicting the way human agents do think. Counter to views he advanced later in his career (in *The Minute Logic* of 1902, 2.195–200), he also dismissed the prescriptive view that they are 'normative laws' regulating how we ought to think. Concerning the normative view, Peirce had the following to say: 'But why ought we to be logical? Because we wish our thoughts to be representations or symbols of fact. It is evident therefore that logic applies to thought only in so far as the latter is a symbol. It is to symbols, therefore, that it primarily applies. Now by recognizing this fact it becomes plain at once that the objects of these laws cannot but comply with the laws; and hence that the whole idea of their being "normative" laws is false' (W1:166).

G. Frege followed Peirce in opposing Mill's view that laws of logic are laws of psychology. Peirce and Frege agreed that logic is a science of objectively true principles imposing preconditions on thinking. Frege, however, did not dispute the claim that logic is concerned with the way we ought to think. He took the position that the prescriptive force of logical laws is derivative from logical laws understood as objective truths. We ought to use as principles guiding our reasoning any true principles, whether they are truths of logic or physics and whether we know what these truths are or not. In this sense, logical laws are prescriptions concerning how we ought to reason (Frege 1967, 12–13).

By way of contrast, Peirce contended that a failure to comply with the laws of logic is a failure to reason symbolically – that is, to reason at all.

A normative dimension does, of course, creep into Peirce's view. Representations need not be symbols capable of conveying information. Icons and indices fail to do so. But inferences and the propositions that are their premises and conclusions are symbols carrying information. To consider, receive, or communicate information, symbolic representations satisfying the syntactic and semantic requirements of logic are needed. Thus, Peirce like Frege would concede that inquirers ought to conform to logical requirements; but the goals to be promoted by such conformity are understood differently. For Frege, we ought to conform in order to use truth-preserving rules of inference. For Peirce, we ought to conform in order to make inferences.

Peirce and Frege agreed that the formal constraints on symbolization guarantee the truth-preserving validity of deductive inferences but fail to guarantee truth-preserving validity of inferences where true laws of physics are used as rules of inference. Consequently, Frege's view that we should conform to the laws of logic in order to groove with the truth seems virtually equivalent to Peirce's view that we should conform to the laws of logic in order to achieve successful symbolic representation.

Appearances, however, are deceiving. Frege was content to restrict logic, to deductive logic whereas Peirce was not. For Peirce, successful symbolization came in two varieties: On the one hand, symbolic representation (by means of a proposition) may fail to carry *new* information but might instead elaborate or 'explicate' the implications of the information already available (W1:458). On the other hand, such symbolic representation could add to the available information and, in this sense, be 'ampliative.' Hence, when a proposition is a conclusion of an inference, it is explicative if it fails to add to the information already carried by the premises and is ampliative otherwise.

According to the early Peirce, information is carried by 'symbols.' These symbols may be terms, propositions, or arguments. A term singles out an object or set of entities (its denotation, extension, or breadth) by specifying a set of properties (its connotation, intension, or depth) which those objects share (W1:272–86, 454–71, and W2:70–86).

Consider, then, the proposition that all men are risible. This proposition conveys information by declaring the extension of 'risible' to include the class of men and the intension of 'man' to include the property of being risible. A proposition fails to convey any new information if the extensions (intensions) of the subject and predicate terms already coincide. In that case, the subject and predicate terms carry the same information.

An inference is ampliative if and only if the hypothetical proposition claiming that the conclusion is true if the premises are true carries new information additional to that already available to the inquirer.

The interesting feature of Peirce's early view of ampliative inference is that the information terms carry and, hence, their intensions and extensions depend upon the information an inquiring agent already has. If, for example, agent X is in a state of ignorance, where, as far as he or she believes, it is possible that some men are risible and others are not, the intension of 'risible man' is greater than that of 'man' and the extension of 'man' is at least as great as that of 'risible man.' But if the inquirer should change his or her belief state by coming to the conviction that there are no risible men, Peirce insisted that the intensions, as well as the extensions of 'man' and 'risible man' come to coincide (W1:275–7).

Compare this with the way Frege motivated his distinction between *Sinn* and *Bedeutung*. He invited his readers to suppose that the Morning Star is identical with the Evening Star. He then asked why the sentence 'The Morning Star is identical with the Evening Star' carries more information than 'The Morning Star is identical with the Morning Star' (Frege 1952, 56–7).

Peirce would have regarded Frege's question to be confused. Under the supposition that the Morning Star is identical with the Evening Star, the information conveyed by the two identity claims is the same. Neither proposition adds any new information to the information already available. Consider the inference from 'The Morning Star is larger than the Sun' to 'The Evening Star is larger than the Sun.' Frege would require an account of the ampliative character of this inference (on the supposition that the Morning Star is identical with the Evening Star). According to Peirce, however, under the same supposition, the inference is explicative – not ampliative. Peirce would concede that when the inquirer is in suspense as to the identity of the Morning Star and the Evening Star, the inference is ampliative. But when the identity is assumed true, the inference from the one to the other does not enlarge the information available and, hence, is not ampliative.

Frege's distinction between sense and reference (or the corresponding distinction between explicative and ampliative inference) agrees (roughly) with Peirce's 1867 distinction between essential breadth and depth (W2:79–80) – that is, with the distinction between intension and extension in a state of maximal ignorance.[1] But when the state of belief is more substantial, Frege would continue to classify inferences with respect to whether they are explicative or ampliative in the same way. Otherwise Frege would have thought that the distinction carried an unacceptable level of psychologistic baggage. Peirce would have disagreed.

For example, according to the early Peirce, the inference from the Morning Star being larger than the Sun to the Evening Star being larger is ampliative if one is in suspense as to whether the Morning Star is or is not identical to the Evening Star. If one takes the identity statement for granted, it is non-ampliative. According to Frege, the inference should be ampliative in both cases.

None the less, there is no psychological consideration entering into the distinction between ampliative and explicative inference relative to a body of information. The premisses and conclusion of an inference are propositions. The information can be represented symbolically by a 'theory' – that is, a set of propositions closed under deductive consequence. Proposition C is inferable explicatively from P_1, P_2, ..., P_n *relative to theory K* if and only if C is deducible from K and the P_i's. And deducibility can be characterized in semantic and syntactic terms. Ampliative inference is inference which is not explicative. Hence, it can be characterized formally as well. There is not the slightest whiff of psychologism in Peirce's approach.

To be sure, only explicatively valid inferences are such that the truth of their premises guarantees the truth of their conclusions in virtue of formal properties of the inference relative to the information already available. To ascertain how well ampliative inferences support their conclusions requires appeal both to factual considerations and to the aims of inquiry in ways that cannot be fully characterized in semantic and syntactic terms. Peirce was prepared to focus on the question of how one ought to reason ampliatively because he thought that in inquiry we ought to acquire new information ('more truth') as well as avoid error (W1:285). He thought that the validity of ampliative inference is a formal and, hence, a logical question because the necessary and sufficient conditions for being an ampliative inference adding information to that already available are formally specifiable. Such validity does not mean that the premises of the ampliative inference provide sufficient support for the conclusion to warrant adopting the conclusion on the basis of the premises. For the early Peirce, a valid inference is one which lends support to some degree or other to the conclusion (W1:438). Only in the case of explicatively or deductively valid inference did he claim that the support would be maximal.

To sum up, for Peirce, explicative inferences include valid deductive inferences but are not exhausted by them. Inferences where the premises do not deductively imply the conclusion but do so relative to the information already available to the inquirer are also explicatively valid. However, from the point of view of the inquirer all and only explicative inferences are truth preserving relative to the information available to the inquirer in virtue of semantic considerations alone. Peirce contended that ampliative arguments can also be valid on the basis of formal considerations alone even though they are not truth preserving relative to the information available.

By way of contrast, Frege held that legitimate inferences ought always to be truth preserving. Logic should focus, therefore, on those inferences that are truth preserving on the basis of formal considerations alone. Moreover, the truth-preserving status of the inferences should be independent of the information available to the inquirer. Hence, only valid deductive inferences in the strictest sense should fall within the province of logic.

Peirce divided ampliative inferences into two subcategories: inductive and hypothetic. These types differ formally from one another with respect to the formal conditions necessary and sufficient for their validity. Both the Harvard Lectures of 1865 and the Lowell Lectures of 1866 identify the formal conditions of inductive and hypothetic inference in terms of the relations of these inferences to deductively valid categorical syllogisms. Thus, corresponding to a valid syllogism in Barbara there is a valid inductive form exchanging the major premiss of the syllogism for the conclusion. The corresponding valid hypothetic inference exchanges the minor premiss for the conclusion. Inductive and hypothetic inferences are formally valid in the 'unpsychologistic sense' but they are not truth preserving. Peirce regarded the formal differences between these two types of ampliative inference as reflecting different kinds of explanatory arguments obtained when one makes these inferences. He contended that only putative ampliative inferences meeting the formal conditions necessary and sufficient for inductive or hypothetic validity can be relevantly assessed with respect to the strength of such inferences.

Thus, Peirce did not recommend grooving with the truth in the sense in which Frege later on did. He did not prescribe reasoning in conformity with true laws whether we believe them or not. Inquiry, as he explicitly declared later in 'The Fixation of Belief,' is concerned to settle doubts – that is, increase information. Ampliative logic could offer 'formal' – that is, semantic – conditions for the validity of ampliative inferences seeking to meet this demand.

On the other hand, scientific inquiry, as Peirce also maintained, seeks not only to increase information but to obtain new information that is error free. (See Harvard Lecture X of 1865, W1:285.)[2] Peirce never thought criteria for ampliative inference that achieve a legitimate trade-off between increasing information and avoiding error could be specified in formal terms. He was undeniably interested in the questions of avoiding error and acquiring new information; but identifying principles for avoiding error or even assessing degrees of reliability were not within the province of logic as he construed it in 1865. Thirty-seven years later, he modified his conception of logic to allow such normative and methodological questions within the domain of logic.

3 Probabilistic Logic

F.P. Ramsey prefaced his well-known 'Truth and Probability' of 1926 with a citation from Peirce, and there are expressions of sympathy with Peirce's ideas registered elsewhere in the paper (Ramsey 1990, 52–94). Ramsey's essay, however, is customarily celebrated for its pioneering contribution to the project of deriving numerical representations of the utility and subjective probability judgments of expected utility maximizers from information about their preferences. Peirce was an opponent of what is nowadays called 'Bayesianism.' He would have had little sympathy with Ramsey's insistence that rational agents should have numerically determinate credal-probability distributions over any space of possibilities they consider. It should be emphasized, however, that no matter what importance Ramsey may have attached to his representation theorems, within the framework of his paper these theorems played an ancillary role. Ramsey, like Peirce, and in opposition to Russell and Keynes (and by implication to Frege), was interested in a conception of logic that encompasses both explicative and ampliative reasoning.

In his *Treatise on Probability*, J.M. Keynes declared his ambition to do for probability logic what Russell and Whitehead had done for deductive logic (Keynes 1921, ch.1). Like Russell (and Frege), Keynes regarded deductive entailment as an objective relation between premisses and conclusion which recognizes inferences from premisses to conclusion to be formally valid and truth preserving. Keynes's ambition was to develop a probability logic licensing inferences from premisses to probability judgments where the relation between premisses and conclusion is also formally valid and truth preserving.

Ramsey's essay is devoted to rejecting Keynes's vision of a probability logic and to making some positive suggestions concerning what might be meant by probability logic. In so doing, Ramsey was backing away from the views of logic prevailing at Cambridge under Russell's influence and moving closer to Peirce's ideas. Ramsey's construction of a betting-rate interpretation of belief probabilities was intended to serve an illustrative role helping to explain what he had in mind for a probability logic.

When an inquirer's total evidence and background information is K, and relative to K the agent has a degree of belief r in hypothesis H (in the sense of a degree of personal or subjective probability), one might, if one likes, speak of an 'inference' from K to the judgment that H is probable to degree r; but, if one does, the notion that the inference is truth preserving makes no sense. The alleged 'conclusion' of the inference lacks a truth value – that is, is neither true nor false. This point is emphasized by Ramsey. Yet Ramsey thought that the network of probability judgments made by an agent at a given time could be subjected to requirements that constitute requirements of probabilistic consistency or coherence (Ramsey 1990, 78–9).

After explicitly appealing to Peirce's distinction between explicative and ampliative reasoning (1990, 82), Ramsey contrasts a 'lesser logic which is the logic of consistency or formal logic' with the 'larger logic, which is the logic of discovery, or inductive logic.'

What we have now to observe is that this distinction in no way coincides with the distinction between certain and partial beliefs; we have seen that there is a theory of consistency in partial beliefs just as much as of consistency of certain beliefs, although for various reasons the former is not so important as the latter. The theory of probability is in fact a generalization of formal logic; but in the process of generalization one of the most important aspects of formal logic is destroyed. If p and $\bar{q}$ are inconsistent so that q follows logically from p, that p implies q is called by Wittgenstein a 'tautology' and can be regarded as a degenerate case of a true proposition not involving the idea of consistency. This enables us to regard (not altogether correctly) formal logic including mathematics as an objective science consisting of objectively necessary propositions. It gives us not merely the ἀνάγκη λέγειν, that if we assert p we are bound in consistency to assert q also, but also the ἀνάγκη εἶναι that if p is true, so must q be. But when we extend formal logic to include partial beliefs this direct objective interpretation is lost; if we believe pq to the extent of 1/3 and $p\bar{q}$ to the extent of 1/3, we are bound in consistency to belief $p\bar{q}$ also to the extent of 1/3. This is the ἀνάγκη λέγειν, but we cannot say that if pq is 1/3 true and $p\bar{q}$ is 1/3 true, $\bar{p}$ must be 1/3 true, for such a statement would be sheer nonsense. There is no corresponding ἀνάγκη εἶναι. (Ramsey 1990, 82–3)

Peirce displayed no explicit concern with formulating a logic of consistency for degrees of belief. One aspect of this topic, however, engaged his interest throughout his career. Consider the case of a prospective visitor to Madeira who wanted life insurance for the duration of his one-year sojourn there. Suppose it is known that the chance is 0.9 of an Englishman visiting Madeira surviving for a year and that the chance is 0.1 of a consumptive visiting Madeira surviving for a year. The applicant for insurance is known to be an English consumptive. The problem facing the insurer is to ascertain a fair premium to charge.

This question is a special instance of the general problem of determining the fair betting rate and, in this sense, the subjective, belief, or credal probability an agent ought to assign to a hypothesis concerning the outcome of an experiment (the English consumptive surviving a year's visit to Madeira) given the agent's full beliefs about chances. So construed, the examination of this issue concerns the 'logic of consistency' for credal probability. Ramsey's discussion focused on the requirement that credal-probability judgments ought to obey the formal requirements of the calculus of probability. I call this requirement the 'principle of credal coherence.' Ramsey to the contrary notwithstanding, it is at least entertainable that the logic of consistency for credal probabilities includes other requirements as well.

Both John Venn in *The Logic of Chance* (Venn 1866) and Peirce in his 1867 review of Venn's book (W2:98–102) agreed that an agent's knowledge of objective chances or physical probabilities (which they interpreted as specifying what the relative frequencies of outcomes of repetitions of experiments would be were large series of such repetitions realized) should ground judgments concerning fair betting rates in specific cases. They were reluctant, however, to admit that these judgments are judgments of credal probability – anxious as they were to resist using the idea of subjective, epistemic, or credal probability.

Peirce's official position was that probability is a property of inferences of a given kind. It is the long-run relative frequency with which inferences from true premisses would yield true conclusions (Lowell Lecture III, 1866, W1:400–1). Consequently, he could not admit the notion of a probabilistic logic of the sort Ramsey was advocating that regulated degrees of belief.

To be sure, in 1865 Peirce wrote that the theory of probabilities 'is closely allied to the subject of logic, if not actually a part of it' (W1:189). His reference appears to be to the formal calculus of probabilities which he saw as closely related to Boolean algebra. There is no implication that the formal calculus applies to degrees of belief as Ramsey's principle of credal coherence requires or that there is an additional principle of direct inference regulating degrees of credal probability.

However, in 1866 Peirce did discuss statistical inductions from data to estimates of statistical probabilities or chances and claimed that they correspond to explanatory syllogisms. He did not say so then, but such syllogisms would have to be what he later called 'probabilistic' or 'statistical' and would look like direct inferences. In 'Deduction, Induction and Hypothesis' of 1878, Peirce did regard a facsimile of direct inference to be a form of deduction (W3:324–5), but the form in which he presents the inference is problematic in several respects.[3]

In 'The Doctrine of Chances' of 1878, Peirce explicitly addressed the problem of the single case. He clearly recognized that when decision makers assess decision problems in single cases, they need not be concerned with average benefits accruing from making decisions of one kind in a series of repetitions of similar decision problems. He suggested instead that to be 'logical' the decision maker should behave as if he were concerned with long-run benefits in such a series of repetitions (W3:276–89, and Levi 1980b, 130–4). Finally, in 'A Theory of Probable Inference' of 1883, Peirce explicitly admitted that direct inference yields a conclusion where the associated probability is the 'modality' with which the conclusion is drawn (W4:426n) and, hence, is to be construed as something like a subjective or credal probability. Moreover, the inference in question is regarded as one of two species of deductive inference, the other being demonstrative inference:

A cardinal distinction between the two kinds of inference is, that in demonstrative reasoning the conclusion follows from the existence of the objective facts laid down in the premises; while in probable reasoning these facts in themselves do not even render the conclusion probable, but account has to be taken of various subjective circumstances, – of the manner in which the premises have been obtained, of there being no countervailing considerations, etc.; in short, good faith and honesty are essential to good logic in probable reasoning. (W4:410)

However, even if the subjective circumstances allowing for probability are present, it is still the case that in probable deduction, the conclusion is only probable. (W4:411)

Notice that the conditions under which one is warranted in assigning a probability to the conclusion cannot be fully specified formally but include so-called subjective considerations – in particular, the requirement that given the background information the premises invoked constitute the total relevant information. In effect, Peirce had abandoned his conception of *deductively* valid inference as being fully characterizable in semantic or formal terms alone.

In the 1883 paper, Peirce also explicitly acknowledged that in general such modes of inference are 'apagogical inversions' of syllogisms that are not demonstrative but are rather probable or statistical – that is, direct inferences. Thus, Peirce recognized that in order for the account of inductive and hypothetic inference he was proposing in 1883 to work, he needed to allow for an account of direct inference that regarded the probability judgment in the conclusion to be the 'modality with which the conclusion is drawn rather than part of the content' and that this conception of direct inference played a similar role in inquiry to necessary inference and, hence, should be regarded as a species of deduction.[4]

The 'principles of direct inference' endorsed by Peirce in 1883 cannot be derived from Ramsey's principle of credal coherence. Yet, if principles of direct inference are legitimate, they belong to the logic of consistency for credal probabilities and supplement the principle of credal coherence.[5]

There are other ways one might seek to add constraints to the logic of probabilistic consistency. P.S. Laplace and A. de Morgan invoked principles of insufficient reason or indifference. Venn and Peirce rejected such principles.

Both Venn and Peirce took the position that if all that was known about the applicant was that he was English, the fair betting rate on his life should be 0.9. If, again counter to fact, all that was known was that the applicant was a consumptive, the fair betting rate should be 0.1. In either of these cognitive situations, a degree of belief in Ramsey's sense would be licensed by the underwriter's convictions concerning the chances and his information about the applicant according to direct inference.

In the case under consideration, the underwriter knows too much about the applicant. He knows he is an English visitor to Madeira and also that he is a consumptive visitor. Knowing one without knowing the other licenses a direct inference to a numerically definite judgment of subjective probability grounded on knowledge of chance. But once the underwriter knows both bits of information, he cannot invoke either the information about chances of surviving a year among consumptive visitors or chances among English visitors. He needs information about chances of survival among English consumptive visitors. Without such information, the principles of probabilistic coherence and direct inference make no determinate recommendation as to what the credal probability of the applicant surviving the visit to Madeira for year would be.

In his 1867 review of Venn's *The Logic of Chance*, Peirce took the position, in effect, that no judgment of credal probability should be made unless it could be grounded in knowledge of fact – that is, of chances or objective statistical probability. Appeal to insufficient reason was an unacceptably a prioristic way of assigning credal probabilities. For Venn and Peirce the principles of credal coherence and direct inference constitute a complete set of constraints on credal consistency.

Although Venn disavowed insufficient reason, Peirce complained that Venn was, none the less, a backslider into the 'conceptualistic' view of de Morgan and Laplace. Venn allowed that an insurer who knew that the visitor to Madeira applying for insurance is an English consumptive could be fairly sold insurance at the betting rate of 0.9 and also at the betting rate of 0.1 or, for that matter, any mixture of the two. Venn cannot be accused of invoking insufficient reason; but he can be charged with allowing the insurer to adopt any numerically definite degree of belief between 0.1 and 0.9. Because it allows the decision maker to make such a credal-probability judgment based solely on his or her interests and personal hunches, Peirce thought the view contained a whiff of the a prioristic conceptualism found in the use of insufficient reason. Doing so need not violate credal coherence and direct inference; but it fails to meet the additional demand imposed by Peirce that no numerically definite judgments of credal probability be made unless they can be grounded in knowledge of chance or statistical probability. Peirce's view is an instance of what I call 'objectivist necessitarianism' (Levi 1980a). In the absence of such grounding, Peirce argued, 'credence and expectation cannot be represented by single numbers' (W2:102).

To sum up, a logic of consistency for credal-probability judgments might invoke a principle of credal coherence with or without supplementation by principles of direct inference and insufficient reason.

Necessitarians forbid making probability judgments more determinate than can be derived from a logic of consistency for credal probability.[6] Different versions of necessitarianism emerge from selecting different subsets of the three principles just cited.

Laplace, de Morgan, Venn, Peirce, Ramsey, and de Finetti all endorsed the principle of coherence. Of these only Venn and Peirce endorsed direct inference. Only Laplace and de Morgan endorsed insufficient reason. Laplace and de Morgan appear to be necessitarian. Because numerically definite probability judgment is not grounded in knowledge of facts, Peirce considered it 'conceptualistic.' Peirce was also a necessitarian. But he rejected insufficient reason and replaced it with direct inference allowing for the grounding of numerically definite probability judgment in knowledge of facts. Venn, Ramsey, and de Finetti were not necessitarians. They allowed for an element of personal judgment. They were conceptualists but for a different reason than Laplace and de Morgan were.

No matter how these issues are sorted out, they concern what Ramsey called the logic of consistency. Both Peirce and Ramsey claimed that there could be a logic of consistency for probabilistic as well as deductive inference. Ramsey contended that such a logic would not coincide with a logic of truth, at least in the case of ampliative inference. Ramsey rightly recognized this as a deviation from the views of Keynes and as calling for a critical rethinking of the conception of logic advocated by Russell (or, for that matter, Frege).

The similarity between Peirce's view and Ramsey's is not, however, complete. Note has already been taken of the fact that Peirce did not think that rational agents always ought to have numerically definite degrees of belief. But, as I am interpreting him, he did think that there are constraints on the judgments of credal probability an inquirer ought to have relative to his or her information about chances. To this extent, the subject matter of Peirce's account of what Ramsey called 'the logic of consistency' coincides with Ramsey's. It applies to constraints on an agent's credal-probability judgments. Where Ramsey and Peirce differ is that, for Ramsey, such constraints concern ampliative inference, whereas by the time Peirce was prepared to acknowledge officially that he endorsed principles of direct inference, he insisted that they were principles of explicative or deductive and not ampliative inference (W4:420–1). Consequently, insofar as induction and hypothesis were, for him, the two species of ampliative inference, neither of these kinds of inference concerned assigning credal probabilities to propositions on the basis of the available knowledge or evidence. And insofar as Peirce insisted on a logic of induction and hypothesis, his understanding of logic was more ample than Ramsey's. These points require a closer scrutiny.

4 Ampliative Inference as Change in Commitment

Inference, whether it is ampliative or explicative, involves a change in belief. According to Peirce's belief-doubt model of inquiry, inference is implicated in the removal of the doubt that provides the incentive to inquiry. Removal of doubt is, after all, a change in the inquirer's state of belief. Prior to instituting such a change, the inquirer makes a distinction between what he regards as settled and what is open to question or doubt. At the termination of inquiry, the distinction is altered in some way. Some claims which were open to doubt become settled. And claims which were initially settled might become doubtful.[7]

Suppose that at t_0 Mario is convinced that Albany is north of New York and that 'is north of' is transitive. At t_1, Mario learns somehow that Montreal is north of Albany but fails to put two and two together and to believe that Montreal is north of New York. This he manages to do at t_2. The transition from t_0 to t_1 and the transition from t_1 to t_2 both involve a change of belief. But the first shift illustrates what Peirce would have called an ampliative inference. New information was added to Mario's belief state. The change from t_1 to t_2 by way of contrast is merely explicative or non-ampliative. It does not yield new information.

According to this perspective, there is a sense in which Mario did not change his state of full belief in the interval from t_1 to t_2. He was already committed to being certain that Montreal is north of Albany at t_1; for the negation of this proposition is incompatible with what he consciously took for granted by that time. The change which took place between t_1 and t_2 was Mario's fulfilling the commitment he had already undertaken (Levi 1991, ch. 2). There is no change in his commitment to a distinction between what is settled and what is conjectural or between what is seriously possible and what is not. With this terminology in place, we may say that ampliative inference involves a change in doxastic commitment, whereas explicative inference involves a change in doxastic performance – that is, success in fulfilling doxastic commitments.

The distinction just drawn between change in commitment to a state of full belief and change in the extent to which such commitments are fulfilled may be generalized to credal-probability judgments. An agent's commitments to a state of full belief call for his or her satisfying the requirement that he or she be certain of all the logical consequences of his or her full beliefs. An agent's commitments to a state of full belief cum credal state of credal-probability judgments supplements this requirement with the constraints that the principle of credal coherence and direct inference be satisfied together with credal caution. These constraints are all aspects of a logic of consistency in Ramsey's sense. Any change in either full belief or credal-probability judgment which improves the agent's performance in fulfilling commitments meeting these constraints is explicative inference.

Ampliative inference involves a change in commitment from one state (ideally) fulfilling these commitments to another such state.[8] Explicative inference involves no change in commitment but rather a change in the extent to which commitments already undertaken are fulfilled. Direct inference is explicative in this sense. Moreover, in 1883 Peirce said it was explicative. He could not have claimed this legitimately by appealing to the account of extension, connotation, and information he offered in the 1860s. As Ramsey had pointed out, probabilistic reasoning is not truth preserving because credal-probability judgments lack truth values. Even so, if one keeps in mind that change in information is a species of change in doxastic commitment and change in credal-probability judgment is another such species, a probabilistic logic of consistency including direct inference is explicative and not (as Ramsey suggested) ampliative. Peirce emphasized, I surmise, this aspect of the ampliative-explicative contrast in dealing with probabilistic reasoning. For Ramsey, as for Frege, the truth-preserving feature of explicative inference remained salient and so he drew the contrast in a different way.

5 Direct Inference and Induction

Peirce's recognition of direct inference as a species of explicative inference played a central role in improving his understanding of induction and led eventually to a reconsideration of the way he classified inferences into deductions, inductions, and abductions. To see this, we shall look a little more closely at his understanding of induction and hypothesis in the 1860s.

At that time, Peirce held that inductive inferences have the formal structure of arguments whose premisses are conclusions and minor premisses of syllogisms in Barbara and whose conclusions are the corresponding major premisses. Hypothetic or abductive inferences have the formal structure of arguments whose premisses are conclusions and major premisses of syllogisms in Barbara and whose conclusions are minor premisses. Peirce allowed also for inductions and abductions to be obtainable from valid syllogisms in the second and third figure by such 'apagogical inversion.'

Thus, if the major premiss or 'rule' of the syllogism is 'All cloven-hoofed animals are herbivorous' and the subsumption or minor premiss is 'Neat, swine, sheep and deer are cloven hoofed,' one may validly deduce 'Neat, swine, sheep and deer are herbivorous.'

According to the early Peirce, one could also validly (in the sense explained previously) make the inductive inference from 'Neat, swine, sheep and deer are cloven hoofed' and 'Neat, swine, sheep and deer are herbivorous' to the conclusion that 'All cloven-hoofed animals are herbivorous.' This is a form of inference which increases information by increasing the intension of 'cloven-hoofed animal' and increases the extension of 'herbivorous animal.'

Peirce also required that the neat, swine, sheep, and deer should be a random sample from the cloven-hoofed animals. By a random sample Peirce meant at the time that 'being cloven hoofed was the only condition that consciously guided us in the selection of these animals' (W1:433). Peirce thought that 'it was a fair presumption when we are conscious of no disturbing condition, to suppose that there is none' (ibid.). This view conflicts with Peirce's critique of Venn. If we select from the cloven hoofed according to the criterion of randomness given and find out that the sample consists of neat, swine, sheep, and deer, we are conscious of some condition – to wit, that we have selected neat, swine, sheep, or deer. Moreover, we do not know whether it is a 'disturbing' condition or not. The problem is precisely like the issue of the English consumptive planning to visit Madeira. Even if he had been selected at random from the English, if we know that he is a consumptive, the question arises as to whether this is a disturbing condition. In Venn's and Peirce's example, the only way to find out is to ascertain the chance of an English consumptive visiting Madeira surviving a year. If it is the same as the chance of an English visitor to Madeira surviving a year, the fact that the given person is a consumptive is not disturbing. Otherwise it is. In his review of Venn's *Logic of Chance*, however, Peirce was quite insistent that we cannot presume that no disturbing condition is present just because we neither know nor believe that a given condition we believe to be present is disturbing.

Precisely the same point holds in the case of the neat, swine, sheep, and deer even if they had been selected at random in Peirce's sense. Peirce should have worried about this. Otherwise, even though the form of the induction formally meets the requirements Peirce lays down for the validity of inductions, it cannot qualify as a legitimate ampliative inference. There is no way to reason, as Peirce apparently wanted to do, that the chance is high that someone following inferences such as the one he considers will be approximately correct in the long run a large proportion of the time.

Not only should Peirce have worried about the nuisance information, but I believe he did so. He went out of his way to assert that disjunctive predicates like being a neat, a swine, a sheep, or a deer are not symbols even though the disjuncts are. Disjunctions of symbols are not symbols and cannot carry information. It follows that such disjunctive predicates (which Peirce considers to be signs with denotation but without connotation) cannot carry relevant information and are no longer a nuisance. Peirce never justified the denial of symbolic status to truth-functional compounds of symbols, but in the 1860s, he often asserted it. There appears to have been no good reason for his introducing this restriction on symbolization except the need to remove nuisance information standing in the way of his account of induction.

By the time 'The Probability of Induction' of 1878 and 'A Theory of Probable Inference' of 1883 were written, Peirce no longer spoke of disjunctive terms. Instead, he represented inductive inference as the following of a rule which is adopted in advance of its implementation. Thus, if the design of random sampling from the cloven-hoofed animals is known to have a high chance of yielding a representative sample before implementation and *before it is known whether neat, swine, sheep, or deer will be selected*, one can via probabilistic deduction or direct inference accord a high degree of credal probability that whatever the outcome of following the rule in the specific case might be, one will obtain a correct answer. After one has made the random selection, found out that neat, swine, sheep, and deer were selected – all of whom were not only cloven hoofed but herbivorous – and responded according to rule by adding the information that all cloven-hoofed animals are herbivorous, one can no longer make a probability judgment concerning the correctness of the conclusion reached by following the rule in the particular case. The disjunctive character of 'neat, swine, sheep or deer' does not prevent the term from carrying information and, in this case, prevent the term from carrying nuisance information. At best, one can say that either the conclusion reached is correct or, if wrong, repetition of the experiment will with high probability reveal it. (W4:417).

Strictly speaking, the induction is not a species of inference at all and should not be construed as an apagogical inversion of even a statistical syllogism, as Peirce said it was. In Peircean induction, one has changed from one state of belief to another in response to experimental or observational inputs and according to a rule or program which the inquirer has chosen in advance. The data serving as inputs do not provide intermediate premises from which the final belief state is obtained according to the rule.[9]

The only argument involved in all of this is the reasoning involved in reaching the judgment before experimentation that, whatever the outcome, the probability of avoiding error in following the rule is high, which is a direct inference from knowledge of chances and the assessment that the information promised from following the rule is worth the risk of error. But the conclusion of this reasoning is not the conclusion of the induction. Rather, it is the recommendation for using data as input in reaching an inductive or ampliative conclusion. The direct inference involved is explicative. The decision to use the rule is based on a consideration of means and ends and is, in this sense, methodological.

6 Three Tasks in Inquiry

Peirce never abandoned speaking of deduction, induction, and abduction as species of inference. But his conception of inference, of the distinction between explicative and ampliative inference, and of the distinction between deduction, induction, and abduction underwent significant changes.

There is a way to rationalize Peirce's new conception of explicative inference in keeping with Peirce's conception of inquiry. He could defend this change on the ground that explicative inference had a specific *task* to perform in inquiry – to wit, make explicit the testable consequences of conjectures and the reliability of rules of procedure. Even if it remained possible for Peirce to retain some kind of formal characterization of the contrasts between deduction, abduction, and induction, the change Peirce had made in the 1880s in this characterization indicated that the guiding consideration controlling how inferences are classified now focused on the functions such inferences performed in the various tasks involved in inquiry.

By the time he wrote *The Minute Logic* in 1902–3, Peirce had explicitly recognized this point and had convinced himself of the relative unimportance of formal characterizations of induction and abduction in terms of permutations of the premisses and conclusions of syllogisms. He began to reclassify inferences by reference to the tasks performed in inquiry in a more thoroughgoing way. In particular, he recognized that inferences he had classified as abductions closely resemble inductions in the tasks they perform and ought to be reclassified as a species of induction (2.102; see also Levi 1980b, 129–130, and K.T. Fann 1970). Abductions were construed as attempts to identify potential solutions to problems on the basis of the available information. They are conjectures. Deduction elaborates the testable ramifications (both demonstrative and probabilistic). Induction is the activity of selecting a solution to the problem from the conjectures obtained via abduction on the basis of the testable consequences obtained by deduction.

My contention is that Peirce had already started on this path in 1883 when he revamped his conception of deduction to include statistical deduction. I suggest that this change itself was prompted by Peirce's adoption of the Neyman-Pearson rationale for confidence-interval estimation as the basis of his conception of induction in 1873 and 1883. The introduction of confidence-interval estimation was in turn provoked by the difficulties with nuisance information in direct inference which Peirce had sought to avoid by withholding symbolic status from disjunctive terms in the 1860s. By the turn of the century, Peirce had managed to revamp his understanding of induction and hypothesis more in keeping with the views adumbrated in 1883. This change led to an abandonment of key elements of the unpsychologistic definition of logic advanced in the 1860s as the science of the forms of symbolization and to an inclusion of methodological concerns within the province of logic. By 1902, Peirce had come to the conclusion that logic is, indeed, a normative science that includes an account of the goals of inquiry. He reclassified many of the arguments he had originally considered hypothetic or abductive as species of induction. He explicitly acknowledged that his efforts to offer formal characterizations of induction and abduction in terms of permutations of syllogistic arguments were unsatisfactory and that his doctrine of intension and extension of symbols was less important than he had originally suggested.[10] Instead, deduction, induction, and abduction were regarded as different types of tasks involved in inquiry.[11]

Given this task-oriented characterization of the trichotomy between deduction, induction, and abduction, Peirce abandoned his attempt to offer a formal characterization of valid inductive and abductive inferences. He could still say that induction and abduction are species of logic. For Peirce, the domain of logic covered induction and abduction as well as deduction at the end of his career as it had in the 1860s; but logic was no longer the purely formal science he advertised it to be in the 1860s. The change in his view was not due to a shift in his interests from formal to methodological questions. He always had interests in both. But he had initially thought that he could offer an account of the differences between deduction, induction, and abduction in formal terms which would do justice to his ambition. Driven by the difficulties that the question of the reference class posed for direct inference and, in virtue of that, for inductive inference, Peirce was led to modify the way he classified inferences as deductive, inductive, and abductive and to do so in methodological rather than formal terms. But as the Rabbis say in *Ethics of the Fathers*, 'one sin begets another.' When Peirce appreciated the importance of what he was doing, he enlarged his conception of logic to encompass methodological issues so as to preserve the view that there are logics of abduction and induction. Peirce embraced the view that logic is a normative science not merely in the sense that it provides critical standards for how one ought to reason but that it offers critical standards designed to identify the ends of inquiry as well as the means for realizing them.

Notes

1 I agree with Skagstad (1981, 128) that Peirce did not endorse a contrast between sense and reference of the sort favoured by Frege. But I do not think that Peirce's dissent would derive from his maintaining that meaning and reference are identical. The passages cited by Skagstad on page 128 seem to be reiterations of Peirce's insistence that any distinction between sense and reference is always relative to the information conveyed by a symbol – that is, its interpretant.

2 William James's later vision of a trade-off between seeking truth and shunning error in fixing belief is already articulated in Peirce's 1865 lecture.

3 The syllogism Peirce used has the 'rule' or major premiss 'The beans in this bag are 2/3 white.' The 'case' or minor premiss is 'this bean has been drawn at random' that

Peirce rephrased as 'this bean has been drawn in such a way that in the long run it would turn out white 2/3 of the time.' I suggest that this means that the chance or objective probability of obtaining a white bean on a single draw is equal to the percentage of white beans in the bag. The form of this argument is deductive in the sense of a necessary or analytic inference provided that random selection is interpreted in the fashion just indicated and that an additional premiss is adopted stating that sampling is with replacement and beans do not change colour during the period of the trial. But even if we grant that these assumptions suffice to give us a deductive argument in the strict sense, Peirce's endorsement of the claim that one can equate the rate at which one should bet on a white bean being drawn on a specific occasion should equal the chance cannot be derived from deductive logic alone.

4 Peirce also admitted that his past practice of attempting to convert statistical syllogisms into necessary inferences yielded 'apagogical inversions' that are also necessary and are, according to Peirce, 'of no particular interest' (W4:426n).

5 To be sure, one could insist as B. de Finetti (but not Ramsey) did that the concept of physical probability or chance is meaningless so that the issue of determining credal probabilities on the basis of information about chances cannot arise. Principles of 'direct inference' or statistical syllogism cannot, from de Finetti's point of view, contribute to a logic of consistency for belief probabilities.

6 In Levi 1980a, a credal state is representable by a set of permissible real valued functions. The set is required to be non-empty (credal consistency) and convex (credal convexity). Strict Bayesians, like de Finetti, Ramsey, and Laplace and de Morgan before them, assumed that such sets should be single membered as well (credal uniqueness). I took for granted the least controversial requirement on the permissibility of permissible credal probability functions that might be a candidate for a principle of what I called inductive logic (probability logic might have been better). I followed Peirce in registering sympathy for a principle of direct inference and in being hostile to principles of insufficient reason. Authors who share my sympathy (either explicitly or tacitly) for credal coherence disagree about the status of the other two principles. Suppose, however, that a conception of what constitutes a complete inductive logic is endorsed. Necessitarianism is the requirement that all probability functions satisfying the conditions of inductive logic should be permissible.

7 How Peirce understood the distinction between what is settled and what is open to question is one of the more problematic aspects of his philosophy. *Prima facie* to take extralogical *H* for granted at time t is to discount the logical possibility that *H* is false as not a serious possibility. From the inquiring agent's point of view, *H* might be false in the sense that its falsity is a logical possibility and also in the sense that the agent is capable of changing his or her mind and coming to doubt that *H* is true by moving to a position of suspense as to its truth or to a full conviction that it is false. This capacity to change one's mind is accompanied by a capacity to think

hypothetically and counterfactually about situations where H would be false. And not only are we capable of changing our minds, but Peirce would have insisted that sometimes we should do so. Our convictions are, in this sense, corrigible. In spite of this corrigibility, I maintain (Levi 1980a, chapters 1–3, and 1991) that, according to the agent who takes H for granted, there is no serious possibility that it is false in a sense which guides the agent's current deliberations and inquiries. The inquirer assigns H credal probability 1 and regards H as part of his or her background information or evidence. In this sense, the inquirer judges what he takes for granted to be infallibly or certainly true.

I have argued elsewhere (Levi 1980a, ch. 3 and 1991), that Peirce's messianic realism (which presupposes as a goal of inquiry progress to the true complete story of the world and as a hope that scientific methods of inquiry can, in the End of Days, realize the goal) implies that epistemic infallibilism is inconsistent with corrigibilism. Cheryl Misak (1991) seems to think that Peirce's realism does not have this implication. And she also argues that my textual evidence for his embracing the equation of incorrigibilism with infallibilism is questionable. I think she is right about the texts I argued. Thanks to K.L. Ketner, Peirce's 1898 lectures at Harvard from which the passages are taken are in an edition that makes it plain that what otherwise looks like a blatant betrayal of the belief-doubt model is a critical response to James's 1897 lectures on 'The Will to Believe' (Peirce 1992). Misak is, none the less, mistaken about the tension between Peirce's messianic realism and his commitment to the belief-doubt model. Peirce's belief-doubt model of inquiry advanced in 'The Fixation of Belief' and elsewhere is, to my way of thinking, the most original contribution Peirce made to philosophy. It is the aspect of his thought that James and Dewey shared with him. This model presupposes a conception of taking propositions for granted that acknowledges the consistency of epistemic infallibilism and corrigibilism – counter to messianic realism. Dewey and James solved the tension by abandoning messianic realism. In my judgment, they threw out the baby with the bathwater by dismissing truth as a value in inquiry altogether. There is another alternative. One can finesse the conflict between epistemic infallibilism and corrigibilism by substituting for Peirce's messianic realism a secular realism which regards avoidance of error as a common feature of proximate goals of efforts to change states of belief (Levi 1991, ch. 4:10). Peirce's conception of progress towards the true complete story of the world is abandoned (just as recommended by James and Dewey) for the sake of preserving what is valuable in his philosophy – to wit, his belief-doubt model of inquiry. But in contrast to Dewey, a realism which, like Peirce's, regards truth as an important cognitive value is retained.

By replacing Peirce's messianic realism with a secular realism, the coherence of the belief-doubt model of inquiry can be saved, truth can be seen as a goal of inquiry, and clarity can be restored to Peirce's distinction between what is settled for the agent and what is conjectural.

8 Such changes are analogous to the sorts of changes envisaged in thermodynamics or in economics from one equilibrium state to another while ignoring the transitional intermediate states of disequilibrium.

9 In contrast to Peirce, I would not call this process a species of inference at all, precisely because one does not first add the data reports to the state of belief or information and then justify adding the conclusion. Such a procedure is what I have called 'deliberate' or 'inferential' expansion. By way of contrast, Peirce's procedure appeals to 'routine' expansion. Data are used as input (not premisses) in a program previously adopted for adding new information to a state of full belief. As I have suggested (in Levi 1980a, chs 2 and 17, and 1991, ch. 3), routine expansion is the sort of process involved in exploiting the testimony of the senses or of witnesses in acquiring new information. In 1980a and 1980b, I also pointed out that the Neyman-Pearson rationale for confidence-interval estimation is a rationale for routine expansion and that Peirce's conception of induction is as confidence-interval estimation. Peirce seems to restrict expansion to routine expansion in his later writing.

10 Recall that, for the early Peirce, the form of an inductive inference is a permutation of the form of a valid syllogism where the major premiss of the syllogism is the conclusion of the induction. Hypothetic inferences involve taking the minor premiss of the syllogism to be a conclusion. Thus, Peirce could and did insist that he was able to offer accounts of the formal properties of both inductive and hypothetic inferences. He regarded the study of these properties as well within the province of logic. He wanted to maintain that in order to obtain successful symbolic representations which carry new information – that is, are ampliative – inductive and hypothetic inferences would perforce have to be of the forms he identified for them. He did not claim that meeting the formal requirements would insure the truth of the representations obtained even if the premisses of the inferences are true.

11 When facing a question, one task is to identify potential answers to the question and to assess how well they gratify the demands for information raised by the question. This is the task of abduction. Abduction is neither explicatory inference nor ampliative inference. It neither improves doxastic performance nor changes doxastic commitment. Deduction derives consequences of the conjectures posed as potential answers to the question which are amenable to test. It is explicative. Induction uses the results of tests to render a verdict on the potential answers and thereby (at least on some occasions) to change doxastic commitment.

References

Fann, K.T. 1970. *Peirce's Theory of Abduction*. Martinus Nijhoff.
Frege, G. 1952. *Translations from the Philosophical Writings of Gottlob Frege*. Edited by P. Geach and M. Black. Oxford: Blackwell.

Keynes, J.M. 1921. *A Treatise on Probability.* London: Macmillan and Co.

Levi, I. 1980a. *The Enterprise of Knowledge.* Cambridge, Mass.: MIT Press.

– 1980b. 'Induction as Self Correcting According to Peirce.' In *Science, Belief and Behaviour*, edited by D.H. Mellor, 127–40. Cambridge: Cambridge University Press.

– 1991. *The Fixation of Belief and Its Undoing.* Cambridge: Cambridge University Press.

Misak, C.J. 1991. *Truth and the End of Inquiry.* Oxford: Clarendon Press.

Peirce, C.S. 1931–58. *The Collected Papers of Charles Sanders Peirce.* 8 vols. Edited by C. Hartshorne, P. Weiss, and A. Burks. Cambridge, Mass.: Belknap Press of Harvard University Press.

– (W) *Writings of Charles S. Peirce.* 5 vols. Edited by M.H. Fisch, E. Moore, and C.J.W. Kloesel et al. Bloomington: Indiana University Press.

– 1992. *Reasoning and the Logic of Things.* Edited by K.L. Ketner. Cambridge, Mass.: Harvard University Press.

Ramsey, F.P. 1990. *Philosophical Papers.* edited by D.H. Mellor. Cambridge: Cambridge University Press.

Skagstad, P. 1981. *The Road of Inquiry.* New York: Columbia University Press.

Venn, J. 1866. *The Logic of Chance.* London: Macmillan and Co.

The Logical Foundations of Peirce's Indeterminism

PAUL FORSTER

Positively the most important part of the most advanced sciences, Mechanics and Astronomy, has been merely metaphysical, twisting things into shape.

C.S. Peirce, 'Private Thoughts' (W1: 9, 1868)

Discussions of Peirce's indeterminism (the view he called 'tychism') have yet to address two important interpretive problems.[1] First of all, Peirce has been admired for being among the first, if not the first, to develop an indeterministic metaphysics. Yet Peirce's arguments for this view, published in 1893 in 'The Doctrine of Necessity Examined' (6.35–65, 1892), are widely deemed inadequate.[2] This fact raises the question of how so precocious a metaphysical thesis could have developed from such flimsy arguments.

Accompanying this question is a related biographical puzzle. Estimates of the date of Peirce's discovery of indeterminism range from 1884 (the time of his first paper on cosmology, entitled 'Design and Chance') to the early 1890s (when the series of papers in which Peirce presented tychism to the world appeared in the *Monist*).[3] If these estimates are right and if, as Ian Hacking (1990) has persuasively argued, Peirce's indeterminism is the product of a new style of reasoning, one that embodies possibilities literally unthinkable a century before, then it is important to consider what could have led Peirce at about age fifty to this unprecedented and radical position.

This paper addresses both of these questions by outlining the broader philosophical foundations of Peirce's indeterminism and by tracing its intellectual roots. First, by way of background, I will summarize the view of chance and necessity to which Peirce is responding. Second, I will argue that, contrary to received opinion, indeterminism is not a relatively late development but rather is among Peirce's earliest philosophical discoveries. A close reading of the

Lowell Lectures of 1866 (delivered twenty-five years before the *Monist* series and eighteen years before 'Design and Chance') will show that Peirce was crafting his indeterminism from the beginning. Third, I will discuss Peirce's early effort to work through the logical foundations of this view. This discussion will show just how far Peirce had advanced in his early writings in developing his indeterminism. What is more, it will demonstrate that Peirce's indeterminism was not initially based on the cosmological arguments he published in 1893, but rather emerged out of his early theory of statistical inference. Finally, I will consider the intellectual influences that led Peirce to indeterminism so early in his career.

Design, Chance, and Necessity: The State of the Art

When Peirce sketches the history of the rise of statistical methods in science he begins, appropriately, with Adolphe Quetelet (6.297, 1893). Quetelet's aim is to do for the human sciences what Newton did for physics; his innovation is the extensive application of probability theory to these sciences.

Quetelet's approach rests on two fundamental principles. The first is the law of causality: 'that constant causes necessarily produce constant effects, all other things being equal' (Quetelet 1969, 6). An important corollary of this law is that if constant causes should produce different effects, then, laws being immutable, it must be that all other things are not equal; that there has been some change in the conditions under which the law operates that influences its effect. For Quetelet, this law is fundamental to physics and must be adhered to in the human sciences as well.

Although, for Quetelet, everything can in principle be causally explained, the infinite variety of experience is beyond the comprehension of finite minds. The study of individuals in their indefinite particularity yields only isolated facts. The aim of science, however, is to ascertain predictive *laws*. Correlations among phenomena are to be viewed as the resultant of predominant 'constant causes' in conjunction with relatively minor 'accidental causes.' Thus all scientists emulate the astronomer who seeks to reduce planetary motions to general laws and minor perturbational forces.

Quetelet's second axiom, the 'law of accidental causes,' states that accidental causes give rise to variations in phenomena that are normally distributed about a mean value that is itself fixed by laws that define some general class (Quetelet 1848, 17). From this law it follows that the greater its deviation from the mean, the rarer a phenomenon's occurrence. It also follows that the effects of accidental causes, though influential in individual cases, cancel out over the species taken as a whole. Thus by averaging data collected over a large sample of individuals within a class, scientists can abstract the constant causes that form the essence of a species or group (Quetelet 1969, 6). The arithmetical mean of all traits in some class (the group of Frenchmen, for example) constitutes the ideal type of that group (a '*l'homme moyen*') which is analogous to the centre of gravity in matter (Quetelet 1981, 3).

For Quetelet every science deals with averages of this type; even the results of direct observation are subject to variability calculable by means of the error curve. Consequently, scientific results are inevitably probabilistic. Knowledge of the constant causes that define a class cannot yield exact predictions about any particular member since individuals cannot escape the contingencies of accidental causes. None the less, because the effects of contingencies are subject to constraints (as reflected in their being normally distributed about a mean) laws do apply to individual cases within limits of error calculable by the theory of probability (Quetelet 1969, 7).

The view that general kinds are groups of individuals normally distributed ensures that all phenomena admit of analysis by the theory of probability, or, doctrine of chances. At the same time, the law of causality implies that all events are necessitated by their antecedent conditions. Peirce would later see an irony here, but for Quetelet none arises. The distinction between accidental and constant causes enables us to keep both laws. In retrospect, the important prior question is why one might think it *necessary* to keep both laws.

An influential answer to this question is provided by Henry Buckle, whom Peirce also cites in his history of statistical methods of inquiry (6.297, 1893). For Buckle, chance events involve abrogations of law; they are appearances without antecedent causes (Buckle 6). To admit the reality of chance would be to hold that the universe is unlawful and thus unintelligible. However, on Buckle's telling, history shows that appeals to chance are 'most natural only to a perfectly ignorant people' (ibid). As knowledge progresses, the world becomes more predictable and controllable. Thus 'in the ordinary march of society, an increasing perception of the regularity of nature destroys the doctrine of Chance, and replaces it by that of Necessary Connexion' (ibid. 7).

This reply typifies the view of chance and causation prevalent among scientifically inspired intellectuals at the time of Peirce's earliest writings. The main tenets of the view are as follows:

i) Explanations of phenomena are to be modelled on mechanics, the key feature of which is that from a small number of universal laws, and complete knowledge of the state of the universe at a particular instant, all prior and subsequent states of the universe can be deduced.

ii) The doctrine of absolute chance (the view that chance is part of the furniture of the universe) implies that laws of nature are abrogated. Thus it is not only an unscientific, but an *anti-scientific*, view. The same can be said of theories positing free will or miraculous intervention. Insofar as these imply the abrogation of laws, they are at odds with a scientific conception of the universe.[4]

iii) The law of causality, however, is not an ad hoc assumption peculiar to science; it is a principle fundamental to both rational thought (the comprehension of events) and rational action (which requires the formation of reasonable expectations). Thus advocates of the thesis of absolute chance are enemies not just of science, but of reason itself.

iv) Properly construed, chance is not an objective feature of reality. Probabilistic claims measure our subjective uncertainty resulting from ignorance about the specific accidental conditions that cause particular events. Such claims feature in science only because complete knowledge of the state of the universe is beyond our capacity as finite knowers.

v) Since absolute chance implies that the universe is chaotic and since the statistical laws discovered in astronomy or sociology, for example, are none the less *regularities*, the results of science, even though probabilistic and inexact, support rather than undermine determinism.

Peirce calls this view 'Necessitarianism.' Peirce not only questions the foundations of this view in his Lowell Lectures of 1866, but, as I will argue, he uses indeterminism as the basis of this challenge.

Peirce's Lowell Lectures: The Critique of Necessitarianism

It is important to emphasize how pervasive necessitarianism is among prominent writers in the nineteenth century. The view is endorsed with varying degrees of qualification by Kant, Whewell, Laplace, Mill, Spencer, and Herschel, and by members of the Cambridge Metaphysical Club such as John Fiske and Chauncey Wright.[5] Yet this consensus is supported by a bewildering array of philosophical justifications. For example, there is disagreement over whether the fundamental axiom of science is the principle of causality (as is argued by Quetelet, Buckle, Herschel, Laplace, and Wright), the principle of the uniformity of nature (as Mill contends), or the principle of the persistence of force (the candidate of Spencer and Fiske). There are also disagreements about whether these principles are to be justified transcendentally (following Kant, Whewell, and Herschel), or naturalistically, either as the products of evolution (as for Fiske and Spencer) or as the products of induction on direct experience (as for Mill). There is even controversy about whether the denial of these principles is inherently inconceivable (as Kant, Whewell, and Herschel contend), contingently inconceivable (as Fiske and Spencer argue), or conceivable but empirically false (as Mill holds).

By the time of Peirce's earliest work, then, there is the kind of dispute over axioms and foundations among sane and intelligent thinkers that Peirce would later cite as evidence against axiomatic methods of justification in philosophy and science.[6] Given the centrality of mechanics to the argument against appeals to divine intervention, free will, and chance, these disputes about the foundations of science are far from incidental to necessitarians. It is not surprising, therefore, that Peirce addresses these issues in his early lectures on science. What is remarkable is that by that time he had already reformulated the question that necessitarianism was designed to answer.

For the necessitarian, the problem raised by statistical methods is one of reconciliation. A fundamental aim of that view is to find a place for probability in a deterministic world and thereby to legitimate statistical inferences in science. In his Lowell Lectures of 1866, Peirce addresses a different question, namely, does reliance on statistical methods presuppose or imply determinism? Rather than ask *how* science *can* reconcile chance and determinism, Peirce is already questioning whether science *must* reconcile them. While he does not defend indeterminism explicitly in these lectures, we shall see that the mere fact that he is able to raise this issue shows that he has already separated questions of the authority of science as a cognitive pursuit from questions of the merits of determinism as a scientific theory. This means that he had recognized indeterminism as a coherent scientific option.

A large part of the Lowell Lectures is devoted to induction. Induction is important to necessitarianism for at least two reasons. First, on that view, as on Peirce's own, the discovery of laws of nature is the fundamental achievement of science. Second, it is by appeal to the *necessity* of the laws of mechanics that the existence of absolute chance, free will, and divine intervention is ruled out. For both reasons, providing warrant for inferring the existence of necessary laws is vital to the vindication of the authority of science.

Peirce agrees with the necessitarians that probability theory holds the key to understanding induction; laws are generalizations about classes of phenomena based on finite samples of data. Yet, Peirce claims in his lectures, inferences of this kind are at first glance puzzling. After an appropriately selected sample of individuals is examined, the character of the entire population from which it is drawn is inferred. It is only by observation that the character of the members of the sample is known, and there is no direct evidence, observational or otherwise, of the unsampled members of the population. Deductive reasoning from the observational evidence will only explicate knowledge already possessed; it cannot add to it. Yet the opinion about these unseen members is not a guess, but a belief 'found generally to accord with the fact' (W1:394, 1896). The mystery is that: '[in induction] the intellect seizes the premisses afforded by sense, and not merely explicates them, but discovers new facts, such as sense would seem to be needed to find out, and yet those facts are generally true' (W1:394, 1866).

Peirce considers and rejects three theories of the grounds of such inferences. Against theological justifications of induction (such as that of Abby Gratry) Peirce argues that appeals to the nature of God are illegitimate in logic.[7] Against Pierre Laplace's mathematical vindication of induction, he argues that the probability of inductive conclusions cannot be established by a priori reasoning alone.[8] Peirce then examines John Stuart Mill's naturalistic justification of induction. It is Peirce's case against Mill that presupposes the discovery of indeterminism, and thus it demands attention here.

The focus of Peirce's discussion is Mill's claim that induction rests on the principle of the uniformity of nature. Peirce objects that Mill's solution is circular, since the leading principles of induction are presupposed in the vindication of induction. Peirce also argues that Mill's effort to evade this charge rests on ad hoc terminology rather than sound logic. The details are not important here; suffice it to say that if the argument is correct it is sufficient to undermine Mill's view of induction. Yet Peirce carries on to argue against Mill's claim that the uniformity of nature can be proven empirically.

Against Kantians and Cartesians, Mill insists that the falsity of the principle of uniformity is *conceivable* and therefore that the thesis of absolute chance cannot be ruled out on a priori grounds. However, Mill claims that the evidence of regularity disclosed by science proves that nature is uniform. Peirce agrees with Mill that science has discovered laws in nature, but he tries to show that this is not sufficient to establish Mill's principle of uniformity. Mill's evidence is not challenged; rather it is its significance as proof of necessitarianism that Peirce questions.

Against Mill's general claim that the uniformity of nature can be justified by induction, Peirce argues that there are many more irregularities, or accidental relations, than uniformities in nature (W1:417, 1866). Any ripe pear one selects will be sweet, borne on a particular kind of tree, and so on, just like all other ripe pears. Yet for each of these regularities there is an indefinite number of relations true of that particular pear but not all others: it is mine, it grew in a particular orchard, and is now a certain distance from Glace Bay, Nova Scotia: 'Indeed when it is remembered that everything in the world is related to every other in countless ways; it is plain that there is no end to the excess of accidental relations over those which present any regularity' (W:417, 1866). Since irregularities outnumber regularities the empirical evidence does not allow us to conclude that nature follows Mill's principle of uniformity.

Peirce argues that the same goes for Mill's empirical defence of the most general formulation of the principle of uniformity, namely, that the universe is 'so constituted, that whatever is true in one case, is true in all cases of a certain description.' Against Mill, Peirce notes that no law disclosed by science is exactly conformed to in any particular instance without interference from what Quetelet calls perturbational forces. For every scientific generalization there are residual phenomena that the law fails to explain, and thus no truly universal law has ever been found (W1:420, 1866).[9]

Notice that in neither of these two arguments is the evidence in question. Mill admits the existence of 'accidental relations' and is well aware of the probabilistic character of scientific results (Mill 1973, 275).[10] However, whereas Mill wants to show that determinism can explain away accidental relations and 'irregularities' by appeal to the necessitarian view of chance, Peirce is concerned to challenge the notion that all scientific evidence of regularity *must* be viewed as evidence of determinism.

This is also apparent in Peirce's response to another version of the principle of uniformity, namely, that everything belongs to a natural kind. Peirce argues that to say natural kinds exist is to say that some non-analytic universal judgments are true. For if this were the case, then there would be classes of objects with properties in common other than those which are implied by the definition of the class. These would form natural, as opposed to conventionally defined, kinds. Since these non-analytic universal propositions express uniformities in nature, rather than definitional truths, Peirce writes: 'it seems to me likely that when he [Mill] defines the uniformity of nature as the fact that whatever is true of one case is true in all cases of a certain description, he means to identify it with the fact that everything belongs to a real kind' (W1:416, 1866). Here again Peirce does not wish to dispute Mill's claim; he acknowledges that it is likely that everything does belong to a natural kind (W1:416, 1866). However, he tries to argue that this does not establish Mill's principle of uniformity and thus does not prove necessitarianism.

Peirce makes his case by examining the claim 'All humans are mortal,' which is a non-analytic universal truth. To assert this claim is to say that of the four possible groups defined by the presence or absence of humanity and mortality, one group has no members, that is, no objects are both human and immortal. But this fact, says Peirce, marks a dissymmetry, or irregularity, in nature. On the other hand, if one half of humans were mortal and one half immortal, there would be no universal generalizations linking humanity and mortality, yet nature would possess a striking symmetry or regularity. Thus, concludes Peirce, the uniformity of nature is independent of the existence of non-analytic universal truths and thus independent of the existence of natural kinds.

Peirce offers a second argument for this conclusion. He notes that the claim that 'All humans are mortal' states that each person will die; indeed, Peirce says an endlessly existing thing is unimaginable. To say that something non-contradictory is unimaginable is to say that it denotes no objects, but this is *not* to predicate any uniformity of nature. Thus, again, Peirce concludes that the uniformity of nature does not follow from the existence of non-analytic universal truths and thus necessitarianism is not implied by the existence of natural kinds.[11]

As a final attempt to argue this point, Peirce offers the following illustration. Suppose a blackboard is covered with dots, with each dot representing an individual. Let circles be drawn around individuals with any common trait. The intersection of the circle drawn around animals and the circle drawn around rational things will comprise the set of rational animals, which is the typical definition of 'humanity.' Members of this intersection will form a natural class if they can be enclosed within a third circle, since this would signify that the members have a universal character (mortality, for example), in addition to the traits listed in its definition. Peirce continues: 'Now imagine the board to be all covered with circles, of every size, and in the most irregular manner. Do you not see that the utter irregularity itself occasions every part of the board to be included in some segment surrounded by many circles – that is to be a natural class. Here is no uniformity; yet there is a natural classification. Natural classes then cannot constitute a uniformity in nature' (W1:420, 1866).

Since natural classes might exist everywhere even when regularities and uniformities do not, Peirce concludes, evidence of the former does not suffice to prove the uniformity of nature.

We do not have to endorse, or even understand fully, these arguments to appreciate their significance as a response to necessitarianism. Peirce agrees with the necessitarian that the existence of laws is required of any intelligible world. He also agrees that the actual world is intelligible and that science has discovered that laws of nature exist.[12] Therefore, if he is able to argue against Mill that the evidence of regularity in nature disclosed by science does not *suffice* to prove necessitarianism, he must already have conceived of a possibility not open to the received view of chance and causality; namely, that the intelligibility of reality does *not* demand that the laws of nature be *necessary*. Thus Peirce has recognized that denying determinism does *not* commit him to the view that the world is chaotic and unknowable. Having realized that the existence of chance is *not* incompatible with the existence of laws (W1:421, 1866), Peirce was, at this time, well on his way to a metaphysics of probabilistic laws.

This will become even more evident after examining Peirce's early efforts to develop a logical foundation for indeterminism.

Peirce's Early Work on Logic: The Foundations of Indeterminism

For the necessitarian, the principles of the uniformity of nature and of universal causality perform at least two crucial functions. First, they ensure the universal applicability of scientific reasoning and thereby bolster the claim that science can provide an exhaustive understanding of reality. Second, because these axioms are not ad hoc assumptions made by scientists but rather conditions underlying *all* rational thought, they legitimate the claim that necessitarianism rests on neutral epistemology, rather than a scientistic or an anti-theological ideology. While Peirce is not a necessitarian, he is a firm believer in the universality and neutrality of science. As we shall see, Peirce, in his early writings, attempts to carve out a logical space for indeterminism by reinterpreting the axioms of necessitarianism while at the same time preserving their status as fundamental principles of rationality.

For the necessitarian, the principles of uniformity and causality are the grounds of scientific inferences. Peirce's reinterpretation of these principles is based, accordingly, on his own theory of inference.

Peirce argues that inferences are of three irreducible forms: 'Deduction', 'Induction,' and 'Hypothesis' ('Abduction' would not be included until some time after 1893). Each form of inference is a permutation of a standard deductive syllogism, as follows:[13]

Deduction		Induction		Hypothesis	
All S is P	(rule)	M is S	(case)	All S is P	(rule)
M is S	(case)	M is P	(result)	M is P	(result)
∴ M is P	(result)	∴ All S is P	(rule)	∴ M is S	(case)

Deduction merely explicates the premises and does not yield new empirical knowledge.

In induction a 'rule' is inferred from a 'case,' describing a sample from some population, and a known 'result,' describing a common trait among members of the sample.[14] The inferred rule is a law relating these two facts. Induction therefore answers 'how'-questions since it 'informs us upon what principle it is that certain things have a common character ...' (W1:427, 1866).[15]

Hypothesis is what Peirce would later call 'Qualitative Induction.' When it is noticed that an object possesses several traits characteristic of some general class, it is inferred that the object possesses *all* of the characteristics typical of that class. Thus, hypothesis is also reasoning from a sample to an entire population; however, the sampled units are properties not individuals.

Hypothesis explains a known result, in terms of a known rule, by inferring that the relevant condition, or case, obtains. Thus hypothesis reveals '*why* a certain class should have a certain common character ...' (W1:427, 1866); it is reasoning about causes and effects (W1:428, 1866).[16]

With this theory of inference in hand, Peirce redefines the uniformity of nature in terms of the conditions that make hypothesis and induction possible:

> There is still another sense in which we might speak of the uniformity of nature. If we select a good many objects on the principle that they belong to a certain class and then find that they all have some common character, pretty much the whole class will generally be found to have that character [this is simply a description of induction]. Or if we take a good many of the characters of a thing at random, and afterwards find a thing which has all these characters, we shall generally find that the thing is pretty near the same as the first [this is a description of hypothesis].
>
> It seems to me that it is this pair of facts rather than any others which are properly expressed by saying that nature is uniform. We shall see that it is they which are the leading principles of scientific inference. (W1:420, 1866 [parenthetical remarks added]).

Since Peirce's forms of inference are irreducible, we can refer to the condition that makes induction possible as the principle of the uniformity of nature and to the condition that makes hypothesis possible as the principle of causality. In both cases, however, they involve the claim that sound inferences from random samples to entire populations are possible. Having thus reformulated these necessitarian axioms in terms of the logic of statistical inference, Peirce needs to show they are strong enough to preserve the autonomy and universality of science.

Peirce secures the universal applicability of these principles, and hence of science itself, by appeal to the methodological maxim that it is never legitimate to block the road of inquiry. For Peirce, the aim of inquiry is to render phenomena intelligible. For an inquirer to conclude that a phenomenon is ultimately inexplicable is tantamount to attempting to render it intelligible by offering a theory that denies its intelligibility; as a result any such theory is self-defeating. More generally, Peirce claims that any theory that implies that there are domains beyond the scope of inquiry is methodologically flawed (W2:175–6, 1868). Since rational inquirers must presuppose that success is possible, they must assume the principles of uniformity and causality, since these principles make scientific inquiry possible.

Peirce defends the autonomy of these principles from non-scientific interests, and thereby defends the neutrality of science, by demonstrating that they neither rest on, nor imply, any material truths about reality; they are purely formal presuppositions, 'not laws of *nature* but the conditions of knowledge in general' (W1:422, 1866). Put another way, logic, according to Peirce, can establish that the principles of uniformity and causality must hold in any intelligible world, but it cannot (since logic is non-empirical) establish that any such world exists.

In support of this view Peirce argues that the principles cannot be established by experience and thus do not rest on facts about nature. As formulated by Peirce, the principles involve terms like 'pretty much,' 'generally,' and 'a good many' and thus, Peirce argues: 'are so vague that you cannot bring them to any touchstone of experience. They rather insinuate a uniformity in nature than state it. And as insinuation always expresses the state of feeling of the person which uses it, rather than anything concerning its objects, so we may suppose these principles express rather the scientific attitude than a scientific result' (W1:421, 1866).

The principle of causality is unfalsifiable for the further reason that putative counter-examples are never to be construed as evidence against the principle, but rather as anomalies to be investigated, or, problems to be solved. Thus: 'causality evades verification. It cannot be brought to a conclusive test. *There is no case whatever supposable which if it occurred could be said to show that the hypothesis failed* ... Accordingly all thought of proving the law by experience is preposterous' (W1:222, 1865).

Not only does Peirce claim that the principles of uniformity and causality are established independently of experience, he argues that they do not *impose* any particular metaphysics on experience. The principles of uniformity and causality demand only that sound reasoning from samples to populations be possible. This requires the existence of regularities,[17] but Peirce argues that the laws required need only govern the form or pattern of events in the long run, not the order in which events occur. Statistical generalizations express only the 'ratio of the number of occurrences of a specific event to the whole number of occurrences of a supposed *certainly* known generic event of which the first is a special kind' (W1:395, 1866). As a result, the truth of a statistical law depends only on the relative frequency of events in the long run, not on any particular sequence or order of occurrences. Certain courses of experience (getting 1,000 sixes in a row with a fair die, for example) are ruled out, not as being absolutely impossible, but only as (in varying degrees) improbable. What is more, the statistical law exemplified by successive rolls of a fair die is, unlike a deterministic law, compatible with a wide variety of sequences of outcomes; the law 'would hold with one set of numbers as well as with another' (W1:422, 1866). Thus, says Peirce, it has the character of a formal, rather than a material, law.

Furthermore, neither the principle of uniformity nor the principle of causality as formulated by Peirce specifies what the degree of regularity must be. This feature is in stark contrast to necessitarianism. For Peirce, laws can be expressed as conditionals of the general form: 'If event E occurs under conditions C, result R occurs, $p\%$ of the time.' The necessitarian axiom that 'like circumstances will produce like effects' will hold if and only if p is 100, in the case of affirmative laws, or 0, if the generalization is negative. Peirce's principles, although compatible with determinism, do not place *any* restriction on p, and therefore do not impose any particular degree of regularity on the universe. Thus the argument establishing the ontological *neutrality* of Peirce's principles of statistical inference at the same time demonstrates the *partiality* of necessitarian metaphysics. Rather than reduce chance to necessity and thereby eliminate it, Peirce's logic views necessary laws as special cases of probabilistic laws. Since Peirce's principles are compatible with every possible degree of regularity, he claims they are formal laws, not material ones (W1:422, 1866): 'But as the laws which we have mentioned, that as is the sample so is the whole and that the sameness of a number of characters manifests identity, are laws which could hold so long as there were *any* laws, though only formal ones, it is plain that no alteration in the constitution of the world would abrogate them, so that they are themselves formal laws, and therefore not laws of *nature* but the condition of knowledge in general' (W1:422, 1866).

In these early writings Peirce does not develop these ideas further. However, it is interesting to note that his view contains within it a reconceptualization of the relation of cause and effect. As noted above, Peirce insists that it is an inescapable methodological maxim that every event is to be explained. He also says that a 'fact is *explained* when a proposition – possibly true – is brought forward, from which that fact follows syllogistically ...' (W1:426, 1866). Causes are inferred by hypothesis: on the basis of an observed result and a known rule it is inferred that the relevant condition, or case, obtains, since that would render the occurrence of the known result intelligible. However, so far as Peirce's logic of hypothesis is concerned, the relevant rule may be a statistical law. Such laws *determine* their results, albeit probabilistically and not invariably, and their cases describe initial conditions that render such determinations operative. Thus cases inferred by hypothesis are rightly considered as necessary antecedents (even if not in every case sufficient to produce the result) and are therefore justly labelled causes. However, since only universal laws link cases to results invariably, necessity is only a special limiting case of causation. Thus, on Peirce's early view, the universal applicability of hypothesis (that is, of the principle of causation) does not entail necessitarianism.

There is, however, a difficulty lurking in the logic of indeterminism presented thus far. According to necessitarianism, absolute chance is an inherently inexplicable abrogation of law; it is therefore at odds with the laws of rational thought. Peirce avoids this problem, in part, by arguing that the laws of thought are inherently statistical. However, this argument does not eliminate the problem. For Peirce, chance falls under the category of Firstness (6.32, 1891); it is, like feeling, simple, unanalysable, and inexplicable. Thus, a metaphysics of chance would seem to violate Peirce's own logical strictures on positing inexplicable phenomena.

Peirce did not address this issue directly until 1893 when it was raised by Paul Carus. However, it is important to recognize that Peirce's reply relies only on the foundations established in the early work on logic described above; no new logical or conceptual apparatus is introduced.

In the first place, the thesis of absolute chance contradicts necessitarianism not by denying the existence of laws altogether, but only by denying the universality of deterministic laws. To admit of the reality of chance is to deny that *every* event in the universe is *precisely* determined by law. Thus, the issue for Peirce is not whether laws exist or not, but rather to what degree events are governed by laws.

Second, Peirce insists that chance is not a property of *events*, but of their relations; specifically, their relative frequencies. Thus, on Peirce's view chance enters into explanations, not as a material condition of laws (that is, not as a property of events) but as a formal principle linking rules to their results by means of their cases, albeit in a less than exact manner.[18] Therefore, for Peirce, chance is not a mechanism or entity, but a relation among events characterizable by the logic of probability. As a result, the *operations* of chance are both lawful and intelligible.

But is the admission that chance is inexplicable not logically pernicious? Peirce's answer is no. Chance is the absence of deterministic law. But Peirce insists that the absence of some general trait requires no general explanation: 'Chance, according to me, or irregularity – calls for no explanation. If *law* calls for a particular explanation ... surely the mere absence of law calls for no further explanation than is afforded by the mere absence of any particular circumstance necessitating the result, thereby accounting for the coincidence it presents. It would be highly absurd to say that the absence of any definite character must be accounted for, as if it were a peculiar phenomenon, simply because the imperfection of language leads us so to talk of it' (6.612, 1893). According to Peirce, laws delimit possibilities. Chance is the absence of *necessary* determining constraints, that is, the absence of laws that rule possibilities out absolutely. In the passage quoted above, Peirce claims that although laws require explanations, possibilities do not. To understand his point, recall that for Peirce facts are explained 'when a proposition – possibly true – is brought forward, from which that fact follows syllogistically ...' (W1:426, 1866). To explain the absence of law (irregularity) would require that it appear as the result of some syllogistic argument. But this would involve subsuming the irregularity under some general rule, thereby rendering it lawful. Thus, to demand an explanation of irregularity and unlawfulness is self-contradictory. Hence, the inexplicability of chance is *mandated* by logic, not in violation of it.

It might seem, however, that Peirce's logic is not metaphysically neutral after all, since it requires that the world be lawful in order to be intelligible and thereby seems to rule out a priori the possibility of a chaotic universe. It is important to remember, however, that logic, because it is formal, cannot rule any matter of fact in or out. It does reveal the conditions of an intelligible world and that regularity is such a condition, but logic alone cannot establish that an intelligible world exists; a chaotic universe is therefore possible.

On the other hand, Peirce argues that a chaotic universe would be absent of all regularity. In such a world induction and hypothesis could not function since, *ex hypothesis*, the requisite conditions would not be fulfilled. These forms of inference would not be invalid, only inapplicable. They would yield no knowledge, not because they are logically flawed, but because there would be nothing to know (W2:254, 1869). Since knowledge would not be possible and since, for Peirce, to be *real* is to be the object of a true proposition, an unknowable chaos could not be real. Thus logic also shows that it is contradictory to claim that *reality* is chaotic.[19]

Putting these two conclusions together leads to Peirce's bizarre final view that a chaotic universe is *possible* but *unrealizable*.[20] Chaos has a level of being greater than that of pure nothing but less than that of real things.[21]

I have argued, on the basis of questions raised and arguments presented in the Lowell Lectures, that Peirce had discovered indeterminism by 1866. I have also argued that in his early writings on the logic of science Peirce goes a long way towards developing the logical foundations of indeterminism. By way of conclusion, I shall explore the factors that might have led Peirce to such a radical and precocious view so early in his career.

The Roots of Peirce's Indeterminism

Peirce's familiarity with statistical methods throughout his formative years no doubt explains their importance in his philosophy. But it remains startling that he challenged the received view of probability and necessity so early. In 1884, in 'Design and Chance,' Peirce appears to reveal the sources of his indeterminism. First, he claims that his probabilistic metaphysics is 'only Darwinism analyzed, generalized, and brought into the realm of Ontology' (W4:552, 1884). Second, he says that his motive for doubting necessitarianism is that laws require explanations, and he cites the explanation of Boyle's law and the second law of thermodynamics by the kinetic theory of gases as exemplary. Since these facts have led several commentators to conclude that Peirce developed indeterminism on the basis of these theories, this account of the roots of Peirce's indeterminism deserves careful study.

Though Peirce (in a rare display of modesty) confesses his ignorance of the theory of evolution, he was at Harvard during the famous debate between Louis Agassiz and Asa Gray.[22] That debate has direct bearing on the scientific status of necessitarianism. Agassiz, the leading scientific critic of Darwin, held that individual organisms are manifestations of eternal ideal forms. Since no amount of natural variation can alter these forms, new species can be created only by God. He further argued that the species dominant in each epoch are obliterated by geological catastrophes, only to be replaced by new, divinely created creatures. Thus natural history is discontinuous; it is punctuated by the active intervention of the creator.

Gray, on the other hand, argued that evolutionary explanations are methodologically superior to those of special creation theories since they trace the chain of efficient causes much farther back (Gray 11). Evolution is motivated by the desire to extend to the life sciences the well-established principle of physics that there are no sharp breaks in nature (ibid. 101). What is more, evolution best explains the continuity among different species of the same genus, and the fact that within species individuals exhibit a continuous distribution. As a result, Gray insisted, the overwhelming evidence in favour of evolution also undermines Agassiz's theory of special creation.[23]

Gray's view is important for Peirce's metaphysics since evolution plays the same role for Gray that mechanics does for the necessitarian. By establishing the continuity of natural history, evolution underwrites the universal applicability of science and rules out appeals to periodic 'special creations.' What is more, although Gray is convinced of evolution, he is not certain that it is a deterministic theory. He writes: 'Variation is of the nature of an origination ... we cannot predict what particular new variation will occur from any observation of the past ... to introduce necessity here is gratuitous and unscientific ... I agree that, judging from the past, it is not improbable that variation itself may be hereafter shown to result from physical causes, when it is so shown, you may extend out necessity into this region, but not till then' (ibid. 62).[24]

This passage is revealing, not only because Gray foreshadows Peirce's later argument that variety and creativity require indeterminacy, but also because Peirce views Darwinism as founded on statistical methods: 'Mr. Darwin proposed to apply the statistical method to biology ... Darwin, while unable to say what the operation of variation and natural selection in any individual case will be, demonstrates that in the long run they will adapt animals to their circumstances. Whether or not existing animal forms are due to such action, or what position the theory ought to take, forms the subject of a discussion in which questions of fact and questions of logic are curiously interlaced' (W3:244, 1877). The point is that if evolution is sufficient to refute special creation and yet is not itself deterministic, then indeterministic, or statistical, continuity is all the continuity science requires (W1:405, 1866). Evolution seems to offer a third alternative in the debate between advocates of mechanics and advocates of miracles.

While this is a significant result for Peirce, it does not seem to be his inspiration. Darwin repeatedly insists that the use of 'chance' and 'fortuitious variation' in the theory of evolution does not imply indeterminism; these concepts are to be understood in Laplacean fashion (Schweber 266). This was also argued extensively by Chauncey Wright, the senior member of the Metaphysical Club, and echoed by Peirce himself. Indeed, in 1871 Peirce claimed that Darwinism simply extends 'mechanical principles' to familiar phenomena, and thereby contributes to the debasing of morals implied by materialism (W2:485–6). Even in 'Design and Chance' he notes that no evolutionist of any school acknowledges the operation of chance as essential to evolution. Since Peirce does not discuss evolution as an indeterministic theory before 'Design and Chance' and since an indeterministic reading of Darwin would have been too controversial (indeed, explicitly opposed by Darwinians) to ground a metaphysics, it is more likely that Peirce's reading of evolution was a significant application of indeterminism rather than its source.

Peirce also views the kinetic theory of gases as a triumph of statistical methods:

> Darwin proposed to apply the statistical method to biology. The same thing had been done in a widely different branch of science, the theory of gases. Though unable to say what the movements of any particular molecule of a gas would be on a certain hypothesis regarding the constitution of this class of bodies, Clausius and Maxwell were yet able, by the application of the doctrine of probabilities, to predict that in the long run such and such a proportion of molecules would, under given circumstances, acquire such and such a number of collisions, etc.; and from these propositions were able to deduce certain properties of gases, especially in regard to their heat-relations. (W3:244, 1877)

In 1860, Maxwell (1860/1965) derived his velocity distribution law, which states that collisions among molecules in a gas produce a distribution of molecular velocities resembling the error curve. Using this law and calculations of the mean free path of molecules (Clausius's term for the average distance a molecule moves before coming within the sphere of action of another molecule), he was able to derive Boyle's law, among many other properties of gases.[25]

Peirce cites Maxwell's theory as an example of how the operation of chance can give rise to laws. He was also quick to note the connections between Quetelet's social physics, Maxwell's kinetic theory, and Darwin's theory. However, it does not seem that Peirce was initially inspired by these developments, either. Peirce makes no mention of gas theory in the writings leading up to 1866. Also, as in the case of Darwinism, there is no indeterministic interpretation of the kinetic theory for him to appeal to. The use of probability by Maxwell and Clausius is universally interpreted in necessitarian fashion.[26] Furthermore, throughout the 1860s Maxwell's statistical approach was controversial even among physicists at the time and thus would not have offered Peirce a secure foundation for his metaphysics.

While there is much to be said about the impact of both the theory of evolution and the kinetic theory of gases on the development of Peirce's metaphysics, these theories could have been taken as support for indeterminism only *after* indeterminism had been established on more solid ground. More importantly, Peirce provides no detailed discussion of these theories as support for indeterminism in the period leading up to the Lowell Lectures of 1866.

While a more complete survey might produce further potential sources, there is no obvious precursor, and Peirce certainly mentions none, who is sufficiently well known and whose views are sufficiently secure to underwrite so radical a metaphysical view.[27] There is, however, a route to indeterminism through logic itself.

The most influential thinker in Peirce's early life has no connection to statistics at all. It is from Immanual Kant that Peirce inherited his distaste for psychologism and for naturalistic justifications of logic. By Kant, Peirce was convinced that attempts to justify the methods of science by appeals to empirical results are viciously circular. Questions of the foundations of science are prior to, and independent of, any empirical scientific results, including astronomy and mechanics. Early on, therefore, Peirce was moved by Kant to seek an architechtonic foundation for scientific reasoning, one which insists that logic is prior to metaphysics in the sense that it determines the form of knowable reality independently of empirical science (W1:57–84, 1861).

By 1866 Peirce had also become persuaded of the centrality of statistical reasoning to natural science. Having been immersed in techniques of statistical inference throughout his formative years, Peirce (unlike Quetelet and Laplace) was able to take the scientific status and value of these methods for granted and use the logic of statistical inference as the ground of his theory of inquiry. Given his view of the importance of statistical methods to science, and his facility with those methods, it is not surprising that he would come to the conclusion that prior to Kant's question about the possibility of *necessary* (that is, synthetic a priori) judgments is the more general question of the possibility of *synthetic* judgments (for Peirce, probabilistic judgments) *per se*.[28]

In this context, Boole's *Laws of Thought* is particularly significant. By 1866 Peirce had inherited Boole's refutation of Laplace's attempt to reduce statistical inferences to a form of deduction. It was on that basis that Peirce came to view induction and hypothesis as distinct and irreducible forms of inference. In the process, Peirce accepted Boole's frequency interpretation of probability. On that view, probabilistic claims describe the relative frequency of some kind of event in *relation* to a broader containing class of events. Thus, these claims refer to matters of external fact, specifically to regularities in nature, not, as for Laplace, to internal psychological states such as subjective expectations or degrees of belief.[29]

In essence, then, Peirce learned from Kant that foundational issues in logic have metaphysical implications. However, for Peirce, the relevant logic was supplied by Boole.[30] A key feature of that logic is the thesis that probability claims are objective descriptions of regularities in nature of the general form 'If event E occurs under conditions C, result R will occur $p\%$ of the time' (of which necessary laws are a special case). This interpretation of probability combined with a Kantian view of the connection of logic and metaphysics leads to a conception of regularities in nature that allows the *possibility* of real statistical laws. Since Peirce also saw a direct connection between necessitarianism and what he took to be the debasement of morals resulting from nineteenth-century materialism, and since he saw in indeterminism a way to preserve free will while refusing to endorse any form of dualism, this indeterministic metaphysics would be a particularly compelling theory for him to pursue.

Conclusion

The foregoing is far from a complete analysis of Peirce's indeterminism. Nothing in the position presented suggests Peirce's later view that laws of nature themselves evolve. What is more, the view presented does not suggest that events can occur in *violation* of the laws of nature, yet Peirce would later argue that this is what the evolution of law demands. In short, chance, as described here, is no more than 'that diversity in the universe which laws leave room for'; this is the 'transitional' view Peirce claims to have passed through on the way to his final version of tychism (6.602, 1893).

What I have argued is that Peirce's indeterminism is grounded by his theory of statistical inference. I have also argued that Peirce had developed the logical foundations of indeterminism by the time of his Lowell Lectures in 1866. Thus, it ranks as one of his earliest philosophical discoveries. From both the conceptual and historical points of view, then, it is evident that 'chance' is as pervasive in Peirce's thought as he claims it is in the universe.

Notes

1 I would like to thank the following for their comments: Margaret Morrison, Ian Hacking, Isaac Levi, Don Ross, Angus Kerr-Lawson, Joe Macdonald, and Andrew Lugg.
2 See, for example, Goudge (1950, 109, 272–93), Gallie (1952, 214ff), Hacking (1990), Hookway (1985), and most recently, Cosculluela (1992).
3 Murphey (1993, 333) cites the late 1880s or early 1890s; Hartshorne (1941) says Peirce was still a determinist as late as 1890. For Goudge the pivotal year is 1892 (195ff, 219), while Rosensohn (1970, 63–9) says the thesis developed from 1879 to 1885. Hauser (W4:lxx) and Esposito (1980, 153) recognize early discussions of chance, but each begins his story of tychism with 'Design and Chance' written in 1884.
4 Buckle argues that free will is the doctrine of chance applied to the mind. 'Free' acts are said to be caused by a will which is undetermined. This view is at odds with the existence of laws of human behaviour. A true science of human behaviour views actions as the results of motives that have causes; 'therefore, if we were acquainted with the whole of the antecedents, and with all the laws of their movements, we could with unerring certainty predict the whole of their immediate results' (Buckle 13).
5 Mill originally rejected Laplace's account of probability, but he revised his criticism after Herschel forced him to change his interpretation of Laplace (see Strong 1978). His final position is that causality is derived from the principle of the uniformity of nature, which is the most basic and best warranted principle of thought (Mill 275). Darwin's views on this are detailed in Schweber (1977). For the remaining authors see the following: Laplace (1951, 3), Whewell (1967, 66, 178–84), Herschel (1850, 366–73), Spencer (1945, 134–45, 162–70), Fiske (1890, vol. 1, 286–7), and Wright (1971, 71).
6 Proponents disagree not only about foundational matters. For example, whether this view is inherently materialistic and whether it is compatible with progressive evolution is hotly debated. In addition, Spencer and Fiske deduce progress from the persistence of force, yet Wright argues that progress is an anthropomorphic fiction. Darwin also views evolution as non-teleological (Schweber 310). Herschel endorses necessitarianism and design but rejects Darwinism (which he disparagingly referred to as the 'law of higgledy-piggledy') (ibid. 314).
7 The theologian explains the reliability of induction by appeal to the benevolence of God. Peirce objects, first, that even if correct, the question of *how* induction works remains unanswered. Logic must uncover the principles of induction in order to know exactly what has been ordained, and under what conditions it is reliable. Second, he claims that knowledge of God is too crude to be used as a basis for deductions about His effects. Third, theology is a branch of inquiry. To legitimate inductive methods by appeal to results obtained with them is circular. Finally, this

approach undermines natural theology, since if induction presupposes God's benevolence its results cannot be appealed to as proof of His existence.

8 Mathematicians view induction as a species of deduction. Peirce argues that all such attempts run afoul of cases in which we have no prior experience of the phenomenon in question. Laplace argues that in cases of a trial with two outcomes, such as a coin toss, where the relative frequency of the outcomes is unknown (that is, where we have no idea if the coin is fair), there is no more reason for thinking the next toss will be heads than there is for thinking it will be tails. This balanced state of mind is to be represented by assigning a probability of one-half to each outcome.

The general principle here is that equal possibility implies equal probability. Peirce objects to this principle, since it treats as equivalent cases of ignorance and cases in which we positively *know* that the probability of each outcome is one-half. When it is known that the coin is fair it is rational to bet even money on heads since we are assured of winning as often as we lose in the long run. In the case of ignorance, however, there is no such assurance. As a result, the rational course is to abstain from wagering at all.

Furthermore, Laplace's principle yields inconsistent results. Suppose A and Z are distinct outcomes and that events of type A are of two kinds: B and C. According to Laplace's rule, A and Z are equally probable. However, so are B and C, *per impossibile*.

Peirce concludes that 'no correct cyphering can begin with ignorance and land us in knowledge of a probability' (W1:404, 1896). Since calculation of probabilities by deduction requires prior knowledge of the relative frequencies of outcomes, induction cannot be reduced to deduction.

9 Peirce argues that the scientific quest for such laws is inexplicable and unwarranted if the principle of uniformity is to be justified by observation alone (W1:420, 1866). Later he argues that '[t]hose observations which are generally adduced in favor of mechanical causation simply prove that there is an element of regularity in nature, and have no bearing whatever upon the question of whether such regularity is exact and universal or not. Nay, in regard to this *exactitude*, all observation is directly *opposed* to it; and the most that can be said is that a good deal of this observation can be explained away. Try to verify any law of nature, and you will find that the more precise your observations, the more certain they will be to show irregular departures from the law' (6.46, 1892; emphasis added).

10 Mill describes these accidental relations, as 'coincidences from which we have no ground to infer uniformity – the occurrence of a phenomenon in certain circumstances without our having reason on that account to infer that it will happen again in those circumstances. This, however, when looked closely into, implies that the enumeration of the circumstances is not complete … It is incorrect, then, to say that any phenomenon is produced by chance' (275). Thus, such coincidences are rigidly determined by law. This is also the argument given by Chauncey Wright (1971, 131).

11 On the other hand, Peirce continues, if we consider universal propositions which we *can* imagine to be false, such as 'No man has two heads,' 'you will *generally* find that now and then an exception to it occurs. It must be admitted that there are exceptions, to almost every rule. Thus many of the characters which seem to belong to a class universally only belong to a part of it. We cannot know how far this limitation extends; it seems probable that there really are natural classes and that nearly everything belongs to one. But does this bare circumstance constitute any uniformity?' (W1:419, 1866; emphasis added).

12 'Now all law may, in one sense, be contingent. But that there should be knowledge without the existence of law, that there should be intelligence without anything intelligible, all admit to be impossible' (W1:423, 1866).

13 The conditions under which these inferences are valid are summed up in their leading principles. For example, induction and hypothesis require that the sampling involved be random and that the relevant trait be 'predesignated.' For a more detailed discussion of Peirce's theory of scientific inference see Forster (1989).

14 As for Quetelet, induction enables inquirers to distinguish individual traits from those common to every member of a population. It thereby determines which traits of individuals are reliable *signs* of the characteristics that typify some group. Thus, Peirce claims, the product of induction is a natural classification (W1:426–7, 1866).

15 Once again, Peirce insists that the sample must be randomly drawn, that it must be sufficiently large, and that the common trait among the members of the sample must be 'predesignate.' For more on this see Goudge (1950, 158–63).

16 The following is a case of hypothesis:
   1) This sand formation is in the shape of a footprint.
   2) People walking on beaches leave footprints.
   3) Thus, this sand formation was caused by a person.
   The conclusion is merely hypothetical.

17 These principles imply that finite groups of objects in a class are capable of serving as signs of the traits of the entire class. Since, as Peirce would later argue, it is nonsensical to claim that a law has a character that can never be manifest, there must be, for every law, some finite set of instances which manifests it (2.784, 1902).

18 The mode of operation of chance is that of final rather than efficient cause, since it ordains a general pattern of events, which no amount of individual variation can disrupt (W3:8, 1872).

19 Furthermore, since a chaotic world would have no connections among its elements (no Secondness), it would not, strictly speaking, exist. Thus it would also be contradictory to claim that such a chaos is actual.

20 Peirce developed the ontology of modalities very early on (W1:18, 1857; W1:38, 1859).

21 Indeed Peirce tried to show this early on. Laws of the form 'All A are B' exclude possible combinations of characters, that is, they exclude the possibility of an A that is not-B. Were there no laws in the world, no logically possible combination of

characters would be ruled out in this way and thus objects with every possible combination of traits would exist. At the same time, since precisely the same traits cannot be found in two different objects, it follows that 'in a chance-world every combination involving the positive or negative of every character would belong to just one thing' (W3:309, 1878). However, this would amount to a regularity, and thus not be a chaotic world at all. Once again the supposition of a chaotic reality is self-contradictory.

22 Peirce refers to this debate as an example of a dispute that verges on dogmatism (W2:357, 1869–70). He also refers to this debate at (W1:488, 1866), where he calls the Darwinian controversy a dispute between those who ask for causes (i.e., like Gray who defends natural selection) and those who ask for classification (which is the subject of Agassiz's treatise). Peirce thinks his distinction between induction and hypothesis can help end the dispute.

23 Gray tries to establish the scientific legitimacy of evolution and then defend it from Agassiz's charge that it is necessarily atheistic and materialistic. Thus for Gray evolution does rule out special creation, but not the existence of a 'designer.'

24 Gray also writes, 'it is worth noting that, though natural selection is scientifically explicable, variation is not. Thus the cause of variation, or the reason why the offspring is sometimes like the parents, is just as mysterious as the reason why it is generally like the parents. It is now as inexplicable as any other origination' (Gray 316); what is more, 'no one can say how new structures or organs appear, no one can show that they are necessary outcomes of what preceded' (ibid.).

25 Maxwell himself was led to contrast the 'statistical knowledge' provided by his methods with the 'dynamical knowledge' exemplified by mechanics. The former is based on laws that apply to particular cases only on average, within varying limits. Dynamical knowledge is detailed and exact knowledge of the behaviour of each individual. Dynamical knowledge is, for Maxwell, 'the only perfect knowledge' (1969, 439), but statistical knowledge is what science is left with when, as in the case of sociology and molecular theory, 'we are unable to follow the details of each individual case' (1969, 439).

26 As Porter notes, 'Maxwell's discovery that the distribution of molecular velocities will conform to the error function, which introduced advanced probability techniques into physics, had little or nothing to do with his later recognition that the macroscopic gas laws are only probabilistic. There is no more reason to associate epistemological uncertainty with a kinetic theory like Maxwell's, in which molecular velocities are governed by the law of errors, than with that of Clausius, for whom the distribution of velocities was entirely unknown. Maxwell's distribution law for molecular velocities represented unambiguously a contribution to knowledge, and not a demonstration of its limits' (1981, 79).

27 Maxwell's indeterminism was not developed until the 1870s. Both Clausius and Kronig had exploited statistical techniques in the late 1850s, but their work was far

from widely accepted, and not viewed as being incompatible with necessitarianism (see Porter 1986). The work of the most plausible remaining candidates is either too late (i.e., Renouvier, Galton), goes unmentioned by Peirce until later (i.e., Fechner), or is openly criticized (i.e., Hamilton).

28 Peirce describes his approach to logic this way at W2:267–8, 1877.

29 'The rules which we employ in life assurance and in other statistical applications of the theory of probabilities, are altogether independent of the *mental* phenomena of expectation. They are founded upon the assumption that the future will bear a resemblance to the past; that under the same circumstances the same event will tend to recur with a definite numerical frequency, not upon any attempt to submit to calculation the strength of human hopes and fears. Now experience actually testifies that events do, under given circumstances, tend to recur with definite frequency, whether their true cause be known to us or unknown. Of course, this tendency is, in general, only manifested when the area of observation is sufficiently large' (Boole 244–5).

30 As Peirce would later write: 'When in 1866 ... I had clearly ascertained that the three types of reasoning were Induction, Deduction, and Retroduction ... I thought that the system I had already obtained ought to enable me to take the Kantian step of transferring the conceptions of logic to metaphysics' (RLT 146, 1898). That the logic of 1866 was inspired by Boole is clear from the Lowell Lectures of 1866.

References

Ayer, A. 1968. *The Origins of Pragmatism*. San Francisco: Freeman, Cooper and Company.

Boole, G. 1958. *An Investigation of the Laws of Thought*. New York: Dover Books.

Brush, S. 1983. *Statistical Physics and the Atomic Theory of Matter*. Princeton: Princeton University Press.

Buchler, J. 1939. *Charles Peirce's Empiricism*. London: Kegan Paul, Trench, Trubner and Co. Ltd.

Buckle, H. 1871. *History of Civilization in England*. Vol. 1. London: Longmans, Green.

Coscuiluela, V. 1992. 'Peirce on Tychism and Determinism.' *Transactions of the Charles S. Peirce Society* 28:741.

Esposito, J. 1980. *Evolutionary Metaphysics*. Athens, Ohio: Ohio University Press.

Fiske, J. 1890. *Outlines of a Cosmic Philosophy Based on the Doctrine of Evolution*. 2 vols. Boston: Houghton.

Forster, P. 1989. 'Peirce on the Progress and Authority of Science.' *Transactions of the Charles S. Peirce Society* 25:421–52.

Gallie, W.B. 1952. *Peirce and Pragmatism*. New York: Dover Publications Inc.

Goudge, T. 1950. *The Thought of Charles Peirce*. Toronto: University of Toronto Press.

Gray, A. 1963. *Darwiniana: Essays and Reviews Pertaining to Darwinism*. Cambridge, Mass.: Belknap Press of Harvard University Press.

Hacking I. 1990. *The Taming of Chance*. Cambridge: Cambridge University Press.

Hartshorne, C. 1941. 'Charles Sanders Peirce's Metaphysics of Evolution,' *New England Quarterly*, 14, (Mar.): 51.

Herschel, J. 1850. 'Quetelet on Probabilities.' Microform. *Landmarks of Science*.

Hookway, C. 1985. *Peirce*. London: Routledge and Kegan Paul.

Laplace, P. 1951. *Philosophical Essays on Probabilities*. New York: Dover Books.

Maxwell, J. 1965. 'Illustrations of the Dynamical Theory of Gases.' In *The Scientific Papers of James Clerk Maxwell*. NewYork: Dover Books.

– 1969. 'Does the Progress of Physical Science Tend to Give any Advantage to the Opinion of Necessity (or Determinism) over That of the Contingency of Events and the Freedom of the Will.' In *The Life of James Clerk Maxwell*, edited by Lewis Campbell and William Garnet, 434–44. New York: Johnson Reprint Corporation.

Mill, J. 1973. *A System of Logic*. In *Collected Works of John Stuart Mill*, vols 7–8. Toronto: University of Toronto Press.

Murphey, M. 1993. *The Development of Peirce's Philosophy*. Indianapolis: Hackett Publishing Company, Inc.

Peirce, C. 1931. *Collected Papers of Charles S. Peirce*. Vol. 6. Edited by C. Hartshorne and P. Weiss. Cambridge, Mass. Belknap Press of Harvard University Press.

– 1982–93. *Writings of Charles S. Peirce*. 5 vols. Edited by M.H. Fisch, E. Moore, and C.J.W. Kloesel et al. Bloomington: Indiana University Press.

Porter, T. 1986. *The Rise of Statistical Thinking*. Princeton: Princeton University Press.

Quetelet, A. 1848. *Du Système Social*. Paris: Guillaumin et Cie, Librairies.

– 1969. *Treatise on Man*. Gainesville, Fla.: Scholar's Facsimiles and Reprints.

– 1981. *Letters Addressed to H.R.H. the Grand Duke of Saxe Coburg and Gotha on the Theory of Probability*. New York: Arno Press.

Reingold, N., ed. 1964. *Science in Nineteenth-Century America*. Chicago: University of Chicago Press.

Rosensohn, W. 1970. *The Phenomenology of Charles S. Peirce*. Vol. 10. Philosophical Currents. Amsterdam: B.R. Gruner.

Schweber, S. 1977. 'The Origin of the *Origin* Revisited.' *Journal of the History of Biology* 10, no. 2:229–316.

Spencer, H. 1945. *First Principles*. New York: A.L. Burt Company.

Strong, J. 1978. 'John Stuart Mill, John Herschel and the "Probability of Causes." ' In *PSA 1978*, edited by P. Asquith and I. Hacking, 31–44. East Lansing, Mich.: Philosophy of Science Association.

Turley, 1977. *Peirce's Cosmology*. New York: Philosophical Library.

Whewell, W. 1967. *Philosophy of Inductive Sciences*. 2 vols., New York: Johnson Reprint Corporation.

Wright, C. 1971. *Philosophical Discussions*. New York: B. Franklin.

A Tarski-Style Semantics for Peirce's Beta Graphs

ROBERT W. BURCH

I Introduction

The 'Beta' part of Peirce's System of Existential Graphs of 1896 – hereinafter designated by 'EG-Beta' – is a logical system that is at least the equivalent in scope and power of first-order predicate logic with identity (more precisely, with identity but without constants and without functions).[1] The most prominent feature of EG-Beta is a two-dimensional, 'graphical' syntax, which is inscribed on a surface that Peirce calls a 'sheet of assertion.' In this syntax, n-adic (or: n-ary) predicates appear as 'spots' that have n 'hooks.' The graphs of EG-Beta make no use at all of variables, so that EG-Beta is a variable-free syntax for quantified logic. Because of this fact, one might doubt the applicability to EG-Beta of a Tarski-style semantics: a semantics in which the crucial role is played by infinite sequences of members of a domain of interpretation, and in which the crucial notion is that of the 'satisfaction' of well-formed formulae (wffs) by such infinite sequences.[2] For the notion of 'satisfaction' depends on correlating the kth variable of the vocabulary of a logical syntax with the kth entries of infinite sequences of members of a domain; and, with respect to the variable-free syntax of EG-Beta, there obviously can be no such thing as correlating the kth variable with the kth entries of any infinite sequences.

In the present paper, nevertheless, a Tarski-style semantics for EG-Beta is developed that is 'natural' for EG-Beta despite EG-Beta's lack of variables.[3] In this semantics the 'satisfaction' of a graph of EG-Beta is done (or fails to be done) by infinite sequences of members of a domain, as is usual. But the crucial correlation at issue is not between variables and entries of such sequences but rather between 'hooks' (understood to be ordered in some manner) of the graphs of EG-Beta and entries of such sequences. The present paper also sketches the syntax of EG-Beta, along with a deductive apparatus (or a set of 'illative permissions') for EG-Beta. Although the paper hints that the resulting system is both consistent and complete, the paper stops short of actually proving this result.

II   Prominent Features of EG-Beta

The 'hooks' of EG-Beta are instances of a more general graphical feature of EG-Beta: a feature that Peirce calls 'lines of identity.' Such lines are used in Peirce's EG-Beta to indicate two somewhat different logical 'ideas': identity and existential quantification. For the sake of clarity I prefer a slight change from Peirce's favourite graphical syntax. In my own rendering of EG-Beta, I separate the 'idea' of identity from that of existential quantification by using a special 'spot' for existential quantification: a small circle with one 'hook' radiating from it. Thus, where Peirce would use the graph

to mean '(∃x)Fx,' I would use this graph to mean 'Fx,' and I would represent the existential quantification '(∃x)Fx' with the graph

The foregoing should make it clear that in my version of EG-Beta there are structures that correspond to free (unbound) variables, namely 'hooks.' Although some scholars may think for this reason that my version of EG-Beta deviates from Peirce's, I believe that Peirce's ultimate intentions were in accord with my designs. Nevertheless, I make no pretensions in this paper to meticulous Peirce scholarship. Accordingly, Peirce scholars who believe that Peirce intended his EG-Beta to contain structures corresponding only to bound variables should feel at liberty to regard my presentation as my own idiosyncratic extension of Peirce, rather than as a presentation of Peirce himself.

In addition to spots and lines of identity, EG-Beta has several other features that will now be discussed.

First, there is the special spot that Peirce refers to as the 'teridentity spot.' Teridentity may be represented by a point from which three hooks emerge, and its meaning is that three are one; in the standard syntax its equivalent is 'x = y & y = z.'[4]

Second, there is the operation of joining two 'hooks' or lines of identity together, either joining two lines that emerge from the same spot or else joining two lines that emerge from two different spots.

Third, there is the operation of concatenating graphs of EG-Beta into one graph by drawing them on the same sheet of assertion.

Fourth, there is the feature of EG-Beta known as 'cuts.' Cuts are simple closed curves that are used to provide for negation by enclosing whatever portion of a graph be understood to be negated. Thus a 'cut' is EG-Beta's version of what in a more familiar, linear logical syntax would appear as the protocol

$\neg(...)$.

It should be clear from the use in graphs of cuts to provide for negation that in any graph any pair of cuts is such that either the two cuts are wholly outside one another or else one of the two cuts is wholly inside the other. From this fact it follows that any set of cuts in a graph divides the sheet of assertion on which that graph is inscribed into various connected 'areas.'

Fifth, the two-dimensional syntax of EG-Beta is understood in such a way that inscription into the same connected 'area' – as just described – of a 'graph' is understood to indicate logical conjunction.

As we shall see, the presence of the teridentity spot and the possibility of joining together hooks of graphs make it possible in effect to quantify existentially in a graphical manner. It should be clear, then, that EG-Beta can be seen as (at least) a system of predicate logic with identity that does not have constants or functions and that is based on negation, conjunction, and existential quantification. It is variable free, though its 'hooks' do in effect the same job as that done in the standard syntax by variables.

III The Graphical Syntax of EG-Beta

We now undertake to define the graphs of EG-Beta. The completely empty sheet of assertion will be said to be 'the blank graph' or 'the empty graph.' The sheet of assertion with nothing but a single cut inscribed upon it will be said to be 'the pseudograph.' We presuppose ourselves to be in possession of an infinite set of potentially inscribable spots R_i^n for positive integers i and n. Each spot R_i^n will be understood to have radiating from it n hooks. In addition we also presuppose ourselves to possess a special spot 1^3, called 'the teridentity spot,' with three hooks radiating from it. In a graph a hook may be connected to another hook, and if so the hook will be said to be 'joined' (to the other hook). Any hook not connected to any other hook in a graph will be said to be 'free.' A graph consisting entirely of any single spot R_i^n with its n free hooks radiating from it, including the teridentity spot 1^3 with its three free hooks radiating from it, will be said to be an 'atomic graph.' The definition of a graph of EG-Beta will now be given recursively.

0)   The blank graph is a graph of EG-Beta. Likewise, the pseudograph is a graph of EG-Beta.

1)   Any atomic graph is a graph of EG-Beta.

2)   If G is any graph of EG-Beta, and if $\neg(G)$ represents the result of inscribing a cut around the graph G, then $\neg(G)$ is a graph of EG-Beta. In drawing this graph $\neg(G)$, all the free hooks of G – if there are any such – are understood to radiate from inside the cut inscribed around G to outside this cut. Moreover, if G is the blank graph, then $\neg(G)$ is understood to be the pseudograph.

3)   If G_1 and G_2 are any two graphs of EG-Beta, and if $G_1 \wedge G_2$ represents their concatenation (in that order) – that is, the result of inscribing both of them, understood to be in that order, on a single sheet – then $G_1 \wedge G_2$ is a graph of EG-Beta. If G_1 is the blank graph, then $G_1 \wedge G_2$ is understood to be G_2, and if G_2 is the blank graph, then $G_1 \wedge G_2$ is understood to be G_1.

3a) More generally, if G_1, G_2, ..., and G_k are any k graphs of EG-Beta, and if $G_1 \wedge G_2 \wedge ... \wedge G_k$ represents their concatenation (in that order) – that is, the result of inscribing all k of them, understood to be in that order, on a single sheet – then $G_1 \wedge G_2 \wedge ... \wedge G_k$ is a graph of EG-Beta. If any of the graphs G_1, G_2, ..., or G_k is the blank graph, then $G_1 \wedge G_2 \wedge ... \wedge G_k$ is understood to be the concatenation (in the appropriate order) of the remaining graphs.

4)   If G^n is a graph of EG-Beta that contains $n \geq 2$ free hooks, and if $J^{ij}(G^n)$, for $1 \leq i < j \leq n$, is obtained from G^n by joining together the ith and the jth free hooks of G^n, then $J^{ij}(G^n)$ is a graph of EG-Beta.

IV A Tarski-Style Semantics for EG-Beta

In this section and the following three sections of this paper I develop a Tarski-style semantics for EG-Beta. This semantics, it will readily be seen, is 'natural' for EG-Beta even though EG-Beta does not make use of variables. (In the following I confine myself to extensional semantics only.) An Enterpretation (by which is meant an extensional interpretation) for EG-Beta is a pair (D, *), where D is a non-empty set, called the 'domain' of the Enterpretation; where * is a function from the (possible) 'spots' of EG-Beta to sets of n-tuples of members of D; and where, moreover, in particular, * maps the teridentity spot 1^3 to the set of all triples (d_1, d_2, d_3) of members of D such that $d_1 = d_2 = d_3$.

We now define the crucial Tarskian semantic notion of 'satisfaction' with regard to EG-Beta. In particular we shall speak of the satisfaction on an Enterpretation (D, *) of graphs of EG-Beta by infinite sequences $s = (d_1, d_2, ...)$ of members of D. The definition is as follows:

0) If G is the blank graph, then G is satisfied by every infinite sequence $s = (d_1, d_2, ...)$ of members of D; and if G is the pseudograph, then G is satisfied by no infinite sequence $s = (d_1, d_2, ...)$ of members of D.

1) If G is an atomic graph, that is if G is a spot R_i^n, with its n free hooks, then G is satisfied on (D, *) by an infinite sequence $s = (d_1, d_2, ..., d_n, ...)$ of members of D whose first n members are $d_1, d_2, ..., d_n$ if and only if $(d_1, d_2, ..., d_n) \in *(R_i^n)$.

1a) In particular, if G is the teridentity spot 1^3, then G is satisfied on (D, *) by an infinite sequence $s = (d_1, d_2, d_3, ...)$ of members of D whose first 3 members are d_1, d_2, d_3 if and only if $(d_1, d_2, d_3) \in *(1^3)$, that is to say if and only if $d_1 = d_2 = d_3$.

2) The graph ¬(G) is satisfied on (D, *) by an infinite sequence $s = (d_1, d_2, ...)$ of members of D if and only if s does not satisfy the graph G on (D, *).

3) For any infinite sequence $s = (d_1, d_2, ...)$ of members of D, and for any integer $n \geq 0$, let $s_n = (d_{n+1}, d_{n+2}, ...)$ be the infinite sequence of members of D obtained from s by deleting the first n members of s. Let G_1 be a graph of EG-Beta having $n \geq 0$ free hooks. And let G_2 be a graph of EG-Beta. Then the graph $G_1 \wedge G_2$ is satisfied on (D, *) by an infinite sequence of members of D $s = (d_1, d_2, ...)$ if and only if s satisfies G_1 on (D, *) and s_n satisfies G_2 on (D, *).

3a) More generally, for any infinite sequence $s = (d_1, d_2, ...)$ of members of D, and for any integer $n \geq 0$, let s_n be defined as in (3). And, for each i with $1 \leq i \leq k$, let G_i be a graph of EG-Beta having $n(i) \geq 0$ free hooks. Then the graph $G_1 \wedge G_2 \wedge ... \wedge G_k$ is satisfied on (D, *) by an infinite sequence of members of D $s = (d_1, d_2, ...)$ if and only if the following k conditions are met: (1) s satisfies G_1 on (D, *); (2) $s_{n(1)}$ satisfies G_2 on (D, *); (3) $s_{n(1) + n(2)}$ satisfies G_3 on (D, *); ... ; and (k) $s_{n(1) + n(2) + ... + n(k-1)}$ satisfies G_k on (D, *).

4) The graph $J^{ij}(G^n)$, for $n \geq 2$ and for $1 \leq i < j \leq n$, that is obtained from a graph G^n (which contains $n \geq 2$ free hooks) by joining together the ith and the jth free hooks of G^n is satisfied on (D, *) by an infinite sequence $s = (d_1, d_2, ..., d_{n-2}, ...)$ of members of D whose first $n - 2$ members are $d_1, d_2, ..., d_{n-2}$ if and only if there exists some $d \in D$ such that the infinite sequence $(d_1, d_2, ..., d_{i-1}, d, d_i, ..., d_{j-2}, d, d_{j-1}, d_j, ..., d_{n-2}, ...)$, whose first n members are $d_1, d_2, ..., d_{i-1}, d, d_i, ..., d_{j-2}, d, d_{j-1}, d_j, ...,$ and d_{n-2}, satisfies G^n on (D, *).

4a) In particular, the graph $J^{12}(G^2)$ that is obtained from a graph G^2 that contains exactly two free hooks by joining together the first and the second of the two free hooks of G^2 is satisfied on (D, *) by an infinite sequence $s = (d_1, d_2, ...)$ of members of D if and only if there exists some $d \in D$ such that the infinite sequence $(d, d, d_1, d_2, ...)$ satisfies G^2 on (D, *).

We now define the notions of Universal Satisfaction on an Enterpretation (D, *) and Universal Unsatisfaction on an Enterpretation (D, *). A graph G is Universally Satisfied (for which we write 'U.S.') on (D, *) if and only if every infinite sequence s = $(d_1, d_2, ...)$ of members of D satisfies G on (D, *). A graph G is Universally Unsatisfied (for which we write 'U.U.') on (D, *) if and only if no infinite sequence s = $(d_1, d_2, ...)$ of members of D satisfies G on (D, *).

A graph ¬(G) is U.S. on (D, *) if and only if G is U.U. on (D, *), and a graph ¬(G) is U.U. on (D, *) if and only if G is U.S. on (D, *). A graph $G_1 \wedge G_2$ is U.S. on (D, *) if and only if both G_1 is U.S. on (D, *) and G_2 is U.S. on (D, *). And, more generally, a graph $G_1 \wedge G_2 \wedge ... \wedge G_k$ is U.S. on (D, *) if and only if each G_i, for $1 \leq i \leq k$, is U.S. on (D, *).

In general, no graph can be both U.S. and U.U. on a given Enterpretation (D, *). But a graph may be U.S. on one Enterpretation (D, *) and yet not U.S. on another Enterpretation (D′, *′).

In light of (4a) it should be clear that such a graph as $J^{12}(G^2)$ either is satisfied on (D, *) by *every* infinite sequence or else is satisfied on (D, *) by *no* infinite sequence. In other words, such a graph either is U.S. on (D, *) or else is U.U. on (D, *). More generally, in light of (4a), (2), and (3), any graph having no free hooks either is U.S. on (D, *) or else is U.U. on (D, *). In the first case we say that the graph is *true* on (D, *); in the second case we say that the graph is *false* on (D, *). We may here take note that if a graph G has no free hooks – so that both G and ¬(G) have no free hooks – then ¬(G) is true on (D, *) if and only if G is false on (D, *), and ¬(G) is false on (D, *) if and only if G is true on (D, *). Also, for such a graph G, if some infinite sequence s = $(d_1, d_2, ...)$ of members of D satisfies G on (D, *) then every infinite sequence s = $(d_1, d_2, ...)$ of members of D likewise satisfies G on (D, *), so that G is true on (D, *); and if some infinite sequence s = $(d_1, d_2, ...)$ of members of D fails to satisfy G on (D, *) then every infinite sequence s = $(d_1, d_2, ...)$ of members of D likewise fails to satisfy G on (D, *), so that G is false on (D, *).

It should be clear that the blank graph is U.S. – that is, is true – on every Enterpretation (D, *) and that the pseudograph is U.U. – that is, is false – on every Enterpretation (D, *).

Although a graph G having no free hooks must be either U.S. or else U.U. on any Enterpretation (D, *), it is not the case in general that a graph G having $n \geq 1$ free hooks must be either U.S. or else U.U. on any Enterpretation (D, *).

V The Relation Determined by a Graph

The relation $*_D(G)$ determined by a graph G of EG-Beta on the Enterpretation (D, *) is defined as follows. If G has $n \geq 1$ free hooks, then $*_D(G)$ is that subset of D^n (perhaps the null set $\varnothing$) containing all the n-tuples $(d_1, d_2, ..., d_n)$ of members of D such that any infinite sequence $s = (d_1, d_2, ..., d_n, ...)$ of members of D whose first n entries are $d_1, d_2, ..., d_n$ satisfies G on $(D, *)$. If G has $n = 0$ free hooks, then $*_D(G)$ = the truth-value TRUE if G is true on $(D, *)$; and $*_D(G)$ = the truth-value FALSE if G is false on $(D, *)$.

We now state several facts about $*_D(G)$.

0)   If G is the blank graph, then $*_D(G)$ = TRUE; and if G is the pseudograph, then $*_D(G)$ = FALSE.

1)   If G is an atomic graph R_i^j, then $*_D(G) = *(R_i^j)$.

1a)   In particular, if G is the teridentity spot 1^3, then $*_D(G) = I_D^3$, namely the set of all triples (d_1, d_2, d_3) with $d_1 = d_2 = d_3$.

2)   If G has $n \geq 1$ free hooks, then $*_D(\neg(G)) = D^n - *_D(G)$. If G has $n = 0$ free hooks, then $*_D(\neg(G))$ = TRUE if $*_D(G)$ = FALSE, and $*_D(\neg(G))$ = FALSE if $*_D(G)$ = TRUE.

3)   If $G = G_1 \wedge G_2$, then there are four subcases.

3.1)   If neither G_1 nor G_2 has any free hooks, then $*_D(G_1 \wedge G_2)$ = TRUE if and only if both $*_D(G_1)$ = TRUE and $*_D(G_2)$ = TRUE; and $*_D(G_1 \wedge G_2)$ = FALSE if and only if either $*_D(G_1)$ = FALSE or $*_D(G_2)$ = FALSE.

3.2)   If G_1 has no free hooks and G_2 has n $\geq$ 1 free hooks, then $*_D(G_1 \wedge G_2) = *_D(G_2)$ if $*_D(G_1)$ = TRUE; and $*_D(G_1 \wedge G_2) = \varnothing$ if $*_D(G_1)$ = FALSE.

3.3)   If G_1 has n $\geq$ 1 free hooks and G_2 has no free hooks, then $*_D(G_1 \wedge G_2) = *_D(G_1)$ if $*_D(G_2)$ = TRUE; and $*_D(G_1 \wedge G_2) = \varnothing$ if $*_D(G_2)$ = FALSE.

3.4)   If G_1 has n $\geq$ 1 free hooks and G_2 has n $\geq$ 1 free hooks, then $*_D(G_1 \wedge G_2)$ $= *_D(G_1) \times *_D(G_2)$. (Note that '$\times$' indicates the Cartesian Product, and also that for any set S, $S \times \varnothing = \varnothing \times S = \varnothing$.)

3a)   If $G = G_1 \wedge G_2 \wedge ... \wedge G_k$, then $*_D(G)$ is found by repeated application of (3.1) – (3.4). That is to say, $*_D(G_1 \wedge G_2 \wedge ... \wedge G_k) = *_D(\{...[(G_1 \wedge G_2) \wedge G_3] \wedge ...\} \wedge G_k)$.

4)   If $G = J^{ij}(G^n)$, where G^n is a graph with n $\geq$ 2 free hooks and i, j are such that $1 \leq i < j \leq n$, then $*_D(G) = SD^{ij}[*_D(G^n)]$, where SD^{ij} indicates 'Selection' by and 'Deletion' of the ith and j^{th} places of n-tuples, and is explicated in detail as follows.

4.1)   If G^n is a graph with n $\geq$ 3 free hooks, then (i) if $*_D(G^n)$ contains any n-tuples that match in the ith and j^{th} places then $*_D(G) = SD^{ij}[*_D(G^n)]$ = the set of all $(n - 2)$-tuples obtained from the n-tuples in $*_D(G^n)$ by selecting those that match in the ith and j^{th} places, and then deleting from them the entries in these two places and then closing them up to form $(n - 2)$-tuples; (ii) if $*_D(G^n)$ contains no n-tuples that match in the ith and j^{th} places, then $*_D(G) = SD^{ij}[*_D(G^n)] = \varnothing$. (In particular, if $*_D(G^n) = \varnothing$ then $*_D(G) = \varnothing$.)

4.2) If G^2 is a graph with exactly 2 free hooks, then (i) if $*_D(G^2)$ contains any 2-tuples that match in the 1st and 2nd places then $*_D(G) = SD^{12}[*_D(G^2)] =$ TRUE; (ii) if $*_D(G^2)$ contains no 2-tuples that match in the 1st and 2nd places then $*_D(G) = SD^{12}[*_D(G^2)] = $ FALSE . (In particular, if $*_D(G^2) = \varnothing$ then $*_D(G) = $ FALSE.)

VI The Existential Quantifier and Its Semantics

Let G^n be a graph of EG-Beta with $n \geq 1$ free hooks. And let i be such that $1 \leq i \leq n$. Then we let

$$(\exists^i)G^n$$

stand for the graph

$$J^{i, n+1}[G^n \wedge J^{12}(1^3)].$$

If we also let U^1 stand for the graph $J^{12}(1^3)$, then $(\exists^i)G^n$ can be written as $J^{i, n+1}(G^n \wedge U^1)$. This graph is called the 'existential quantification with respect to the ith free hook' of the graph G^n.

We may see that $*_D[(\exists^i)G^n] = DEL^i[*_D(G^n)]$, where DEL^i indicates 'Deletion' of the ith places of n-tuples, and is explicated in detail as follows.

1) If G^n is a graph with $n \geq 2$ free hooks, then $*_D[(\exists^i)G^n] = DEL^i[*_D(G^n)] = $ the set of all $n - 1$-tuples obtained from the n-tuples in $*_D(G^n)$ by deleting from them their i^{th} places and then closing them up to form $(n - 1)$-tuples. (In particular, if $*_D(G^n) = \varnothing$ then $*_D[(\exists^i)G^n] = DEL^i[*_D(G^n)] = \varnothing$.)
2) If G^1 is a graph with exactly 1 free hook, then if $*_D(G^1) \neq \varnothing$, then $*_D[(\exists^1)G^1] = DEL^1[*_D(G^1)] = $ TRUE; and if $*_D(G^1) = \varnothing$, then $*_D[(\exists^1)G^1] = DEL^1[*_D(G^1)] = $ FALSE.

By straightforward computation we can verify the following. Given an Enterpretation $(D, *)$, an infinite sequence $s = (d_1, d_2, ...)$ of members of D satisfies $(\exists^i)G^n$ on $(D, *)$ if and only if there is some infinite sequence $(d_1, d_2, ..., d_{i-1}, d, d_i, ..., d_{n-1}, ...)$ that satisfies G^n on $(D, *)$. In particular, an infinite sequence $s = (d_1, d_2, ...)$ of members of D satisfies $(\exists^1)G^1$ on $(D, *)$ if and only if there is some infinite sequence $(d, d_1, d_2, ...)$ that satisfies G^1 on $(D, *)$. The graph $(\exists^i)G^n$ is U.S. on $(D, *)$ if and only if for every infinite sequence $s = (d_1, d_2, ...)$ of members of D there is some $d \in D$ such that the infinite sequence $(d_1, d_2, ..., d_{i-1}, d, d_i, ..., d_{n-1}, ...)$ satisfies G^n on $(D, *)$. In particular, $(\exists^1)G^1$ is U.S. on $(D, *)$ if and only if for every infinite sequence $s = (d_1, d_2, ...)$ of members of D there is some $d \in D$ such that the infinite sequence $(d, d_1, d_2, ...)$ satisfies G^1 on $(D, *)$.

We can also straightforwardly verify the following. $(\exists^i)G^n$ is U.U. on $(D, *)$ if and only if G^n is U.U. on $(D, *)$. For $(\exists^i)G^n$ is U.U. on $(D, *)$ if and only if there is no infinite sequence $s = (d_1, d_2, ...)$ of members of D such that for some $d \in D$ the infinite sequence $(d_1, d_2, ..., d_{i-1}, d, d_i, ..., d_{n-1}, ...)$ satisfies G^n on $(D, *)$. In other words, $(\exists^i)G^n$ is U.U. on $(D, *)$ if and only if there is no infinite sequence of members of D that satisfies G^n on $(D, *)$.

Hence, by substitution it follows that $(\exists^i)\neg(G^n)$ is U.U. on $(D, *)$ if and only if $\neg(G^n)$ is U.U. on $(D, *)$. And thus it follows that $\neg[(\exists^i)\neg(G^n)]$ is U.S. on $(D, *)$ if and only if $\neg[\neg(G^n)]$ is U.S. on $(D, *)$, that is to say, if and only if G^n is U.S. on $(D, *)$.

Now, let G^n be a graph of EG-Beta with $n \geq 1$ free hooks. And let i be such that $1 \leq i \leq n$. Then we let

$$(\forall^i)G^n$$

stand for the graph

$$\neg[(\exists^i)\neg(G^n)].$$

This graph is called the 'universal quantification with respect to the ith free hook' of the graph G^n. It should be clear how $*_D[(\forall^i)G^n]$ is to be defined in terms of $*_D[(\exists^i)G^n]$. And it should be clear that it was shown in the preceding paragraph that $(\forall^i)G^n$ is U.S. on $(D, *)$ if and only if G^n is U.S. on $(D, *)$.

If we now define the 'existential closure' of a graph G^n of EG-Beta to be the graph $(\exists^1)(\exists^2) ... (\exists^n)G^n$, then, it should be clear, we have in effect shown that a graph G^n of EG-Beta is U.U. on an Enterpretation $(D, *)$ if and only if its existential closure is U.U. on $(D, *)$. And if we also define the 'universal closure' of a graph G^n of EG-Beta to be the graph $\neg[(\exists^1)(\exists^2) ... (\exists^n)\neg(G^n)]$, then, it should be clear, we have also in effect shown that a graph G^n of EG-Beta is U.S. on an Enterpretation $(D, *)$ if and only if its universal closure is U.S. on $(D, *)$.

VII Logical Validity of Graphs of EG-Beta

Let us define a graph G of EG-Beta to be 'logically valid' if and only if G is U.S. on $(D, *)$ for *every* Enterpretation $(D, *)$. Logical validity of a graph G means that G is satisfied by *every* infinite sequence $(d_1, d_2, ...)$ of members of the domain D for *every* Enterpretation $(D, *)$.

Let us now take note of three facts. First, it is obvious that the blank graph is logically valid. Second, as we now proceed to show, the graph $J^{12}(1^3)$ is logically valid. For, let (D, *) be any Enterpretation, and let s = $(d_1, d_2, d_3, ...)$ be any infinite sequence of members of D. Now, s satisfies $J^{12}(1^3)$ if and only if there is some d $\in$ D such that the infinite sequence (d, d, $d_1, d_2, d_3, ...$) satisfies 1^3. But the sequence (d, d, $d_1, d_2, d_3, ...$) satisfies 1^3 if and only if d = d = d_1, that is to say, if and only if d = d_1. Hence there is some d $\in$ D, namely d_1, such that the infinite sequence (d, d, $d_1, d_2, d_3, ...$) satisfies 1^3. Hence s satisfies $J^{12}(1^3)$. And thus the graph $J^{12}(1^3)$ is logically valid. Third, as was shown in effect at the end of the previous section, a graph G of EG-Beta is logically valid if and only if its universal quantification with respect to any of its free hooks is logically valid.

VIII   A Deductive System for EG-Beta

The question arises whether EG-Beta can be presented as a deductive system with axioms and rules of inference. (Peirce, by the way, used the phrase 'illative permissions' to designate what are nowadays called rules of inference.) In this section of this paper, a deductive system suggested by Peirce's writings will be presented and discussed in a provisional way. This deductive system involves two axioms and six rules of inference (illative permissions).[5]

One of the two axioms of the system suggested by Peirce's writings is the same axiom as the single axiom that Peirce uses for the purely propositional part of EG-Beta, the part that Peirce calls 'EG-Alpha.' This is the blank graph, which represents the proposition 'THE TRUE.'

The second of the two axioms of the system suggested by Peirce's writings is the graph

$$J^{12}(1^3).$$

This is the graph obtained by inscribing on the sheet the teridentity spot with two of its three free hooks joined to each other, leaving exactly one free hook. This graph is the form in EG-Beta of what in standard quantificational logic would be written as 'x = x.' It designates the unary universal relation.

Five of the six 'illative permissions' suggested by Peirce's writings for EG-Beta understood as a deductive system are rules of inference that in the first instance were designed for EG-Alpha. In order to understand these permissions, we shall need a bit of preliminary information and terminology. To this end the following five paragraphs are devoted.

We begin by recalling from section II of this paper that in any graph any pair of cuts is such that either one of the two cuts is wholly inside the other or else each of the two cuts is wholly outside the other. We also recall that from this fact it follows that any set of cuts in a graph divides the sheet of assertion on which that graph is inscribed into various connected regions that are called 'areas.'

If two cuts are such that one of them is wholly inside the other; and if there is no third cut wholly surrounded by one of the first two and wholly surrounding the other of the first two; then the two cuts are referred to as a 'Double Cut.' For any double cut there is an annular (that is, ring-shaped) area between its two cuts. This annular area is called the 'annulus' of the double cut. Obviously, the annulus of a double cut may be empty (that is, blank) or may not be empty.

Any area of a graph will have what will be called a 'level-number.' The level number of an area of a graph may be defined as the number of cuts, perhaps 0, that completely surround any point in that area. This number will, of course, be either even or odd. (Note that 0 is an even number.) An area will be said to be an 'even area' or an 'odd area' accordingly as it has, respectively, an even level-number or an odd level-number.

An area A_1 will be said to 'dominate' an area A_2 of the graph just in case either $A_1 = A_2$ or else A_1 completely surrounds A_2.

Given any graph G, any portion of G around which one could draw a cut will be said to be a 'subgraph' of G. In other words, a subgraph of G is any portion of G around which could be drawn a simple closed curve that is either wholly inside or else wholly outside any cut of G. Any subgraph of G obviously will be inscribed on some area or other of G; which area of G on which the subgraph is inscribed is determined by its being that area of G upon which would be inscribed that cut the drawing of which defines the subgraph in question. It is to be noted that G is itself a subgraph of G, and that G itself is inscribed upon the single level-0 area possessed by G.

With these preliminary explanations accomplished, we now are in a position to present the first five of the six 'illative permissions' suggested by Peirce's writings for EG-Beta understood as a deductive system. They are as follows.

1) Double Cut (DC): a double cut with an empty annulus may be inscribed into any area of a graph G provided that its annulus remain empty in so being inscribed; also, any double cut with an empty annulus may be erased from any area of any graph G.

2) Erase-even (Erase): any subgraph of a graph G such that the subgraph is inscribed on any area of *even* level may be erased from that area.

3) Insert-odd (Insert): any graph may be inscribed into a graph G on any area of *odd* level.

4) Iterate (It): in any graph G, any subgraph of G that is inscribed on any area

A_1 of G may be inscribed again (that is, iterated) on any area A_2 of G such that A_1 dominates A_2.

5) Deiterate (Deit): in any graph G, any subgraph of G that is inscribed both on an area A_1 of G and inscribed again (that is, iterated) on any area A_2 of G such that A_1 dominates A_2 may be erased (that is, deiterated) from A_2.

In order that these illative permissions should be used also with EG-Beta and not merely with EG-Alpha, they require certain modifications, as follows.

'DC' is to be understood to allow, in addition to the inscription or erasure of any double cut whose annulus is empty, the inscription or erasure of any double cut whose annulus is empty *except for* being completely traversed by one or more lines of identity.

'Erase' is to be understood to apply to lines of identity on an area of even level in the following way: a short stretch of the line of identity is erased and the two resulting 'end points' of the line are affixed with small circles representing existential quantifications.

'Insert' is to be understood to apply to lines of identity on an area of odd level in the following way: two 'end points' of lines of identity that are affixed with small circles representing existential quantifications are joined into a single line of identity, with the small circles then disappearing.

'It' is to be understood to apply to lines of identity in such a way that they, when 'led' by any small circles affixed to any of their end points, can be extended arbitrarily within a given area A_1 of any graph G and/or extended arbitrarily into any area A_2 such that A_1 dominates A_2.

'Deit' is to be understood to apply to lines of identity in such a way that they, along with any small circles affixed to any of their end points, can be retracted arbitrarily within a given area A_1 of any graph G and/or retracted arbitrarily from any area A_2 such that A_1 dominates A_2.

In addition to the five illative permissions just presented, Peirce's writings suggest for EG-Beta, understood as a deductive system, an additional rule of inference, a sixth illative permission:

6) 'Universal Generalization' (UGEN).

UGEN corresponds to what is often called 'Generalization,' or 'Gen' in standard systems of quantified logic. It goes this way. From any graph G of EG-Beta, having a connected graphical piece G^n with n free hooks, and for i any integer such that $1 \le i \le n$, one may infer the graph G' that is obtained from G by replacing the connected graphical piece G^n with the connected graphical piece

$\neg[(\exists^i)\neg(G^n)]$.

This notation makes use of the 'existential quantifier' $(\exists^i)$, which was explained previously. UGEN allows us to isolate for attention a single connected piece of a multipiece graph, draw a cut entirely around this piece, then attach a circular spot to the free hook in question outside this first cut, then draw a second cut around the graphical piece with the circular spot thus attached.

Now that we have an overview of the system of deduction for EG-Beta that Peirce's writings suggest, let us see that the two axioms and the six rules of inference of this system allow us to derive two further rules of inference. In order to understand the first of these, we need the idea of a completely closed line of identity. Such a line is a line of identity, however complex, each end point of which terminates in a small circle representing existential quantification. The minimal such closed line of identity is simply the circular spot with no ray radiating from it. It represents the proposition '$(\exists x)(x = x)$'. The next least complex such line has two small circles and looks like a barbell; it represents the proposition '$(\exists x)(\exists y)(x = y)$.' The next least complex such line has three small circles and looks like a weathervane; it represents the proposition '$(\exists x)(\exists y)(\exists z)[(x = y) \& (y = z)]$.' And so forth. Obviously, each such closed line of identity represents a logical truth. Now we are ready for the two derived rules of inference of EG-Beta.

1) Closed Identity (CI). Any completely closed line of identity – a line of identity, no matter how complex, having no free hooks – may be either inscribed into or erased from any area. (It is to be understood that the closed line of identity that is either to be inscribed or erased must lie wholly within a single area.)

2) Singly Open Identity (SOI). Any singly open line of identity – a line of identity, no matter how complex, having exactly one free hook – may be either inscribed into or erased from any area. (It is to be understood that the singly open line that is either to be inscribed or erased must lie wholly within a single area *except for* its single free hook, which extends outward to the single level-0 area of the graph.)

CI and SOI are justified as follows. Let us imagine any graph G to be given. G will divide the sheet of assertion into various areas. Now, according to our second axiom, we may inscribe on the level-0 area of the graph the teridentity spot with two of its three free hooks joined to each other, leaving one free hook. Now by an obvious use of Erase, we may produce a closed line of identity and a singly open line of identity as follows.

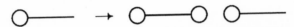

Either, or both, of these lines of identity may then be Iterated on the level-0 area itself and then again Iterated into any area to obtain its inscription into any area of G. Then the original lines of identity may be Erased from the level-0 area, leaving us with our desired result. So much for the clauses of CI and SOI having to do with inscription. As for the clauses having to do with erasure, we simply reproduce on the level-0 area any identity line we want to erase (as we did just previously), and then Deiterate the graph we want erased. Then, we Erase the identity line on the level-0 area. And we have our result.

The significance of the deductive system for EG-Beta suggested by Peirce's writings, particularly in its relations with the Tarski-style semantics developed in this paper, will now be discussed briefly.

It was shown in section VII of this paper that the two axioms suggested by Peirce's writings for EG-Beta as a deductive system are logically valid. It was also shown in section VII that the sixth illative permission of this system, namely UGEN, preserves logical validity. Moreover, it can be proved – although the proof will not be given in this paper – that the first five illative permissions of the system likewise preserve logical validity. From the foregoing facts it follows that all the theorems of EG-Beta are logically valid.

And from the result that all the theorems of EG-Beta are logically valid it follows that EG-Beta, considered as a deductive system in accord with suggestions found in Peirce's writings, is a consistent system. Laying out the details of all the proofs involved in showing this result, however, would involve considerable further exposition, especially of the nature of lines of identity. Thus the proofs must be left for a future presentation.

So also must be left for a future presentation the task of discussing, concerning the presentation just given of EG-Beta as a deductive system, whether this system is complete.

Notes

1 Peirce presented the 'System of Existential Graphs' in various of his writings. Perhaps the best single collection, even today, of Peirce's various presentations of the existential graphs, including the 'Beta' part, is to be found in 4.347–584.

2 An excellent presentation of a Tarski-style semantics is to be found in Elliott Mendelson, *Introduction to Mathematical Logic*, 3rd ed. (Monterey, Calif.: Wadsworth and Brooks/Cole 1987), 46–54.

3 Peirce probably originally intended the existential graphs to have a 'game-theoretical' semantics, a semantics, that is to say, in which the crucial idea is that of a game-like procedure in which two 'players' determine a truth value for a graph. See Robert W. Burch, 'Game-Theoretic Semantics for Peirce's Existential Graphs,' *Synthese* 99, no. 3 (June 1994): 361–5.

4 The fact that teridentity is expressed in the standard logical syntax by 'x = y & y = z' does not imply that triadic relations are in general reducible to dyadic ones. For, as I have shown, the construction of the proposition 'x = y & y = z' presupposes teridentity or some other 'non-degenerate' triadic relation. See Robert W. Burch, *A Peircean Reduction Thesis: Foundations of Topological Logic* (Lubbock: Texas Tech University Press 1991).

5 Peirce provided several different formulations of a deductive system for the existential graphs. See, for example, 4.372–93, 4.415–17, 4.466–71, and 4.485–509. The system presented in section VIII of this paper combines various of Peirce's suggestions into a 'generic' deductive system.

The Tinctures and Implicit Quantification over Worlds

JAY ZEMAN

> ... one must keep a bright lookout for unintended and unexpected changes thereby
> brought about in the relations of different significant parts of the diagram to one
> another. Such operations upon diagrams, whether external or imaginary, take the
> place of the experiments upon real things that one performs in chemical and physi-
> cal research. Chemists have ere now, I need not say, described experimentation as
> the putting of questions to Nature. Just so, experiments upon diagrams are ques-
> tions put to the Nature of the relations concerned. (4.530)[1]

The diagrammatic nature of mathematical reasoning suggests that as my power
to create diagrams increases, so too will my capacity for fruitful mathematical reasoning. Peirce's own work involved an unending series of experiments
with different diagrammatic notations, all interesting, some difficult, some
extremely fruitful. And the diagrammatic notations available are not only a
function of some kind of 'internal mental activity.' As Dewey has noted,
'Breathing is an affair of the air as truly as of the lungs; digesting an affair of
food as truly as of tissues of stomach' (Dewey 15); so, analogously, is mathematical reasoning an affair of the diagrams available as truly as of the 'mind'
(which is then not limited to something inside the head, but includes the relevant diagrams, 'external' as well as 'internal'); so does mathematical reasoning
have its 'alembics and cucurbits' just as surely as does chemistry. In doing
mathematical reasoning, we make of the diagrams 'instruments of thought,'
and advances in the technology of diagrams can directly affect our patterns of
reasoning. I can imagine Peirce spending hours (and dollars) in a modern art-
ists' supply store, marvelling at the rainbow of pencils and pens of all types
and the diagrammatic possibilities that this technology opens up. And what
would he think of the contemporary computer? A handy tool for writing a
paper such as this, or for quickly doing all sorts of calculations, indeed. But

also a medium for doing *logic*, for facilitating the examination and understanding of the process of mathematical reasoning.

Without going into great technical detail (about computers and programming), I will sketch out an approach to Peircean logic employing the graphical capabilities of the modern personal computer. Only a limited graphics capability is required – essentially, just the garden variety VGA; for better video resolution and greater diagrammatic flexibility, certain supersets of VGA are appropriate, but all we assume is the 18-bit red-green-blue (RGB), 256 colour scheme native to the VGA. I have done a considerable amount of programming in this environment and have found that, indeed, the diagrams involved are fruitful in presenting 'unintended and unexpected changes thereby brought about in the relations of different significant parts of the diagram to one another.'

In 'Peirce and Philo' (forthcoming), I point out that Peirce viewed the *de inesse* conditional as an instantiation of an integrating abstraction which he called the 'hypothetical'; he held that his development of notation for quantification was necessary to treat adequately of the hypothetical, and as I note, in 1902 he remarks that 'the quantified subject of a hypothetical proposition is a *possibility*, or *possible case*, or *possible state of things*. In its primitive state, that which is *possible* is a hypothesis which in a given state of information is not known, and cannot certainly be inferred, to be false. The assumed state of information may be the actual state of the speaker, or it may be a state of greater or less information. Thus arise various kinds of possibility' (2.347).

In the context of the existential graphs (EG), quantifications are handled by transformations involving the 'line of identity' (LI); LIs are 'implicitly quantified variables' (Zeman 1964, 1967). The signs Peirce calls 'selectives' are also implicitly quantified variables; a selective (usually a letter of the alphabet, but possibly some other sign) may be attached to a hook (of a 'spot,' or predicate; a hook is the graphical equivalent of a blank in a predicate) or to the end of a LI; the set of identical selectives in a given graph is treated as the set of identical quantified variables in the scope of their common binding quantifier in standard algebraic logic. Thus, that set of selectives is an alternative notation for a ligature connecting the points to which the selectives are attached, and any 'rules for selectives' would be derived from the appropriate rules for LIs.

We find Peirce (in 4.518 ff) introducing a peculiar type of selective in one of his discussions of modality in a graphical context. Although it would be fascinating to follow him through the development of this notion, we will reserve this for another occasion. Suffice to say for now that he here treats states of information as values for selectives (i.e., for 'quantified variables'), and even develops (4.521) a ligature or concatenation of LIs to serve as such (implicitly) quantified variables. He also presents a sign 'to express that a state of information B follows after a state of information A' (4.522); this is cut from the same cloth as is 2.347 and other places where he deals with the hypothetical. So *states of information* can be represented by selectives attached to hooks (which would have to be of a peculiar kind) associated with graphs; the effect of attaching a selective *x* to such a hook on a graph *g* is to assert that 'There is a state of information *x* such that *g* (or the proposition expressed by *g*) holds at *x*.'

Peirce is here, of course, very close to the contemporary idea of possible-world semantics. I propose in this paper to develop this Peircean idea in a natural Peircean context. The notion of 'selective for a state of information' will be given another representation, one that is, in fact, employed by Peirce, although not fully developed in some of the directions we will go here. In the 'Prolegomena to an Apology for Pragmaticism' (PAP 4.530–72), Peirce explores a diagrammatic notation which, among other things, will enable us to deal with 'states of things' in a variety of modalities:

> When any representation of a state of things consisting in the applicability of a given description to an individual or limited set of individuals otherwise indesignate is scribed, the Mode of Tincture of the province on which it is scribed shows whether the Mode of Being which is to be affirmatively or negatively attributed to the state of things described is to be that of Possibility, when Color will be used; or that of Intention, indicated by Fur; or that of Actuality shown by Metal. Special understandings may determine special tinctures to refer to special varieties of the three genera of Modality. Finally, the Mode of Tincture of the March may determine whether the Entire Graph is to be understood as Interrogative, Imperative, or Indicative. (4.554)

My suggestion is that a tincture in the sense of PAP be taken as a *selective* for a state of information, or a state of things, or a state of affairs. This would mean that tincture in a broader sense will be a line of identity for states of affairs, much as is displayed in 4.522 and 4.523; the scribing of a graph on an area belonging to a tincture would be like attaching that 'peculiar kind of hook' to the LI which is the tincture.[2] Whether thought of as a selective or as a line of identity, then, the tincture would be an implicitly quantified variable which draws its values from a domain of states of affairs, or of *possible worlds*! In ordinary algebraic modal semantics, we commonly make use of a binary predicate which takes statements as one argument and terms or term-variables for 'possible worlds' as the other; if we take '@' as such a relation, then (corresponding to use of the hook to which attach selectives or ligatures for states of affairs) the algebraic

(1) $\exists x(\alpha @ x)$

will be read 'Proposition α is true at some world x'; we would accomplish the same assertion in this version of 'tinctured existential graphs' by scribing α on an appropriate area of the tincture corresponding to the variable x.[3]

A tincture has, literally, two sides, called by Peirce the *recto* and the *verso* of that tincture. Based on this fact, as we shall see, we interpret a tincture in the diagrammatic system of VGA256 graphics to be a pair of colours $<x, y>$ where x and y are either colour indexes or are RGB colour representations.[4] Peirce comments that 'Should the Graphist desire to negative a Graph, he must scribe it on the *verso*, and then, before delivery to the Interpreter, must make an incision, called a *Cut*, through the Sheet all the way round the Graph-instance to be denied, and must then turn over the excised piece, so as to *expose* its rougher surface carrying the negated Graph-instance' (4.556; emphasis added). This would be represented in more ordinary notation by

(2) $\sim\exists x(\alpha @ x)$

which is the same as

(3) $\forall x \sim (\alpha @ x)$

Although in PAP Peirce tells us that 'We are to imagine that the Graphist always finds Provinces[5] where he needs them' (4.553), he is not tremendously clear about how we are to interpret and work with these provinces (which are thought of as overlying each other) in the most general case. 'Cuts' as discussed in 4.556, however, do give us one pretty clear picture of access to other tinctures. These cuts may be thought of as penetrating down through the current sheet and into an underlying province, and so permitting us to 'get at' new tinctures.

A tincture is a variable with a structure: as we have indicated, we think of it as having a *recto* and a *verso*. These 'sides' draw their values from the *recto–verso* pairs of individual sheets of assertion (SAs), each of which represents a 'state of affairs,' or 'possible world.' We have mentioned that in the context of VGA256, each tincture may be thought of as a pair $<R, V>$, whose members may be either VGA256 colour indexes or RGB colour representations. Where R and V are colour indexes (0–255), we will take them as *bit-wise (logical) complements* of each other with respect to 255 (= 0xFF = 1111 1111 binary). When they are RGB colours drawn from among the $64^3 = 262,144$ colours available in this mode, the pair associated with the tincture may also be thought of as

$$<<r_R, g_R, b_R>, <r_V, g_V, b_V>>$$

The triples making up this pair are the red, green, and blue values for the *recto* and *verso* respectively.[6] Our understanding is that these are colour complements of each other (in the sense that $r_V = 63\text{-}r_R$, and so also for green and blue), so that the *recto-verso* pair are complementary colours (as <red, cyan>, <blue, yellow>, etc.). A basic map of the colours upon which we will draw in the present discussion is shown in Figure 1.[7]

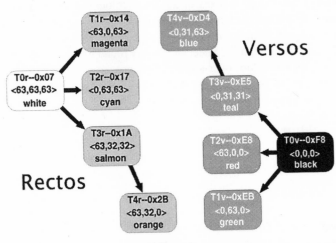

Figure 1

This diagram designates *rectos* and *versos* for five tinctures, which will be known respectively as Tincture 0, Tincture 1, and so on; the tinctures shown are for present purposes only; many other patterns are possible. In terms that Peirce uses in PAP, we might think of our Tincture 0 as a *metal* ('*Argent,*' most likely) and the other four as *colours* (4.553).

The relationship between *metals* and *colours* – indeed, between tinctures in general – is left vague in PAP; the arrows in Figure 1 display a fairly natural relationship between tinctures which we will describe at some length later. Now, Peirce discusses tinctures and their placement as follows:

Every part of the exposed surface shall be tinctured ... The whole of any continuous part of the exposed surface in one tincture shall be termed a Province. The border of the sheet has one tincture all round; and we may imagine that it was chosen ... in agreement between the Graphist and the Interpreter at the outset. The province of the border may be called the March. Provinces adjacent to the March are to be regarded as overlying it. Provinces adjacent to those Provinces, but not to the March, are to be regarded as overlying the provinces adjacent to the March, and so on. We are to imagine that the Graphist always finds Provinces where he needs them. (4.553)

Peirce is not, unfortunately, too explicit about how the various 'Provinces' are bounded, nor about how we relate different provinces to each other. The interpretation of 'tincture' we are suggesting will tie the operations on tinctures to the rules for LIs and 'ligatures' in general. Let us at present work with a limited manner of dealing with tinctures; though other ways of approaching the matter may be developed, the approach I will suggest is a start, and is consistent with the way that Peirce approached modality and 'possible worlds.' In a paper from the same year (1906) as PAP, Peirce discusses an 'Improvement to the Gamma Graphs'; which 'improvement gives substantially, as far as I can see, nearly the whole of that Gamma part which I have been endeavoring to discern' (4.578). He is employing colours here in a slightly different manner than in PAP: 'In working with Existential Graphs, we use, or at any rate imagine that we use, a sheet of paper of different tints on its two sides. Let us say that the side we call the *recto* is cream white while the *verso* is usually of somewhat bluish grey, but may be of yellow or of a rose tint or of green' (4.573). The notational improvement he has in mind includes this colour difference, so that when we perform a cut in the gamma context, 'the cut may be imagined to extend down to one or another depth into the paper, so that the overturning of the piece cut out may expose one stratum or another, these being distinguished by their tints; the different tints representing different kinds of possibility' (4.578). This echoes remarks of Peirce's in the 1903 Lowell Lectures. There, in trying to describe the relationship between 'actual existent fact' and 'possibility,' he remarks that

although the universe of existential fact can only be conceived as mapped upon a surface by each point of the surface representing a vast expanse of fact, yet we can conceive the facts [as] sufficiently separated upon the map for all our purposes; and in the same sense the entire universe of logical possibilities might be conceived to be mapped upon a surface. Nevertheless, if we are going to represent to our minds the relation between the universe of possibilities and the universe of actual existent facts, if we are going to think of the latter as a surface, we must think of the former as three-dimensional space in which any surface would represent all the facts that might exist in one existential universe. (4.514)

The 'strata' of possibility in 4.578 are continuous with each other, but may be approximated by the pages of a book, or a stack of sheets. This analogy may also be applied to the tinctures of PAP; the cuts of the logic we are working with are then cuts indeed, going down to some appropriate level of paper in the book, 'always find[ing] Provinces where [we] need them.' For our present purposes, then, we will access tinctures by cutting down to them, and overturning the little stack of papers thus freed; the bottommost of the layers cut is the one we are accessing 'through the cut,' and so what is displayed in the cut, once the stack of paper thus freed is overturned, is the *verso* of that accessed layer. Tinctures other than the one on top (very likely, the alpha-beta sheet of assertion, representing the 'actual existent universe') are then seen only within cuts – a condition that extends recursively to any area of the graphs involved; passage from one tincture to another will always be via a cut, from the *recto* of one tincture to the *verso* of the other, or vice-versa.

This mode of display dictates much of what can happen with the rules of inference for ligatures when they are applied to tinctures; in particular, it affects the rules for iteration and deiteration. Note that when a graph containing LIs is iterated, an exact copy of the graph is scribed in the same area as the original, or in an area enclosed by at least the same cuts as the original; this permission is just the same as the alpha rule of iteration-deiteration. An additional permission is that LIs which are *unenclosed in* the graph being iterated may be attached by ligature to the copies of those same LIs in the graph-instance resulting from the iteration; for example, as in Figure 2.

Figure 2

Both the transformation shown and its inverse are permitted by this rule. Note that if a ligature is *enclosed in* the graph being iterated, that graph may be iterated only in simple alpha style; else the two graphs in Figure 3 would both give rise by iteration to Figure 4.

Figure 3

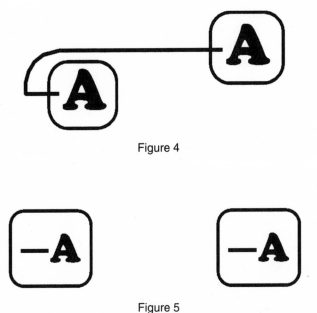

Figure 4

Figure 5

This result would suggest that the two graphs of Figure 3 are equivalent, which they are not. Although alpha iteration of the right graph in Figure 3 results in the two identical graphs of Figure 5, when we interpret the translation (into standard logical notation) of the graph including these two, the situation is complicated by the fact that LIs must be translated using quantifiers and variables:

(1) $\exists x A x \wedge {\sim}\exists x A x$

But, although the xs in the above are alphabetically the same, they are discontinuous with each other (as are the LIs in Figure 5); this discontinuity is emphasized by the fact that

(2) ${\sim}\exists x A x \wedge {\sim}\exists y A y$

is logically equivalent to (1).

Now, we have noted that *new* tinctures will be accessed only via cuts; this means that if I am working in an area on the *recto* of Tincture 0, I would encounter another tincture (say Tincture 1) as follows; Tincture 1 is here what we will call 'isolated,' which is to say that it does not occur on the sheet of assertion outside of the shown enclosure:

Figure 6

Figure 7

If I apply alpha iteration to the graph of Figure 6, the result would *not* be Figure 7. This last graph would be the analogue in tinctures of Figure 4; Figure 6 is the analogue in tinctures of the *right-hand* graph in Figure 3. The identification of quantified variables implicit in the sameness of colour in both subgraphs of Figure 7 could not result from an iteration of Figure 6. The proper result of such an iteration is Figure 8, where the tincture represented here by *red* (the *verso* of Tincture 2) is entirely new to the total graph (if there are any isolated tinctures [*other than* Tincture 1]) 'hidden' in p, they must be similarly changed in the copy of the graph iterated).

Figure 8

The iteration rules for tinctures, based on the beta rules, may be stated as follows:

Itr$_\gamma$: A partial graph may be iterated in the same area or inward. *Isolated tinctures* in the original will be changed in the copy to *new tinctures accessible*[8] *to the tincture of the area to which the iteration is performed.*

Dit$_\gamma$: A partial graph which might have resulted from Itr$_\gamma$ may be deiterated.

Although movement from Figure 6 to Figure 7 would represent illegal manipulations of the LI which is Tincture 1, there are times when maintaining or making colour identifications of areas will be perfectly okay. Before we examine some such, however, let us consider some interpretations of graphs involving tinctures. As a first such example, consider the graph in Figure 6. It starts on the *recto* of Tincture 0, which we may think of as the 'ordinary' SA. Reading inward, we cross a cut into the *verso* of Tincture 1. The tincture there is a selective for 'possible worlds,' and the formula p is scribed on that *verso*. The effect is the same as

(3) $\sim\!\exists w(\, p \,@\, w)$

This is strongly suggestive of certain interpretations of modal propositions in standard modal semantics; also, Peirce's own intended use of the tinctures (especially of those he called 'colours') is to express modality; various interpretations and rules of transformation which have been suggested for the tinctures (see Roberts 1974, Zeman 1974) would, in fact, result in reading the graph in Figure 6 as 'p is impossible,' or

(4) $\sim\!Mp$

Although this reading is attractive, and is indeed the direction we are going here, it is not yet supported by formula (3). The standard 'relational' semantics[9] requires an 'accessibility relation' between possible worlds; say Rxy, which would intuitively read 'world x has access to world y.' Intuitively, of course, 'access' can mean a great variety of things, depending on the kind of modality we are dealing with. Once we have the relation R, we can extend our use of the predicate @ to include modal functions:

$$(L\alpha) @ b \text{ iff } \forall w(Rbw \supset \alpha @ w),$$

and

$$(M\alpha) @ b \text{ iff } \exists w(Rbw \wedge \alpha @ w).$$

The colours (from VGA256) which we employ here give us a ready-made path to the accessibility relation. Suppose that we have two tinctures (worlds), u and v, associated respectively with the *recto–verso* pairs $<a, b>$ and $<c, d>$. With colour h (in terms of red, green, blue) as $<r_h, g_h, b_h>$, we say that (colours) $e \leq f$ iff $r_e \leq r_f$ *and* $g_e \leq g_f$ *and* $b_e \leq b_f$; we might say in this case that e is a *subcolour* of f. Then (with u as $<a, b>$ and v as $<c, d>$):

$$Ruv \text{ iff } c \leq a$$

(equivalently, $b \leq d$, by the relationship between colours representing *rectos* and *versos*). This is not the only possible meaning of R, of course, but is a good natural one for these initial efforts. Loosely speaking, then, '*recto*-colours' have access to their 'subcolours,' and '*verso*-colours' are accessed by their subcolours. In interpreting a tinctured graph we will take the relation R to be asserted for a given tincture at the outermost point at which that tincture appears; this tincture will thus be accessed by the one immediately enclosing it. This access is, of course, in addition to those which follow from the properties of R.

For present purposes, we begin our graphical-logical work on the basic (alpha-beta) SA, whose tincture is Tincture 0 (in PAP terms, *Argent*).[10] This tincture[11] is the 'base,' representing the 'possible world' in which our graph-work is thought of as beginning. Access to Tincture 0 is obtained on the very first *recto* – its own – which we encounter (unlike access to the other worlds we deal with in this presentation,[12] which we find only by cutting down to them and overturning the resultant stack of sheet-pieces). Considering Tincture 0 to be a selective (or part of a LI), its presence, even when blank, is a claim that 'There is a world, a universe of discourse, in which certain (as yet) indefinite propositions are true.' Following the procedures used, say, in semantic tableaux for quantifiers, we may assign a name to this world – let us call it 'a' – provided that name has not been used before (and so designates an entirely indefinite[13] world). Given this name, the graph of Figure 6 would now have the interpretation

(3') $\sim\exists w(Raw \wedge (p @ w))$

which would be equivalent to asserting $\sim Mp$ in the world represented by Tincture 0, that is, world a. Lp would be represented (as holding in the *Argent* world) in these terms by Figure 9.

Figure 9

Magenta is the *recto* of the same tincture whose *verso* is green; since the cut within which the magenta appears is within the area of the green, there is no problem with tincture identity. Thought of as a line of identity,[14] Tincture 1 simply extends inward across the green-to-magenta cut, and the quantification implicit in it is determined by the position of its outermost (green) portion. This tincture is accessed, as we have noted, by Tincture 0. With a as the (indefinite) name of Tincture 0, we have, as the ordinary logic interpretation of Figure 9:

(5) $\sim\exists w(Raw \wedge \sim(p @ w))$

This, of course, is equivalent to

(5') $\forall w(Raw \supset p @ w)$

which is equivalent to asserting *Lp* in the *Argent* world.

Figure 10

In what follows, we shall perform some graphical transformations (deductions) involving tinctures, and as we go we shall introduce appropriate rules for tinctured gamma graphs based on the alpha and beta rules (see Appendix). As with most such graphical deductions, our first step will be a simple use of rule $Dc_{+\alpha}$, giving Figure 10.

At this point we may introduce variants of the double-cut rules which will apply in the tinctured graphs. Since a tincture is a LI or selective, Tincture 1 in Figure 9 is like a LI with its outermost portion in the space between the two cuts in that figure. By the beta rules, then, those two cuts might not be placed or removed as a double cut. In Figure 10, however, Tincture 0 begins outside the outermost cut and continues through the annular space into the innermost cut; considered as a LI, it would not prohibit the making or erasing of the double cut. Based on the beta rules, the double-cut rules for tinctures are:

$Dc+_{\gamma}$: A pair of cuts with nothing between them but blank SA, and with the same tincture outside the outer cut, between the two cuts, and within the inner may be scribed around any graph ('rule of positive double cut for tinctures').

$Dc-_{\gamma}$: A pair of cuts with nothing between them but blank SA, and with the same tincture outside the outer cut, between the two cuts, and within the inner may be erased from around any graph ('rule of negative double cut for tinctures').

The next step will to be to use the (alpha) rule of insertion in odd to obtain

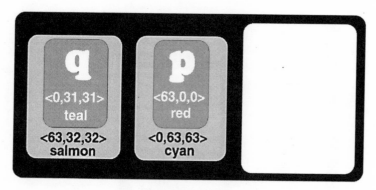

Figure 11

Figure 11. This rule is unaltered by the tinctures. An application of the rule of iteration appropriate to tinctures is now required. The partial graph containing *q* in Figure 11 is of Tincture 3. This tincture is *isolated* in this graph – its outer-most occurrence is just where we see it. By the reasoning which led to Figure 8, an iteration of this graph must result in a replica with an entirely new tincture (Tincture 1), giving Figure 12.

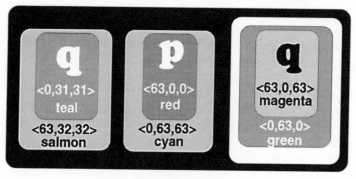

Figure 12

We may in turn iterate the partial graph containing *p* in the same manner, but to a different area, giving Figure 13. The new tincture chosen for the iterated instance is Tincture 4, which, I note, is accessible to Tincture 3 (see Figure 1) by the concept of accessibility we have discussed.

So far the iterations follow, as we have noted, the reasoning leading to Figure 8. But now a new twist appears. The just-iterated partial graph (which is of Tincture 4; as indicated in Figure 1, Tincture 4 is *accessible to* its enclosing

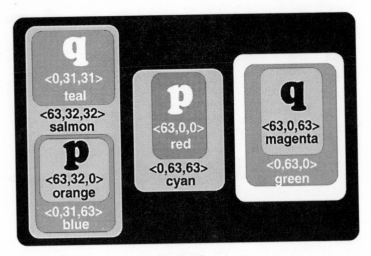

Figure 13

Tincture 3) is now entirely within an area of Tincture 3. The outermost area of the just-iterated graph is *oddly enclosed* in the overall graph. Tincture 3, thought of as a LI, may be extended inward by beta-iteration, and then, by beta-join-in-odd, connected to the LI which is Tincture 4 in this graph; these tinctures are thereby identified, as in Figure 14.

Following the above reasoning, we may state tincture rules corresponding to the beta rules for insertion in odd and erasure in even

Ins$_\gamma$: A tincture t on any *verso*, along with the same tincture in all areas within the enclosure of that *verso*, may be identified with a tincture *which accesses* t and which *totally surrounds* t.

Ers$_\gamma$: A tincture t on any *recto*, along with the same tincture in all areas within the enclosure of that *recto*, may be replaced by a tincture *accessible to* t and entirely new to the whole graph.

We might further alter the graph of Figure 14 by applying the rule of negative double cut in Tincture 1 and the rule of positive double cut in Tincture 0; this gives Figure 15.

This is the graphical equivalent of

(6) $L(p \supset q) \supset (Lp \supset Lq)$

In similar fashion, we might have found graphical equivalents of formulas such as

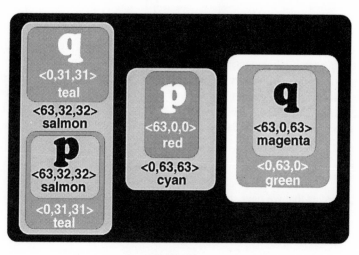

Figure 14

(7) $L(p \land q) \supset (Lp \land Lq)$

and

(8) $(Lp \land Lq) \supset L(p \land q)$

Figure 15

Note that with the rules as we have them, if a graph A is constructible on Tincture 0, then it will be constructible on any *recto*. Now, although other agreements might be arrived at between 'Graphist' and 'Interpreter' (4.552), one reasonable such agreement, and the one that we will take as applying to the tinctured graphs with which we work here, is, then, that all logical transformations which can be applied in '*Argent*' may be applied in all the colours to which *Argent* has access. Thus, where ⊢ A @ w means that A holds at w by virtue of the rules of transformation for *EG*, we will have, for a the *Argent* world

(9)   If ⊢ A @ *a* then ⊢ ∀w(*Raw* ⊃ A @ w)

which means that we have the equivalent of *necessitation*:

(10)   If ⊢ α, then ⊢ *L*α

With this, and with (6), we then also have the equivalent of

(11)   If ⊢ α ⊃ ß then ⊢ *L*α ⊃ *L*ß

Expressions (6)–(11) mean that the logic we are dealing with contains the equivalent of Segerberg's (1971) normal modal logic K, or, equivalently, Sobocinski's T° (see Zeman 1973).

Figure 16

In addition, Figure 16 will result from the alpha rules alone. Then, by Ers$_\gamma$ applied to the left (twice-enclosed) white *recto*, we get Figure 17 (the

Figure 17

change in the *recto* takes its enclosed *verso* along with it from Tincture 0 to Tincture 1).

Since Tincture 1 is accessible to Tincture 0, Figure 17 is the graphical equivalent of

(12) $Lp \supset p$

The logic we are dealing with then contains the equivalent of the modal system T.

Figure 18

We may carry this a bit further; if we take the graph of Figure 10 and first perform an application of Ins$_\alpha$ to get the partial graph in Tincture 1, and then perform Itr$_\gamma$ to get the replica of that partial graph (in Tincture 3) in the inner *recto* area, we have Figure 18. This figure may be further modified by an application of Ins$_\alpha$, giving us Figure 19.

Figure 19

And by an application of Itr$_\gamma$, this becomes Figure 20.

Figure 20

Given the conventions we have adopted regarding tincture and access, access is a transitive relation; the tincture of the just-iterated partial graph (which is accessible to the area onto which it is iterated, by Itr_γ), is accessible to the tincture on which *that* tincture stands, and so the graph of Figure 20 is the equivalent of

(12) $Lp \supset LLp$

and the graphical system we are dealing with includes the equivalent of the Lewis-modal S4.

So we have the basis of modal logic within the tinctures of PAP. It is clear that many variations could be produced by altering the very natural access between worlds we have used; if we restrict ourselves to shades of grey (where $r = g = b$, for example, we get a version of Prior's Diodorean modal logic (see Zeman 1973, 229 ff). There is much to be examined here – where, for instance, do the 'furs' of PAP fit in? But for now, we have presented an exercise in experimentation on diagrams which is, I believe, faithful to Peirce's own approach.

Appendix: Rules for Graphs

Alpha and Beta

Ins_α: On any *verso* (area enclosed by an odd number of cuts) any graph may be scribed ('rule of insertion in odd').

Ers_α: On any *recto* (area enclosed by an even number, including 0, of cuts), any graph may be erased ('rule of erasure in even').

Itr_α: Any graph *g* may be iterated (scribed again) in the same area or inward, that is, into any area enclosed by at least all the cuts that enclose the original instance of *g* ('rule of iteration').

Dit_α: Any partial graph which might have resulted from Itr_α may be erased, regardless of how it is enclosed ('rule of deiteration').

$Dc+_\alpha$: A pair of cuts with nothing between them but blank SA may be scribed around any graph ('rule of positive double cut').

Dc_α: A pair of cuts with nothing between them but blank SA may be erased from around any graph ('rule of negative double cut').

In addition to the above, the following hold for beta:

Ins_β: On any *verso*, LIs may be joined at will.

Ers_β: On any *recto*, LIs may be severed at will.

Itr_β: If *g* is iterated by Itr_α and *g* has LIs with parts unenclosed in its original area, those LI parts may be connected by LI to the corresponding parts of the iterated replica of *g*. As a specific subcase of this rule, the end of an LI unenclosed in *g* may be extended to any area to which *g* might be iterated. Also, a 'point of teri-dentity' – a branch – may be extended from any point on a LI.

Dit_β: Any partial graph which might have resulted from Itr_β may be 'undone.'

$Dc+_\beta$:   A pair of cuts with nothing between them but blank SA and LIs which pass from completely without the outer cut to completely within the inner may be scribed around any graph.

$Dc-_\beta$:   A pair of cuts with nothing between them but blank SA and LIs which pass from completely without the outer cut to completely within the inner may be erased from around any graph.

Tinctures

Ins_α and Ers_α apply unchanged to tinctured EG; the tincture of the *recto* or *verso* involved does not matter. Itr_α and Dit_α are subcases of the corresponding γ-rules (specifically, they apply when there are no 'isolated tinctures' in the partial graph to be iterated). Similarly, the double-cut rules for alpha are the special cases of the corresponding γ-rules. We tentatively will take the beta rules to hold as stated, observing, of course, any tincture-connected provisos associated with the iteration–deiteration and double-cut rules.

A tincture t is isolated in a (partial) graph *g* iff there is no occurrence of t in the whole graph outside of *g*.

Although the meaning of 'access' among tinctures might be developed in a variety of directions, for present purposes, let us first suppose that we have two tinctures (worlds), *u* and *v*, associated respectively with the *recto–verso* pairs <*a, b*> and <*c, d*>. With colour *h* (in terms of red, green, blue) as <r_h, g_h, b_h>, we say that (colours)

$$e \leq f \text{ iff } r_e \leq r_f \text{ and } g_e \leq g_f \text{ and } b_e \leq b_f;$$

we might say in this case that *e* is a *subcolour* of *f*. Then (with *u* as <*a, b*> and *u* as <*c, d*>),

$$v \text{ has access to } u \text{ iff } c \leq a$$

(equivalently, $b \leq d$, by the relationship between colours representing *rectos* and *versos*).

Ins$_\gamma$:   A tincture t on any *verso*, along with the same tincture in all areas within the enclosure of that *verso*, may be identified with a tincture *which accesses* t and which *totally surrounds* t.

Ers$_\gamma$:   A tincture t on any *recto*, along with the same tincture in all areas within the enclosure of that *recto*, may be replaced by a tincture *accessible to* t and entirely new to the whole graph.

Itr$_\gamma$:   A partial graph may be iterated in the same area or inward. *Isolated tinctures* in the original will be changed in the copy to *new tinctures accessible to the tincture of the area to which the iteration is performed.*

Dit$_\gamma$:   A partial graph which might have resulted from Itr$_\gamma$ may be deiterated.

Dc+$_\gamma$:   A pair of cuts with nothing between them but blank SA, and with the same tincture outside the outer cut, between the two cuts, and within the inner may be scribed around any graph.

Dc−$_\gamma$:   A pair of cuts with nothing between them but blank SA, and with the same tincture outside the outer cut, between the two cuts, and within the inner may be erased from around any graph.

Notes

 1 Citations from the *Collected Papers* 1931–58 will follow the form indicated at the beginning of this volume.

 2 In 4.528, Peirce gives us notation for expressing some relationships of graphs (propositions) to sheets of assertion (universes of discourse).

 3 '@' may be taken as a relation between propositions and 'possible worlds'; our intuitive reading of

$$\alpha \ @ \ b$$

would be 'proposition α at [holds at, is true at] "world" b.' @ will, of course, have the following properties:

Where p is any 'atomic' formula, $p \ @ \ b$ iff p is assigned true at 'world' b

$$(\alpha \wedge \beta) \ @ \ b \text{ iff } (\alpha \ @ \ b) \wedge (\beta \ @ \ b)$$
$$(\sim\alpha) \ @ \ b \text{ iff } \sim(\alpha \ @ \ b)$$

So far as quantifiers are concerned,

$$(\forall x Bx) \ @ \ b \text{ iff } \forall x(Bx \ @ \ b).$$

4 We shall shortly explain these terms.

5 'The whole of any continuous part of the exposed surface in one tincture shall be termed a Province' (4.553).

6 The correlation between *colour index* and *colour* is arbitrary or, we might prefer to say, 'user-defined.'

7 Limitations on the presentation of this material dictate that we tag the colours with identifiers to avoid having to visually discriminate between the shade of grey that represents blue, for example, and that which represents red. In the diagram of Figure 1, 'T*n*r' designates the *recto* of Tincture n, while T*n*v designates its *verso*; the rest of the first line gives the VGA256 colour index in hexadecimal; the '0x' prefix is a C-language convention for hexadecimal. If the colours are imagined as laid out on a 16×16 matrix with columns (counted from the left) mapping the first digit and rows (from the top) the second digit of each index, the colours will be laid out in approximately the pattern given in Figure 1. The second line in each box gives the <red, green, blue> proportions of each colour, and the third line gives an intuitive colour designation, for reference, e.g., 'blue,' 'yellow,' or 'red.' These names are in no way part of the graphs in which they appear, but are for convenience in recognizing the tinctures involved. The letters representing graphs – e.g., 'p,' 'q,' 'r,' 'A,' 'B,' – will be considerably larger than the colour identifiers. In tinctured graphs, lettering on *verso* will generally be white, and on *recto*, lettering will be black.

8 We shall shortly give meaning to this word.

9 Which is connected with the 'normal' modal logics of Segerberg 1971, 74ff.

10 This tincture's *recto* colour is <63, 63, 63> – white – the fullest saturation of red, green, and blue available in VGA256. Any other colour will be included in white, and so Tincture 0 will have access to any of the other tinctures we discuss.

11 Again, presumably *Argent*; appropriately, metallic silver appears sometimes white and sometimes black.

12 Which follows generally the suggestions of 'An Improvement on the Gamma Graphs' (4.573ff). This involves, as we have noted, cutting down into the SA to find other levels of possibility. PAP suggests a somewhat different picture, in which the base tincture is defined by the province at the 'March' of the graph (4.553), and provinces in other tinctures are thought of as overlying that base and each other (and so being accessible, perhaps, directly rather than only through cuts – Peirce does not give much detail on this). Ibid.

13 I am making an effort in this to stay as close as possible to Peirce's own uses of terms such as 'indefinite.' For further remarks on Peirce's logic of the indeterminate, see Zeman 1988.

14 I admit here to using the expression 'line of identity' where Peirce might have preferred 'ligature.' I don't think that any confusion will result.

References

Dewey, John. 1988. *Human Nature and Conduct: 1922; The Middle Works of John Dewey, 1899–1924.* Vol. 14. Edited by Jo Ann Boydston. Carbondale: Southern Illinois University Press.

Peirce, Charles Sanders. 1931–58. *The Collected Papers of Charles Sanders Peirce.* 8 vols. Edited by C. Hartshorne, P. Weiss, and A. Burks. Cambridge, Mass.: Belknap Press of Harvard University Press.

Roberts, Don. 1974. *The Existential Graphs of C.S. Peirce. Approaches to Semiotics* 27. The Hague: Mouton.

Segerberg, Krister. 1971. *An Essay in Classical Modal Logic.* Uppsala. Photocopied typescript.

Zeman, J. Jay. 1964. *The Graphical Logic of C.S. Peirce.* PhD diss., University of Chicago.

– 1967. 'A System of Implicit Quantification.' *Journal of Symbolic Logic* 32:480–504.

– 1973. *Modal Logic.* Oxford: Clarendon Press.

– 1974. 'Peirce's Logical Graphs.' *Semiotica* 12, no. 3:339–56.

– 1988. 'Peirce on the Indeterminate and on the Object: Initial Reflections.' Paper presented at conference On the Background of Contemporary Philosophical Logic, Miami, Mar. 1987. *Grazer Philosophische Studien* 32:37–49.

– Forthcoming. 'Peirce and Philo.' In *Studies in the Logic of C.S. Peirce*, edited by N. Houser, Don Roberts, and James Van Evra. Bloomington: Indiana University Press.

Pragmatic Experimentalism and the Derivation of the Categories

SANDRA B. ROSENTHAL

It is generally held that Peirce's philosophy incorporates diverse methods for obtaining the categories, a priori deduction from mathematical principles, and phenomenological inquiry. This diversity is in turn held to evince different systems chronologically developed,[1] or a conflict between naturalist and transcendentalist strains of his thought.[2] The present paper will first attempt to show that one method, the phenomenological method, is at work in Peirce's derivation of the categories, though he of course did not use this term until late in his career, and to decipher the distinctively pragmatic character of its dynamics with the implicit pluralism it involves. The remainder of the paper will then examine the significance of this view of Peirce's phenomenology for interpreting his understanding of the nature of the metaphysical enterprise and the dynamics of its relation to his phenomenology.

The phenomenology Peirce develops could be called hermeneutical phenomenology, but perhaps, in the context of his pragmatism, experimental phenomenology is a more appropriate label, and one which points more directly to its key pragmatic features. Peirce's categories of 'Firstness,' 'Secondness,' and 'Thirdness' will be seen to be an interrelated set of meanings, abductively generated as a tool for focusing on the richness of experience in order to elicit its illusive, 'intangible' (1.535) but pervasive textures, 'traits' (1.288), 'tones or tints' (1.353). And, as with all sets of meanings, it is necessary to distinguish their abductive, creative genesis within experience, the logical priority of these abductively generated meanings for the future delineation of experience, and the verification of the adequacy of their application in the ongoing course of experience.

These experimental dynamics can best be brought to light by first examining in just what sense Peirce's phenomenology' simply scrutinizes the direct appearances' or confines itself to 'honest, single-minded observation of the appearances' (1.287). First, it involves 'pure observation' in the sense that it does not make judgments concerning the reality of what is observed. As he states, 'Phaneroscopy is the description of the phaneron; and by the phaneron I mean the collective total of all that is in any way or in any sense present to the mind, quite regardless of whether it corresponds to any real thing or not' (1.284). In this sense, it is concerned with phenomena in their dimension of firstness (5.122). When Peirce claims that his phenomenological derivation of the categories is an experiential derivation, he is 'taking experience in its broadest sense,'[3] and to include not only experience of the real world but experience of ideal worlds, of illusion, and so on (7.535; 7.527). In brief, as Peirce states, 'In high philosophy experience is the entire cognitive result of living, and illusion is, for its purposes, just as much experience as is real perception' (7.527); it 'includes interpretations quite as truly as it does the matter of sense' (7.538).[4] Thus experience in the context of Peirce's phenomenology cannot be understood in the more restricted Peircean sense in which 'the world of experience' is equated with 'the world of fact' (1.321).[5] Phenomenology involves pure observation, then, in that it observes the entire range of experience, possible and actual, without judgments of objectivity.

Phenomenology is further concerned with the observation of appearances in that it does not impose upon the experiences the frameworks of any of the sciences. Thus Peirce points out that though the psychologist and the astronomer look upon the same world as the phenomenologist, what they observe is different (8.297). It is in this sense that one needs the ability to see what presents itself, just as it is. As Peirce stresses, one needs the 'observational powers of the artist who sees the appearance of the snow in the sunshine as a rich yellow rather than as the white which his theory tells him he ought to see' (5.42).

Yet, though phenomenology is pure observation in the above two senses, there is, for Peirce, no observation without the directing focus of meanings. Phenomenology, for Peirce, consists strictly in the observation and classification of whatever seems to be before the mind at any given time. It provides the 'ultimate analysis of experience.' In order to classify and analyse, there must first be the creative formation of meaningful structures which provide the delineations for classifications and the tools of analysis. Interpretive, legislative elements must enter into the phenomenological focus on experience as it appears in order for an 'observing' mind to grasp and delineate its pervasive textures. This point is well summarized in Peirce's claim that 'It is the genius of the mind, that takes up all these hints of sense, adds immensely to them, makes them precise, and shows them in intelligible form' (1.383). Within the context of Peirce's radical rejection of the spectator theory of knowledge it is not possible to focus on any aspect of experience independently of interpretive elements.

There are, then, highly interpretive elements at work in Peirce's phenomenology as the 'pure observation' of what appears as it appears. From this backdrop the following discussion will turn to the experiential elements involved in his so-called transcendental strain or his 'logical deduction' of the categories.

That Peirce was strongly influenced by Kant is undeniable, but this does not lead to some version of a transcendental deduction of the categories. Here, as elsewhere, Peirce's Kantianism is a radically transformed pragmatic version, and it rules out both intuitionism and formalism. This point can best be developed by first turning to Peirce's own account of his relationship to Kant and to his more Kantian-sounding claims.

Peirce observes that since Kant, the importance of the fact that systems have been constructed architectonically has been recognized, yet its full significance has not been adequately apprehended (6.9). He clarifies this point via a critique of past philosophical systems in which 'an idea which has been found interesting and fruitful has been adopted, developed, and forced to yield explanations of all sorts of phenomena. Just as if a man, being seized with the conviction that paper was a good material to make things of, were to go to work to build a papier mâché house' (6.7). Meanwhile, the remaining systems of philosophy have consisted of reforms, sometimes quite radical, in light of problems found within an accepted position. But, he states, 'this is like partially rebuilding a house' (6.8). Peirce then goes on to correct this misapprehension with the following continuation of his analogy:

> When a man is about to build a house, what a power of thinking he has to do before he can safely break ground. With what pains he has to excogitate the precise wants that are to be supplied! What a study to ascertain the most available and suitable materials, to determine the mode of construction to which those materials are best adapted, and to answer a hundred such questions Now without riding the metaphor too far, I think we may safely say that the studies preliminary to the construction of a great theory should be at least as deliberate and thorough as those that are preliminary to the building of a dwelling house. (ibid.)

Peirce's specific recommendation for those who wish to form an opinion about fundamental problems of philosophy is that they should examine all areas of human knowledge so that they understand the nature of the materials a philosophical theory must concern itself with, and only then turn to the nature of philosophical problems and the best way of solving them (6.9). And, his point concerning this type of empirical survey is geared towards the specific recommendation that one engage in a systematic study of the conceptions which are capable of building a good philosophical theory and their interrelation and uses (ibid.). After looking at many different disciplines and giving a brief 'hint at their nature' in providing conceptions 'serviceable for philosophy,' Peirce turns to the examination of logic and finds analogous conceptions. Any phenomenological survey must include a phenomenological examination of logic, for as Peirce states in a letter to James, phenomenology is the analysis of 'what kind of constituents there are in our thoughts and lives,' taking thoughts in the logical sense which has 'nothing to do with psychology' (8.295).[6] In turning to his phenomenological focus on what constituents there are in our thoughts, he states that: 'Among the many principles of Logic which find their application in Philosophy, I can here only mention one. Three conceptions are perpetually turning up at every point in every theory of logic, and in the most rounded systems they occur in connection with one another. They are conceptions so very broad and consequently indefinite that they are hard to seize and may be easily overlooked. I call them the conceptions of First, Second, Third' (6.32). Recognizing the tentative and vague nature of the experiences which give rise to the abductive generation of the categories, Peirce can express the wish that in the future students will retrace the ground he has covered and present their results to the community (6.34).

Only in light of such a vague and empirically grasped recognition of these distinct conceptions can Peirce abductively create the interpretive structure which allows him to claim that 'We find then a priori that there are three categories of undecomposable elements to be expected in the phaneron: those which are simply positive totals, those which involve dependence but not combination, those which involve combination' (1.299). This is not a Kantian fixed a priori, but rather this claim is 'a priori' in that, although it is abductively generated in the light of past experience, it is logically prior to the analysis of ongoing experience. It is a tool created to bring to experience for the interpretation of experience, one which can be discarded for another if it does not work adequately, and which is thus like the conditional or hypothetical certitudes of mathematics. As he stresses, phenomenology, as a science which does not 'aim to declare that something is positively or categorically true ... must, if it is to be properly grounded, be made to depend upon the Conditional or Hypothetical Science of Pure Mathematics,[7] whose only aim is to discover not how things actually are, but how they might be supposed to be' (5.40).[8] The tool dictates what we must find if we use it; *if* we use it, *then* certain things must follow, for it legislates for the interpretation of experience. But, it may be found pragmatically useless in that too much of experience cannot be incorporated into it.[9] Thus, after asserting the 'a priori' nature of the categories, Peirce is led immediately to suggest, 'Now let us turn to the phaneron and see what we find in fact' (1.299). And he stresses that in turning to the phaneron, each of the categories has to find its justification in its usefulness within experience (1.301), for the categories cannot be regarded as final 'as Kant thought' but must be put to the test by an independent examination of the facts (1.374).[10]

Peirce, then, can emphatically point out the uselessness of transcendentalism (W1:72–3), yet hold to an a priori dimension in the formulation of the categories, for there is a dimension which legislates the manner in which we focus on experience. Like all interpretive tools, the categories of phenomenology arise out of experience but in turn are legislative for the analysis of experience. They are not handed down from on high; nor are they pure inductions from experience. Rather, they emerge as a creative, interpretive framework through which to focus on the entire gamut of 'whatever is in any way present to mind.' Thus is that Peirce can claim that with his interactional, synechistic understanding of subjective-objective, the issue of the a priori 'gains new life' (6.590).

It is in the context of these dynamics that Peirce's partial agreement with Kant concerning congenital tendencies of the mind in relation to the categories must be understood (1.374). Indeed, Peirce goes so far as to hold that the pragmatist cannot deny a doctrine of innate ideas (5.504). But, contrary to traditional notions, Peirce's pragmatic transformation of innate ideas or congenital tendencies of mind does not indicate absolute structures. What he means by this claim is that the pragmatist must hold to the embeddedness within behaviour of dispositional tendencies, which are for him, of course, the core of interpretive structures. Dispositional tendencies, however, are always 'tendencies in relation to' or a 'readiness' in relation to 'given circumstances' (5.480). Thus, what is emphasized by innate ideas or congenital tendencies is the pragmatic interplay of interpretive categories and the conditions of their formation and retention.

A categorial set is not something fixed, final, or absolute. Rather it is a tool which, though it is legislative in being applied, is itself further developed or refined in the very process of legislating, for its adequacy must be continually tested by future observations. As Peirce states, the materials supplied by the categories must be able 'to predict many more things which new observations can alone bring to the test' (6.34). These new situations serve both to verify, and to demand revision of, the categories.

These experimental dynamics can be well exemplified by turning more directly to the relation of the categories to Peirce's analysis of logic. Though this relationship is generally held to point towards the 'formalist' strain of his thought, yet a brief sketch of its history points towards the ongoing pragmatic, processive, open-ended nature of categorial determination developed above.

Peirce's interest in the interactive relationship among three irreducible conceptions is something he brought to his understanding of logic. Indeed this was already developed in 1861 in terms of the 'I,' 'It,' and 'Thou.' As he stated in 1861:

> If conceptions which are incapable of definition are simple, I, It, and Thou are so. Who could define either of these words, easy as they are to understand? Who does not perceive, in fact, that neither of them can be expressed in terms of the others? ... Though they cannot be expressed in terms of each other, yet they have a relation to each other, for THOU is an IT in which there is another I. I looks in. It looks out, Thou looks *through*, out and in again. I outwells, It inflows, Thou commingles ... The I, the IT and the THOU are . . . in Three different worlds. (W1: 45–6)

And, in an 1866 paper, Peirce relates the I, It, and Thou to the three references of a sign. Further, as Murray Murphey well observes concerning that paper, it 'suggests that the terms "Firstness," "Secondness," and "Thirdness" were first derived from the names of the pronouns and only later matched with the number of entities connected by the relations.'[11]

In Peirce's ongoing development and revision of the categories, culminating in his revised list of categories presented in 1885 in the paper 'One, Two, Three: Fundamental Categories of Thought and of Nature,' which views the categories squarely in terms of monadic, dyadic, and triadic logical relations, the continuity of terminology tended to hide the substantive changes taking place. Thus Murphey claims that, while 'Extensive revisions of position pass unnoticed under a shell of changeless terminology,' the revision of the categories was in fact so substantial that new names should have been provided to avoid confusion.[12] It would seem that Peirce's triadic divisions influenced the way he approached mathematical/logical issues. Yet, in their application to this area, to be verified by their workability, the early categories legislated were found inadequate, and as a result were altered, partially in a substantive sense, partially in the sense of a clarification and sharpening of originally too-vague intentions (4.3). Further, though it was not until 1885 that Peirce distinguished formal and material aspects of the categories, this lack of distinction in the earlier categories, far from pointing towards their pure formality, is indicative of the inseparable intermingling of the two dimensions. Indeed, Peirce's writings point to the fact that the impetus for his ongoing revision of the categories came not only from discoveries in logical theory but also from problems connected with his theories of cognition and reality. Recognizing the difficulty of this ongoing project, Peirce states, 'I will endeavor to convey to you some idea of the conceptions themselves. It is to be remembered that they are excessively general ideas, so very uncommonly general that it is far from easy to get any but a vague apprehension of their meaning' (ibid.).

It would seem that Peirce's three categories brought into significant focus in a general sense the new observations involved in examining the logic of relatives, yet were revised because of their inability to deal adequately with this new area under examination. And there is of course a big difference between revising the categories in light of their inadequacy to accommodate the new data of the logic of relatives and the claim that they are *deduced from* the logic of relatives.[13] David Savan points out that Peirce clearly vacillates as to whether to rest logic upon observation or to rest observation upon logical procedures, and that 'Peirce is tempted to suggest that the issue is only verbal.' Yet this issue, Savan continues, is 'so central to his thought that he cannot accept this escape, even as a last resort.'[14] What Peirce did not adequately see was that no clear-cut answer could be given because of the dynamic interplay between the two. The categories are derived from experience yet legislative for the analysis of experience, while at the same time subject to revision in light of experience. These experimental dynamics hold in the area of logic as well as in all other areas of experience. Developments in any area of human experience are brought into focus through the categories, but may themselves demand categorial revision. This is not a vicious circle but an exemplification of the cumulative process involved in the pragmatic, experimental interplay between meanings and experience.

Phenomenology, precisely as experimental phenomenology, displays this pragmatic interplay. What is involved in the experimental nature of phenomenology is an organization of experience in ways which work in grasping universally pervasive tones or textures of what appears as it appears, tones or textures which are continually put to the test in future observation of phenomena. These categories which work have arisen through the creativity of abductive processes based in part on the thorough study of the various disciplines to obtain a 'hint at their nature' and, once developed, can be applied back to these disciplines in forms and terminologies relevant to each, though in their very application they are subject to the test of continual workability.[15]

The failure to recognize Peirce's halting and never clearly defined use of the above method leads to the often-raised question as to whether he was attempting an empirical justification of the categories or an a priori deduction of them. If a dichotomy is made in this way, then the problems attributed to Peirce's method do in fact arise. If the method is empirical, then we cannot know that the categories have universal application. Alternately, if the method reduces to a rational assertion, the categories have universal application 'by fiat' but seem somewhat arbitrary in their application to experience.[16]

The vague recognition of some of the features of Peirce's halting, never clearly defined, pragmatic, experimental method involved in categorial inquiry leads Dewey to note that Peirce's analysis of the phaneron has a logical dimension to it.[17] Similarly, Thomas Goudge points out that 'in reality Peirce's phaneroscopy is a double-edged sword, possessing at once both its rational and empirical edge.'[18] It is precisely Peirce's pragmatic interrelation and transformation of 'rational' and 'empirical' factors in his phenomenology which are incorporated in the dynamic interplay between meanings abductively formulated and legislative for experience, and the vague experiences which give rise to them and which, as made precise through these interpretive or legislative tools, serve to judge them adequate or inadequate.[19]

If, as Peirce holds, the dynamics of experimental method allow for alternative interpretations which are continually open and subject to revision, then he must allow for the possibility of alternatives to the categories of firstness, secondness, and thirdness. This, however, is precisely what he does hold. Peirce nowhere indicates that his categories are absolute or eternal and in fact states quite clearly that though his selection may probably be the most adequate, alternative series of categories are possible (1.525, 526). Or, as he elsewhere states of his categories, 'I do not claim nor opine that this set comprises all indecomposable[20] and almost universally recurring ideas, but merely that it is *one* such set having a peculiar importance of its own, perhaps, on the whole, greater than that of any other set' (MS296:16; emphasis added). Again, he notes that at every step 'conceptions are met with which presumably do not belong to this series of ideas' (1.525). Indeed, as to his three universal categories of firstness, secondness, and thirdness, he states that there is perhaps 'no very good reason for thinking that they are more universal than the others' (1.526).

It may here be objected that Peirce's frequent emphasis on the possibility of alternative categorial sets, while indicative of his fallibilism, does not involve pluralism. Thus, one might argue that a doctrine of categories, *if* correct, would be definitively and uniquely so. But pluralistic implications are contained in the fact that Peirce can claim *both* that his set of categories is probably the *most* adequate, and also that not only are alternative series of categories possible, but that 'at every step' features are met with which do not fit his categories or 'series of ideas,' for his set does not 'comprise all.' And, since his set may well be the *most* adequate, but yet does not comprise all, presumably by their very nature categorial sets *cannot* do so, thus allowing for alternative possibilities. Even the most adequate set of categories will not rule out the possibility of grasping the phenomenon in different ways which work in grasping features which overflow the bounds of that set of categorial distinctions. It has been seen that what one finds is partially dependent upon what one brings, and that alternative ways of bringing will lead to different discriminations within the rich textures of the phenomenon. Some ways of discriminating within the phaneron are better than others, but none can be exhaustive of its richness, and other categorial sets may be 'equally universal.' Peirce's experimental phenomenology, then, is not only fallibilistic, but incorporates an inherent pluralism, for there are in theory always alternative, perhaps equally adequate, perhaps better,ways of organizing the phenomena because of the creative abstractive nature of the categories and the richness of the phaneron.

The discussion thus far has focused on the development of Peirce's categories through a pragmatically oriented 'experimental phenomenology.' It is now time to turn to an examination of Peirce's move from the categories as phenomenologically descriptive of the textures, tones, or tints of experience to the categories as metaphysically assertive of reality, and to the dynamic experimental nature of this move which both founds the speculative categorial claims of metaphysics and gives further confirmation to the adequacy of the categories as phenomenological.

Peirce holds that 'Metaphysics is founded in phenomenology but goes beyond it.' The nature of this 'going beyond' is found in his posing of the 'problem of metaphysics': 'We must begin by asking whether the categories can be admitted as simple and irreducible conceptions; and afterward to go on to ask whether they cannot all be supposed to be real constituents in the universe' (5.82). His conclusion seems evident from his statement that the 'premisses of nature ... though they are not the perceptual facts that are premisses to us, nevertheless must resemble them in being premisses. We can only imagine what they are by comparing them with premisses for us' (5.119).[21] This stress on analogy with perceptual facts in the move to metaphysics is important in two respects. First, experiences of perceptual facts, while manifesting the three categorial features found in all experience, are that special part of experience which serve as signs of an independently real universe, and metaphysics 'endeavors to comprehend the Reality of Phenomena' (5.121). Second, it would seem that perhaps Peirce's metaphysical discussions of the three categories and their interrelation are not to be understood as an attempt to provide literal descriptions.

Peirce can give an affirmative answer to the above posed question concerning the problem of metaphysics because there is, for him, no gap between the categories as phenomenological and as ontological, for there is no gap between experience and reality.[22] The epistemic and ontological unity at the heart of experience is expressed by Peirce in a telling criticism of Kant: 'That time and space are innate ideas, so far from proving that they have merely a mental existence, as Kant thought, ought to be regarded as evidence of their reality. For the constitution of the mind is the result of evolution under the influence of experience' (MS14, Article 23:33). Indeed, Peirce's pragmatic transformation of the doctrine of innate ideas which points, as indicated earlier, to the nature of the dynamics of phenomenological inquiry, points even more directly to the interrelation of the categories as phenomenological and as metaphysical. Dispositional tendencies are tendencies of a concrete organism in interaction with a natural universe, and it is this epistemic and ontological interactional unity which is ultimately emphasized by Peirce's pragmatic, dynamic understanding of innate ideas.

What appears within experience, then, is also the appearance of the independently real; there is no ontological gap between appearance and reality. As Peirce observes, 'Synechism ... will not admit a sharp sundering of phenomena and substrates. That which underlies a phenomenon and determines it thereby is, itself, in a measure, a phenomenon' (7.629). Further, it is at the same time 'to me' that it appears and reflects my intentional link with the externally real. Thus Peirce can say that 'Perhaps it may reconcile the psychologist to the admission of perceptual judgments involving generality to be told that they are perceptual judgments concerning our own purposes' (5.166). The epistemic and ontological unity of these two dimensions can be seen from Peirce's position that though the generality of perceptual judgments reflects our own purposes, yet 'since no cognition of ours is absolutely determinate, generals must have a real existence' (5.312). For Peirce, these are 'two sides of the same shield' (1.420). Or, as he eloquently summarizes his position, though 'everything which is present to us is a phenomenal manifestation of ourselves,' this 'does not prevent its being a phenomenon of something without us, just as a rainbow is at once a manifestation both of the sun and of the rain' (5.283). The general features manifest in the phenomenological dimensions of experience and embodied in the categories of phaneroscopy throw us outward onto the reality within which we are embedded. Or, as Peirce states, the 'list of categories' is 'applicable to being' (1.300).

To examine further the nature of the categories for Peirce, let us turn to the issue of just what the metaphysical categories are intended to be 'about'. Or, in Peirce's terminology, what is one talking about when one talks of 'truths of being?' (1.487). This problem can best be met by a somewhat negative approach. Peirce's pragmatism warns us that most metaphysical claims are combinations of empty words defined in terms of each other with no real conceptual content, or else are absurd (5.423). Thus, if metaphysical discussion is to be of value it must be not about empty words but about meaningful concepts. In speaking of empty words, Peirce points out that,

Certain very metaphysical and eminently intellectual notions are absolutely simple. But though these concepts cannot be defined by genus and difference, there is another way in which they can be defined. All determination is by negation; we can first recognize any character only by putting an object which possesses it into comparison with an object which possesses it not. A conception, therefore, which was quite universal in every respect would be unrecognizable and impossible. (5.294)

And 'being' is precisely such an 'unrecognizable and impossible concept,' which is about empty words, for it can be defined, 'for example, as that which is common to the objects included in any class, and to the objects not included in the same class' (ibid.). Or, as Peirce more succinctly sums up his views on 'being': 'The conception of being, therefore, plainly has no content' (1.548). Thus, it can be seen that being, for Peirce, is an 'empty concept' or, in more exact terms, 'being' is not a concept at all, but merely a term to which we can give no meaning, for as indicated above, a concept to which no empirical content can be given is, in fact, no concept at all. Metaphysics, then, is not about 'being qua being' but rather about *categories of* being, which is quite another matter. Thus, he states that 'there are three *modes* of being' (emphasis added) which are manifested phenomenologically (1.23). Peirce's statement that the materials supplied by firstness, secondness, and thirdness can account 'for the main features of the universe as we know it' (6.34) is perhaps more true to his intentions than his statement that the categories are 'applicable to being.' The categories do not indicate distinct realms of being, but rather discernible features which help in understanding the interrelated characteristics of the universe in which we are embedded.

These metaphysical categories involve neither spectator attempts to grasp reality 'as it is' independently of our modes of interpreting, nor related attempts to transcend our perspectival condition by a move to an absolute perspective which somehow contains all other perspectives. Rather, they are products of creative, abductive attempts to articulate features of reality in a way which can accommodate the various tones or textures to which we are attuned. Like all interpretive tools, the metaphysical categories are perspectival and subject to revision in terms of their workability in accounting for features of reality which intrude within experience and which pervade the tones and textures of experience. Peirce's mode of eliciting the phenomenological categories and his subsequent application of them to metaphysical reality indicates an awareness of these characteristics. In the last analysis, however, Peirce confounds the independence of reality as it intrudes within experience with our workable interpretations of it. This confusion is evinced in his statement that 'Metaphysics is the science of Reality. Reality consists in regularity. Real regularity is active law ... Thirdness' (5.121). Thus, 'metaphysics, as I have just remarked, treats of phenomena in their Thirdness' (ibid.; 5.124). Peirce then goes to deliberate pains to elaborate a metaphysics which gives equal play to firstness, secondness, and thirdness (6.342).

The above clarification shows that Peirce's argument commits the fallacy of equivocation. In one sense reality is an affair of thirdness, for it is only through interpretive concepts or categories that there is an objective reality *as known*, be it the reality grasped by the metaphysician or the reality of common-sense objects and facts as the outcome of our everyday perceptual judgments. And, concepts and categories are best characterized as exemplifications of thirdness. To clarify this interpretive process, however, Peirce describes independent reality as characterized by firstness, secondness, and thirdness. Peirce's equivocation here helps clarify the two distinct concepts of reality which pervade his writings in general, the reality with which perception begins and the reality with which it ends;[23] that is, the real in its independence of human noetic activity (5.565) and the categorized reality with its known objective properties, reality as the 'end product' of the interpretive perceptual process (5.316). Thus, reality for Peirce is both that which is independent of what anyone may think (5.405), and that which will be an object represented in the ultimate opinion of mankind (5.407).[24]

In light of the above discussion it can be seen that while metaphysics is dependent upon phenomenology and hence on the categories phenomenology establishes, yet metaphysical claims concerning the realities represented by metaphysics' own categories legislate, and must prove adequate for, the analysis of the experience of reality. Further, the adequacy of the metaphysical categories in their own right gives added verification to the categories of phenomenology in which they are grounded. Thus, though metaphysics presupposes phenomenology for its categories, the adequacy of the metaphysical categories, which are verified through the intelligibility they introduce into our experience of the real, helps verify the adequacy of the phenomenological categories. If the categories are inadequate for metaphysics then they are inadequate for phenomenology, for reality appears in the phenomena, though when we are focusing on the phenomena it is not judged as reality. Peirce's metaphysical claims, then, are rooted in the phenomenological interpretive descriptions of experience and help verify their adequacy. There is an experimental dynamics operative in the articulation of the phenomenological categories, in the development of the metaphysical categories, and in the relation between the phenomenological and metaphysical categories. The fallibilism and pluralism indicated above in Peirce's 'experimental phenomenology' hold *mutatis mutandis* for the metaphysical context which it founds.

At this point, one may object that Peirce's position seems to have become involved in an arbitrary circle with no firm roots anywhere. It is true that though his metaphysics attempts to understand the independent element which enters, along with a conceptual element, into our sense of empirical reality, what this independent element is like can be determined only from within experience; and it is also true that how we understand our experience will in part be influenced by the ontological categories in terms of which we approach it. But such a self-corrective method is not viciously circular; nor is it circular at all. Rather, it is a cumulative process, noted earlier in the context of Peirce's phenomenology, based on the pragmatic interplay at every level between concepts or categories and experience. Our interpretive concepts and categories at all levels, then, have arisen out of past experience and have been made prescriptive for the interpretation of future experience. This type of mutual feedback is surely not arbitrary; indeed, it harmonizes quite well with the conception of scientific method as indicating a self-corrective rather than a 'building block' enterprise. And it is to the scientific as well as the metaphorical nature of metaphysics that the discussion will now turn.

Peirce holds that the attitude of metaphysics 'toward the universe is nearly that of the special sciences from which it is mainly distinguished, by confining itself to such parts of physics and psychics as can be established without special means of observation. But these are very peculiar parts, extremely unlike the rest' (1.282). According to Buchler, 'What these "peculiar parts" are we never find expatiated in Peirce.'[25] And, in the too frequently asserted claims of the supposed 'scientism' of Peirce's position, the peculiarity of metaphysics seems to be virtually ignored. Though it is true that Peirce never explicitly clarifies this point, he perhaps gives the clue to that peculiarity in his statement that metaphysics 'rests upon a kind of phenomena with which every man's experience is so saturated that he usually pays no particular attention to them' (6.2). Thus, the data for metaphysics differ from those of science precisely because the former are so pervasive of our every experience that their presence is often not recognized. This difficulty can be dealt with through the painstaking method of experimental phenomenology which provides, ultimately, a clearer focus on the data from which metaphysics begins.

We see then that metaphysics, like science, rests upon observation. This, however, does not mean that metaphysical assertions are open to direct verification in experience, for neither are the objects of science open to direct observation. Only the experiences which form the starting points of its creative abductions and which serve to verify them can be directly observed (ibid.). It is enough for the experimental character of a science that its conceptions and theories are necessary for a more satisfactory explanation of certain phenomena which are directly observed.[26] Thus, the conclusions of neither metaphysics nor science are directly observed in experience. In metaphysics, its 'conclusions' or theories result from speculative extrapolation from the pervasive textures of experience.

Peirce observes that the assumption which underlies metaphysics is not very different from the assumption which underlies the possibility of scientific success, for 'All the categories portend to' is to 'suggest a way of thinking; and all the possibility of science depends upon the fact that human thought necessarily partakes of whatever character is diffused through the whole universe, and that its natural modes have some tendency to be the modes of action of the universe' (MS284:68–9). Anticipating a possible objection here he observes, 'I hear you say: 'This smacks too much of an anthropomorphic conception.' I reply that every scientific explanation of a natural phenomenon is a hypothesis that there is something in nature to which the human reason is analogous' (1.316). As Peirce states in speaking of anthropomorphism:

> I heartily embrace most of the clauses of that doctrine if some right of private interpretation be allowed to me. I hold, for instance, that man is so completely hemmed in by the bounds of his possible practical experience, his mind is so restricted by being the instrument of his needs, that he cannot, in the least, *mean* anything that transcends those limits ... For let him try ever so hard to think anything about what is beyond that limit, it simply cannot be done. (5.356)[27]

Thus, that which transcends experience in either science or metaphysics is anthropomorphic in the sense that we can think of it only in terms of our experience. In both science and metaphysics, we proceed to hypothesis via analogy from experience to the conditions which account for it. Both science and metaphysics rest on observation but proceed to explanatory frameworks. Peirce prefers to say that science and metaphysics are anthropomorphic, but what he means is not that the 'matter' of either science or metaphysics is of the nature of our experience but that we can understand it or even conceive of it only as in some way analogous to our experience.

Philip Weiner has aptly noted that Peirce 'boldly generalized the role of imagination,' making it the 'source of all the sciences.'[28] Imaginative, metaphorical thinking is involved in much more than science and metaphysics for Peirce, however. As he states, 'Metaphysics has been said contemptuously to be a fabric of metaphors. But not only metaphysics, but logical and phaneroscopical concepts[29] need to be clothed in such garments' (MS283:132). And ultimately, for Peirce, metaphor is involved not just in the above disciplines but in the very fabric of thought, for he holds that words and conceptions in general require metaphor, most of which relate to human conduct (MS870:6). In terms of his own metaphor, 'a pure idea without metaphor or other significant clothing is an onion without a peel' (MS283:132). All awareness goes beyond what is given in experience, and thus, he stresses, even 'When I say to myself the stove is black, I am making a little theory to account for the look of it' (MS403:22). Metaphysical thought, like scientific thought, is continuous with the dynamics of common-sense perception. The imaginative flight of metaphysics does not form a tension with Peirce's pragmatic theory of meaning, but rather arises from it. As Peirce insists: 'If pragmatism is the doctrine that every conception is a conception of conceivable practical effects, it makes conception reach far beyond the practical. It allows any flight of imagination, provided this imagination ultimately alights upon a possible practical effect; and thus many hypotheses may seem at first glance to be excluded by the pragmatical maxim that are not really so excluded' (5.196).

Because the data from which metaphysics sets out are the characteristics which pervade all experience, scientific and non-scientific alike, its conclusions must be more comprehensive and hence less verifiable than the conclusions of scientific theory; but the difference is not essentially one of kind. The difficulty of either formulating or verifying a metaphysical theory does not mean that metaphysical speculation will eventually halt. Peirce points out that 'you might as well pass a law that no man shall jump over the moon, it wouldn't forbid him to jump just as high as he possibly could' (5.356). As he summarizes, 'we need to think of the universe as intelligible, and furthermore, we shall do so' (MS290:30–1). Nor should it end; Peirce takes his stand here with a question of his own: 'Do you think, reader, that it is a positive fact that "Truth, crushed to earth, shall rise again," or do you think that this, being poetry, is only a pretty fiction?' (1.217). That metaphysical endeavour is rooted inhuman 'need' and is highly imaginative in nature does not, for Peirce, detract from the intellectual urgency of its development. He aptly recognizes that any scientific person who claims not to require metaphysics occupies a position loaded with inadequate and uncritical metaphysical presuppositions. In short, as Peirce sums up the problem of metaphysics, 'The best that can be done is to supply an hypothesis, not devoid of all likelihood, in the general line of growth of scientific ideas, and capable of being verified or refuted by future observers' (1.7), at least in some sense. Concerning his own positive metaphysics, Peirce claims that it goes a long way towards proving a philosophy that is compatible with physical science (1.6).

In contrasting the metaphysical perspectives of Peirce and Whitehead, Victor Lowe notes that 'Pierce's position seems to be a kind of scientism,' while for Whitehead, 'Metaphysics is nothing but the description of the generalities which apply to all the details of practice.'[30] According to the present view of Peirce's method of metaphysics, however, this latter characterization could well be applied to him. It is precisely the point of Peirce's phenomenologically founded metaphysics that 'everything of which we are conscious, as enjoyed, perceived, willed, or thought, shall have the character of a particular instance of the general scheme.'[31] Perhaps it is just the awareness of this role, coupled with the recognition that metaphysical statements are speculative extrapolations from experience, which leads Peirce to use such blatantly anthropomorphic language.[32]

Peirce's metaphysical discussions are couched in highly speculative, metaphorical, and anthropomorphic language not in spite of the nature and limits of meaningfulness imposed by his pragmatism but because of them. His metaphysical discussions are highly metaphorical precisely because he recognizes them to be metaphorical or imaginative extrapolations from experience. As John E. Smith has aptly captured this point, 'Peirce was acutely aware both of the extent to which metaphysics involves "extrapolation" and of the unavoidability of this sort of reasoning if we are not to deceive ourselves concerning the ultimate assumptions behind what we believe.'[33] It has been noted that Peirce's formulation of his ideas often 'converts a perfectly reasonable doctrine into something which seems utterly outrageous.'[34] And, indeed, if on the one hand Peirce's claim to be scientific in his metaphysics is taken too narrowly, or on the other his metaphorical assertions are taken too literally, then his doctrines will seem outrageous and often contradictory.

The above examination has attempted to understand Peirce's pragmatic method, or method of experimental inquiry, as the context within which his doctrine of the categories can be interpreted. His method of categorial development reveals the experimental nature of phenomenology, of metaphysics, and of the relation between their respective claims. And, one can see in this development an exaggeration of the experimental method by which we have meaningful everyday experience. There is an exaggeration of the metaphorical, imaginative, creative features of the meanings which arise out of past experience through abductive fixations of experience, and which legislate for the analysis of future experience. Further, there is an exaggerated attentiveness to what appears in experience, to its pervasive features or textures, an attentiveness which both founds the categories and serves to verify their adequacy. And, as Peirce has been seen to point out, the claims of his experimental phenomenology, and hence the claims of the metaphysics which it grounds, are fallibilistic and open to alternative categorial possibilities. There is an in built pluralism here which is not merely a step towards final agreement but is inescapable because of the concrete richness of the textures of experience, the abstractive nature of the classificatory focus required, and the creativity involved in obtaining this classificatory focus. It is because of both this fallibilism and this inherent pluralism that Peirce could claim that he received 'the pleasure of praise' from what 'was meant for blame,' when 'a critic said of me that I did not seem to be absolutely sure of my own conclusions' (1.10).

Notes

1 Murray Murphey, *The Development of Peirce's Philosophy* (Cambridge, Mass.: Harvard University Press 1961).
2 Thomas Goudge, *The Thought of C.S. Peirce* (Toronto: University of Toronto Press 1950).
3 Peirce similarly uses the term 'existence' in a broad sense as well as in the more narrow sense which limits it to 'one of the three Universes' (MS137:2–4).
4 Peirce emphasizes that this 'matter of sense' is 'a hypothetical something which we never can seize as such, free from all interpretative working over' (ibid.).
5 In 5.37 Peirce states that he will not restrict phenomenology to the observation of experience, but he is there hitting what he considers to be Hegel's muddling of secondness and thirdness, 'fact and essence,' and thus uses experience in a more limited, technical sense.
6 By psychology here Peirce means explanations 'by motions and changes of the brain,' 'a sort of physiology of the mind.'
7 Phenomenology is also dependent upon mathematics in that it requires 'the generalizing power of the mathematician who produces the abstract formula that comprehends the very essence of the feature under examination purified from all admixture of extraneous and irrelevant accompaniments' (5.42).
8 As he again objects to Hegel in a way not unrelated to the objection indicated in note 5; 'A phenomenology which does not reckon with pure mathematics, a science hardly come to years of discretion when Hegel wrote, will be the same pitiful club-footed affair that Hegel produced.'
9 The nature of 'a priori' certitude in Peirce's philosophy as a distinctively pragmatic concept, and its relation to mathematical reasoning, is developed by me in some detail in 'Mathematical Necessity, Scientific Fallibilism, and Pragmatic Verificationalism: The Peircean Synthesis,' *International Philosophical Quarterly* 24 (1984): 1–19. The way this distinctively pragmatic a priori is operative in all of the pragmatists is discussed in some detail in my book, *Speculative Pragmatism* (Amherst: University of Massachusetts Press 1986; paperback ed. Peru, Ill.: Open Court Publishing 1990).
10 Since he is here referring to the triad in psychology, the facts will be psychological facts.
11 Murphey, *Development of Peirce's Philosophy*, 88.

12 Ibid., 89, 319. This general point is made concerning both the move to the New List and to the revised list.

13 Goudge, *Thought of C.S. Peirce*, 80, 268ff.

14 David Savan, 'On the Origins of Peirce's Phenomenology,' in Philip Weiner and Frederic Young, eds, *Studies in the Philosophy of Charles Sanders Peirce* (Cambridge, Mass.: Harvard University Press 1952), 194.

15 As Peirce applies his categories to various areas, 'In psychology Feeling is First, Sense of reaction Second, General conception Third, or mediation. In biology, the idea of arbitrary sporting is First, heredity is Second, the process whereby the accidental characters become fixed is Third' (6.32).

16 See Murphey, *Development of Peirce's Philosophy*, 368.

17 John Dewey, 'Peirce's Theory of Quality,' *Journal of Philosophy* 32 (1935): 702.

18 Goudge, *Thought of C.S. Peirce*, 77.

19 André De Tienne, in 'Peirce's Early Method of Finding the Categories,' concludes, after a detailed examination, that the method can best be characterized as 'critical common-sensist retroduction.' *Transactions of the Charles S. Peirce Society: A Quarterly Journal in American Philosophy* 25 (1989): 385–406. Although his analysis takes him in a direction different from that offered here, he sees that 'some of the germs of Peirce's pragmaticism were already at work in his "New List of Categories"' (ibid., 405).

20 Peirce holds that the 'several very broad classes of phanerons are so inextricably mixed together that no one can be isolated, yet it is manifest that their characters are quite disparate' (1.286). The traits, or classes of phenomena are thus separable by precision, by attending to one element and neglecting others. See 1.353. Further, though Peirce speaks of 'elements,' what is intended is not analysis into elements but the tracing out of relations (1.294).

21 When Peirce speaks in this passage of premisses and conclusions, he is indicating the direction of abduction, not deduction, or in other terms, the order of discovery, not the order of logical analysis. Thus, the premisses are the observed data, while the conclusions are the abductive hypothesis from the data.

22 There is implied here a rejection of ontological phenomenalism, an issue which concerns the objective reference of the contents of awareness. Ontological phenomenalism holds that the contents of awareness – at whatever level of complexity they are grasped – are either the only reality there is or the only reality which can be known, rather than a grasp of a 'hard,' external, independent reality.

23 There is intended here no ontological or numerical distinction between these two dimensions of reality.

24 The nature of this 'ultimate opinion' is itself open to quite conflicting interpretations.

25 Justus Buchler, *Charles Peirce's Empiricism* (New York: Octagon Books 1966), 151.

26 See Nynfa Bosco, 'Peirce and Metaphysics,' in Edward Moore and Richard Robin,

eds, *Studies in the Philosophy of Charles Sanders Peirce: Second Series* (Amherst: University of Massachusetts Press 1964), 352.

27 Emphasis in original.

28 Philip Weiner, 'Peirce's Evolutionary Interpretations of the History of Science,' in Moore and Robin, eds, *Studies in the Philosophy of Charles Sanders Peirce: Second Series*, 145.

29 Richard Bernstein notes Peirce's own 'extremely fertile imagination' at work in the very grouping of the various and diverse phenomena which are brought together under each of the three categories. 'Action, Conduct, and Self-Control,' in Richard J. Bernstein, ed., *Perspectives on Peirce* (New Haven and London: Yale University Press 1965), 73.

30 Victor Lowe, 'Pierce and Whitehead as Metaphysicians,' in Moore and Robin, eds, *Studies in the Philosophy of Charles Sanders Peirce: Second Series*, 444.

31 A.N. Whitehead, *Process and Reality* (New York: Harper and Brothers 1957), 4.

32 Helmut Pape notes that 'Peirce's claim that all human thought has an anthropomorphic character' has methodological implications and implies an idealistic metaphysics. 'Laws of Nature, Rules of Conduct and Their Analogy in Peirce's Semiotics,' *Transactions of the Charles S. Peirce Society: A Quarterly Journal in American Philosophy* 20 (1984): 211. While the anthropomorphic character of thought has implications for the method of metaphysical endeavour, however, it need not, as Pape holds, require the *content* of metaphysics to be that of objective idealism.

33 John E. Smith, *Purpose and Thought: The Meaning of Pragmatism* (New Haven: Yale University Press 1978), 126.

34 Murray Murphey, 'On Pierce's Metaphysics,' *Transactions of the Charles Sanders Peirce Society* 1, no. 1 (1965): 13.

Classical Pragmatism and Pragmatism's Proof

RICHARD S. ROBIN

It is commonplace to think of pragmatism in terms of its two principal varieties, one of which stems from Charles Peirce and the other from William James. The first alone is deemed classical, for what sets Peirce apart, both in kind and degree, is his enthusiastic embrace of a philosophical tradition traceable to classical Greek philosophy, onto which is grafted the notion of a right method, a method unabashedly scientific. 'I stand before you an Aristotelian and a scientific man,' Peirce once declared (1.619). It is this amalgam of the classical and the modern, the old and the new, that will be brought to bear on one of the remaining puzzles of Peirce scholarship, namely, the proof of pragmatism, which Peirce claimed to have and which he promised to publicize but never did.

Let it be noted at the outset so as to avoid inflated expectations that the sought-for proof is neither deductive nor inductive. Nor is it transcendental. Rather, it has that special character related to a coherentist defence, which in itself is a reflection of an underlying architectonic conception of philosophy. This is to say that the whole of Peirce's philosophy is implicated and, in fact, comes into play.

The story, briefly, dates from the Harvard Lectures of 1903 when Peirce spoke of his lingering doubts that the truth of pragmatism would be favourably resolved. What doubts remained concerned only his ability to present cogently the argument for its truth. However, nothing more was said directly on the subject until two years later when Peirce published in *The Monist* the first of three articles on pragmatism. According to the original plan, the first article would explain the doctrine, the second would provide the illustrations, and the third, entitled 'The Basis of Pragmaticism,' would contain the proof. The first two articles appeared as planned but the third did not. Instead, what was published appeared under the title 'Prolegomena to an Apology for Pragmaticism,' and reflected the altered circumstances. From the title one might gather that the proof would follow in a subsequent article, and in fact at least one other article was projected. Several references to a 'next' article followed: one of them in a letter (dated 7 December 1907) to Francis Russell in which Peirce mentions that the article in question 'is the most difficult to present of any I have written. It is the first part – the lemma – to my proof of the truth of pragmatism' (L387). Many months elapsed between the appearance of the 'Prolegomena' article and the letter to Russell. It is evident that Peirce was struggling with the proof. In any case, the 'next' article never materialized. In its place are numerous manuscript pages identified as either drafts of 'The Basis of Pragmaticism' (MSS279–84, c. 1905) or drafts of later attempts to fashion the proof (MSS296–300, c. 1907–8). These drafts are all incomplete and unpublished, but together they yield considerable background information.[1]

At least we know the reasons for Peirce's dissatisfaction with the argument of his two earlier articles on pragmatism in *Popular Science Monthly* of November 1877 and January 1878 ('The Fixation of Belief' and 'How to Make Our Ideas Clear'). Initially he said that that argument was the kind of argument one might expect to find in a popular journal 'to whose readers any defense of so broad a proposition would have been impenetrably obtuse if it had not begged the question,' for, as Peirce went on to say less defensively, the argument was 'entirely built upon making man's belief to consist in that proposition upon which he would be satisfied to base his conduct insofar as that proposition should bear upon it' (MS296). In other words, beliefs were modes of action, with no distinction so subtle that it does not yield a difference in practice – a difference in some sensible result. Peirce had made pragmatism depend on a theory of belief which treated belief as if it were a behavioural phenomenon. Now he saw the behavioural theory as the problem. How can pragmatism – presumably a logical doctrine – rest comfortably upon a psychological base? Put in another way, the earliest version of Peirce's theory of inquiry made the resolution of doubt by belief *the* motivation for inquiry. The question now was whether this was motivation enough.[2]

Apart from the reversal of the justificatory roles of logic and psychology, what basis was there in psychology for thinking that all human beings ever want are sensible or practical results? Doesn't science in the pure practice of it aim at something else? Doesn't ethics demand a loftier ideal? Peirce was also questioning the viability of his earlier nominalistic metaphysics, as he was also questioning his earlier commitment to a 'subjective' theory of the modalities.

Precisely this kind of questioning forced the reconsideration that eventually led Peirce to a reformulation of pragmatism. Originally, the pragmatic maxim was a logical rule for the clarification of concepts in terms of conceivable practical bearings, from which it followed that if existential propositions are the outcome of conceivably performable tests and if concepts are nothing more than some set of operations, then saying that 'something is real' is merely saying that certain data are observed. The new formulation mentions a higher grade of clarity that is achieved only so far as it is remembered 'that the only ultimate good which practical facts to which it directs attention can subserve is to further the development of concrete reasonableness; so that the meaning of the concept does not lie in any individual reactions at all, but in the manner in which those reactions contributed to that development' (5.4). This reformulation of the original maxim avoided earlier psychologizing, substituted realistic convictions for nominalistic ones, and articulated a higher ideal for human motivation than personal satisfaction. Peirce effectively transformed pragmatism into pragmaticism, and then sought and claimed a proof for the latter.[3]

The turn-about is especially evident when one considers the now classic example of the 'hardness' of a diamond. 'Suppose, then,' Peirce said, 'that a diamond could be crystallized in the midst of a cushion of soft cotton and should remain there until it was finally burned up. Would it be false to say that the diamond was soft' (5.403)? Without pausing, he answered his own question: 'there is absolutely no difference between a hard thing and a soft thing so long as they are not brought to the test' (ibid.). Subsequently (twenty-five years or so later), he recanted: 'I myself went too far in the direction of nominalism when I said that it was a mere question of convenience of speech whether we say that a diamond is hard when it is not pressed upon. I *now* say that the experiment will prove that the diamond is hard as positive fact. That is, it is a real fact that it *would* resist pressure, which amounts to extreme scholastic realism' (8.208). Notice how the relation between antecedent action and consequent experiential experimental expectation shifts from the indicative conditional to the subjunctive and contrafactual. Thus, 'if a substance of a certain kind should be exposed to an agency of a certain kind a certain kind of sensible result would ensue' (5.457). Here Peirce is making a commitment to real kinds (generals) and to real modality, inclusive of real possibility and real necessity (ibid.). 'Hence, before we treat of the evidences of pragmatism, it will be needful to weigh the pros and cons of scholastic realism. For pragmatism could hardly have entered a head that was not already convinced that there are real generals' (5.503).

Far from turning his back on his patriarchal models, Aristotle and Scotus, Peirce set out to save metaphysics from its own excesses. He aimed to replace transcendental metaphysics with a scientific one which was beholden to a rule or maxim that demanded experimental consequences for determining the admissibility of hypotheses. Just as there was no difficulty about accepting unobservable entities in science, so, too, there was no difficulty about accepting the concept of universal categories as genuinely hypothetical once their empiricist credentials were established in virtue of their relevancy (confirmability/falsifiability) for every item of every experience. Peirce repeated time and again that metaphysics could and indeed should be an observational science, differing from the special sciences only by the breadth of its observational base.[4]

Rejecting nominalism provided both the motivation and the direction for exploring anew the question of being. That exploration yielded three universal and irreducible yet hypothetical modes of being – ontological categories – which are designated 'Firstness,' 'Secondness,' and 'Thirdness,' distinguishable by their monadic, dyadic, and triadic character, respectively. 'First is the conception of being or existing independently of anything else. Second is the conception of being relative to, the conception of reaction with, something else. Third is the conception of mediation whereby a first and second are brought into a relation,' that is, by a third (6.32). Thirdness is the mode of being of law and potentiality. The continuum (continuity being another name for generality) is the prime example. The concrete reasonableness referred to before is, in the terminology of the categories, the thirdness of thirdness. Given that terminology, scholastic realism is concerned exclusively with the category of thirdness.

Herewith we have the context for Peirce's remark that pragmatism 'would essentially involve the truth of synechism' (5.145) – the cosmological analogue of the mathematical conception of continuity – which he depicts variously as 'the keystone of the arch' (8.527) and as the 'master key' (NEM4:XI). Presumably the role of continuity in the proof of pragmatism was addressed in the eighth and last lecture of the Harvard series, an afterthought, we presume, since it was originally unscheduled. Unfortunately that lecture, which bore the title 'Multitude and Continuity,' is missing. Only references to it and to an early partial draft survive. Neither the references nor the draft pages are especially helpful.

The Monist drafts widen our perspective on Peirce's search for a proof. The later drafts concentrate on his system of existential graphs as well as on his semiotic theory, both of which are barely mentioned in the drafts of 'The Basis of Pragmaticism.'

The attention Peirce lavishes on the graphs is a clear signal that they will play a prominent role in the presentation of the proof itself, although he admits in one place that the graphical system 'makes no essential difference in my argument for the truth of Pragmaticism' (MS296). But that some role would be assigned is not surprising, since the graphs are supposed to give us a moving picture of the action of thought and thereby represent the three kinds of reasoning: deductive, inductive, and abductive. The system of existential graphs is assumed to have the capability of determining whether what commonly belongs to all significations of concepts is or is not that which pragmatism supposes.

The ostensible reason for introducing the graphical system was to facilitate an inquiry into the indecomposable elements of our ideas, an inquiry which Peirce relates directly to the question of what characteristics are to be considered essential to a sign in general. As his categories came into play so did his semiotics, the central truth of which is that all thought takes place in signs.

Pragmatism's relationship to semiotics follows from the fact that pragmatism is the theory of general intellectual concepts, that is, of the nature of the significance of general terms, and, as such, falls within the scope of semiotics, which studies as widely and exactly as possible the relations of all signs to their significations.

Although pragmatism is associated with one kind of sign which signifies growth, or self-development, of thought, namely, the symbol, Peirce is advising that the more general study, semiotics, be accorded a 'good generous margin of breadth' (MS296, variant page) for the reason that a proper grasp of pragmatism requires a proper grasp of its semiotical background. Besides, that broadened study acts as insurance against the chance that something will be missed.

More of the background emerges upon close examination of the drafts of 'The Basis of Pragmaticism.' In them one finds Peirce concentrating on *Philosophia prima*, cenoscopy, which is made to rest on mundane, everyday experience and whose principal conclusions involve few leaps, 'passing,' as Peirce puts it, 'with [as] slight a gap as possible from familiar to unfamiliar' (MS283). In equating philosophy with cenoscopy, Peirce is also acknowledging the commonsensical presuppositions of philosophical inquiry.

Common sense is one of two components of Peirce's critical commonsensism. The critical component is mostly alluded to and, as one might guess, principally in connection with idioscopy (the special sciences), whose point of departure is the unfamiliar, the new, and sometimes surprising data. It is evident that this critical component is as much a part of the general background of Peirce's alleged proof as the common-sense component is, or, for that matter, anything else. For one way of thinking about pragmatism is to think of it as effecting the transition from what is vague, instinctive, and uncontrollable to what is mainly clear and basically subject to our control. That the worldly truth is by no means final is the fallibilistic conclusion which, in conjunction with common sense, safeguards against the twin philosophical errors of taking too much for granted and not enough.

The framework created by combining affirmation with criticism is surely an essential part of the story. Common sense introduces the indubitability ingredient via beliefs whose indubitability consists in *not* being doubted. Belief qua belief isn't the problem; belief challenged is. Since no belief is absolutely immune to challenge or criticism, all beliefs are eminently fallible. In 5.212

Peirce affirms that 'the elements of every concept enter logical thought at the gate of perception and make their exit at the gate of purposive action; and whatever cannot show its passports at both those gates is to be arrested as unauthorized by reason.' Perceptual experience is as close as one gets to indubitability; purposive action is critically guided rational action. Critical commonsensism effectively establishes the boundary conditions for all serious discussion, including pragmatism's defence.

While Peirce's general focus – appertaining to situating pragmatism – is cenoscopy, his specific focus is its mid-portion – the normative sciences – for the obvious reason that pragmatism is a principle of logic, and logic, broadly conceived, is one of the normative sciences. Logic is grounded in ethics, which in turn is grounded in aesthetics. Peirce's immediate aim is to fix the location of pragmatism vis-à-vis the normative sciences. His ultimate aim, however, is to fix pragmatism vis-à-vis all the sciences, that is, to locate pragmatism as exactly as possible within that classificatory scheme of the sciences that includes the normative ones. His earlier classificatory schemes did not do so, and hence it is only the later ones, which more nearly approximate the time of Peirce's reassessment of pragmatism and his search for its proof, that interest us. Presumably, pinpointing the location of pragmatism by reference to those later schemes will facilitate its proof. In the draft pages under examination Peirce warns against the 'absurdities' resulting from philosophizing unarchitectonically and calls for an architectonic 'beyond what Kant dreamed of' (MSS280–1). Therefore a closer look at a classificatory scheme hierarchically ordered by principle dependence is both warranted and mandated.

Recall that pragmatism makes the *summum bonum* consist in a process of evolution in which the existent increasingly embodies those generals that are recognized as reasonable. The discovery of the *summum bonum* is the business of aesthetics. For something 'to be aesthetically valuable, it must have a multitude of parts so related to one another as to impart a positive simple immediate quality to their totality' (5.132). The particular quality of the total is irrelevant (ibid.). But not irrelevant is 'the impress of Reasonableness that Creates' (MS310, 1903). In categorical terminology the total unanalysable impression of a reasonableness that expresses itself creatively is 'the Firstness that truly belongs to a Thirdness in its achievement of Secondness' (ibid.). Aesthetics provides us with a schematized wholeness or unity that underlies directly the ethical demand for social harmony and indirectly the logical commitment to knowledge and truth, realizable in both instances by a community of social agents in the guise of investigators reaching for consensus.

Aesthetics cuts across the categorical divisions much as pragmatism tends to cut across logical divisions. Exemplifying firstness, aesthetics is beholden only to phenomenology. It exhibits a clear relationship between art and iconicity. Signifying their objects in virtue of resemblance, icons are the only kind of sign suited to conveying feelings generally. Moreover, the condition for aesthetic feeling is a sort of simplicity: minds in the right frame, suitably unburdened, unbiased, and hence capable of objective observation or judgment. This objectivity is important because it caps the justificatory process, which begins with logic's dependence upon a normative science immediately higher on the scale than it is. 'The instant that an aesthetic ideal is proposed as an ultimate end of action, at that instant a categorical imperative pronounces for or against it ...' (5.133). Peirce adds: 'So then, it appears to me that any aim whatever which can be consistently pursued becomes, as soon as it is unfalteringly adopted, beyond all possible criticism, except the quite impertinent criticism of outsiders' (ibid.). Indubitability attaches to aesthetic pronouncements of the suitably objective kind in much the way that indubitability attaches to the commonsensical presuppositions of inquiry. Indubitability is not proof strictly, since indubitable propositions may be false. But seeking a proof which follows from more evident premises is unnecessary. 'Proof,' Peirce admonishes, 'does not consist in giving superfluous and superpossible certainty to that which nobody ever did or ever will doubt, but in removing doubts which do, or at least might at some time arise' (3.432).

But as already indicated, the categories of secondness and especially thirdness have essential ties to Peirce's aesthetic theory, which proposes as our chief end the actualizing of ideas of the 'immortal, ceaselessly prolific type' (2.763). That end consists in the 'development of embodied ideas' (5.402); that is to say, 'the one thing whose admirableness is not due to an ulterior reason, is Reason itself comprehended in all its fullness, so far as we can comprehend it' (1.615). In short, the *summum bonum* is in a state of incipiency or growth (1.615); it must be general and still possess unity (1.613); and if adopted, it must be an end which can be consistently pursued (5.133). This brings us around to pragmatism, for 'the pragmaticist does not make the *summum bonum* to consist in action, but makes it to consist in that process of evolution whereby the existent comes more and more to embody those generals which were ... said to be *destined*, which is what we strive to express in calling them *reasonable*' (5.433). The stamp of approval which aesthetics finally bestows is far from arbitrary, since diversified and accumulative experience bears upon it.

Pragmatism is supported, so to speak, from above and below. From above, it acquires its justification from aesthetics and from principles more general than the ones it provides as it dictates to the sciences that stand beneath it. From below, pragmatism gains that extra measure of support from that reasonableness that impresses itself via a logic that works itself through the special sciences, each of which has its own wellspring and whose conclusions represent the nearest one gets to the truth about real objects. Pragmatism is, in short, supported by a whole network, in this case represented by the classificatory scheme.

The pieces of the puzzle are there. What is required is to integrate them. When this is done, the puzzle of Peirce's proof will be essentially solved. Peirce, of course, was painfully aware of what he had to do, certainly by the early 1890s, when he sought to interest a publisher in a multivolume work, still in the making, to which he had already assigned the title 'The Principles of Philosophy.' An advertisement, or prospectus, privately printed, gave a rather detailed account, volume by volume, of its contents. Bringing unity to his thought was the main objective. The principle of continuity would play a key role; a philosophical encyclopedia on the order of Hegel's would be its chief outcome. What would have been Peirce's *magnum opus* was doomed at the start; not enough support was generated by his advertisement to permit the work upon it to move forward.

Some ten years later, closer to the time of his most intensive efforts to find a proof of pragmatism, Peirce established his priorities once more, on this occasion as part of his Carnegie Institution grant proposal. Financially burdened, feeling the pressure of advancing age, and generally frustrated by his past failures to publish in any systematic way, he asked for the chance 'to draw up some three dozen memoirs each complete in itself, yet the whole forming a unitary system of logic in all its parts,' the whole upon a scientific basis. The memoirs would concentrate upon familiar themes: the classificatory scheme of the sciences; the defence of mathematical method, in particular, the defence of the method of infinitesimals; the phenomenological categories; the priority relations obtaining among the normative sciences of aesthetics, ethics, and logic; the definition of logic as formal semiotics; the several divisions of logic; and scientific metaphysics. The grant proposal was rejected.[5]

What the outcome would have been had Peirce received the grant from Carnegie is anyone's guess. Yet Peirce's penchant for triadic analysis suggests that it might have had at least a Hegelian cast, not so much in its details as in its structure. Indeed his many references to Hegel, including his defence of philosophers with Hegelian proclivities, provide ample evidence of some influence. In fact, he prefaced his dissatisfaction with his original version of pragmatism by observing that that version plays into the hands of all those, including fellow pragmatists, who wish to denigrate the absolute. He entered the long-standing dispute between Royce and James over the question of the absolute on the side of Royce, an absolutist with whom he disagreed on some points of logic and other technical matters, but to whom he paid the highest compliment for having achieved a position in *The World and the Individual* 'nearer to the genuine upshot of pragmatism than ... any other pragmatist' (MS284).

Peircean pragmatism rejects the foundation metaphor. To be sure, the scientific process is self-corrective, but not by reason of some allegedly unshakable foundation upon which science rests. Peirce's recourse was to align himself with coherence theorists, with their egalitarian view with regard to the possible sources of warrant. All sources are inferential, so that whatever justification there is depends entirely upon a network of inferences. Enough of Hegel survives in Peirce to suggest that at bottom Peirce's argument – or rationale – for pragmatism depends upon coherency. The analogy which recommends itself is not that of an edifice resting on more or less secure foundations but of a richly textured, highly complex mosaic which, when contemplated in the right way, is aesthetically fulfilling.

Phenomenology, normative sciences, evolutionism, synechism, semiotics, and so on, when taken individually, have their own credibility or lack of it. But they relate to each other as well, sometimes in perplexing ways, sometimes in supportive ways. It is this tangled web of relations that Peirce sought greater unity for. How those parts came together is not always clear, even to Peirce himself. It is instructive, however, to find Peirce commenting in one of the manuscripts with which we have been particularly concerned that the relation of his categories and his system of existential graphs was not immediately evident to him. Apparently he had arrived at each quite independently of the other. Then he goes on to say, 'the fact of the entire concordance adds to the confidence in the correctness of both' (MS296, variant page).[6] The key word is 'concordance' ('coherence' would have served as well).

The general strategy advocated is that of uncovering more of those concordances and of deepening, where possible, existing ones. An authenticated pragmatism depends upon the success of this venture, especially so since it is tempting to regard pragmatism as its focus. For to deny the centrality of pragmatism carries a certain element of implausibility in view of the enormous intellectual energy Peirce devoted to cognitive questions, to the analyses of the belief-habit-action complex, to understanding the nature of scientific methodology. Add to this his self-characterization as a logician (in the broad sense) and as a man of science. Any serious understanding of Peirce's efforts at systemization requires a 'handle,' some starting place, an initial perspective beyond what commonsense convictions supply. Arguably, the pragmatic perspective suffices, on balance, at least as well as – perhaps better than – the alternatives.[7]

Starting points are just that; the arrival point matters most. Putting aside for the moment the question of beginnings, where an adjustment in the system of relations becomes necessary under pressure of new experiences, the adjustment may occur anywhere. If and when such an adjustment is necessitated, Peirce – so it seems – would have been reluctant to scrap his pragmatism, as he would his categoriology, semiotics, doctrine of the normative sciences, and classificatory scheme of the sciences, though the last suggests a problem. The classificatory scheme admits of a linear ordering of priorities, with phenomenology prior to the normative sciences and those sciences prior to metaphysics, and with metaphysics placed in a seemingly unwelcome dependency relationship. However, treating the classificatory scheme as merely heuristically valuable serves to restore the balance, a suggestion which is acceptable if the same holds for the rest. Indeed, the interrelationships exhibited are so profound and basically reciprocal as to make the priority question moot – in any case, circumventable by an approach best described as coherentist with holistic features.

The relevant coherency theory is not subject to the isolation criticism, which admits of no empirical grounding. Rather, as already indicated, coherence refers to the systematic set of inferentially related beliefs mutually supportive of each individual belief. The isolation criticism is met by integrating the empirical requirement in such a way that it still remains the case that all beliefs, including so-called empirical ones, derive their authority from inferential relations with other beliefs. That individual beliefs are not sustainable on their own is, of course, the holistic component.

Certainly there is a strong presumption for thinking that Peirce's theory of scientific inference accommodates the holistic aspect of scientific change. Indeed, the parallel with Quine's holism, especially its singular commitment to empiricism, is to some extent apt. But Peirce is not Quine. Quine's quasi-historical account of empiricism, much of which would have been congenial to Peirce, concludes with his denigration of first philosophy prior to science.[8] Quine's positivism (epistemological questions are the province of one or another of the natural sciences) has no counterpart in Peirce, who remains faithful to his philosophical forebears in the classically realistic tradition, with the proviso that questions concerning which generals are real had to be settled by science alone. Furthermore, whereas Quine's conception of science as a descriptive enterprise leaves him with the nasty problem of dealing with normativity (what should one believe?), Peirce gladly accepts the challenge by treating logic as if it were a normative science. What is at stake here is a broadened understanding of science and a widened holistic scope.

Peirce's anti-positivism was not always apparent to everyone. The original formulation of the pragmatic maxim was thought by some to be compatible with, even anticipatory of, the extreme reductionist program of Carnapian positivism (the basic terms of which are sensory experience, logic, and set theory). The reformulation of the maxim and much else dispute this. Peirce was a metaphysical realist, a position which precludes the extension of coherentism beyond the concept of justification (for which consistency and mutual supportability are sufficient) to that of truth. Reference (frequent) to real objects created no special problem for him. Those objects presupposed by cognitive inquiry do not require proof, or, put differently, they have their proof in the absence of genuine doubt. Peirce championed Scottish common-sense realism and defended a correspondence theory of truth of Aristotelian origin.

We are left with unfinished business. The proof is still in the making, and if there is one, it will be the product of collaborative effort. That effort has and continues to take several forms, one of which, only apparently negative, is consumed with exposing problems inhibiting unification. A pivotal problem in this regard is centred in the philosophy of continuity (synechism), for which a modal logic dealing with probability is required. Peirce made a start, but the modal component of his existential graphs was not completed.[9] Furthermore, continuity implicates infinitesimals. As we know, Peirce defended the method of infinitesimals against the then (even now) prevailing opinion of mathematicians. It is an open question whether present-day non-standard analysis will settle the question in Peirce's favour. The future also holds the fate of Peirce's cosmological speculations, many of which have thus far proved remarkably prophetic, particularly with regard to the quantum revolution in physics, although admittedly some have not. His whole cosmology remains at risk, however, in view of the changing face of scientific fact.

Christopher Hookway, too, wonders whether the system of existential graphs, if completed, would vindicate Peirce on the matter of pragmatism's limitation of inference to induction, deduction, and abduction.[10] Indeed, as Hookway notes, Peirce anticipated this problem as early as c. 1905 in correspondence with the Italian pragmatist Calderone, and again as late as 1911, when he wrote: 'I am unable yet to *prove* that the three kinds of reasoning I mean are the *only* kinds of sound reasoning; though I can show reason to think that it can be proved, and *very strong* probable reasons for thinking that there is no fourth kind' (NEM3:177–8). The obvious question is what Peirce meant by 'prove' as against 'strong probable reasons.' Does he have deduction in mind in the one case and something on the order of inductive confirmation in the second? These questions are raised against the background of his intent not to undermine the triadicity thesis.

The puzzle is reawakened by an opinion of Fitzgerald: 'The proof of pragmatism was not a search for pragmatism itself – he was already in possession of this – nor was the search for facts which would suggest the truth of pragmatism. Rather it was a search for a way of integrating the pragmatic principle into his findings in the antecedent and more general parts of science.'[11]

Apparently, Fitzgerald himself is in search of a deductive proof. Peirce's problem, as he sees it, is simply making explicit the more general grounds (semiotics) for pragmatism. A subsection of one of the chapters of Fitzgerald's book is entitled 'The Formal Basis of Pragmatism.' Here we find Fitzgerald claiming that 'Peirce's later researches into pragmatism were analogous to the inquiry into the foundations of mathematics.' But then in light of this claim what do we make of Peirce's insistence that pragmatism be treated as any hypothesis which is put to the experimental test by drawing out its consequences? For Peirce the problem of justifying pragmatism is at least the problem of 'finding an inductive confirmation of its validity' which MS300 makes clear. Justification lies in the consequent parts of the system of science Peirce envisaged as much as in the antecedent parts, that is, in the formative details issuing gradually and cumulatively from the successes of the various idioscopic sciences as much as in the general facts having their origins in mathematics and phenomenology, or, as Fitzgerald would have it, semiotics. In fairness to him, Fitzgerald is one of the earliest to attempt to view pragmatism whole by relating it to the totality of Peirce's thought. His book engages characteristic features of Peirce's thought and could be taken as attempting, albeit indecisively, a reconstruction of the proof.

Other problems are locatable across the spectrum of Peirce's architectonic, and scholarly effort to deal with them is now paying off in the details contributed to the picture of the architectonic we already possess. More details and more clarity and refinement can be expected as the scholarly effort continues.

These interlocking efforts to come to terms with the whole Peirce, which we take to be synonymous with coming to terms with pragmatism's proof, bring to mind the cable metaphor Peirce introduced in a *Journal of Speculative Philosophy* article of 1868 (intended for republication in 1893) when he wrote that philosophy should heed 'the multitude and variety of its arguments ... [not] the conclusiveness of any one. Its reasoning should not form a chain which is no stronger than its weakest link, but a cable whose fibers may be ever so slender, provided they are sufficiently numerous and intimately connected' (5.265). The context, significantly, is Peirce's denunciation of Cartesian individualism (the solitary seeker) and his endorsement of the Scholastic, communal model (the community of seekers). The involvement of so many renders the project essentially a community affair.

The invitation to study Peirce comprehensively is certainly not new. It is almost the standard response to the question of Peirce's proof. But how could it be otherwise in view of what Peirce says explicitly about the architectonic design and construction of pragmatism?

Just as a civil engineer, before erecting a bridge, a ship, or a house, will think of the different properties of all materials, and will use no iron, stone, or cement, that has not been subjected to tests; and will put them together in ways minutely considered, so, in constructing the doctrine of pragmatism the properties of all indecomposable concepts were examined and the ways they could be compounded. Then the purpose of the doctrine having been analyzed, it was constructed out of the appropriate concepts to fulfill that purpose. In this way, the truth of it was proved ... There is no other independent way of strictly proving it. (5.5)

Hartshorne and Weiss took the lead in virtue of instinct and editorial practice.[12] Subsequently, Thompson remarked that the proof 'would amount to a kind of elucidation of most of Peirce's philosophy and formal logic' and thereby set the agenda.[13]

How are we to conclude? By cautiously predicting that when the scholarly process is farther along there will emerge a more credible, classically oriented philosophy, faithful to its own history and yet keeping pace with new developments, increasingly inclusive and comprehensive, dominated as always by a synoptic vision, edging ever closer to the promised proof.

Notes

This paper is a revised version of my contribution to the Peirce symposium arranged by the American Philosophical Association, Eastern Division, Washington, D.C., December 1988.

1 Max Fisch has done more than anyone to dramatize the problem of proof by making us aware of much of the relevant chronology. See his 'The "Proof" of Pragmatism,' in K.L. Ketner and C. Kloesel, eds, *Peirce, Semeiotic, and Pragmatism* (Bloomington: Indiana University Press 1986).
2 Admittedly, Peirce was very early influenced by the Kantian conception of architectonic philosophy as well as by the significance Kant attached to formal logic. But he did not always identify logic with formal logic. Probably sooner rather than later he settled on his own semiotic theory of logic. In any case, the evidence of the manuscripts cited indicated that his commitment to logic, formal or semiotic, was not, even in the early years, so solid as to prevent the intrusion of psychological elements into his analysis. His subsequent unhappiness over this development should not be construed as support for a Kantian architectonic grounded in formal logic.
3 Whether the reformulation represents a revolution in Peirce's thought is questionable. There were, after all, realistic elements in place prior to the *Popular Science* series. Is it a mere curiosity that the term 'pragmaticism' was abandoned soon after it was put into use? – a practice I have chosen to follow, except of course

when the term occurs in quoted material. Let calling attention to the doctrinal issues the term introduces suffice for our purpose.

4 Reference to an observational base should not obscure the fact that Peirce stands closer to the Greek notion of experience than to the modern Lockean one, which for him is nominalistic.

5 For this remarkable but ill-fated proposal, see Carolyn Eisele, ed., *Historical Perspectives in Peirce's Logic of Science*, 4 vols (Berlin: Mouton 1985), 2:1022–41.

6 Peirce does not say specifically in what the concordance consisted. One presumes it involved parallel triadicity at the very least.

7 The centrality question is subject to debate. Joseph Esposito, for example, stresses the triadic theory of categories, with much effect, in his *Evolutionary Metaphysics* (Athens, Ohio: Ohio University Press 1980).

8 W.V. Quine's version of the history of modern empiricism, along with pertinent references to Peirce, is found in his 'The Pragmatist's Place in Empiricism,' in R.J. Mulvaney and P.M. Zeltner, eds, *Pragmatism: Its Source and Prospects* (Columbia, S.C.: University of South Carolina Press 1981), 21–39.

9 Murray Murphey draws attention to this problem in his chapter on Peirce in E. Flower and M. Murphey *A History of Philosophy in America*, 2 vols (New York: Putnam 1977), vol. 2. In his influential *The Development of Peirce's Philosophy* (Cambridge, Mass.: Harvard University Press 1961), he argued that Peirce produced successively several systems without achieving a satisfactory final one.

10 Christopher Hookway, *Peirce* (London: Routledge and Kegan Paul 1985), 261.

11 John J. Fitzgerald, *Peirce's Theory of Signs as Foundation for Pragmatism* (The Hague: Mouton 1966), 249.

12 Charles Hartshorne reflects on the decision of the editors of *The Collected Papers* to reject the chronological approach in favour of the systematic one in his autobiography *The Darkness and the Light* (Albany: State University of New York 1990), 175.

13 Manley Thompson, *The Pragmatic Philosophy of C.S. Peirce* (Chicago: Chicago University Press 1953), 250.

The Logical Structure of Idealism: C.S. Peirce's Search for a Logic of Mental Processes

HELMUT PAPE

I Introduction

There is something mysterious, obscure, and, for some people, even repulsive about the idealism in Peirce's philosophy. In fact, very often people talk about rather different theses when they talk about Peirce's idealism.[1] Is it

i) a metaphysical thesis about the nature of reality *in toto*, that is, the thesis that the ultimate reality is mental? or,

ii) an epistemological (Kantian) thesis grounded in a theory of mind about the way in which the structure of mind and mental activity relates to its objects, that is, the thesis that the categorical structure of our minds determines the order and the structure of our knowledge about the world? or,

iii) a logico-semiotical thesis claiming that logical and semiotical laws are not only true independent of factual or material truth but are providing the structure for all sorts of material truth; that is, the thesis that all important distinctions are distinctions of semiotical or logical form?

If you ask whether Peirce is a metaphysical, epistemological, or logical idealist, you will probably find evidence for all three varieties of idealism. In this paper I will defend the claim that one of Peirce's contributions to modern philosophy is a unique fusion of all three kinds of idealism under the guidance of what I will call 'logical idealism' (LI). As I will argue in this paper, Peirce's metaphysics, his 'pragmatistic idealism' (8.284, 1904), is a realistic theory of mental processes based on a special interpretation of logic. This, I take it, is what Peirce tried to convey when in 1898 he remarked in a lecture: 'What is reality? Perhaps there isn't any such thing at all ... But if there is any reality, then, so far as there is any reality, what that reality consists in is this: that there is in the being of things something which corresponds to the process of reasoning, that the world *lives*, and *moves*, and *has its being*, in a logic of events' (NEM4:343–5).[2]

This passage, obviously, states some version of logical idealism. But which one? Clearly, the first step gives us the thesis of logical idealism: If there are real things their being corresponds to the process of reasoning. The second step is a difficult one: What does it mean to say that the being of the world consists in a 'logic of events'? This seems to imply a highly controversial and difficult, albeit interesting move: An idealistic account of the ontological structure of the world can be developed only in terms of a theory that is valid for both the processes of reasoning and the course of events. Note that this account does not imply any naïve metaphysical reading of logic – say, any proposal that tries to convert quantification theory with identity into some sort of ontology. Instead, Peirce claims that idealism achieves a consistent account of reality only insofar as it describes the logical properties which thoughts and things as events in space-time, that is, processes of reasoning and, say, movements of my body, have in common. Reality, viewed in this way, is a deeply conditional, temporal relation between the logical structure of thought and events. But are there any interesting logical properties which thoughts and movements have in common? Do Peirce's logic of relations and his semiotics indeed build on an account of mind and matter viewed as events? If so, then we should be able to give an account of Peirce's idealism as a theory that allows us to connect mind and matter via a logic of events.

If this hypothesis about the structural isomorphism of logical and material processes is the core of Peirce's logical idealism, how do epistemological and metaphysical idealism fit in? Or, are they different stages of one logical idealistic argument? Why was Peirce never understood as an idealist who provided a logically independent framework for some varieties of metaphysical idealism, such as objective idealism? To give a fair account of these problems and difficulties, let us take a look at the methods and the themes from which Peirce's arguments for idealism evolved.

There is no way around admitting that from 1891 onwards C.S. Peirce explicitly stated in his most important published writings on metaphysics that he was an objective idealist because he held that 'the one intelligible theory of the universe is that of objective idealism, that matter is effete mind, inveterate habits becoming physical laws' (6.25, 1891). Although he insisted that metaphysics must have a logical basis, and used the expression 'objective logic' to suggest that his idealism is an application of his logic in a rather extensive sense, many of his interpreters have ignored his claim or refused to take his words seriously. Again, one may easily misunderstand what 'logic' means here. 'Logic' for Peirce comprises semiotics (speculative grammar), the theory of valid arguments (critic), a theory of methods (methodeutic), and presupposes phenomenology and mathematics. When Peirce talks about 'objective logic' he wants to say that his idealism is the thesis that logical principles have a metaphysical meaning because they are phenomenologically justified in a way that provides a basis for philosophy independent of the sciences. That is to say, they structure and develop the content of experience in general, even of our everyday experience. This claim adds something very natural to Peirce's idealistic interpretation of logic: metaphysics itself rests on logic *and* on a formal, phenomenological analysis of experience. Peirce's phenomenology, therefore, naturally complements his idealistic reading of logic. This combination makes sense because an objective reading of logic does not itself require or determine a specific phenomenological justification of each metaphysical thesis, although the phenomenological meaning may secure the basis for it. We may use logical and mathematical principles in building theories about the most pervasive structures of experience: in this way, a phenomenological basis will complement a metaphysical interpretation of logic by giving it a neutral evidential basis which is independent of any specific science. For this reason Peirce sometimes describes experience as a scientifically neutral and independent realm from which his idealism follows, if we apply logic to it: 'Indeed, Idealism, in the sense in which Objective Logic, as I understand it, is Idealism, may be defined as the doctrine that nothing exists but phenomena and what phenomena bring along with them and force upon us, that is Experience, including the reactions that experience feels and all that logically follows from experience by Deduction, Induction, and Hypothesis.'

Immediately after this passage, Peirce discusses an objection to one of his idealistic theories in metaphysics, his tychism, in a way that shows how logic and phenomenology may complement each other. Tychism is the thesis that chance is real and plays a crucial role in the evolution of the physical universe. Tychism, taken by itself, is not capable of being inferred from phenomenological evidence, because we cannot experience that an event has happened by chance. In answering this objection Peirce specifies the conditions under which a metaphysical thesis can be introduced *without* a phenomenological justification. His example is chance events required by his cosmological thesis that the universe has its origin in a state of chance events: 'the single sporadic event in point of fact does not exist ... but it *begins* to exist; ... The points of discontinuity at its [the universe's] origin and extinction are not full existence; and therefore are according to my form of Idealism not obliged to be phenomenal.'

This strategy is characteristic of Peirce's idealism: In a case where a phenomenological justification is not available, we have to use logical and mathematical principles directly in building a theory, *provided these formal principles have an independent phenomenological basis.* Chance, for him, is not a phenomenological property of single events, but a general property of classes of events only. If we were to restrict our methodology to the phenomenological arguments, chance would be an unjustifiable fiction. Instead, Peirce uses a logical or mathematical account of chance, for example, one adapted from probability theory. For as he says, 'although the fact that a given event is casual cannot be inferred, yet the operation of chance itself is part of the regularity of nature and can be inferred.' This is the typical Peircean rule in doing philosophy: always try to introduce a formal type of law, if you go beyond phenomenological evidence. Let us try to interpret the following passage as the result of this rule. With the following remarks Peirce concludes his discussion of an objection to tychism from which the above quotations were taken: 'For I hold that potentialities have a being, though they are not actual; ... I stand in the Aristotelian ranks here. I maintain that we directly contemplate this ideal world and when we open our eyes we perceive in the world about us that which corresponds to the freedom of the ideal world. It is true that reflection is required to enable us to recognize it. But that reflection *recognizes* it, and assures us that we *saw* it from the very first impression of sense.' (All three quotations are from lecture notes, MS942, *c.* 1898; NEM4:144–5, for the lecture series from which the first quotation about the logic of events belongs.)

Read by itself, Peirce's claim that reflection on sense experience reveals to us that we do perceive 'potentialities' and even 'the freedom of the ideal world' might be understood as a queer mixture of epistemological idealism and Platonism, in some respects somewhat close to Malebranche's and Berkeley's immaterialism. But in the context of the argument and quotations given above this judgment is quite wrong. Rather, this passage voices the claim implicit in Peirce's discussion that in metaphysics we have to use logic and mathematics to describe the general properties of possible instances – 'real potentialities' – directly without being restricted to individual cases. When we pass to a nonphenomenological, formal interpretation of general properties of our experience of sets of objects or classes of instances, for example, by using probability theory or a logic of relations, this provides us with the metaphysical means to deal in a general way and more freely with a subject matter. This move will allow for a larger number of possible conclusions and will make it hard to decide about specific cases. The point here is not the undecidability, but that we introduce properties, such as relations, probability ratios, of a type that are, to some degree, independent of the individuals to which they apply, but rather create something that integrates *them* into a new type of ordering. Conclusions about ratios, relations, and so on, will apply to some domain, for which they are valid, but cannot be reduced to properties of individuals.

How is it that deductive reasoning is at all possible? Even deductive reasoning, especially in more complex cases and where higher-order predicates are invoked, requires that we decide which theorems, rules, and premisses are relevant to us. In this sense, we are free from the restriction to individual cases, their properties, and conclusions. Or, as Peirce puts it, 'all deductive reasoning, except ... non-relative syllogism – requires an act of choice; because from a given Premiss, several conclusions – in some cases an infinite number – can be drawn' (6.595, 1893).

There is a special moral I want you to draw from this example. We substantiated Peirce's thesis that there is freedom in the ideal world and that 'potentialities' are real by turning to the property of the non-predicability of probability ratios to the individuals in the universe of discourse for which this ratio holds. This formal property of non-predicability, in turn, requires an act of choice. Therefore, there is a freedom which is due to the generality of the type of reasoning invoked. In order to get back to the topic of idealism in Peirce, I want to generalize from this example in a somewhat drastic and unjustified way. I want to propose the problematic hypothesis that:

For every major claim in Peirce's idealism there is some mathematical, phenomenological, logical, or methodological principle or conjunction of several such principles justifying the introduction of the particular metaphysical claim or theory in question.

This thesis (or some version of it) is neither new nor original.[3] For it says simply that Peirce followed his own metatheoretical and architectonical principles which he codified in his classification of the sciences and in statements such as the following that 'metaphysics consists in the results of the absolute acceptance of logical principles ... as truth of being' (1.486). In what follows I will use 'logic' and 'logical' in a sense close to Peirce that covers semiotical, logical, and methodological principles and theories.

In the rest of the paper I will not argue for this claim directly and in detail. It would really take the length of book to do so.[4] Such a book would have to include a careful study of Peirce's rather demanding theory of quasi-Scotistic theory of logical form. In order to be able to argue for his idealism as a metaphysical theory Peirce has to assume, all the way through his philosophical career, say, from his 1867 'On a New List of the Categories' onwards, that:

– all relevant distinction can be accounted for in terms of distinctions of form;
– all distinctions of form are distinctions of logical form, with as much help from mathematics to provide us with a new type of form as we proceed;

and that:

– all logical forms are capable of being realized in all types of physical, physiological, and mental manifestations.

This theory put in a nutshell and stated in all its radical generality says (MS293, 1906): 'Form is that which makes anything such as it is, while matter makes it to be.' Any somewhat complete study of Peirce's metaphysics – and at present there is none at hand – would have to focus on the internal assumptions and theses of Peirce's theory of logical form and how they apply in semiotics. As we will see shortly, the difference between versions of his idealism is one of emphasis, scope, and selective force in an ontological interpretation of some forms as giving the correct 'logic of events' connecting things and thoughts. But this is not my topic, nor do I have the research for a paper on Peirce's theory of logical form ready at hand.

Rather, what I plan to do in this paper is to take another route which will bring us as close to our goal as we can get from a different vantage point: I will develop two external arguments for the adequacy of the logical interpretation of Peirce's idealism. The task of the next section is to introduce Peirce's unique kind of idealism, namely 'logical idealism.' In the third to sixth sections, I will do the following: In the third section, I will describe the type of everyday experience and the intuitions which support and motivate Peirce's idealism. In the fourth section, I will try to show that many features of Peirce's logic – his graphical logic and logic of relations in particular – and his theory of the categories may be understood as theories that were designed to capture some of the evidence of idealistic aspects in everyday experience which Peirce recognized. The fifth section is devoted to the crucial role that triadic identity plays in the semantic model undergirding Peirce's idealism, while the concluding section points out the ethical dimension of triadic identity, especially the teleological meaning of Peirce's idealistic conception of the object of a sign.

II Different Types of Idealism and the Primacy of a Logic of Mental Processes

The fact that Peirce's idealism is not a well-developed and codified theory but consists in a few papers, manuscripts, and reflections has stimulated the fantasy of his interpreters. Almost all of them assembled their own versions of Peirce's idealism. He has been described as an 'epistemological idealist' (Murphey), 'transcendentalist' (Goudge) or a 'semiotic idealist' (Savan, McCarthy), and an 'absolute idealist' (Almeder). I want to add to this list of idealisms in the hope that the denomination 'logical idealism' which I propose will capture more of the sustainable and original aspects of Peirce's idealism – that is, the semiotical, especially the logical aspect – and exclude inadequate characterizations that should be given up – such as transcendentalism, epistemological idealism, and absolute idealism. The last three do not apply to Peirce's philosophy because they misidentify arguments and theses of some of Peirce's unfortunate formulations of his logical or objective idealism. As you may have noted, 'objective idealism' is conspicuously missing from my list. This is so because I think that objective idealism is a problematic metaphysical hypothesis which is independent of Peirce's logic, and of his logical idealism, too. Furthermore, objective idealism has to have a special status because it is a theory which Peirce explicitly defended in a published statement. Logical idealism is, then, if you wish, an artefact, an abstraction. Its task is to capture some of the claims of objective logic, that is, that logic describes the formal structure of experience and reality, to which it assigns a metaphysical significance, while stopping short of the ontological commitments of objective idealism.

What is the relation between objective idealism and logical idealism? Both are metaphysical theories. But only logical idealism may be characterized by what I will call the 'Thesis of logical idealism,' (The.LI) for short:

(The.LI): *That mind is an emergent process that creates an irreducible identity, that is, triadic identity, and has an ontological priority over matter is equivalent with the thesis and that there is a mathematico-logical formalism for the logic of mental processes which comprises the logic of all forms of valid argumentation and inference describing physical reality and the irreducible identity of mind as a process.*

Peirce claimed that metaphysics should be based on logic – and not the other way around. Therefore, the validity of logic cannot depend on metaphysics[5] or there would be a vicious circle. The characteristic thesis of objective idealism can be independently defended, but it has to have a logical basis, and in this sense objective idealism implies some *use* of logical theory to which logical idealism itself assigns significance. In contrast, Peirce's objective idealism may be described by a quite different thesis – (The.OI) – in the following way:

(The.OI): *The physical is a degenerate version of the mental such that there are some properties of mental processes which both of them share. The sameness of the physical and the mental can be explicated only in terms of logical form understood as a constitutive principle.*

Note that (The.OI) does not imply absolute idealism. The latter may be rendered, if we assume in accordance with Peirce some appropriate logical basis for this type of idealism, in the following fashion:

(The.AI): *The logical form of the physical is identical with the logical form of the mental.*

It is true that (The.AI) also implies the truth of some version of (The.LI). And objective idealism as characterized by (The.OI) does so as well. But I don't think that every form of (The.LI) has to imply any one of the two other types of idealism. I admit without any reservations that there are numerous texts where Peirce defends a version of (The.LI) that already seems to imply some version of (The.OI). The question whether logical idealism implies (The.OI) turns on the question of what the validity of a logical system in a metaphysical sense means and why Peirce so often did not distinguish logical and objective idealism.

The last part of the question is liable to receive a very short and straight-forward answer. Imagine you are a defender of (The.LI). Then you are convinced that metaphysics and ontology should be developed by generalizing semiotical and logical principles, and you also argue for the hypothesis of objective idealism. But in metaphysical contexts you will surely be tempted to exaggerate the importance of logic. That is to say, in some weak moments when you forget about your strict methodology of expanding logical conceptions into metaphysical ones without assuming the metaphysical validity of their interpretation from the outset, you will treat the validity of a logical system as *evidence* for a specific metaphysical claim. However, this not really harmful, if it is only a metaphorical way of expressing the methodology of LI in a colourful and abbreviated way. I take it that this is what Peirce does when he refers to talking about nature as 'syllogizing' (NEM4:344) or when he describes the universe as God's vast argument. He would indeed have committed a fallacy if he had described some metaphysical doctrines as *justifying* the validity of some piece of logical theory.[6] Let us now turn to the first part of our question: how to understand the philosophical significance of the validity of some logical systems. If the mental and objective validity of a logical system by itself would imply the truth of objective idealism, metaphysics is indeed in danger of collapsing into logic. It should be possible to give – and Peirce is aware of this – an interpretation of logic in terms of the ontological structure of reality independent of its formal validity. After all, the use of logical principles and laws as constitutive principles describing the structure of being is an interpretation that selects only some logical principles and restricts their formal validity. For all we know, the formal validity of some logic of mental processes and valid argumentation may even be due to a queer sort of cosmological accident establishing an arbitrary link via an omnipotent evil demon. Such a strange sort of accident might relate human minds to reality without there being any true correspondence between the structure of our logic of mental processes and reality. We have no basis on which we could possibly decide that such a sceptical hypothesis about logical validity is a truth or a falsehood – that is, as long as we defend (The.LI) alone.

The point of logical idealism is that the validity of a logical system provides a characterization of mind as well as a way of describing some logical structure which may be treated *as if* it were related to the ontological structure of reality, if we are engaging in metaphysics. This implies that objective idealism is a possible hypothesis – but not more. The crucial point here is that we don't have to assume (The.OI), that the ontological structure of the physical is a degenerate form of the mental, if we affirm (The.LI). That is to say, we may use (The.LI) as a problematic hypothesis, suspending judgment about the ultimate ontological structure of reality. That the validity of logic gives us a clear-cut sense in which nature is intelligible is nothing but a methodological *as if* principle for metaphysics. In fact, for Peirce the *as if* principle is crucial for LI: 'Philosophy ... postulates that the processes of nature are intelligible. *Postulates*, I say, not assumes. It may not be so; but only so far as it is so can philosophy accomplish its purpose; it is therefore committed to *going upon* that assumption, true or not. It is the forlorn hope' (MS956, 1890; emphasis added).

Only on the ground of this postulate Peirce propagates his version of objective idealism and claims that logic is the right kind of basis for it. Peirce does *not* argue that objective idealism is true because natural processes *have* a logical structure identical with processes of reasoning. Rather, his argument is that only insofar as we are able to act according to our knowledge about nature do the two *processes become identical*. With regard to our action, there is no room for metaphysical doubt left – or we would rob ourselves of the possibility of building pragmatic philosophy on the distinction that it is one thing to believe and a categorically different thing to act according to a conception: 'But as far as the process of nature is intelligible, so far is the process of nature identical with the process of reason; the law of being and the law of thought must be practically assumed to be one. Hence, in framing a theory of the universe, we shall do right to make use of those conceptions which are plainly essential to logic' (ibid.). As can be seen from the quick movement of the argument in this passage, in Peirce logical and objective idealism are not far apart. However, I claim that they can be separated in principle.

But I now want to leave the abstract level of comparison between different types of idealism.

III Everybody's Idealism

What is it like to be an idealist? What are the evidential resources, rooted in our rich everyday experience of human life, on which some versions of idealism may base its arguments? There should be some trivial sort of idealism, everybody's idealism, so to speak, that may be built into our natural languages or is genetically built into our cognitive habits. One such intuitive starting point in experience is the tendency to regard us or our mental capacities as able actively to grasp and to choose some properties out of the infinitely many properties that surrounding reality offers us. I don't want even to touch the historical question how to isolate everybody's idealism in the tradition from Plato to Peirce. What I am looking for are idealistic features of common, everyday experiences that practically everybody knows. They should be of such a nature that they provide a puzzling problem and suggest an intuitive solution. In short, they are supposed to provide the sort of evidential material which feeds the holy fire of idealism, if philosophical reflection takes it as its point of departure. Let me give you the following example:

> A few days ago I was walking alongside a little river. A grasshopper, disturbed by my approach, took a huge leap – and fell into the water. The water was running fast and carried it for some yards before it could grasp some little branch which touched the surface of the water. By this time I was again approaching the grasshopper. He jumped again – and fell again into the water. I felt sorry for the poor beast and decided to intervene. I made a few fast steps, kneeled down, and took the grasshopper out of the water.

This story describes a sequence of perceptual judgments, thoughts, decisions, and actions in just the way in which I remember having experienced them. Of course, on the one hand it leaves out some of my perceptions and thoughts: It does not say anything about how I suffered from the heat that day, sweating all the time, nothing about the feel of the stones under my shoes when I knelt down, and it does not mention a train of thoughts about what to say about Peirce's idealism in this paper – that I scratched my head, and so on. Therefore, it might be said that the story describes and selects a series of cognitive activities, such as seeing, feeling a sense of pity, spontaneously deciding what to do next, which are related to a number of physio-biological conditions perceived as relevant for understanding the story, e.g., the flowing of water, the movements of my body, and the jumps of the insect. The story was designed with two things in mind: First, I want the reader to understand a little story about my rescuing a grasshopper. Second, I want to make him or her aware that once we accept a personal, subjective order of experience as an irreducible feature that has to be accounted for philosophically, this story does illustrate some of the intuitions and questions motivating idealism. For how is it possible that a sequence of cognitive activities, events, and actions becomes part and parcel of one experience, 'one story' of one and the same person, of the speaker, of me? If we ask for such an account, it becomes essential to explain how the selection of this sequence of experiences was brought about and how they were experienced by one person who executed an active, unifying role in understanding, thinking, and deciding about the way in which to interrelate, to act upon, and to represent the objects of his experience. One of the general philosophical puzzles about experience to which this story may give rise is this:

How can we explain that persons are able to create an irreducible unity of their experience which correlates, unifies, and represents their experience, thoughts, decisions, and actions that cannot be reduced to a list of the factual components of this experience?

The assumption that there is indeed some irreducible type of comprehensive, subjective unity that pervades and structures all our experiential interactions with the world which we are capable of recounting, remembering, and, in general, representing is an obvious and natural assumption for any philosophical theory that tries to account for it. Indeed, I think it is one of the strongest evidential sources of idealism. The high degree of unification is indicated on the linguistic level by the use of 'I.' Try to remove, even if only on the surface level of linguistic representation, the subject of this story, and it will be reduced to a conjunction of descriptions which does not convey the point that the story does convey. Such a conjunction of descriptive sentences in the common-sense use of such sentences conveys a sort of neutrality, if contrasted with the story told by someone referred to as 'I':

There was a person walking alongside a river. There was a grasshopper that fell twice into the river when that person approached. The person who was walking on the side of the river knelt down and took the grasshopper out of the river.

Although I have eliminated the explicit reference to a person, 'I,' the story is imperfectly reduced to its descriptive content because I used singular terms, tenses, and demonstrative pronouns which implicitly presuppose that there is a person who had some special experiences, and so on. Now imagine that my elimination is a complete success, that is, I achieve a conjunction of descriptions containing no singular terms, only bound variables, logical symbols, predicate variables, and some physical and neurological descriptions. It does not matter that the resulting formula is not even a possible candidate for meaningful use in ordinary discourse. My point is rather this: The fact remains that, if a logician is able to understand this sequence of formal expressions and scientific facts, then we can always add as a sort of transcendental prefix 'I, here, now' to any string of symbols representing his reading of the formula which indicates the fact that there was an unrepresented subjective unity whose operation in the background caused this interpretation.[7] The logician goes through a sequence of mental operations, such as associating, remembering, and so on, combining different types of mental tokens. Whatever his mental computations are, they are *not* what is depicted by the tokens that form the conjunction of descriptive propositional functions in the formula.[8] Now, to generalize:

It holds for every description or logical formula, for example, for every analysis of a piece of discourse expressed in terms of logical notation and scientific descriptions, that for every interpreter of this formula there is an implicit 'I,' 'here,' 'now' referring to the interpreter as performing a sequence of unrevealed mental logical operations in understanding that logical formula.

The primacy of a subjective unity of logical operations is therefore a special case of the thesis that the 'I think here and now that' always demarcates the largest possible scope for propositional functions. The irreducibility and the emergent character of the subjective unity of experience evidenced by our story is also reflected by the fact that there is no way to map the truth-functional logical connectives onto such a description in which a sequence of mental structures unifies a piece of discourse. Peirce's logical idealism is the thesis that it is a worthwhile project to look for a formalism that will capture, at least to some extent, the logical structure of mental operations. In short, that, philosophically speaking, only a logic of mental processes is a logic in a philosophically relevant sense.

IV The Evidential and the Formal Aspects of Peirce's Logical Idealism

What does Peirce's logical idealism do in order to account for the unity of thought and experience in his logical and metaphysical theories? In the idealistic tradition, Kant conceived of the 'original unity of apperception,' that is, 'die ursprüngliche Einheit der Apperzeption,' and the schematism of the categories to account for this operational unity of thought and experience. But Kant did not think that his account could explain all the mental operations structuring human cognition. In the chapter on schematism in the *Critique of Pure Reason* in B 180/181 he admits that much when he states that there is a 'hidden faculty in the depth of the human soul whose real operations we will hardly ever be able to guess from nature.'[9] This 'hidden faculty of the soul' is what does the trick – connecting a sequence of experiences with a judgement about it in general terms. But the function of the 'I think' cannot be completely accounted for if it cannot be explained how descriptive concepts, or propositional functions, relate to individual instances present in experience. The problem which Kant's theory of schematism in the *Critique* did not solve, Kant transferred to his theory of practical reason and his theory of imagination (*Einbildungskraft*).

Peirce decided to take up Kant's problem with the categories in its original setting, in the framework of a logic of mental processes, but drastically reshaped the task. In his answer to this question Peirce rejected several of its explicit and implicit assumptions, the most important of which is probably the rejection of Kant's traditional syllogistic concept of logic and the faculty theory of mind, in particular the assumption that sensibility and reason can be separated in such a way that a series of synthetic activities is needed. Kant's 'initial synthesis' was for Peirce an error due to the faculty theory of mind and is replaced by the general notion of an *initial analysis* which works upon a more or less undifferentiated whole of presented experience into which differentiations are introduced.[10] From his early work in the logic of relatives onwards and even in his late development of a logic of graphs, his semiotics and his theory of the categories can be seen as parts of the answer to what the logical structure of mental processes is.

Peirce stresses, for example, at 4.551 (from MS315, 634), that the operational unity of mental processes can be explained only by describing their relational structure directly, without taking account of reflexive relations. Take the following thesis: All mental processes are expressed in signs and are part of an ongoing process of interpretation by which at least two signs are connected into a unity of one interpretation. This thesis is not a claim of psychology but a thesis about the logical structure of mental processes. But that thoughts have to be instantiated in tokens and that every sign is an entity in which two minds or two sequences of mental continuity become identical are for Peirce two basic facts about the relational form exhibited by mental processes. More precisely, it is just an interpretation in terms of semiotico-mental ontology of the thesis that concepts of all types – monadic and relational concepts alike[11] – can be analysed in terms of operations combining relations with relations. Take the claim of 1906 that 'signs require at least two Quasi-minds; a *Quasi-utterer* and a *Quasi-interpreter*; and although these two are one (i.e. *are* one mind) in the sign itself, they must nevertheless be distinct. In the Sign they are, so to say, *welded*'

(4.551). Two minds 'welded' in a sign are identical because of the connection established by this process of interpretation. This mental identity is very special: It is the product of a logical operation on relations performed by these two minds. To see this, let us take a look at Peirce's paradigm of a logical operation on relations, his relative product (PP). (PP) not only combines two relational concepts in an ordered way, for example, by transforming

1) '– is a brother of –' and '– is a friend of –' (not into '– is a brother of and is a friend of –' but rather) into
2) '– is a brother of a friend of –'

and then applies existential quantification to it –

3) There is somebody x, such that: y is a brother of x and x is a friend of z –

but furthermore assumes that every relation definable in this way belongs to the three elementary relational types and has a relational identity of its own. A thought is the process that establishes a connection between two sequences of mental processes. In doing this it produces an identity of its own which Peirce calls *teridentity*.[12] Teridentity is irreducible and consists in the combination of two co-identities, that is, in the assertion of something equivalent to 'x = y & y = z.' It is obvious that this combination of two co-identities gives us the logical form for what Peirce, when talking about the semiotics of mental processes, calls two quasi-minds which have become welded. This idea of the logical unity of mind (or minds) linked by some sort of logical process is for Peirce the crucial and characteristic property of a reasoning process and has a number of important consequences for the whole of Peirce's philosophy. Therefore, we should expect that it constitutes the point of departure for every piece of theory even vaguely related to his idealism. This holds especially for his work in phenomenology (that is, his theory of the categories), formal logic, semiotics, and metaphysics. Its importance is best grasped in formulating it as the teridentity thesis about mental processes (TTM), that is, about the triadic identity created by some mental processes:

(TTM): *There are some representational mental processes that combine mental sequences of tokens thereby producing executively a relational identity of an entity, or teridentity, which consists in the continuity of what these processes represent.*[13]

(TTM) says that mental processes are processes which stabilize themselves in time, creating a dynamical type of relational identity of the objects they represent. Even syllogistic reasoning[14] can be better understood if it is described in terms of the relational dynamics of mental processes, because any two premisses of a syllogism determine a conclusion only 'by means of their community with respect to the middle term ... a term which as combining the characters of subject and predicate has a triadic element. For *combination is triadism, and triadism is combination*' (1.515, 1896; my emphasis).

If we manage, interpretively, to keep up the connection, by recombining and generalizing over represented objects, all mental processes may eventually form just one ordered continuous sequence of combined interpretations. Even in every partial sequence the dynamic identities of the objects of thinking and other mental activities are a result of the kind of unifying relatedness established by these mental processes. This is Peirce's logical account of the subjective unity of experience: Instead of appealing to an original unity of apperception Peirce argues that

1) on the surface level of consciousness we proceed by creating a consistency of argumentation, and
2) on the underlying, all pervasive level of mental events in time there is a sequential, continuous process that unifies our mind under one aspect or idea.[15]

Although it is not clear how Peirce would have construed this process in detail, it is clear that 'growth of an idea' has an ethical meaning that overrides and structures the logical one. (I will come back to the consequences of this point in my concluding remarks in the sixth section.) Indeed, for Peirce logic has to be based on ethics, and here is the point where both disciplines connect: In the self-controlled development of the idea of *my* identity *and* the identities of the objects I want to understand or act upon, my and their respective identities function as so many kinds of (changeable) purposes governing my mental processes. This is a difficult, consequential problem, and I will come back to this point later. Here it suffices to say that the identity of any object acts as a purpose for all mental processes representing it. That is to say, the teridentity or dynamic identity produced by any mental process representing this object is performed in order to capture an aspect of the complete identity of this object.

Whereas syllogistic reasoning uses the transitivity and convertibility of the identity relation to represent valid reasoning, Peirce suggests that the more basic logical structure of mental processes is a relation of sequence which underlies the relation of growth in interpretive content.[16] The question of the truth of a thought is the question of whether the process of transformation of one thought into another is legitimate, as Peirce points out in 1906: 'The highest kind of symbol is one which signifies a growth, or self-development of thought, and ... accordingly, the central problem of logic is to say whether one given thought is truly, i.e. is adapted to be, a development of a given other or not' (4.9). Any process that creates a dynamic identity, or teridentity, instantiates some relation of sequence that has a strict order: it is transitive and asymmetrical. For the formal part of Peirce's logical idealism it follows that in some sense the concept of a sequence is an undefinable logical primitive. Furthermore, such a sequential relation as 'X is a sign for everything Y stands for' has, as the quotation shows, also a semantic task to perform: it is what presents the identity of the object. I will come back to this point in a moment.

In what sense does the thesis that the relation of sequence is a logical primitive in a logic of relations characterize the logical basis of Peirce's idealism? To my mind it belongs to the very core of his idealism because it exemplifies the way in which Peirce accounts for the idealistic evidence that motivates his philosophy. For, if this thesis is taken as the basic idea for the foundation of logic it becomes the claim that:

(LI.1): *All other types of logical operations, that is, of first-order predicate calculus, must be definable in terms of an intensional logic of sequences of operations applying relations on relations.*

As Robert Burch has shown, already in 1870 Peirce had developed a group of intensional operations which apply relations on relations, such as relative product, relative sum, relative multiplication, the comma operation, and so on, that allow for the development of first-order logic. Understood in the light of (LI.1) Peirce's theory of categories is the thesis that in order to express all possible logical relations we need concepts of only three irreducible types, namely monadic, dyadic, and triadic concepts. Herzberger[17] in 1981 and Burch[18] in 1990 proved that, by placing proper restrictions on definitional resources, a Peircean logic of relations validates this reductionistic claim. In his book *A Peircean Reduction Thesis and the Foundations of Topological Logic*, Burch develops a 'Peircean Algebraic Logic,' PAL for short, a type of intensional logic of relations whose only admissible logical operations apply relations on relations. In his seventh chapter, especially Theorem 7.1–2, Burch proves that in PAL it holds that

1) teridentity is not constructible from monadic, dyadic or n adic identity relations, or any combination thereof, for any $n > 3$;

and

2) all identity relations of a dyadic degree or larger may be constructed by using triadic relations only.

Burch, commenting on this result, remarks, that 'the philosophical significance and potential justification for regarding identity as irreducibly triadic in this way rather than dyadic must remain topics of future works' (Burch's MS, 84). Since logic for Peirce is to provide the basis for metaphysics, the justification for PAL is in terms of the phenomenological analysis of the structure of experience. However, I cannot go into this here. Rather, I assume that every reader of Peirce's writings knows his arguments for the pervasiveness and irreducibility of thirdness as an element of experience.[19] However, the philosophical significance of Burch's result for Peirce's logical idealism – see (The.LI) – and for the task of explaining experiential evidence for idealism comes forward in the light of the consideration developed above. The irreducibility of teridentity in Burch's system of PAL shows that logical idealism does have a formal analogue for the claim that the identity of mental processes is irreducible. It also provides a formal account for what it means when Peirce in semiotics claims that every complete sign-relation creates an irreducibly triadic type of identity for the object of a sign.

In the next section I will explain this theory of the sequential structure of thought and how it relates to Peirce's idealistic semantics.

V Idealistic Logic and Semantics

There can never be an exclusively logical proof that mind is a process which creates an identity which allows for identities with a triadic logical form. In fact, the possibility of such a logical proof would refute Peirce's very mathematico-phenomenological method outlined in the introduction to this paper. A logic of whatever type will be able to show only that some crucial feature of the structure of mental processes might be formalized in such a way that this structural feature becomes the basis for all sorts of valid conclusions. For this reason formal consistency is never sufficient, and again, as in the case of tychism discussed above, the selection of what is considered to be a crucial structural feature of mental processes has to be decided by phenomenological arguments. Later on I will describe in some detail how for Peirce these phenomenological arguments point in the direction of the temporal or sequential character of mental processes as their most crucial, universal feature, and suggest that it is their sequential character which allows for triadic relational identities as the elementary forms of what Peirce in 1898 called the 'logic of events' in which reasoning and reality agree.

But before we can investigate more closely why this is so, there is an important objection to the whole approach of an idealistic logical theory of mind which has to be answered: Is it a sort of psychologistic fallacy, a vicious circle, if we take for granted any feature of mind, for example, the sequential, temporal ordering of mental processes, designing a logical system in such way as to accommodate this very feature? In order to see that Peirce's idealistic logic does *not* commit a psychologistic fallacy, we have to distinguish three levels of argumentation.

On the first level, Peirce's strong anti-psychologism in interpreting the validity of logic is situated and has full force. His anti-psychologism is the thesis that the validity of logic is independent of *any* empirical singular facts about the mind described by the empirical science of psychology and that, quite to the contrary, the validity of logic has to be decided by strictly general and formal criteria alone. Peirce's anti-psychologism is as strong as that of, for example, Russell, Frege, or Husserl. But logic provides a suitable basis for the empirical science of psychology.

This leads us to the second level of argumentation. As soon as logic as a complex formal discipline has been established – admittedly with a little help from mathematics and phenomenology – we might look for a suitable logic of the mind. It is at this stage of argument that Peirce *does* want and *can without circularity* give a formal account of mental phenomena. He may do so by applying logic, the logic of relation in particular, in an interpretive account of mental processes. He has to show that logic as formal system instantiates in its axioms, rules, and syntax a specific account of the general conditions and structure of mental processes.

But to develop such a logic of mental processes, there has to be a third level of argumentation in Peirce's search for a logic of the mind. This level consists in the claim or assumption that there are some general features *which cannot consist in singular facts about mental processes*. These general features of mind provide the starting points which are reflected in the axioms and rules of the formal system: they turn a formal system into a logic of mental processes. If you ask what these crucial structural features of mind are, Peirce will tell you that, phenomenologically speaking, these are the continuity and relation of temporal sequence in particular which are present in all mental processes we might possibly experience. It is these third-level, general mathematical features of experience which have to be accommodated by logic. For example, in MS800 Peirce points out that the formal equivalence between 'P $\rightarrow$ Q' and '~(P & ~Q)' will not do as an analysis (that is, does not give us a complete equivalence) of the sequence of thought-signs, at the occasion of our first act of thinking the passage from one thought to another. When Peirce claims that 'time is the form under which logic presents itself to objective intuition' (6.87, 1898) or that 'no continuum can be apprehended except by a mental generation of it' (7.536, c. 1904), he shows that he wants to treat temporal sequence and continuity as structural features of mental processes which provide ontological restraints for what may count as a logic capable of describing the validity of thought processes.

The extent to which we can allow mathematico-ontological third-level properties of the mind to act as restraints for formal logic will be a question of degree. Clearly, to admit some general mathematico-ontological restraints is unproblematic, if one does not want to exclude in principle a second-level theory, that is, a logical and semiotical analysis of mental processes. Therefore, it is of crucial philosophical importance and eliminates quite a number of objections if we can show that an idealistic concept of mind as an emergent process has a formal analogue that can be developed into a deductively complete system of an intensional, algebraic logic of relations. In what follows I am going to argue, in particular, for the thesis that the irreducibility of triadic relational identity is motivated by an assumption about the way in which all mental activity is structured. This is the way in which I interpret the following statement by Peirce: 'The highest kind of synthesis is what the mind is compelled to make ... in the interest of the synthesizing "I think" itself; this it does by introducing an idea not contained in the data, which gives connections which they would not otherwise have had ... the genius of mind ... shows them in intelligible form ... regarding ... the abstract in a concrete form, by the realistic hypostatization of relations; that is the one sole method of valuable thought' (1.383, 1890). What Peirce describes here as the 'abstract in concrete form' brought about by a 'realistic hypostatization of relations' is a deductively valid form of reasoning which he at other places calls 'hypostatic abstraction' and which is now called class abstraction.[20] This kind of argument may establish a kind of identity as a result of the postulation of an identity of hypostatized or fictional entities. It is a process of reasoning about relations which clearly, as Burch has shown in PAL, presupposes teridentity.[21] Hypostatically abstracted concepts are important for the developed semiotics of the mind. Most of the semiotical concepts in their relation to the comprehensive mental processes to which they belong are abstracted in this way. (In fact, for his theory of the categories Peirce needs other types of abstraction, too.)

Abstracted identities and the representation of mental processes are intimately connected. To show this I want to discuss next two consequences of Peirce's relational identity thesis for the logic of mental processes. As I mentioned above, on the one hand, Peirce has to reject some of the traditional equivalences for the truth-functional connectives. But on the other hand, he must endorse the view that we are always able to analyse concepts, names, and propositions as so many hypostatically abstracted abreviations, fictions, or other representations of the true mental processes. In fact, Peircean semiotics can be seen as a theory which accounts for all representation in terms of concepts abstracted from the sequential deep structure of mental processes. Witness that Peirce in 1906 claims that

> an Argument is no more built up of Propositions than a motion is built up of positions. So to regard it is to neglect the very essence of it ... Just as it is strictly correct to say that nobody is ever in an exact Position ... but Positions are ... *entia rationis* (i.e. fictions recognized to be fictions, and thus no longer fictions) invented for the purpose of closer descriptions of states of motion; so likewise Thought (I am not talking Psychology, but Logic, or the essence of Semeiotics) cannot, from the nature of it, be at rest, or be anything but an inferential process; and propositions are either roughly described states of thought-motion, or are artificial creations intended to render the description of thought-motion possible; and Names are creations of a second-order serving to render the representation of propositions possible. (MS295, 1906)

Such a 'fiction' as a name or a proposition is a useful hypostatic abstraction, *ens rationis*, introduced to mark a class of things, for example, a correlate in a process of thought. It might be called a sort of teridentical creation introduced as a representation of a thought process, representing one aspect of this process.

But what about the complete sequential order of relational operations that is supposed to constitute our mental processes? If our linguistically expressed thoughts ride piggyback on a sequentially ordered sequence of mental operations, we should be able to reveal this deep structure directly, at least in those cases where we want to express a relation of logical dependence between states of our thinking. This is the case where a relation of consequence is expressed by conditional sentences, such as, 'If it rains, the street will get wet.' Let us assume we want to analyse what process of reasoning is performed when we think such a conditional for the first time. Obviously, the ordering of this mental process cannot be analysed in terms of a negation of a conjunction, if we want to do justice to the operation performed in thinking two propositions connected conditionally. This is so because thought takes place in time and involves a real change. Therefore in MS300 (1908) Peirce argues that, at least for a logic of mental processes, it is an error to suppose that 'the concept of Consequence is a special composite of two negations, so that to say, "If in the actual state of things A is true, then B is true," is correctly analyzed as the assertion, "It is false to say that A is true while B is false"' (00049). As an analysis of that sequence of thought movements executing 'If A, then B,' the expression (I) 'It is false that: A is true while B is false' is obviously inadequate. Consider the state of affairs in which (I) is true. In it, A is never true without B being true. That is to say, no change in the thinking of logical dependence occurs. The material conditional cannot be analysed by two negations, because thinking a conditional for the first time establishes a change in our thoughts that leads, for example, from the sequent A to the consequent B. Peirce (ibid. 00049) stresses that the elementary character of the concept of sequence was implicitly assumed in all his writings on formal logic. He then gives the following argument: 'In reasoning, at least when we first affirm, or affirmatively judge, the conjugate of the premisses, the judgment of the conclusion has not yet been performed. There then follows a real movement of thought in the mind in which that judgment of the conclusion comes to pass.' But how could we possibly mirror the 'real movement of thought' by a logic? A few pages later Peirce states that 'reasoning takes place in time,' thereby describing the sequential order of mental processes as a kind of temporal ordering. In fact, this is the converse of an older thesis of his that time is the existential analogue of the relation of logical sequence. This conclusion then supports the interpretation given above. The concept of sequence is undefinable in ordinary logic and is primitive. Therefore, we need a logical system of higher logical power to be able to account for the structural properties of the process which truth-functional connectives symbolize and to represent their sequential ordering on one level. At least to some extent, Peirce found such a structural isomorphic logical system in his graphical logic, which he called 'a moving picture of thought' (ibid. 00022). It is because of this feature of a partial isomorphism with the temporal structure of thought that the graphs also provide a logical semantic account of his idealistic logic of mental processes.

In order to prepare for a proper explanation of why and in which sense the graphs supply a semantic model for Peirce's idealistic logic, I will answer the following question: How it is possible for an ordered sequence of operations on mental tokens to determine the independent objects these feelings or thoughts are about? Any interpretation of Peirce's logical idealism and his semiotics should be able to answer these two crucial questions about the possibility of idealistic semantics:

1) Peirce defines a sign as an entity that is determined by its object to bring out a second sign, the interpretant, that represents the object as being represented by this sign. The *first crucial question for idealistic semantics* is: What does it mean that the object 'determines' the triadic sign relation, if this is not a case of physical causality (which it cannot be since physical causality is a dyadic relation)?

2) Given a semiotic and idealistic approach, why do we need the concept of a real and independent object of the sign; why not rather concentrate entirely on the interpretant, for example?[22]

In solving these problems Peirce builds on the property of transitivity and the order of the relation of sequence in the design of his graphical logic when he formulates the thesis – sometimes this is his convention 0 – that the sheet of assertion on which every graphical form is written is itself a diagram, to the effect that 'the same thing which represents The Truth must be regarded as in another way representing the Mind and indeed as being the Quasi-mind of all the Signs represented on the Diagram' (4.550, 1906). Semantically the crucial property of the graphs is the assumption that the spatial relations of inclusion and exclusion represent all logical relations *instantiated on the surface which at the same time represents the universe of discourse*. That is to say, two signs which occur on the same sheet are by this very fact related to each other and, as signs, represent a relation of coexistence in the universe of discourse. From these two facts it follows that they can be understood only to be *true together in the same universe of discourse*. The two-dimensional continuity of the surface of the sheet is interpreted as a semantic model for the relation that holds in an external universe of discourse, for example, for a relation of coexistence in the universe of discourse under consideration.[23] It should be obvious by now that the originality of Peirce's graphical logic lies not just in its fanciful iconic notation for first-order logic but in its achievement of a quite unique expression of his logical idealism *on both the syntactical and the semantic level* of a logic of mental processes. Even the statement that the graphs are 'iconic' or 'diagrammatic' expresses that they provide an adequate logical semantics for a logic of mental processes revealing the deep structure of mental processes. This semantic dimension of the existential graphs and its importance for Peirce's idealism has been ignored. For this reason I want to discuss it a little bit more closely.

The sheet of assertion – which Peirce also calls the 'phemic sheet' – is a semantic device because it represents the relation of our mental processes to the objects in the domain of discourse. But it also represents the sequence of signs that were written on the sheet and that determine each other.[24] In this way, writing the graphs creates a teridentity: The graphs as a moving picture of thought represent, at the same time, the relation of thoughts to the objects represented. But why is it possible to identify the structure of the mental processes with the ontological structure in the universe of discourse in writing symbols on a sheet of paper? Clearly, the graphically represented identity is not complete. But insofar as it is represented it holds because the phemic sheet 'immediately represents a field of thought, or mental experience, which is itself directed to the universe of discourse, and considered as a sign, denotes that universe. ... on the principle that the logicians call "*Nota notae*," that a sign of the sign of anything, X, is itself a sign of the very same X, the Phemic Sheet in representing the field of attention, represents the general object of that attention, the universe of discourse' (MS300, 00041).

The *Nota notae* principle says that all signs, if related at all, are in a strictly ordered, that is, transitive and asymmetrical, relation to the represented universe of discourse. And this is the way in which the graphs represent the semantic structure of our mental processes: graphs and thoughts exhibit a structure which is isomorphic with the structure of their objects in the universe of discourse, regardless of what kind of objects they are. In representing on the sheet the intentionality of thought, we understand every thought as a representation of some independent object such that our future perceptions, thoughts, and actions will show that the thought, was a true representation of the same independent object: Even if, for example, the spatial ordering of objects in the universe of discourse has changed, our thought still captures the isomorphic intentional structure of thought that remains invariant.

In what sense does the identity relation depend on what is revealed in a process of interpretation? In 1908 Peirce stated that, '"Identity" means a continuity, not necessarily in Place, nor in Date, but in what I may call *aspect*, i.e. a variety of presentation or representation' (MS300). Thus, a continuity in aspects is a continuity in general properties which cannot be reduced to spatio-temporal continuity. If we turn to semiotics, we see at once that the kind of relation between non–spatio-temporal properties that is 'a variety of representation' has to be the abstract teridentity produced in the process of interpretation. In a letter to P.E.B. Jourdain, which also dates from 1908, Peirce stressed that in thinking we control the relation between signs and their objects and that our understanding of logic is thereby relativized to ethics: 'We think in signs; and indeed meditation takes the form of a dialogue in which one makes constant appeal to his self of a subsequent moment for ratification of his meaning in respect to his thought = signs really representing the objects they profess to represent. Logic therefore is almost a branch of ethics, being the theory of the control of signs in respect to their relation to their objects' (Peirce in a letter to P.E.B. Jourdain, 5.12. 1908, NEM3:886).

What exactly does it mean to describe logic – which in this context is tantamount to semiotics – as 'the theory of the control of signs in respect to their relation to their objects'? As I understand this passage it implies the contention that in every sequence of signs a principle of objective unity (POU) is at work. This principle may be stated in the following form:

(POU): *For any sequence of signs, if some sign S2 acts as an interpretant of another sign S1, then there is one and only one object a for which they both stand if and only if it holds that S1 presents immediately an object $y^* = x$ and S2 presents immediately an object $z^* = x$ on the condition that a relation of strict order subsists only if for all other signs SN it holds that S1 is a predecessor of S2 and of all SN.*

If (POU) holds for all signs, Peirce's triadic sign-relation or semiosis, for example, 'A represents B for C,' consists in the fact that a sign and its interpretant are related to one another because they represent the same object. That is to say, (POU) can be seen as describing what it is for a sign and its interpretant to stand for an identical object: the sign in itself and its interpretant constitute a complete sign if and only if they relate to the same object. The contingent identity created by a sequence of signs is teridentity. To create and to sustain a sequence of interpretations that produces the teridentity of its object is to represent an object in a certain aspect. What the object is – the aspect – is at the same time the immediate object that is manifest from our reading of the sign used. Furthermore, as in the case of the non-predicativeness of probabilities, it is not the single interpretation which represents the true character of the individuals in the universe of discourse. Rather: *it is the experientially instantiated form which the sequence of interpretive tokens have to take on in order to represent an independent object more and more fully.* Again, the missing theory of logical form stands in the way of further clarification of this point. But whatever such a theory may tell us, it will remain true that the perception of the form of an ordered sequence of tokens not only constitutes the syntax of the sign-process. To grasp the form also means to understand the triadic identity on which the identity of the represented object is based.

VI Conclusion: Having an Object in Mind

Let us review and generalize what we have got have so far. It seems to me that the following conclusion is rather supported by the argument of this paper: Peirce's idealism is formal but context-bound and, in its basic idea – though not in all of its applications – it is anti-metaphysical. Its being 'anti-metaphysical' is supposed to mean only one thing: The object of a sign is described exclusively in terms of the formal properties of the sign-relation. In this concluding step I will try to show that 'being directed to' and 'being determined by' an object in Peirce's idealistic semantic can be treated as the same semantic relation on which the identity of an object depends.

When Peirce claims that the nature of reality consists in a logic of events that is isomorphic with the processes of reasoning, this is the claim that the best metaphysical theory will give us the form of a historical process of representation. That is to say, nothing is real except what can be represented in a form which is known by considering a sufficiently large segment of a temporal process of interpretation relative to some context of acquaintance: 'Of the two great tasks of humanity, *Theory* ... sets out from a sign of a real object with which it is *acquainted*, passing from this, as its *matter*, to successive interpretants embodying more and more fully its *form*, wishing ultimately to reach a direct *perception* of the entelechy' (NEM 4:240). Earlier, Peirce made it clear that the entelechy of an object is the object in its aspect as a sign, which is complete and perfect because it contains the ultimate interpretant of every sign. But wishing for and going for this type of perfection does not imply that we stand a chance of reaching this aim on all counts. In fact, we do not even have to. The condition that a sequence of signs and interpretants is related to a teridentical object can obtain only if this sequence is 'determined' by one and the same object. And this is the object we are acquainted with before the process of interpretation gets started. In fact it is the qualitative matter of the object which triggers off the process of interpretation. Therefore, there must be a sense in which the sameness of the object is equivalent to its function of determining the sign. What does it mean for an object to determine a sign?

I cannot answer this question here completely, because in order to say what identity described as a continuity of representation means would involve an explanation of what the identity between the final opinion and its object is. Is this identity a sort of mathematical limit? Then Quine's well-known objection (in *Word and Object*) is fatal: the concept of a limit is well defined only for numbers.

But do we really need this specific number-theoretical concept of limit here? I doubt that very strongly. I think that the identity between the ultimate opinion and its object can be explicated in an unobjectionable way if we take a more mundane concept of approximation or determination, to use Peirce's term, suggested by the quotation from the letter above. We speak about 'approximating' a goal, aim, or object. The object of my activity is the state of thing I want to realize. If all semiotical activity is a process directed to a goal, we may say that all cognition and all scientific activity approximate and thereby determine an object in this sense.[25] Accordingly, the identity of the ultimate opinion with the real object would be a case of accepting some state of affairs which has come about as the realization of a goal, aim, or purpose.

The property 'being determined by the object' is a regular and crucial feature of almost all of Peirce's definitions of a sign.[26] Despite its obvious importance this way of implying that there is an implicit teleological causality operative in the sign is a rather undeveloped part of Peirce's semiotics. If there is always an object which determines the sequence of signs and creates the teridentity by realizing the sign-relation, it follows that Peirce is committed to an ontology of teleological objects which have an *esse in futuro*. The teleological object of every sign, therefore, can be created only by an ongoing activity of, for example, the community of the once and future interpreters at their specific historical times. This teleological structure of experience, if it can be realized at all, would have to contain, from the point of view of phenomenological and semiotical ontology, the same mental entities which Peirce's logical idealism supposes as the objects identified by the ultimate opinion. I conclude that Peirce must defend the following rather startling thesis about ontology:

All mental processes, become strictly identical with their independent objects that act as final causes of cognitive and bodily actions realizing them, provided that all interpretations are completed, all cognitive and bodily actions have realized their goals, and there are no more future states of these objects to be brought about.

This ideal limiting state of reality is a fiction in a very strong sense, because it has no physical realization under normal conditions:[27]

It would be a crystalline, changeless state in which time would have a stop, and no object would have an esse in futuro.

But at any moment in finite time our experience and thought will produce for us a teridentity of the mental process we are engaged in, which connects us to an *esse in futuro*. None of these teridentities here and now produced by thought and experience will amount to a strict Leibnizian identity. Teridentity gives us a partial identity of an object representing as a part of it an object's *esse in futuro*. Until the assumption is contradicted by experience we assume that the partial identity represented might be developed into an uninterrupted sequence of teridentities. In this sense every representation of teridentity points to an object which is independent of the representation. It is this uncompletability of the real object which provides an ontological – but anti-metaphysical – argument for the possibility of an unlimited number of interpretations. What is real and what is represented remain distinct as long as we do not assume that it is nothing but a contrafactual possibility within the bounds of theoretical speculations of logical idealism that all interpretations come to an end. Even where Peirce speculates, in a sort of idealistic thought experiment, about such a perfected identity, he is always clear about the contrafactual nature of the possibility which he is discussing. Consider one of the most extreme passages, written in 1904: 'The purpose of every sign is to express "fact," and by being joined with other signs, to approach as nearly as possible to determining an interpretant which would be the *perfect truth*, the absolute Truth, and as such (at least, we may use this language) would be the very Universe' (NEM4:239).

Peirce's logical idealism does not collapse into an objective idealism, let alone into some sort of absolute idealism. For logical idealism, the ultimate identity of reality will always be incomplete. The one and only reality of absolute truth is a regulative idea for the deontology of mental processes that govern our search for knowledge.

Notes

1 For example, R. Almeder in *The Philosophy of C.S. Peirce* (Oxford: Basil Blackwell 1980), leaves out logical idealism and concentrates on his versions of (i) and (ii).

2 I cite the following editions of Peirce's writings. Abbreviations used are as given at the beginning of this volume.

 – *Collected Papers of Charles Sanders Peirce*, 8 vols, edited by C. Hartshorne, P. Weiss, and A. Burks (Cambridge, Mass.: Belknap Press of Harvard University Press, 1931–58).

 – The microfilm edition of the manuscripts of C.S. Peirce as listed in Richard S. Robin's *Annotated Catalogue of the Papers of Charles S. Peirce* (Amherst: University of Massachusetts Press 1967) and in 'The Peirce Papers: A Supplementary Catalogue,' *Transactions of the Charles S. Peirce Society* (1971). In cases where I had, thanks to the generosity of Christian J.W. Kloesel and Nathan Houser, the photocopies of the manuscript that are used in the Peirce Edition project at hand, I give the 000XXX numbering of their version.

 – *The New Elements of Mathematics by Charles S. Peirce,* edited by Carolyn Eisele, 4 vols in 5 (The Hague–Paris: Mouton 1976).

 In addition, 'Peirce 1991' refers to *Charles S. Peirce – Naturordnung und Zeichenprozeß Schriften zur Semiotik und Naturphilosophie,* preface by I. Prigogine, edited with an introduction, pp 13–109, by H. Pape, translated by B. Kienzle (1st ed. Aachen: Rader Verlag 1988; paperback ed.: Frankfurt: Suhrkamp Verlag 1991), which contains most of Peirce's published and unpublished writings on the philosophy of nature.

3 A general version of this thesis, that every major change in Peirce's philosophy is due to a change in his logic, has been proposed by M.G. Murphey in *The Develop-*

ment of Peirce's Philosophy (Cambridge, Mass.: Harvard University Press 1961). However, having other objectives, Murphey does not give a detailed account of the relation between logic and metaphysics.

4 The most extensive defence along this line I developed in the introduction, pp. 11–109, Peirce 1991.

5 'in any event logical questions have to be considered first. But if logic is thus to precede philosophy will it not be unphilosophical logic? Perhaps logic is not in much need of philosophy. Mathematics, which is a species of logic, has never had the least need of philosophy in doing its work.' MS956, *c.* 1890–1.

6 Peirce in his metaphysical writings is well aware that he would be begging the question if he claimed that *only the validity of a logical system provided an independent reason for the validity of objective idealism.* On the other hand, Peirce makes a valid point about the function of logic in his logical idealism when he stresses that physical reality can be explained only if the logical structure of mental and physical processes may be the same: 'Nature only appears intelligible so far as it appears rational, that is, so far as its processes are seen to be like processes of thought' (4.422).

7 The expression 'transcendental prefix' as well as the strategy of this argument, to ask for the degree to which a proposition reveals the mental processes by which was caused, is due to the late H.N. Castañeda. See his treatment of transcendental prefixes in the paper 'The Semiotics of Indicators,' in K. Jacobi and H. Pape, eds, *Thinking and the Structure of the World – H.N. Castañeda's Epistemic Ontology Presented and Criticized* (Berlin/New York: Walter DeGruyter 1990).

8 Of course, it goes without saying that Quine and other analytic philosophers never claim that logical analysis and the elimination of singular terms in a regimented language would yield a truthful picture of thinking. Instead, they warn against any such mentalism and declare their sympathy for behaviourism, vaguely implying that logic is the rational type of behaviour for a philosopher in these mental matters.

9 '... eine verborgene Kunst in den Tiefen der menschlichen Seele, deren wahre Handgriffe wir der Natur schwerlich jemals abraten.'

10 This notion is already used by Peirce in his 'New List of the Categories' in 1868 where 'substance' or the 'IT' is described as 'the present in general' (1.547). In 1890 (1.384), Peirce explains his thesis of the initial analysis of undifferentiated experience in much more clear-cut language, taking issue with Kant: 'Kant gives the erroneous view that ideas are presented separated and then thought together by the mind ... What really happens is that something is presented which in itself has no parts, but which nevertheless is analysed by the mind, that is to say, its having parts consists in this, that the mind afterwards recognizes those parts in it. Those partial ideas are really not in the first idea, in itself, though they are separated out from it ...

When ... we think over them, we are carried in spite of ourselves from one thought to another, and therein lies the first real synthesis.'

11 When Peirce speaks about 'monadic' and with regard to complete propositions even 'medadic,' that is 0-relations, W. Kneale and M. Kneale in *The Development of Logic* (Oxford: Clarendon Press 1962), 432, criticize this terminology: 'it can scarcely be said to give philosophical illumination.' However, if you take into account that this terminology has to serve the project of an intensional relational logic of mental processes, its explanatory value shines: With regard to a complete proposition there is no (medadic) and with regard to a monadic predicate there is exactly one act of relational combination to be performed.

12 In MS300 (1908), Peirce connects his treatment of identity with his theory of the relational form of the connection between concepts. He explicitly rejects the traditional Porphyrian genus-species theory of conceptual combination and adds: 'I hold a different theory; namely that in the first place every composition of concepts is built up by the application of relatives, as, for example, that since one may analyse the assertion "M is a *cousin* of N," into "M has *grandfather* that is a *grandfather* of N" it follows that the conception *cousinship* is a composite of the relation of *grandparentage* with its converse, and in the second place that this composition takes place, as in chemistry, by units of valency, so that each correlate of a relative term is a single individual, and, for example, the relation of being a loving servant is not correctly a mere compound of the relations of loving and of serving, but involves besides two relations of co-identity, or, as I usually call it, *teridentity*' (00048).

13 Cf MS300: '"Identity" means a continuity, not necessarily in Place, nor in Date but in what I may call *aspect*, i.e. a variety of presentation or representation.' (00046–7).

14 When I remark below that Peirce described syllogistic reasoning as limited to some logical properties of the identity (e.g., transitivity and convertibility), this remark is aimed at *non-relational* identity or the theory of idea presented in first-order predicate calculus.

15 'The unity of Thought does not consist in that *Ich denke* which Kant, in his first edition, called the '=x,' and not '*Ich denke,*' or 'I opine.' The unity of thought, if we would view our own consciousness, would probably consist in the *continuity of life of a growing idea*; but as well as we can observe it, it lies in the logical coherency and consistency of argument. For to think is to reason ... Now the unity of reasoning is simply the identity of the object reasoned about. An argument is simply a construction of premises which constitutes a *sign* of the truth of its conclusion ... and the question of what its logic is, is nothing but the question in what mode of representation thosepremises make up a sign of the substance of the conclusion' (MS637, 00023–4, 1909).

16 A metaphysical development on the basis of the logical idealist's view of mind as a

combinatorial process is synechism, 'a regulative principle of logic ... that the form under which alone anything can be understood is the form of generality, which is the same thing as continuity' (6.173, 1902).

17 Hans G. Herzberger, 'Peirce's Remarkable Theorem,' in J.G. Slater, L.W. Sumner, and F. Wilson, eds, *Pragmatism and Purpose: Essays Presented to Thomas A. Goudge* (Toronto: University of Toronto Press 1981), 41–58.

18 Robert W. Burch, *A Peircean Reduction Thesis and the Foundations of Topological Logic* (Lubbock: Texas Tech University Press 1990).

19 In the 'Lectures on Pragmatism' of 1903, Peirce argued that because we can describe the sequence of mental states in perceptual consciousness by means of general statements about relations of sequence, for example, from 'is later than,' we may derive thirdness from experience. Murphey (*Development of Peirce's Philosophy*) objected to this that Peirce simply assumed the validity of some general theorems about relations. However, Murphey's reconstruction was formulated in the PM-style way of formalizing relations and treating them extensionally. Although I cannot argue for this in detail, I think it can easily be proved that Peirce's argument is valid if we construct it as a thesis about the possible applications of 'later than' to single instances of present and future experiences.

20 Intuitively, the basic logical operation for this is the move from an expression in predicate-position, such as 'red' in 'The rose is red,' to an equivalent proposition in which this expression is in subject-position: 'Red is in the rose.' It is obviously deductively valid to conclude that, if there is a red rose, the class of red things has at least one member, namely, this rose. For a good account of the fruitfulness of Peircean hypostatic abstraction, even in empirical concept formation, see Thomas L. Short, 'Hypostatic Abstraction in Empirical Science,' *Grazer Philosophische Studien* 32 (1988): 51–8.

21 That the identity of an operation is presupposed and can be introduced before an abstraction is applied is more prominent in Peirce's discussion of mathematical operations. In this context Peirce argues that 'the mathematician conceives an operation as something itself to be operated upon. He conceives the collection of places of a moving particle as itself a place which can at one instant be totally occupied by a filament, which can again move, and the aggregate of all its places, considered as possibly occupied in one instant, is a surface ...' (1.83, 1896)

22 In fact, D. Greenlee, in *Peirce's Concept of a Sign* (The Hague: Mouton 1973) argued that Peirce's semiotics should be developed without the concept of an object of a sign, and A.J. Ayer, in *The Origins of Pragmatism* (London: Macmillan 1968), 166, thought that the concept of an object was the greatest obstacle for a consistent account of Peirce's theory of signs. The difficulties that Ayer and Greenlee have with the idea that every sign has an independent object that determines it are due to the fact that both of them are ontological nominalists, whereas Peirce devised his

semiotics by assuming a realist interpretation of the dynamical teridentity involved in the sign-relation.

23 Note that in his use of tinctures to represent different modalities (e.g,. in 1906, 4.530–84, MS 292–5: possibility, actuality, and intendedness) by different universes of discourse that differ from one another by restrictions on the type of consistency for sentences that can be true in them, Peirce anticipates possible-worlds semantics. The possible, the actual, and the intended universe of discourse are distinguished by the fact that in the actual universe both the *tertium datur* and the law of non-contradiction hold; in the possible and the intended universe either one them does not hold.

24 Rolf George, in a paper titled 'Taking Thoughts One at a Time – Peirce on the Linear Progression of Thought in Reasoning,' *Philosophy of Mind – Philosophy of Psychology*, Proceedings of the 9th International Wittgenstein Symposium (Vienna 1985), 551–7, has argued that Peirce is too successful in designing the existential graphs as a type of deductive system in which all proofs are progressing linearly. This has the effect that we cannot come back to a possible deductive conclusion of a set of premises once we have decided to use the premises to prove another conclusion. But what George stresses holds only if we think one sequence of thoughts determined by only one, stand-alone deductive algorithm. This is not Peirce's idea of a logic of mental processes. All distinct deductive sequences are connected with each other by means of non-deductive or non-monotonic second-order inferential steps, such as hypostatic abstraction, abductive, and inductive arguments. The choice of the proof-strategy is governed by a self-control which acts as a sort of meta-principle for structuring the strategy of a proof. The logical and semiotical problems of self-control I have discussed more extensively in 'Artificial Intelligence, G.W. Leibniz and C.S. Peirce: The Phenomenological Concept of a Person,' *Études Phénoménologiques*, 9/10, S. (1988): 113–46.

25 This is the definition which in 1904 Peirce gave to the notion of an object which he used in his classification of the scienes: 'one should remark that the common use of the word "object" to mean a *thing*, is altogether incorrect. The noun *objectum* came into use in the XIIIth century, as a term of psychology. It means primarily that creation of the mind in its reaction with a more or less real something, which creation becomes that upon which cognition is directed; and secondarily, an object is that upon which an exertion acts; also that which a purpose seeks to bring about; also, that which is coupled with something else in a relation, and more especially is represented as so coupled; also, that to which any sign corresponds' (MS693A, 33).

26 The object's causal role is stressed in a definition which Peirce gives in MS318 (1907), at the end of a detailed discussion of his concept of an object: 'a sign is anything, of whatsoever mode of being, which mediates between an object and an interpretant; since it is both determined by the object *relatively to the interpretant*,

and determines the interpretant *in reference to the object*, in such wise as to cause theinterpretant to be determined by the object through the mediation of this "sign"' (MS318, 44).

27 But only for normal conditions in space and time: J.D. Barrow and F.J. Tipler, in *The Anthropic Cosmological Principle* (Oxford: Oxford University Press 1986), have imagined a quantum mechanical model for which such a state is the terminal point, which they call the Omega Point, of cosmological evolution: 'At the instant the Omega Point is reached, life will have gained control of *all* matter and forces not only in a single universe, but in all universes whose existence is logically possible; ... life ... will have stored an infinite amount of information, including *all* bits of knowledge which it is logically possible to know. And this is the end' (677).

Charles Peirce and the Origin of Interpretation

CARL R. HAUSMAN

It is a well-known Peircean principle that thoughts are signs, and thinking is semiosis or sign processing. However, semiosis does not spring full-blown into consciousness. Moments of experience that appear to be meaningful must originate somewhere and at some time. Where and when does this origin occur?[1] Is a sensation and what is sensed, a red patch, for instance, a pure given that remains to be interpreted? Is the red patch that is given for sensation already an interpreted datum? Or is there a third possibility? Even if interpretation has taken place and the red patch that appears is an interpreted datum, is there nevertheless an underlying chaotic or unordered manifold of experience that is not subject to interpretation? These questions bring into focus the topic of the following discussion.

I believe that one of Peirce's insights is that there is a rudimentary interpretive experience present even in what seems to be presemiotic activity. He recognized that consciousness, the activator of interpretations, is present in incipient form at a so-called lowest level of mental life, namely, sensation or brute feeling. Locating original interpretive action at the level of brute sensuous feeling is possible for Peirce in light of his synechism, that is, the view that continuity pervades the intelligible world. However, Peirce's insistence on the pervasiveness of semiotic experience does not commit him to a semiotic idealism. His view includes a conception of a condition of external constraints, an extrasemiotic condition or 'dynamical object.' Thus, Peirce's conception of meaningful experience has a twofold base of objectivity. On the one hand, there are the semiotic systems that we bring to our experiences and, on the other, there are presemiotic constraints, the sources of which are dynamical objects.

Before developing these points and considering how the discussion bears on some of the controversies that are alive in current philosophical literature, I should add a preliminary observation. Although the iconic, indexical, and symbolic functions of signs will be mentioned, I shall not treat the origin of semiosis in terms of the evolution of icons into symbols. Instead, I shall probe behind even the iconic level and concentrate on Peirce's ideas about the origin of pre-judgmental and judgmental activities in perceptual experience.

With these preliminary comments in mind, let us turn to the main question, How does interpretation originate?

I Peirce's View of the Place of Interpretation in Perceptual Experience

Peirce regards perception as the key to inquiry. Inquiry – indeed, all knowledge – arises with perception. If all inquiry is essentially interpretive, then its key, perception, must reveal the initial stages of interpretation. Perception is an activity that includes stages. It begins with percepts and is developed into perceptual judgments. Perceptual judgment introduces critical control and serves as the beginning of *explicit* interpretation. Once critical control is introduced with perceptual judgment, some degree of hypothetical inference is present, the heart of which lies in what Peirce calls 'abduction.'[2]

However, perceptual judgment, it must be emphasized, is one stage or component of the broader mental activity, perception, which also includes another component, the percept. Peirce's conception of percepts is crucial to our topic. But what are they? One meaning of the term 'percept,' which I name 'percept-one,' refers to the experiential dynamic seeds of forthcoming perceptual judgments. Percepts in this sense must be distinguished from the notion of sense impressions or any kind of sense data introduced by the British empiricists, that is, hard, discrete, and determinate 'atoms' of experience that are firm building blocks for generalization. (Such data are already interpreted.) However, Peirce's percepts-one do constrain the way perception develops and thus constrain the judgmental component of perception. They may be encountered in moments of surprise, when an experienced object is different from an anticipated object (see, e.g., 5.53).[3] Or they may be encountered as parts of an experienced field that compels us to perceive them one way rather than another. A thing perceived as a red patch is something that constrains the perceiver to see a patch rather than a ball and red rather than green. (The red patch is the kind of thing referred to by the traditional empiricists' term 'sense impression.') Yet the percept initially encountered, percept in sense 'one,' does not announce itself as a determinate, classifiable object. It is not an identifiable red patch. A percept in sense 'one' is rather an unclassified focus of resistance or centre of constraints on interpretation.

It may be helpful to think of percepts in this first sense as belonging to the categories of firstness and secondness when these are considered in abstraction – or, more accurately for Peirce, when they are prescinded – from the category of thirdness or mediated interpretation. Thus, percepts-one are givens that are undifferentiated sheer qualitative aspects of experience. They are discriminated, although not classified. Yet they also exhibit Peirce's secondness, because they are brute as givens – they are resistant to efforts of the will to force them out of awareness. At the same time, in terms of Peirce's semiotics proper, sense-one percepts are ready to function iconically insofar as they are qualitatively independent of considerations of what caused them and of anything to which they might belong – yet in being independent of causal considerations, they are not therefore abstractions from temporal (and often spatial) locations at individual moments in actual experiences. Thus, they also function indexically insofar as they have an impact that forces attention beyond them to other experiences.

However, there is another sense of 'percept' in Peirce's scheme that gives percepts more than the status of brute initiating conditions of perception.[4] Percepts in this second sense are reached after judgment has done its work. In this second sense, the term 'percept' refers to the product of perceptual judgment. For example, Peirce refers to a perceived inkwell as a percept. Such an object is classified and therefore must be an interpreted object that provisionally terminates a judgmental act. The inkwell is what is perceived after the thing (percept [1]) constrains interpretation so that the thing is judged to be an inkwell. Thus, percepts (2) result from the transformation of percepts in the first sense. This transformation takes place within the process of judging, and it is through this process that the uninterpreted but compulsive phenomenon confronted by consciousness becomes an object of a completed judgment. In terms of Peirce's categories, percepts in sense 'two' are thirds.

Perceptual judgment, then, begins with sense-one percepts, which, it seems, are completely dumb. They are vague with respect to character, and they await sufficient determination that is required for them to be identified and thus intelligible. However, it is important to notice that they are experienced objects, and, although as yet uninterpreted, they are not things-in-themselves that are independent of consciousness and with no possibility in principle of being made intelligible. This is to say that they are not objects separated from our minds so that they remain forever mysterious. In fact, there is reason to suggest that Peirce saw in them a primitive, or at least a proto-interpretive, element. In more than one place, he refers to percepts as what are real and at the same time as what are semiotic. For instance, in discussing reals – the term 'real' referring to objects that are ordinarily considered to be independent of thoughts – he says that 'Reals are signs' and that they are not by nature different from consciousness. If I am correct about the two senses of 'percept,' then Peirce must here refer to percepts in both senses. As real, they are percepts-one. As signs, they are percepts-two. However, even as percepts-one, they must be disposed to constrain experience, even if the constraining does not (yet), in this brute state, have direction or purpose.

In a puzzling but fascinating and suggestive passage, Peirce indicates that a percept as a real thing is a 'sciousness' rather than a consciousness. The passage is as follows: 'Reals are signs. To try to peel off signs & and get down to the real thing is like trying to peel an onion and get down to onion itself, the onion per se, the onion an sich. If not consciousness, then, sciousness, is the very being of things; and consciousness is their co-being.'[5] This notion of sciousness, I think, points to the extent to which Peirce sees interpretation shading off into the most brute data that confront consciousness. A sciousness is an object of consciousness that is prior to one's explicit awareness of being conscious. (Sartre thought of this as prereflective consciousness.) Another way to characterize such an experience is to say that it is conscious activity that, if not explicitly, is at least peripherally aware of itself. Returning to the example of the red patch, it seems that what constrained interpretation from the beginning must have been an incipient interpretation (a sciousness). The sciousness pushed interpretation away from the judgment that it was a green ball or black cylinder. And its pressures on interpretation were such as to lead to the judgment that this thing was a red patch.

A comment that Peirce makes in a different context reinforces the role of sciousness in brute experience. At one point, where he is discussing how traces of thirdness or genuinely interpretive thought may be present in prediscursive thinking, he says that, at the prediscursive level, there is 'Pure Self-Consciousness' that is a 'germ of thought' (5.71). If pure self-consciousness is non-discursive and immediate, then, again we seem to have the germ of thought seeded in percepts – that is, in reals, which are sciousnesses.

It seems, then, that as a sciousness, a percept has a twofold function that enables it to be raised to the level at which it can be subjected to judgment. Thus, as Peirce says in another place, a percept brings with it a 'double consciousness' of Ego and Non-Ego (5.53). The non-ego aspect of consciousness, I believe, is his sciousness, while the ego side of consciousness points towards judgment and is at the first stages of the activation of consciousness. Similarly, he suggests that 'Immediate Perception' (5.55) is a prereflective and prediscursive attribution of quality to an experienced object (5.57). As prediscursive, it is brute. As attributive, it begins judgment. The incipient red patch, a percept (1), for example, is brute insofar as it is not yet interpreted, but it also contributes to the attribution of a quality to an object and thus to interpretation. It constrains our taking it to be something in some respect and, subsequently, it constrains us to see it with respect to being red.

In addition to the two sorts of percepts that begin and conclude perceptual judgment, perception includes still another component. The projection of interpretation into percepts in the first sense is made possible by what Peirce calls the 'percipuum.' The percipuum links brute percepts and conscious, discursive thought that is exemplified in perceptual judgment. The percipuum is the initial percept as immediately interpreted. By 'immediately interpreted,' I take it, Peirce had in mind an occasion within perception that readies brute percepts for fully activated, mediating interpretation. Thus, the percipuum looks in opposite ways – on the one hand towards what is brute, towards percept (1), and on the other hand towards what controls perception through hypothetical and in turn critical activity in the form of perceptual judgment. The percipuum, then, bridges both the judgmental activity and the percept in sense one. It does this as a stage of development in which thought is initiated, meaning that embryonic interpretation, incipient judgment, begins its work so that fully interpreted percepts (2) can be signs for fully articulated perceptual judgments.[6]

It is clear that the percipuum activates judgments about percepts, thus explicitly activating the full semiotic-interpretive process. At the same time, the percepts linked to judgment by percipua are instances of *sciousness*. Thus, percepts in sense 'one' bear at least infinitesimal (and incipient) marks of semiosis.

In trying to make the case for the presence of interpretation in percepts, I have said that sense 'one' percepts or *sciousnesses* press interpretation to move one way or another. However, as perceptual judgment explicitly enters perception, there is another constraining condition on interpretation. This condition lies in funded systems of signs that have arisen with prior interpretations. These semiotic conditions contribute to the hypothetical activity of perceptual judgment, which begins a process of identifying and selecting similarities between what is confronted and what occurred in past observations. Such identifying and selecting is the first stage of judgment. It is a phase in an interpretive activity that leads to results that are integrated within a system. And it is at the stage of fitting into a system that sense 'one' percepts have been transformed into the termini of perceptual judgments, as percepts in sense 'two,' which have been given determinate location within a system of signs.

Let us now look more closely at the role of percepts (1) understood as *sciousnesses* by considering how interpretation transforms them into elements within systems through an activity of perceptual attention and interpretation.

II The Continuity within Perception

Peirce's notion of *sciousness* indicates that the initiating percepts themselves are not wholly brute, but instead have a brute yet embryonic initiating interpretive component, both aspects of which constrain and propel the transformation of percepts (1). Thus, the percept as a *sciousness* is an incipient sign. However, incipient signs should not be thought of as separated from genuine signs, which emerge as perception evolves. For Peirce, percepts and perceptual judgments lie in a continuum, as should be expected, given his commitment to synechism.

Just as percepts-one are *sciousnesses* and are not absolutely dumb, so we ought to avoid regarding them as separated from the continuum of mental activity in which they occur. Likewise, the percipuum is a component within the continuum of mental activity. The percipuum is the percept as immediately interpreted and is a phase of the continuum that leads to triadic or explicitly discursive interpretation. For Peirce, this initially mediating activity of the percipuum is thus internal to the experience out of which it arises. Further, the activity that evolves from the stage of the initiating percept-one into judgment is a moment in a continuum of infinitesimal increments – a continuum without gaps, as Peirce argues in 'The Law of Mind' (6.107–26). It is because of this continuity that the interpretive moments of hypothetical judgment shade off into all levels of experience. And it is because of continuity that he can say that there is 'Interpretation *in Feeling*' itself (8.185). Feeling, then, is fundamentally an initiating phase in an evolving process.

In spite of their continuity, however, Peirce does mark the distinctions among the phases, percept-one, percipuum, judgment, and percept-two. And this brings us to another Peircean insight.

Peirce's analysis depends on his own special way of marking distinctions. Everything that has been said about the status of percepts-one presupposes an abstraction or, more precisely for Peirce, a prescision, from a richer experience – from experience that is shot through with thirdness as well as secondness. Thus, pre-interpreted brute experience is not a presupposition for interpretation, but instead has direct experiential force. Qualitative presences are events within the richer experience of perceiving that there is a felt resistance that prompts the prescinding of some given compulsive experiential condition from its context. Peirce's conception of prescinding discriminates an aspect of experience that is encountered in an actual experience including mediated experience, resistance, and qualitative immediacy.[7]

Peirce's suggestions that there are internal relations among these aspects of experience seem to imply that there is no extraconceptual, mind-independent condition that contributes to constraints on interpretation. In other words, Peirce seems to be a conceptualist or a semiotic idealist of some sort. However, I do not think that conceptualism or idealism follows for Peirce. And the reason for rejecting conceptualism is absolutely crucial to seeing the full force of his insights. This reason lies in the notion of the dynamical object. The dynamical object provides externality (without a duality of internal-external sources) in the form of a constraining from one side of what we experience. It is the condition of brute resistance, and it is manifest in firsts that are present in seconds, or events. That is, it is manifest in the pressures of qualitative experiences that resist in one way or another the ways we perceive. Dynamical objects are not unrelated to mind, but rather are conditions for each instance of mental activity so that each semiotic process is constrained by a presemiotic initiating force that resists complete insulation or the internalizing of semiosis within itself.

It may be helpful to introduce an illustration. Suppose that one of my teeth aches when I drink liquids. I interpret this as a sign of some impairment or malady. Thus, an interpretant is determined in which my pain is regarded as a representation or sign. The pain is an index of something. In turn, my dentist is able to refine this sign after learning that the pain occurs only when the offending liquids are hot. He says that the pain is a sign of bacterial infection. Thus, according to Peirce's semiotics, the pain is now a more refined index linked with symbolic activity. This index refers to an infection, which is understood as the effect of bacteria that produce gas and thus pressure inside the tooth.

What initiates this semiotic process is a pole in a dyadic, causal relation. It is the activity of the bacteria that causes gas, which in turn causes pressure and the felt pain. The initial condition contributes to the origin of a series of dyadic relations, and the outcome is a series of interpretive acts. Thus, my report of pain determines a mental representation of the pain for both the dentist and me. My report is indexically related to the pain, which *caused* my reaction and is expressed in the report, just as the bacterial gas caused the pain. However, once I reacted, interpreting the pain as an index of something and reporting this to the dentist, triadic relations were invoked, because the dentist understood general laws or regularities that are applicable to the correlation of pain, hot liquid, the behaviour of gases, and so on. This knowledge enabled the dentist to determine a mediating connection between symptom and cause. The pain is an indexical sign of bacteria with respect to, or by virtue of, the laws of bacterial activity.

Without probing the complexities of the example further, it is possible to apply it to the origin of interpretation as it is conditioned by a dynamical object. The originating dynamical object is a condition that, in time, is first manifested in the experience of pain. The dentist's representation of the pain as a symptom or effect construes the pain as an immediate object, which is the dynamical object as interpreted. In this case, the immediate object is recognized as the pain, the dynamical object itself being that which constrains experience and is interpreted as pain, and thus as an immediate object. However, as indicated earlier, constraints are also present in the system of signs that constitute what the dentist knows about toothaches, bacteria, and so forth. Thus, interpretation yields a complex immediate object, namely, the dynamical object interpreted as bacteria and gases. Because of the dentist's role, the dynamical object as initially manifest in pain has been brought into the dentist's interpretive sights. Its interpretation in the form of the immediate object then can be developed in terms of the laws of toothache infections rather than, for example, the laws of fractured teeth.

The interpretation of the cause of gas as bacteria, of course, depends on prior interpretation expressed in biological classifications. Yet those interpretations themselves had constraining forces that contributed to determining the understanding of them. They were phenomena interpreted as certain kinds of organisms rather than as fluid, for example. Thus, they were not immune to other external conditions or dynamical objects that pressured interpretation. These pressures were then interpreted in terms of general classificatory schemes that placed the objects to be understood in a biological realm rather than in a material domain or physical system that manifests no life.

The illustration also can be applied to percepts, percipua, and judgments. The felt pain is initially present as a percept in sense 'one.' The beginning response by which the felt pain is represented as a pain that has some source is the percipuum. Within the percipuum, the felt pain is raised to the status of an immediate object, that is, the pain as represented to consciousness. The interpretation of the pain as an index of infection and in turn as a symbolically understood sign of bacterial action is the development of the percipual action into judgment. Finally, the pain understood as a specific symptom of bacterial infection is a product of judgment, and belongs to generality or thirdness, the category under which symbolic semiosis functions. Judgmental activity arises with the introduction of the dentist's as well as the patient's knowledge of causality, conditions of felt pain, bacterial action, and so on. The result is an interpreted percept, or a percept-two, which in this case is an intelligible complex percept of pain and its cause, bacterial infection.

The main purpose of this rather extended illustration is to bring out the importance of Peirce's insights concerning the function of dynamical objects and the continuity and growth of interpretation from percepts-one into the outcome of perceptual judgment. Pushing this further would require examination of Peirce's theory of continuity that relies on the notion of infinitesimals. For Peirce, new intelligibility arises from some of these infinitesimals, so that the evolution of meaning or interpretation is found to be emergent.[8] However, Peirce's conception of infinitesimals is matter for another study. At this point, let us leave the illustration and return to two other aspects of Peirce's semiotics that reinforce this account of the emergence of semiosis out of percepts.

Peirce says in the early essay, 'On a New List of Categories' that interpretive moments appear in the simplest acts of predication. Predication, or attributing a property to an object, requires a hypothetical act of abstracting a quality from the object and then applying it to the object. Now, if this point drawn from Peirce's early writing is transferred to his later remarks on perception, it seems to me that what follows, first, is that in order for predication to occur, discrimination or an act of focusing within experience is necessary. Further, because the percipuum provides an immediate interpretation of the initiating percept, the percipuum should be thought of as requiring an act of attending that is prior to comparison and predication. Only if such attending to something in the field of awareness occurs can predication take place. Percepts (1), then, are present in a perceptual field and become linked to percipua at the moment they are selected within and divided from other possibilities in their contexts. And when attribution takes place, a classificatory act is initiated.

The second point to be added is that in classifying, attention, I think, must be abductive, which means that the percipuum begins a creative discovery of what is given in the field of experience. If so, then a sense-one percept must be the seed of creative discovery, which is then taken up and expressed in the percipuum. And, as already indicated, the outcome of percipual activity is judgment, which becomes integral to discursive, mediating thought.[9] These additional points, of course, deserve to be explored further. The way focusing and attending to a field of experience contribute to the emergence and evolution of semiosis is a study in its own right. And the role of abduction as a creative discovery that is present at the very origin of meaning is perhaps even more crucial to understanding Peirce. However, I must bring these comments to a conclusion. In doing so, I would like to add some suggestions about where the discussion has led us.

Before I make these suggestions, however, it is proper to raise an issue concerning the significance of this account of interpretation – or, more accurately, my attempt to state and develop some aspects of Peirce's account. It may be asked whether Peirce, or my account, explains the process of interpretation. Does the account tell us how percepts are transformed into judgments? Although my purpose here is not to propose an account of Peirce on perception in terms of proposing an explanation, this question poses a challenge and should be answered, even though all too briefly.

III Peirce's Account and Its Explanatory Function

Whether Peirce's view of the origin of perception constitutes an explanation cannot effectively be addressed without reflection on what is expected of an explanation, or what kind of answer is wanted when one asks, 'How does such-and-such happen?' Is this a demand for a psychological or a biological theory? Is it a demand that philosophy be as specific as the special sciences in saying how something occurs? Consideration here of this issue obviously will only scratch the surface; the problem of explanation and prediction is extremely complex, and I can only suggest what I believe are some of the general expectations assumed when one asks for an explanation.

One expectation of an answer to the question 'How?' is that an explanation refers to causes and that predictions can be made on the basis of referring to these causes in conjunction with references to circumstances. Another way to put this is to say that an explanation should offer a statement of laws and correlated circumstances that enable the thing to be explained (the explanandum) to be predicted or deduced. If this is the kind of explanation asked for, then Peirce's account does not offer an explanation. It does not consist of a theory that makes possible predictability and deduction of specific instances and the properties of percepts and perceptual judgments. As I shall point out in a moment, Peirce's discussion does not intend this.

A second expectation supposed by the question 'How?' is that the explanandum be assigned a place in a larger framework – a system or scheme. The strongest version of this sense of explanation is that the explanandum should follow necessarily from more general rules, principles, or laws, and that the thing to be explained itself should lead to or be instances of patterns of necessary consequences (an objective idealist such as Brand Blanshard might expect this requirement), or further laws or rules.

At this point, an additional problem that might be posed by a possible critic should be faced. It seems clear that the second as well as the first sense of 'explain' could make prediction possible. If the thing to be explained can be deduced, then surely it, or the kind of thing it is, could be predicted, assuming sufficient knowledge of laws and circumstances. However, in both kinds of explanation, even the strongest sense, there remains the issue of how precise such predictions must be. To predict an illness on the basis of knowledge about one's general health and exposure to infection is not to predict the specific severity or exact time of the illness. Nor can the exact movement of a thunderstorm be predicted on the basis of radar information and other types of data. Even the most exact predictions in the physical sciences leave room for deviation. The point in mentioning this is not to engage the problems of determinism or anti-determinism but to suggest that Peirce's answer to the question of how interpretation originates does not propose specific predictions but rather descriptions of major loci of activity that are assumed to be present when interpretation takes place. What is most important, however, is the point that it is questionable whether specific answers can be given to the question 'How does interpretation arise from percepts?' if this answer is expected to provide causal connections or correlations that would enable one to make predictions of specific outcomes. The purpose of Peirce's account follows from his anti-determinism or acceptance of moments of spontaneity such as are present in abductive processes, moments that are in principle departures whose occurrence and direction are unpredictable.[10] (I use the word 'account' in order to remain as neutral as possible about whether he offers an explanation, because what it is to explain something is at issue.)

Peirce's account does in one sense offer an explanation in that it lays open a view or perspective on the origin and development of the process of interpretation. It identifies the sorts of conditions, the limits of various stages of the process, that must function when rudimentary experiences (percepts-one) turn into more explicit interpretive actions. Further, even if all that Peirce has to say is that synechism holds or that the process takes place in a continuum, this would have a kind of explanatory value in the sense that it may alert those who want to understand how interpretation evolves to avoid the conception of it as in a continuum to be treated in terms of mathematical reasoning in which the continuum is a series of discrete elements. For such a series, the elements are separated by gaps. Thus, every moment either must be related to the moments preceding and succeeding it by an invariant and thus unevolving connection, so that the process can be 'explained,' or each moment must remain separated by a gap for which there is no connection, and thus no 'explanation,' that is, the relations between moments are inexplicables throughout the process.

Some general assumptions are at work when one sets out to understand the evolution of perception, and Peirce's account is at least in part an attempt to dig out the conditions of these assumptions. He provides a framework within which psychologists and perhaps psychoanalysts might look for numerous correlations among different kinds of perception – of physical objects, musical and visual qualities, images, for example – and among these and certain kinds of bodily behaviour, and so on. Peirce himself is not engaged in psychology or any one of the special sciences ('ideoscopy') but in offering a general hypothesis about conditions. What he gives us is a version of the third kind of explanation, to which I now turn.

The third kind of explanation consists of providing a framework or what might be called a 'picture' for gaining a perspective on what is to be explained. For Peirce, the picture should not be a fantasy. It should not be an arbitrarily chosen story or one that simply appeals to taste. It should be at least consistent with generalizations made in scientific theorizing, which, by the way, Peirce also says start out as conjectures. Constructing such a picture is in a sense not unlike offering the second kind of explanation, except that rigorous deductions are not in order. The picture or second kind of explanation is more like a component in a larger scheme, what Peirce hoped for as an architectonic. It would then give the reader a perspective within which to place phenomena such as perception in relation to other phenomena – physical process (following reversible laws) in conjunction with biological and psychological processes (following irreversible laws), and these in relation to a notion of what the universe might be like in its origins and where it might be headed, if anywhere.

It should be obvious, then, that Peirce's perspective and his account are not designed to explain in the sense of strict deducibility, any more than they are intended to make specific predictions. Thus, asking how B evolves from A is not to ask that B be shown to be deducible from A so that knowing A is already to have known B. That is, one is not trying to reduce B to A but to give a picture of what may intervene between the two on occasions when B advances beyond A, that is, when B has properties not present in A and when those properties are departures from the regularities that were functioning before B occurred. And it should be acknowledged, as Peirce acknowledges, that figurative language plays a part in such pictures. Yet, as Peirce also says, figurative language plays a part in abductive leaps in the special sciences.

The issues raised here, it seems to me, are worth probing further; it is time, however, to return to my earlier promise to see Peirce's account in the light of a broader context, a consideration that is consistent with what has just been said about kinds of explanation.

Although I am not presumptuous enough to believe that I can add insights not already found in Peirce, I do want to consider the broader context of the issues raised in the discussion. What I shall add, then, will consist of some very speculative reflections.

IV The Horizon of Interpretation

I have tried to indicate that the answer to the question of where interpretation begins depends on close consideration of what has seemed to be pre-interpreted experience. In order to see the relevance of Peirce's answer to current controversies, it is necessary to reflect for a moment on the question of what is meant by 'interpretation.' The discussion started with the assumption of a strong sense of the term 'interpretation,' namely, the sense assumed in Peirce's insistence that genuine interpretation consists in the mediation or triadic relating of thoughts. Let me call this strong sense 'discursive interpretation.' The course of the discussion also led to the idea of a weaker kind of interpretation. This is suggested by the notion that interpretation may take place prior to explicit triadic thought. Interpretation in the weak sense begins with appreciative attending to an aspect or field of experience that must contain rudimentary interpretive acts, seeds that are fit to be future ingredients in strong, discursive interpretation. Discursive interpretation, or triadic thought, of course, must be continuous with the weak sense of 'interpretation.' What is essential, however, is that this rudimentary, incipient interpretive activity be granted.

If this suggestion has at least some merit, it raises the questions: Is there any wholly pre-interpreted experience? Is there any genuinely pre-interpretive level of experience? Are there actual things, occurrences, or events that manifest Peirce's firstness and secondness and that are in some way prior to the initial impetus that prompts interpretation? Or, put another way, is there some ultimately unknowable substratum of experience – contrary to Peirce's repudiation of the conception of anything unknowable in the final sense? Put even more radically, are there specific, structured things in the world that are prior to percepts-one and that can never be known in themselves – again, contrary to Peirce's philosophical perspective? In short, does Peirce presuppose a wholly independent level of precognitive experience? I think the answer is no. All experience is a mixture of the categories so that we experience in the midst of thirdness. Thus, it is imperative to notice that Peirce's discussions of firstness and secondness are discussions of what has been prescinded or abstracted from a total experience. This total experience includes more than any one of the levels that are prescinded for analysis. Prescinding, however, is not to presuppose an experience prior to actual experience, a possibility that is contrary to Peirce's insistence that what is conceptualized must enter experience. To prescind is to abstract from an intertwining of all three categories within a continuum. And what is thus abstracted is still something experienced and understood to be an ingredient in the richer whole of the continuum. Moreover, apart from prescinding, Peirce refers to an actual experiential presence of qualitative feeling and brute resistances. Indeed, there is a pervasive fringe of actual experience that is distinguishable within every total experience, even though discussion of it requires prescinding. Thus, what is prescinded, in its experiential presence, is inseparable from at least incipient interpretive acts. There is neither a finally unintelligible, pre-interpreted stratum nor an intelligible and thus structured world of things and events that is antecedent to or independent of thought.

However, in spite of this denial, and even though there is no experience that is totally devoid of interpretation, it does not follow that Peirce was a semiotic idealist. Perhaps this point can be emphasized in terms of an image. Let me suggest that precognitive, that is, prediscursive, experiential, qualitative and compulsive pressures for Peirce may be regarded as a horizon at which intelligibility arises. As Peirce put it in 'On a New List of Categories,' thinking is initiated through a demand to bring the manifold of inchoate experience to unity (1.545–59). Thus, the move towards making the horizon intelligible is the move of bringing an aspect of the field into focus – an act of attending to a segment of it. The pre-interpreted beginning, then, becomes no longer foreign to the interpreted experience. Focusing attention articulates the link needed between the other side of the horizon and the inner side of the horizon. Focusing, in other words, links the side categorized in terms of secondness, and pointed to by Peirce's notion of the dynamical object, with the side that is to come to the fore as his immediate object or the object interpreted by thought. The far side is the condition of brute seconds, and the inner side is the outcome of attention and abductive or imaginative experience that can be brought into relations.

The notion of the horizon suggests a janusian condition of cognitive experience and, I would add, of the structure of the world.[11] At this horizon, the world to be interpreted appears as a range of transcendent conditions. When contemporary theories of knowledge and metaphysics push the outward-facing Janus to an extreme, Janus is supposed to look at this transcendent side as an independent world that remains to be conquered by thought. When the inward-facing side of Janus is pushed to the extreme, Janus is supposed to look at a world that is not transcendent but is a pure presence. In this case, Janus abandons the hope of seeing an outer side, turning away from it in disdain, as if it could not be there. The only world is a world that is ours and not an other's. Its constraints are ours alone, which is to say that they are subject to and are within the mental processes of the community of inquirers.

The direction and emphasis we give to one or both sides of the janusian horizon determines the philosophical stance we adopt. The first stance, which imposes an extreme emphasis on the outer side, gives us traditional realism, by which I refer to a view that the ideal of knowing is to match thought with the specific structure of an independent reality. On the other hand, the second philosophical outlook, which stresses the inner side, gives us conceptual and linguistic insulation, or, in other words, conceptualism, or, at best, internal realism. Thus, we are cut off from an unknowable, independent reality, and we reject or ignore entertaining even the possibility that there is a condition of extralinguistic, extraconceptual constraints on our insulated world of interpretation.

However, I do not think we must choose between these two extremes. When pushed more gently, the transcendent, outer side of the horizon need not be severed from the horizon, as it is for both of the extreme views. The outer side may instead be regarded as having a constraining role without needing to be a determinate and structured world. The outer side may still force thought one way rather than another, even though it is not hypothesized to be a structured, independent reality. We need not look towards the horizon by facing exclusively in one of the two opposite directions. In approaching transcendent conditions on the horizon, then, there is a way in between the extremes, and this way, I think, is the way of Peirce. Let me conclude this discussion with a brief expansion of the Peircean way of avoiding the two janusian extremes.

V   Conclusion

This third way is linked to the suggestion made earlier about pre-interpreted experience. For Peirce, there is after all no purely or absolutely brute experience. We do not and cannot even begin experiencing anything of which we are aware – that is, we cannot begin experiencing consciously, where consciousness is still not reflexive – without acting in the midst of interpretation, even if interpretation is of the most rudimentary sort and is an infinitesimal moment of abduction. This experiential presence that cannot escape some increment of interpretation is the horizon to which I have referred. Thus, the direction of a Peircean account of the origin of interpretation leads to the conclusion that there is no uninterpreted experience. However, this is not an anti-realist view. The crux of the Peircean account is the point that although the fringe of experience is experienced, and thus, in at least the weak sense, is interpreted, all interpretation is under constraints. One source of these constraints is Peirce's dynamical object. To be sure, the constraints are experienced negatively so that their force on interpretation must occur as resistance rather than as positive, characterized direction. Yet each moment of resistance limits the positive direction that can be taken, and this suggests an external condition, which is the dynamical object. This is what functions on the outer side of the horizon. And it is what stands at the most fundamental level of the conditions of interpretation.[12]

Notes

1 The following discussion is an extensively revised version of a paper presented at meetings of the Académie du Midi, June 1993, in Tuchan, France.
2 The specific role of imagination and/or abduction in the inventiveness of scientific genius has been discussed at some length by a few others, including my colleague Douglas R. Anderson, in *Creativity and the Philosophy of C.S. Peirce* (Dordrecht/ Boston/ Lancaster: Martinus Nijhoff Publishers 1987), see especially ch. 3.
3 Charles S. Peirce, *Collected Papers of Charles Sanders Peirce*, 8 vols, edited by C. Hartshorne, P. Weiss, and A. Burks (Cambridge, Mass.: Belknap Press of Harvard University Press, 1931–58), see especially vol. 1, para 253. Abbreviated references to the *Collected Papers* will be in the form given at the beginning of this volume.
4 I have discussed Peirce's analysis of perceptual judgment and the senses of the term 'percept' in my *Charles S. Peirce's Evolutionary Philosophy* (Cambridge and New York: Cambridge University Press 1993), 154–8, and in an earlier version of this discussion in 'In and Out of Peirce's Percepts,' *Transactions of the Charles S. Peirce Society* 26, no. 3 (Summer 1990): 271–308. A seminal essay on Peirce's account of perception is found in Richard J. Bernstein, 'Peirce's Theory of Perception,' in Edward Moore and Richard Robin, eds, *Studies in the Philosophy of Charles Sanders Peirce: Second Series* (Amherst: University of Massachusetts Press 1964), 165–89.
5 A letter, VB2a(1) CSP-FCR (no. 42) Milford, Pa. To Russell: 7/3/05. I am indebted

to Douglas Anderson for alerting me to this passage. After writing this, I should add, I discovered that Joseph Brent considered the same passage in his *Charles S. Peirce: A Life* (Bloomington and Indianapolis: Indiana University Press 1993).

6 An interesting comparison – one that I had in mind in earlier versions of this paper – would suggest that this perceptual activity is a rudimentary stage of thought corresponding to R.G. Collingwood's imaginative experience, which is both creative, perhaps in Peirce's sense of abduction, and considered by him to be the first and necessary stage of all thinking. *Principles of Art* (Oxford: Clarendon Press 1938).

7 I think that this account of the integral relation of prescinding to a rich, qualitative experience is suggested by Peirce's early paper 'On a New List of Categories.'

8 One of Peirce's discussions of infinitesimals in continua that I have in mind is found in Peirce's 'Law of Mind' (6.112–26). I have discussed this topic in my *Charles S. Peirce's Evolutionary Philosophy*, ch. 4.

9 It would be interesting in an expanded study of this locus of originating cognition to consider Peirce's notion of degeneracy. Thus, one might say that degenerate thirds, present in firsts as degenerate symbols, yet functioning in terms of iconic signs, are clues to degenerate, discursive-cognitive interpretation functioning in abductive predication or percipual activity.

10 Peirce's position on the presence of spontaneity (essential to his tychism) is argued in 'The Doctrine of Necessity Examined' (6.35–65). And his claim that his spontaneitism offers a kind of explanation (explanation in a 'general sense') is presented in this paper and in the one succeeding it, 'Evolutionary Love' (6.287–317). Both papers are from *The Monist* series of 1890.

11 The term 'janusian' was suggested to me some time ago by Albert Rothenberg, both in conversation and in his writing, in particular, in *The Emerging Goddess: The Creative Process in Art, Science, and Other Fields* (Chicago: University of Chicago Press 1979).

12 The interplay of negative resistances and positive directions is discussed in the appendix to my *Metaphor and Art* (Cambridge and New York: Cambridge University Press 1989). This discussion should be pursued, I now think, in terms of the issue whether the universe is at bottom random, that is, consisting of a reality constituted by randomly acting subatomic particles or energy foci. The upshot of such a consideration, however, would not affect the point, which is Peirce's insight that some condition that is independent of any particular system of thought and perhaps also all systems of thought constrains those systems.

Sentiment and Self-Control

CHRISTOPHER HOOKWAY

1 Reason and Sentiment

Peirce makes apparently conflicting remarks about the relations of reason and sentiment. Sometimes they are quite sharply contrasted. When discussing the a priori method of settling opinions in 'The Fixation of Belief,' he comments that it makes opinion a matter of taste or fashion. His argument for the view that this introduces a capricious or accidental element into the fixation of belief rests on the observation that 'sentiments in their development will be very greatly determined by accidental causes,' and he suggests that someone who notices that a belief has been caused by something 'extraneous to the facts ... will experience a real doubt of it so that it ceases to be a belief' (W3:253).[1] It thus appears that reflective inquiry could not survive the discovery that 'sentiment' has a role in how it is carried out.

A slightly different view emerges when Peirce discusses the demands of practical life and the sources of religious belief. In the Cambridge Conferences Lectures of 1898,[2] and elsewhere, he argues that reflective, self-controlled inquiry employing the method of science cannot produce the sort of 'living belief' required for action, producing instead a kind of tentative, detached assent which is fully aware of its own fallibility. Living belief depends upon instinct, common sense, and 'sentiment.' His position, which he describes as 'conservatism' and 'sentimentalism,' acknowledges the role of sentiment in the formation of (real) belief: but the consequence of this recognition is not the living doubt that he predicted in 'The Fixation of Belief' or any kind of sceptical gloom. The consequence is, rather, a deep mistrust of reason and reflection in connection with any matters of vital importance.

But there are other passages in which Peirce claims that sentiment has an ineliminable role even in reflective deliberation and scientific inquiry.[3] In 'The

Doctrine of Chances,' we learn that induction rests upon the altruistic 'logical' sentiments of faith, hope, and charity: and it is noteworthy that this paper is a sequel to 'The Fixation of Belief,' where he had claimed that an origin in sentiment was fatal to a belief's stability. And in 1868, he wrote that an altruistic 'sentiment' which is 'entirely unsupported by reasons' is 'rigidly demanded by logic' (W2:272). A number of passages from towards the end of his life similarly emphasize the 'sentimental' basis of all reasoning.

Peirce's discussion of these topics is related to his later concern with *self-control*. Rationality involves self-control: an agent is rational to the extent that he or she is able to monitor actions and deliberations, taking responsibility for how well they are conducted and for their successes and failures. Anything limiting such self-control in carrying out an activity prevents our carrying it out in a fully rational manner, and limits the degree to which we can be held responsible for its upshot. Pragmatist logicians typically study logic and methodology by applying this truism about rationality to the forms of conduct which are the primary concern of logic: inquiry and deliberation. A rational agent is better equipped to regulate those 'activities,' having the ability to distinguish good deliberations from bad and being motivated to repudiate those inferences and methods of inquiry which do not come up to scratch.

One might see Peirce's late insistence that logic depends on ethics and aesthetics as a recognition of this. The attempt to ground logic in the other 'normative sciences' is part of a search for an understanding of norms which could provide a unified model of self-control, and hence of rationality; and it was central to his attempt to defend pragmatism in the Harvard Lectures of 1903. Later developments in his thought display a growing sense of the demands and complexities of self-control. For example, one might naturally judge that if some of our beliefs and responses are instinctive, or if our reasoning is influenced by our sentiments or emotions, this limits our self-control and rationality. But Peirce increasingly insisted that instinct and sentiment were *required* for rational self-control rather than being in conflict with it. Thus, in 1898, he affirmed that 'reasoning and the science of reasoning strenuously proclaim the subordination of reasoning [evidently including scientific reasoning] to sentiment' (1.673). This affirmation is connected with the claim from the 1870s that not only does 'logic' require 'altruism,' but it calls for a trio of logical *sentiments*: rational self-control depends upon emotion and affect.

This paper examines some of Peirce's mature views about the requirements of rational self-control:[4] it investigates why he thinks that 'sentiments' or emotions are required for self-control and why he denies that this should lead us to feel alienated from our deliberations. The topic is a large one, and the paper cannot deal with all the issues it raises. It is organized around the interpretation the claims about induction, altruism, and the logical sentiments in 'The Doctrine of Chances' (especially in sections 2, 3, and 7), but it also considers some other claims about sentiment and rational evaluation.[5] These topics are surprisingly little discussed: although there is an extensive secondary literature devoted to Peirce's claims about instinct and altruism, few authors have paid much attention to his account of sentiment and emotion. The main exception to this generalization is David Savan's important and insightful paper 'Peirce's Semiotic Theory of Emotion';[6] and section 6 appeals to some of his suggestions to formulate the theses I wish to defend.

2 Altruism and Induction: Eliminating the Self

In 'The Doctrine of Chances,' Peirce makes use of three related but distinct theses. The first is that the scientific method can be used to settle doubts and answer questions only by someone who is a member of a community of inquirers; since all reflective reasoning employs the 'method of science,' it follows that a sense that one belongs to such a community is a precondition of rationality. The second is that science and rationality require a distinctive ethical outlook. Reliance upon induction, probabilities, and statistical reasoning in ordering our opinions demands altruism: 'to be logical men should not be selfish' (W3:284). This altruism requires a high degree of unselfishness: 'he who would not sacrifice his own soul to save the whole world is, as it seems to me, illogical in all his inferences, collectively' ((W3:284).[7] Moreover, and thirdly, this altruism should be manifested in *sentiment*: logic and scientific rationality call for three benevolent 'dispositions of the heart' (W3:285).

Peirce's argument for these views depends upon his understanding of probability. Very roughly, a probability statement is a 'guiding principle' which determines a genus of arguments. If the chance of a coin coming up heads when tossed is 0.47, then 'it is a real fact' that 'a given mode of inference sometimes proves successful and sometimes not, and that in a ratio ultimately fixed.' Consider the inference: the coin was tossed, so it will have come up heads: 'As we go on drawing inference after inference of the given kind, during the first ten or hundred cases the ratio of successes may be expected to show considerable fluctuations; but when we come into the thousands and millions, these fluctuations become less and less; and if we continue for long enough, the ratio will approximate toward a fixed limit' (W3:280–1). He proposes to define the probability of a mode of argument as 'the proportion of cases in which it carries truth with it.' This analysis explains the rationality of relying upon probabilities when the inference form in question is one which will be 'repeated indefinitely.' But, he worries,

> An individual inference must be either true or false, and can show no effect of probability; and therefore, in reference to a single case considered in itself, probability can have no meaning. Yet if a man had to choose between drawing a card from a pack containing twenty-five red cards and a black one, or from a pack containing twenty-five black cards and a red one, and if the drawing of a red card were destined to transport him to eternal felicity, and that of a black one to consign him to everlasting woe, it would be folly to deny that he ought to prefer the pack containing the larger proportion of red cards, although, from the nature of the risk, it could not be repeated. It is not easy to reconcile this with our analysis of the conception of chance. (W3:281–2)

If reliance upon 'probable deductions' is defended by arguing that, *in the long run*, the policy of drawing such inferences will serve us well, then it is hard to see how employing this policy *on a single occasion* can be defended. We might add (and note for further reference) that if reliance on such deductions receives this sort of 'practical' vindication, it is hard to see how, on any particular occasion, it can warrant belief in its conclusion. At best we ought to have the reflective thought that 'going by' such inferences will, in the long run, pay off; but that thought has no relevance to the present case where no such 'long run' is relevant to our decision.

Peirce appears to argue as follows: although *I* can carry out only one inference of the sort described, *we* can carry out lots; and so, by relying on probabilities I adopt a policy which, although it may not benefit *me*, ought, if consistently carried through, to benefit *us*. The conclusion then drawn is that if I care about how well the community at large will do, the inferential policy which may condemn me to everlasting woe can be rationally endorsed.

The problems stem from an account of probability judgments which encourages us to understand the rationality of using probabilities as a guide to life in terms of the consequences of adopting a general policy of doing so but which makes it hard to explain the wisdom of drawing just one such inference. And I note, as Peirce does not on this occasion, that it is then hard to see how someone drawing such inferences in a reflective manner can adopt the conclusion as a *belief*. But Peirce's suggestion that my sense that it would be rational for me to choose the red pack in the case described provides evidence of how profoundly I am imbued with love of mankind is, on the face of it, crazy. Suppose choosing a red card brought me eternal bliss at the expense of everlasting woe for all the rest of mankind.[8] We can see how altruism and a capacity for self-sacrifice could lead someone to choose the black card in such circumstances. But we can also see how, if he is rational and guided by self-interest, the probabilities require him to choose the red one. It is hard to see how Peirce can explain the rationality of this self-interested choice.

We need to distinguish the use of probabilistic reasoning in science from its role, in everyday life, in settling what Peirce was later to call 'vital questions.' I assume that a choice which determines whether I obtain eternal bliss or everlasting woe concerns a 'vital question.'[9] As we noted in the first section, Peirce often insisted that when we confront matters of vital practical or moral importance, we should trust to what he variously called instinct, sentiment, and common sense rather than to deliberate, self-controlled reasoning to solve our problems. Insisting that 'all sensible talk about vitally important topics must be commonplace, all reasoning about them unsound, and all study of them narrow and sordid' (1.677), he claimed that, concerning such matters 'reasoning is at once an impertinence towards its subject matter and a treason against itself' (1.671). His defence of a form of 'sentimentalism' or 'conservativism' stressed that wisdom requires us to trust our instinctive or sentimental responses to vital issues rather than the rationalizations of reflective deliberation.[10] Sentiment, he supposed, reflects the wisdom of the centuries; it guides our desires and actions without being subject to critical self-control.

The matter is otherwise in science, where we try to subject our reasoning to rigorous control, reflecting on the rules we use and on their legitimacy: 'I would not allow sentiment or instinct any weight whatsoever in theoretical matters, not the slightest.' So, during the 1890s at least, Peirce drew a sharp distinction between theory and practice: theory belongs with reason, self-control, and mistrust of 'sentiment or instinct'; but in connection with practical or 'vital' issues, reasoning and reflection are false gods, and wisdom requires sentiment and instinct to rule. If the example of the black and red cards presents a vital question, and if Peirce can show that we rely upon instinct or sentiment in coping with it, it is unclear that anything follows about the role of sentiment and instinct in reasonings (including probabilistic reasonings) which employ the method of science. Peirce's example is irrelevant to the philosophical point he wishes to make.

However, this distinction between scientific issues and vital questions probably exaggerated Peirce's considered opinion even at the time. We have already noted some passages in which he stresses the role of sentiment in reasoning, but we should now add another component of his position: his view of science takes very seriously the idea that we carry out scientific investigations as members of a community. From the 1860s, he claimed that the concept of reality 'essentially involves the notion of a COMMUNITY, without definite limits, and capable of a definite increase of knowledge' (W2:239). It does so because it is defined in terms of a consensus that is 'fated' or 'destined' to occur among members of such a community. We value our own contributions to scientific inquiry not for the truths we uncover in the short run, but for the contribution they make to the eventual progress of the larger scientific community towards the truth. And this response is reflected in a highly social conception of the self: in 1898 he affirmed that 'we' are 'mere cells of the social organism'; the concept of the self becomes necessary only as conflict of testimony obliges us to find somewhere to locate error; and to be a self is to be a possible member of some community. It is not controversial that seeing oneself as a member of community involves an ethical commitment: one's own good is more closely tied to the good of other members of the community than to that of outsiders.[11] And the organic metaphors that Peirce favoured are inconsistent with an attempt to ground these moral commitments in an individualistic contractarian manner: if my link to other members of my community is more immediate than such an individualistic picture would allow, it is plausible that it is manifested in sentiment.

To return, now, to our problem of probabilities: why should we allow probabilities to guide our conclusions about particular cases? The question has two forms: one about the role of such reasoning in practical matters; the other about the role of such reasoning in science. And the comments I have just made suggest that the questions will have different answers.[12] In connection with practical matters, we have an instinctive habit of going by probabilities, and many generations of experience have confirmed us in this practice. The uncertainties that arise when we ask what legitimates it simply confirm the folly of expecting much help from reason in connection with vital questions. In science, where rational reflection is in place, the 'altruistic' solution may not be absurd: in science, according to Peirce, the value we attach to our own efforts is inseparable from an awareness that we are contributing to the eventual success of the community to which we belong. Peirce's example was unfortunate (a result, I suspect, of the unsettled state of his thought in the 1870s): he considered a vital or practical question; and he responded to it as if it raised a scientific question dependent on rational self-control. He *ought* to have insisted that in science, where alone rational self-control is possible, our practice of reasoning depends upon our membership of a community of inquirers bound together by these fundamental altruistic 'logical sentiments.' And in that case, his cited claim that instinct has no sway over theoretical matters is itself a misstatement of the view that we should not trust our instincts about the *truth* of particular claims and hypotheses. Sentiment and instinct still ground our inferential policies by holding together the scientific community.

This diagnosis helps to make sense of a puzzling passage immediately following the announcement that those unprepared for self-sacrifice are illogical in all [their] inferences collectively.[13] As Isaac Levi reports, Peirce 'removes all the teeth from the demand for altruism':[14] 'Now it is not necessary for logicality that a man should himself be capable of the heroism of self-sacrifice. It is sufficient that he should recognize the possibility of it, should perceive that only that man's inferences who has it are really logical, and should consequently regard his own as being so only so far as they should be accepted by the hero. So far as he thus refers his inferences to that standard, he becomes identified with such a mind' (W3:284). Applied to the case of the pack of cards (and indeed to any vital question) this view seems plain crazy: why should thoughts about such heroes have any influence upon the practical decision one makes at all? But if we think of someone relying upon probability judgments in the course of carrying out scientific investigations, it articulates a more familiar and respectable thought. We need think only of someone whose investigations are wholly motivated by thoughts of tenure, prestige, or financial gain, but who acknowledges that these benefits will be secured only if his inquiries meet standards that would recommend themselves to someone possessed of the true scientific spirit – and thus, according to Peirce, capable of true heroism. The idea of a scientific community is integral to scientific activity even if one is not wholly motivated by a sense of one's identity within such a community; although Peirce would, of course, deny that the person just described is possessed of the true scientific spirit.

3 Altruism and Reason

Hilary Putnam has recently credited Peirce with identifying a fundamental problem about rationality:[15] we all agree that it is rational to rely upon probabilities on particular occasions – let us express this fact by saying that probabilities are motivating. The problem is to say why; and Peirce's example of the pack of cards appears to show that it is not enough to say that a general policy of acting on probabilities will have the result that one acts on a reliable basis on the majority of occasions. Rather than talking of motivation, we might also talk of consolation: if I choose the predominantly red pack but then pick the black card, then I am unlucky but my exposure to everlasting woe is not my fault; if I choose the predominantly black pack and pick a black card, then I should hold myself responsible for my demise. Why?

As I understand him, Putnam dislikes Peirce's solution to his 'puzzle': he sees the appeal to 'altruism' and the 'community' as a desperate device for rescuing the strategy of justifying going by probabilities by pointing to the long-term results of doing so; it is analogous to rule utilitarianism in ethics. One justifies relying upon the probability by reasoning: 'Maybe I am not going to benefit by adopting this rule of action, but I am contributing to a policy that will benefit the community as a whole, so my action will have good consequences.' The 'rule utilitarian' answer is that I have chosen according to a rule, the general adoption of which would lead to the best overall consequences. And the problem is to explain why I should be motivated or consoled by that.

Putnam's favoured answer to the problem about probabilities would appeal to 'an *underived*, a *primitive* obligation of some kind to be reasonable ... which – contrary to Peirce – is *not* reducible to my expectations about the long run or my interest in the welfare of others or my own welfare at other times';[16] and he makes a Wittgensteinian appeal to the bedrock where his spade is turned. But – contrary to Putnam – it is not obvious that Peirce makes this strong reductive claim. The references to altruism and the long run seem to favour Putnam's interpretation, but the importance attached to instinct and sentiment might give us pause. When Peirce discusses the role of instinct and sentiment in settling vital questions, it seems clear that they make the rightness of acting in one way rather than another *immediately* evident: there is no place for rational justification or calculation, which are both inappropriate where instinct and sentiment hold sway. That leaves it very puzzling what role altruism has in this immediate, sentimental response, but we shall understand Peirce's position only when we see how our instinctive sentimental attachment to an inference or course of action can itself be a form of 'altruism.' Applying this insight to the case of probabilities, Peirce seems to want a position which combines two features. First, the rightness of going by probabilities is phenomenologically immediate: we find it instinctively or sentimentally correct. But second, these immediate sentimental responses stand in some intimate relation to 'altruism.' There may yet be ingredients in the Peircean position which Putnam would dislike, but I suggest that it avoids the crude reductionism he finds in it. However, addressing this issue must wait until we have cleared some more of the ground: we shall return to it in section 7.

It is interesting to ask how far Peirce's solution to his problem is a form of nominalism.[17] Even if we understand probabilities as propensities, as determining what would happen in various possible trials rather than what does happen in actual trials, it still attempts to explain the rationality of acting on the basis of a probability by reference to a wider class of (actual or possible) applications of the probability judgment in question: we are to consider what *would* occur if we *were* to act on this probability in an indefinite range of possible cases. The problem is to understand how that can be motivating – or how it can provide consolation as we pick the black card from the predominantly red pack. Possibly we avoid this problem only if (with Putnam) we acknowledge that rationality is an irreducible element of our experience; the reasonableness of going by probabilities is not to be understood in means-end terms at all – it is not enough simply to talk about possible means-end relations, or about 'would-bes.' If this view is correct, it again places Peirce's focus on sentiment in an interesting perspective. If rationality requires us to perceive the appropriateness or reasonableness of conclusions, inferences, or procedures *immediately* (if we require immediate awareness of these forms of thirdness), must this awareness be suffused with *sentiment*? In the remainder of this paper, I want to sketch some reasons for favouring an affirmative answer to these questions. If I am successful in this, then Peirce's view may be close to the one that Putnam presents as an alternative and preferable stance.

4 Fallibilism, Immediacy, and Self-Control: Mimicking Foundationalism

All this talk of *immediacy* may suggest a kind of foundationalism which, we all know, is foreign to Peirce's epistemology. In this section I shall argue briefly that the project of mimicking (without endorsing) foundationalism is fundamental to much of Peirce's later philosophy.[18]

The claim that scientific activity rests upon 'altruism' is connected to this insistence that one should hold a detached, uncommitted attitude towards current opinions, whether they be conclusions of probabilistic inferences or the current deliverances of induction and the scientific method. Belief, we noticed, 'has no place in science': this statement appears to suggest that we should take such a detached, uncommitted attitude towards *any* opinion obtained through the scientific method. Now this suggestion raises a question about the epistemological status of a host of beliefs that we rely upon in doing science. For example, a Peircean 'scientist' must be committed to the existence of other inquirers who make up the scientific community and a host of common-sense and perceptual beliefs about the world; she must accept that scientific progress is possible and believe that by working hard and well she can contribute to it; she must be confident of the items of background knowledge used in constructing experiments and making observations; she must be confident that her sense of plausibility (her abductive sense) will serve the cause of progress and believe that attempting to contribute to scientific progress is a worthwhile and sustainable life even if she makes no permanent discoveries, and so on. And since self-control requires reflection on the methods and inference patterns involved and the ability to satisfy oneself that employing such inferences will contribute to achieving one's aims, materials must be available for carrying out these monitoring reflections.

Peirce appears, then, to confront a dilemma. We might suppose that our confidence in the methods of science or in the possibility of making progress is grounded in distinctively philosophical reasoning: the philosophers Peirce denigrates as 'transcendental apothecaries' (2.113) would defend a kind of epistemological or methodological dualism – we have a priori knowledge of the possibility of progress or of the adequacy of induction, or we defend it by claiming that it is presupposed by rational reflection and self-control. But Peirce is anxious to avoid any suggestion of there being non-scientific knowledge of reality; and the point about presupposition may give grounds for hoping that progress is possible but gives no grounds for believing that it is.[19]

But the alternative suggestion, that such knowledge is grounded scientifically, appears equally unattractive if belief has no place in science. For if we are to take an uncommitted attitude towards the knowledge which grounds our participation in scientific activity, affirming only that it is useful to accept such things at this stage of scientific activity, then problems of (at least) two kinds arise. One might think that a regress or circle was in the offing: if my 'assurance' that I can contribute to scientific progress is viewed as the result of a practical policy – having such an assurance is defended as a means of contributing to scientific progress – then it presupposes some sort of assurance that progress can be secured. And even if that problem can be overcome, so that it is 'tentative and uncommitted' all the way down, it is hard to understand how anyone could be motivated to carry out scientific activity: unless I can be confident that I am making a contribution, the rationality of scientific activity is hard to understand. There is a danger that a living confidence in the value and possibility of science is required to engage with the will, in order to motivate someone to undertake scientific discoveries; but that having such living confidence indicates that one lacks a true scientific sensibility.

What this leads to is a first description of the strategy involved in Peirce's later work. In effect, he wants to *mimic* an epistemological dualism without fully endorsing one. Without claiming that we have a special non-empirical non-scientific source of knowledge, he wants to explain how we have a basis of confidence and certainty which serves as a starting point for controlling and evaluating scientific inquiries. And this confident basis must not be merely subjective: we must be aware of the value of scientific activity and we must be confident of the value of our contribution. If we were certain of fundamental commitments, inferences, and perceptual judgments while reflectively aware that no opinion deserves more than detached assent, then we might reasonably feel alienated from our cognitive ventures. My conjecture is that an appeal to sentiment is required in order to avoid such sceptical alienation: we require a kind of acceptance of fundamental commitments which is neither grounded in non-scientific inquiry, nor detached and tentative, nor undeserved. Such acceptance is possible only if these commitments enjoy a sort of secure immediacy, and my claim is that, in Peirce's view, an appeal to logical sentiments is intended to provide this.

Before elaborating upon this claim, it will be useful to list some themes involved in Peirce's attempt to simulate epistemic dualism. We shall mention three such themes, all of which are relevant to understanding the role of sentiments in rationality. First, Peirce betrays his Kantian allegiance by appealing to regulative ideas or hopes, claiming at one point that all the laws of logic are hopes. We have no grounds for belief, concerning any question we propose inquiring into, that it has a definite answer which inquiry would eventually settle on. But inquiry would falter unless, when considering such a question, we hoped that it would have a definite answer; so it is a sound practical policy to rely upon such 'hopes.' Inquiry and deliberation rest upon a framework of assumptions and standards which function as hopes; and inquirers incur the obligation eventually to explain why those hopes were, in fact, warranted. One task of (properly scientific) metaphysics is to provide an account of reality which explains why those hopes were in fact correct.[20] Although these themes became prominent in Peirce's thought only after the mid-1890s, they were implicit in the early discussions of probabilistic reasoning: one of the logical sentiments was *hope* that the scientific community would endure for long enough to benefit from the policy of drawing inferences on the basis of probabilities.

A tension may be suggested by these remarks which will be important, a kind of ambiguity in the idea of a 'hope.' If it corresponds to the Kantian notion of a 'regulative idea,' then hopes are likely to be tentative and uncommitted. We are conscious that we have no basis for accepting the truth of what we hope for; but we resolve to behave as if it were true since that provides our best chance of success in our endeavours. 'Sentiment' suggests something less detached, less subject to rational assessment, something that Peirce elsewhere called 'a living hope.' The question to bear in mind is: what force is there in this additional claim that this hope is a 'sentiment'? And part of the answer is: it is hard to see how the mere hope that scientific progress is possible, defended on the grounds that if it is not possible, full, rational self-control is impossible, could *motivate* someone to scientific activity and to valuing rational self-control. We need to understand how hope engages with the will, and we shall find that linking hopes with sentiments suggests a way of accounting for this.

The second component in Peirce's attempt to mimic epistemological dualism exploits his claim that there are 'pre-logical sciences.' Although they use the scientific method (induction, deduction, and the rest), they are not subject to logical self-control and yield 'practically infallible' knowledge. One of these sciences, in fact, needs no foundations at all: mathematics. Although we can make mistakes in carrying out proofs, and there is thus a limited fallibility, mathematics is not answerable to an independent reality: we cannot raise normative issues about whether our mathematical techniques may not conceal from us the true nature of an independent world of mathematical objects; and our inability to do so is supposedly connected with the claim that mathematics is concerned with the full range of possibilities and not just with the real world. I do not want to say anything more about mathematics here.[21] But we should note that another pre-logical science, fundamental to Peirce's account of epistemic norms, is ethics: logic is to draw on the results of ethics (and aesthetics) in grounding our inferential practice.

Third, Peirce appeals to a range of *acritical judgments*, of which two sorts are relevant. Perceptual judgments, like 'That book is red,' although fallible, are certain and not normally subject to critical self-control. This means that it is impossible to take a detached attitude towards them: their acceptance is not grounded in a practical policy, since it results from no policy at all. Second, we possess many 'common-sense certainties' which are equally acritical and certain: these are mostly vague but present a general view of ourselves, our surroundings, and the relations between them, and offer a sort of 'folk psychology' and an evolving 'folk physics' which ground our scientific endeavours.[22] Since they are not subject to rational self-control, they are certain; but they are also 'empirical,' resulting from an inchoate mass of experience collected over many generations. Any attempt to *state* what justifies them will distort and underestimate the mass of experience upon which they have depended. Once again, they contribute to Peirce's attempt to mimic an epistemological dualism within a perspective which claims that only the 'scientific method' provides knowledge of reality: he says, indeed, that recognition of such common-sense certainties is what 'Kantism' comes to when we abandon the horrors of the transcendental perspective. These too link with our theme. Peirce describes such commonsense certainties as 'instincts' and links them with sentiments; we have to understand why it was important for him to do so.

5 Sentiment and Self-Control

Peirce's most detailed explanation of the role of sentiments and emotional responses in reasoning is found in a lecture delivered to the Lowell Institute in Cambridge in 1903 (1.91ff). Peirce's target is the German logicians who attempt to ground logic psychologically by appeal to a feeling of logicality. Noting the parallels between such views and those who ground ethics in a feeling of approval, and recognizing that such views lead to subjectivism and relativism, Peirce undertakes to 'describe the phenomena of controlled action' and to make sense of the role of feeling in deliberation and action. Those he criticizes are rightly sensitive to the role of feeling and pleasure in these phenomena, but they misinterpret this role by insisting that only pleasure or the thought of it can motivate people to act. We do not treat inferences or ends as good because they give us pleasure; rather, they give us pleasure because we find them good. We take pleasure in doing what we find to be good, but we do not do it for the sake of this resulting pleasure. The cases Peirce considers involve practical deliberation, but the points he makes apply to more theoretical inquiry as well. Moreover, although pleasure is not an emotion, it is plausible that our sentiments and emotions are primarily manifested in feelings such as pleasure and displeasure.

Employing his categories, Peirce contrasts three ways in which we reflect on our 'ideals of conduct.' Certain kinds of conduct have 'an esthetic quality': we judge them 'fine,' taking pleasure in their firstness. Our ideals can conflict, and we find such inconsistencies 'odious' and strive to eliminate them: we consider them in their secondness. And, third, we explore what living by such an ideal would be like, assessing in detail the aesthetic qualities and potential conflicts of the consequences of accepting such an ideal. Deliberation about the acceptability of such ideals can lead us to a general intention to adopt them: we propose rules and strategies designed to enable us to carry out these general intentions. The use of expressions like 'esthetic quality' and 'odious' shows that the endorsement of ideals and repudiation of inconsistencies does not take the form of propositional assent: our judgment is manifested in feeling.[23] Indeed, our conscious formulation of an ideal and our decision to adopt it depend upon evaluations which are primarily sentimental, primarily a matter of feeling. It is only by trusting such aesthetic responses that we can formulate plans and direct our lives.

The same holds when we reflect upon our attempts to achieve our ideals and goals. Recognition that we acted as we decided and that this accorded with our general intentions and ultimate ideals takes the form of 'a judgment and a feeling accompanying it, and directly afterward a recognition that feeling was pleasurable or painful.' Notice that the pleasure *follows* the judgment: we do not notice the pleasure and conclude that we acted well; we judge that we acted well and thus feel pleasure. Our actions are not carried out for the sake of the pleasure we derive from reflecting on their success. The pleasure is a kind of non-discursive acknowledgment of the goodness of our ends and the successes of our actions. As David Savan argued, Peirce defends a cognitivistic account of the emotions and sentiments: our feeling of pleasure is a cognitive state. Our pleasure in our action is the form taken by our knowledge that we acted reasonably and appropriately. Ideals inform our conduct and can be interpreted in our feelings even if they are not precisely articulated or formulated.

Philosophical aesthetics and ethics (both pre-logical sciences) do not offer help in resolving practical issues: they attempt to describe and explain our capacities for aesthetic pleasure and self-controlled action by investigating what it is possible to admire unconditionally, and what it is possible to adopt as an ultimate end for conduct: ethics considers 'as a matter of curiosity, what the fitness of an ideal of conduct consists in, and to deduce from such definition of fitness what conduct ought to do.' Peirce comments that many people doubt the 'wholesomeness' of such study: his own view appears to be that so long as we recall that it is a purely theoretical study and (I suppose) don't allow it to alter our habits of living, no serious harm is likely to be done. Skipping many obscurities and complexities, Peirce's view is that what can be admired without reservation, and what can be sought as an ultimate aim, are reason and its growth. Our sense of pleasure in our deliberations responds to their rationality and to the reasonableness of our ideals. Our conscience constrains us to 'make our lives more reasonable,' and Peirce concludes: 'What other distinct idea than that, I should be glad to know, can be attached to the word 'liberty'? We take pleasure in acting and reasoning freely and reasonably.

Peirce is trying to develop an account of how the role of sentiment and feeling in reasoning and inquiry does not reveal the limits of rational self-control. That we trust our logical sentiments can be a sign of our wisdom and rationality: our instinctive sense of what actions and reasonings are to be trusted can reflect our grasp of what is required of a reasonable agent. This connection between sentiment and rationality, according to Peirce, explains why turning our back on reflective self-control in connection with vital questions diminishes neither our rationality nor our freedom. Our sentimental attunement to the demands of reason exceeds our intellectual understanding of what rationality involves.

If a habit or attitude of mine is not subject to self-control, then it becomes possible for me to feel alienated from it, seeing it is an obstacle to my living freely and rationally. The role of the sentiment of pleasure in the operation of such a habit or attitude disarms such alienation; it is the self's acritical acknowledgment of its mental functioning. Secondly, and connectedly, it is one of Peirce's theses about emotions and sentiments that they are interpreted in other emotional attitudes: they spread. The pleasure I take in an inference spreads into approval of larger inferences which draw on this one and into sentiments of approval towards actions which depend upon the inference. Our sentimental reactions form a coherent and intelligible system which contributes to the unity of the self.

Peirce's view of the emotions receives a clear expression in the 1860s in the *Journal of Speculative Philosophy*. Emotions, he tells us, are 'predicates'; they arise when our attention is drawn to 'complex and inconceivable circumstances' (as when we are guided by instinct or common sense). 'If a man is angry, he is saying to himself that this is or that is vile or outrageous ... passions ... only come to consciousness through tinging the objects of thought ...' and recognizing the state as one of anger is a reflective judgment about it, one that indicates, normally, that the anger is beginning to subside.[24] Thus the logical sentiments are manifested in my making certain inferences with no sense of alienation, in my instinctively judging an inference 'fine' or a proposal 'promising,' and in this sense of the soundness of an inference or judgment 'spreading' to other inferences and hypotheses which depend upon it. The sentiment is a knowing or thinking, but one that is not embedded in a conscious framework of deliberation and reasons; it is not subject to self-control, but its integration with our other aptitudes and practices ensures that its instinctive character does not lead us to repudiate it as an external imposition upon our rationality.

6 Logical Sentiments and Normative Science

As David Savan has taught us, sentiments and emotions are distinguished from other 'cognitive states' by a number of features. They are not subject to rational self-control: in this, they resemble perceptual judgments and differ from scientific hypotheses. They are interpreted in 'affect': they engage with the will, providing imperatives that will motivate us to action. And they 'are not value neutral':[25] as we saw above, when we are angry with someone, we disapprove of him; our love of someone or something is a form of approval. When Peirce argues that reasoning must rest upon sentiment, he claims that some of our epistemic and logical evaluations must be realized in states which share the other features of emotions: they are not subject to rational self-control and they are interpreted in affect. In earlier sections of this paper, we have explored some of Peirce's reasons for thinking that this must be so. The aim of this section is to use some of David Savan's ideas to understand how sentiments serve this role before concluding by returning to the claims from 'The Doctrine of Chances' about the bearing of logical sentiments in the use of probability judgments.

Savan mentions two specific areas where views about the emotions are relevant to Peirce's work. When in 'The Fixation of Belief' Peirce speaks of doubt as being an unsettled state which motivates us to carry out inquiries, he has in mind the way in which confict in our beliefs disturbs our normal easy satisfaction with our opinions, and evokes an emotional response which is interpreted in affect, in a determination of the will. Savan refers to this as 'an affective theory of doubt and belief' (327). When put together with the remarks of the previous section we get a picture of the cognitive agent as someone who (so to speak) trusts his or her cognitive emotions: allowing them to transfer from premisses to conclusions and trusting them to provide guidance about when to question our assumptions and carry out deliberate investigations; feeling confident that they put us into harmony with the good, that the evaluations they express are the ones that rationality depends upon.

In the last section of his paper, Savan writes:

> Our twentieth century has almost lost the sense of a distinction between the emotions and the sentiments. The sentiments are enduring and ordered systems of emotions, attached either to a person, an institution, or, in Peirce's case, a method. Love is the prime example of a sentiment. One who loves will be joyful but also sad, angry, and jealous, and also fearful and careless. But the joy and sadness, jealousy and carelessness, anger and fear are all bound together within one sentiment of love. Just as Peirce spoke of methods of fixing belief, the logical sentiments are ways of fixing emotions. (331)

The inquiring self is commanded by a stable system of emotional attitudes, by fundamental values which govern the instinctive responses which guide his or her reasonings and inquiries. Without such a sentimental grounding, the method of science could not be sustained: confidence in our premises has to produce confidence in our conclusions; surprising conclusions must provoke pressing questions about our premises.

We need this cognitive confidence which only sentiments and their attendant emotions can sustain.[26] It seems to me that David Savan was exactly right when he argued that, for Peirce, the 'aim' of these logical sentiments is 'true stability in our beliefs and in our lives,' asserting that they 'convert the goal of stability into a norm for criticizing, rationalizing and controlling our emotions' (331). Moreover, altruism and the other logical sentiments alluded to above are aspects of love or *agape*, the fundamental logical sentiment: unless we possess this kind of identification of our own good with that of the community (and indeed with that of the universe) we cannot possess the required confidence in our ability to control our emotional responses to beliefs, inferences, and inquiries.

From the late 1890s, Peirce insisted that logic was the third of a trio of normative sciences and that it depended upon ethics and aesthetics. He suggests that, unless we carry out investigations in ethics and aesthetics, our claim to be able to subject our inquiries to rational self-control is in doubt. For logic explains the possibility of rational self-control and logic depends upon ethics and aesthetics. There is no space to explain in detail why he takes this view, but it will be useful to make a comment about it.

We might wonder whether our logical sentiments do in fact serve our cognitive needs, whether trusting them will enable us to arrive at stable answers to our questions and to make progress towards the truth. In fact, Peirce insists that there is no guarantee of such cognitive progress: at best we are rational to *hope* that our inquiries will succeed and to hope that our logical sentiments will serve our purposes. Moreover, reflecting upon my own responses to arguments and methods, I might wonder whether these habits of sentimental response are not idiosyncratic and irrational: am I right to trust my instincts and sentiments? Confidence in inquiry requires both that these hopes are genuinely motivating and that my putative logical sentiments are experienced as expressions of defensible logical and epistemic norms. I have already argued that these hopes can be motivating only if they are manifested in sentiments, in something that engages with the will. But the second worry remains, that the evaluations expressed by my sentiments may not be in accord with the demands of rationality. And the passage from 'The Fixation of Belief' cited in the first paragraph of this paper suggests that Peirce was alert to this problem. Since 'sentiments in their development will be very greatly determined by accidental causes,' we need an understanding of why our logical sentiments can be trusted. Ethics and aesthetics are intended to meet this anxiety: phenomenological reflection upon what I can admire and dislike, upon what can engage with the will and what can disturb it, upon which methods can be sustained and which must be abandoned, enables us to arrive at a description of the values which our sentiments express. By investigating our sentimental responses, inquiries in the normative sciences enable us to understand them and to satisfy ourselves that logical self-control is indeed possible. Once we recognize the role of sentiments in self-control, the need for a systematic account of our right to rely upon our sentiments emerges. Research in the normative sciences then becomes necessary.[27]

Our values and ideals, ethical and logical, are revealed in 'sentimental' judgments; the normative sciences attempt to describe the ultimate ideals by reference to which these sentimental reactions are understood to operate, and by reference to which they interact with our practice of self-control. They are 'theoretical investigations' which help us to understand why our being guided by sentiment, our dependence on intellectual processes which we do not understand or control, does not diminish our freedom or sense that we can control our lives and inquiries. And we have seen Peirce suggest that so long as we are constrained to act or deliberate in accord with 'reason,' our intellectual freedom is not put into question by the fact of our being constrained. So, it seems, ethics and logic must explain how our acritical practices put us into harmony with reason rather than compromising our freedom.

Ethics is concerned with appropriate ultimate ends for the control of conduct; and Peirce's view appears to be that any ultimate end is ethically acceptable which enables the self to function as a rational integrated unity. At one point he says that the only evil is not to possess an ultimate end; but he appears to hold that reflection on the consequences of living by some ends in various possible circumstances will show that they are not capable of achieving the kind of rational unification required for the continued existence of a person. We may question whether such unification has to have the hierarchical structure Peirce describes, that we have to be rationally ordered by reference to a single 'ultimate ideal'; and we may be disturbed by the perfunctory and cavalier fashion in which he carries out his 'ethical' investigation: but it seems clear that this view of the ultimate end is what he has in mind. We seek a specification of our ultimate goal which gives us a theoretical understanding of the nature of our ethical sentiments, which gives us confidence in our right to guide our lives with the illumination they provide.

As well as guiding our conduct in the light of ethical norms, we guide our reasonings in the light of logical norms. Peirce is insistent, first, that it is not obvious that the obligation to subject our deliberations to full logical self-control is traceable to the ultimate ideals of conduct described by ethics; and, second, we are aware of norms, and undergo sentiments, which are answerable to the need for carrying out inquiries and deliberations properly. Hence one task for logic is to formulate the 'ultimate ideal' by reference to which the norms employed in reasoning are defended. And, very quickly, he takes it that the ultimate ideal to which our logical sentiments respond is something like the indefinite *growth* in knowledge and understanding. And this, he thinks, moves beyond the individual: desiring full self-control over one's reasonings requires the kind of wider perspective he has described as altruistic.

7 Altruism and Induction

In conclusion, we must return to our attempts to understand the discussion of the red and black cards in 'The Doctrine of Chances,' and make a suggestion concerning how it should be understood. Our problem concerns how altruism is involved in our sense that it would be rational for someone to prefer the pack made up predominantly of red cards. Recall that one interpretation treats the passage as flawed: since Peirce was then confused about the different demands of rationality in theory and practice, he took an example of someone attempting to solve a vital question and used it to illustrate a point about our reliance upon probabilities when carrying out scientific investigations as members of a scientific community.[28] If we attend to cases where rational self-control has a role, the claims about altruism are less crazy than they appear. We are misled into finding them more peculiar than they are because we forget that Peirce is talking about logical *sentiments*, so that he does not deny that (phenomenologically) we find these inferences and predictive strategies immediately rational. Reflection about the good of the community has no role in our use of probabilities.

This solution leaves unexplained our sense that it *is* rational to prefer the predominantly red pack. Hence we can advance to a more complex or sophisticated picture. We draw the black card from the predominantly red pack, and with everlasting woe beckoning, we feel the consolation that at least we made our choice rationally. This is the product of the habits of inference (habits of sentimentally finding inferences 'fine') that make up our *logica utens*. These habits would not take the form they did unless we also participated in inquiries of a non-vital kind, where rational self-control has a role, and a deference to the interests of the wider community of inquirers is (according to Peirce) appropriate. Thus we receive the consolation of having acted rationally as we advance to meet our fate only because we possess a body of rational habits which genuinely involve 'altruism' in Peirce's sense. Although reflections of an altruistic kind have no application *in this case*, we respond to it as we do only because the relevance of altruistic considerations to other cases is something which engages with (and has influenced the development of) our sense of rationality.

While I see no reason for Peirce to deny this, I suspect that (from his point of view) it is not the whole story. For if this is all that is to be said, then provided I have time to think, I am likely to find my consolation rather shallow: it is the by-product of the operation of a system of cognitive aptitudes whose application to the present case is questionable. The appeal of Putnam's notion of a primitive conception of rationality is clear; and the importance for Peirce of repudiating any reliance upon reasoning and self-control in connection with vital matters seems relevant here too. His conservatism and sentimentalism ought to lead him to pour scorn upon any attempt to interrogate or understand the basis of the consolation we receive when we respond 'reasonably' to vital questions. Perhaps he would agree that we have here a primitive conception of rationality – one that does not need any rational or logical defence. And he could defend this by saying that *in such cases,* 'common sense' insists that we should go by probabilities; the sentimental responses which guide practical conduct and those that guide scientific reasoning are in harmony.

As I have emphasized elsewhere, Peirce employs two conceptions of belief or acceptance whose relations are a complex matter. 'Practical belief' is that on which we act: we trust our beliefs in planning our actions and responding to vital questions. A 'scientific belief' is something which it is reasonable to regard as 'settled' at the current stage of inquiry: it is compatible with such 'belief' that we expect that the 'belief' will eventually be revised or repudiated as inquiry proceeds.[29] It is quite possible that a theoretical proposition might be looked on as 'established' in the second of these senses, while anyone who used it as a basis for action or as relevant to settling vital questions would be deemed unwise. Our strategies for regarding propositions as 'settled' are judged by how well they contribute to furthering the growth of knowledge, whereas our strategies for forming practical beliefs are influenced by how well they enable us to put our lives in order. If 'reasoning' is to have a role in settling vital questions, there must be a substantial degree of harmony between these strategies: 'common sense' (our primitive conception of practical rationality) guides us as to when our 'logical sentiments' can be trusted in connection with practical matters.

In fact, in Peirce's own thought, there is more to be said about the integration of these different elements of our practices. Peirce's later writings employ a religious outlook which leads him to assert that 'your quite highest business and duty, becomes, as everyone knows, to recognize a higher business than your business, ... a generalized conception of duty which completes your personality by melting it into the neighbouring parts of the universal cosmos.'[30] Insisting that 'the very supreme commandment of sentiment is that man ... should become welded into the universal continuum ...,' he emphasizes that this should occur not only with respect to his 'cognitions, which are but a superficial film of his being, but objectively in the deepest emotional springs of life.' However, even if we do not share Peirce's anticipation of this 'joyful Nirvana in which the discontinuities of [one's] will shall have all but disappeared,' his emphasis on the role of sentiments in rationality cannot be ignored. Although this religious outlook may allow a role for 'altruism' even when we are choosing between eternal felicity and everlasting woe, it is important that appeal to the logical sentiments is separable from these religious views and has a fundamental role in Peirce's account of rationality.

Notes

1 There are also passages, to be discussed below, in which Peirce attacks the view, associated with certain 'German logicians,' that logical soundness may be explained by appeal to a 'sentiment of logicality,' or 'logisches Gefühl.' See MS448.

2 These lectures are reprinted as *Reasoning and the Logic of Things*, edited by K.L. Ketner and H. Putnam (Cambridge, Mass.: Harvard University Press 1992). The relevant passages are in the first lecture and are discussed more fully in C. Hookway, 'Belief, Confidence and the Method of Science,' *Transactions of the Charles S. Peirce Society* 29 (1993): 1–32.

3 One further example is provided by Peirce's assertion that 'reasoning and the science of reasoning strenuously proclaim the subordination of reasoning to sentiment'

(1.673, taken from an alternate draft of the first lecture of the Cambridge Conferences, MS435).

4 As such, it is a sequel to Hookway, 'Belief, Confidence and the Method of Science,' and a companion to C. Hookway, 'Mimicking Foundationalism: On Sentiment and Self-control,' *European Journal of Philosophy*, 1 (1993): 155–73.

5 The chronology of these Peircean themes is complex. The claim that sentiment is more trustworthy than reasoning in connection with 'vital' religious or practical matters is found throughout Peirce's writings, as is the claim that science and logic depend upon altruism. However, his ideas about rational self-control and about the importance of the normative sciences developed and matured only (well) after 1890. The later developments were probably required in order to make coherent sense of themes which had always been attractive to Peirce and influential in his thought.

6 David Savan, 'Peirce's Semiotic Theory of Emotion,' in K.L. Ketner et al., eds, *Proceedings of the C.S. Peirce Bicentennial International Congress* (Lubbock: Texas Tech University Press 1981), 319–34. Savan's attempt to place Peirce's ideas about emotions and sentiments in the context of his work in semiotics supplements the present discussion.

7 An almost identical passage appears in writings from ten years earlier, 5.354.

8 In C. Hookway, *Peirce* (London: Routledge and Kegan Paul 1985), a similar worry was raised by considering the absurdity of the response 'I have no interest in the welfare of my fellow human beings, so I may as well choose the predominantly black pack' (215).

9 The contrast between the demands of science and those of vital questions is the main topic of Hookway, 'Belief, Confidence and the Method of Science.'

10 Note that Peirce's desire to ground our everyday moral responses in sentiment does not make him an ally of ethical emotivism. He is not an ethical anti-realist and would, I am sure, have no objection to describing everyday ethical judgments as knowledge; sentiments can be the vehicles of our most secure knowledge. He is not sceptical about everyday moral knowledge but about trusting reflective reasoning in order to solve pressing moral and prudential questions; sentimental judgments are generally ones that it does not occur to us to doubt – and thus ones that we do not need to make objects of inquiry. Such views reflect his affinities with philosophers of the Scottish common-sense school.

11 Except for Peirce, there are no outsiders: 'This community must not be limited, but must extend to all races of beings with whom we can come into immediate or mediate intellectual relation. It must reach, however vaguely, beyond the geological epoch, beyond all bounds' (2.654).

12 These remarks develop an interpretation suggested in Hookway, *Peirce*, 215–16.

13 This form of words is curious. It is unclear what the force is of saying that the illogicality is a property of 'all of his inferences collectively'; does this contrast with

the suggestion that certain specific inferences (the one under discussion, for example) are irrational?

14 Isaac Levi, 'Induction as Self-correcting According to Peirce,' in D.H. Mellor, ed., *Science, Belief and Behaviour: Essays in Honour of R.B. Braithwaite* (Cambridge: Cambridge University Press 1980), 133.

15 Hilary Putnam, *The Many Faces of Realism* (La Salle, Ill.: Open Court 1987), 80ff.

16 Ibid., 84–5.

17 See Ian Hacking's 'The Theory of Probable Inference,' in Mellor, ed., *Science, Belief and Behaviour*, 157.

18 This topic is discussed in more detail, and its philosophical importance defended, in Hookway, 'Mimicking Foundationalism: On Sentiment and Self-control.'

19 These topics receive further discussion in C. Hookway, 'Metaphysics, Science and Self-control,' in K.L. Ketner, ed., *Peirce and Contemporary Thought* (New York: Fordham University Press 1995), 398–415.

20 This theme in Peirce's work is discussed in greater detail in Hookway, 'Metaphysics, Science and Self-control,' and in Hookway, *Peirce*, ch. 9.

21 I have discussed Peirce's philosophy of mathematics in *Peirce*, ch. 6.

22 For examples and further discussions of such judgments, see C. Hookway, 'Critical Common-sensism and Rational Self-control,' *Noûs* 24 (1990): 397–412.

23 A similar claim is found in William James's essay 'The Sentiment of Rationality' in *The Will to Believe*. It is discussed, and used to provide some background to Peirce's view, in Hookway, 'Mimicking Foundationalism.'

24 I am indebted to the discussion of this topic in Savan's 'Peirce's Semiotic Theory of Emotion,' 321ff.

25 Ibid., 328.

26 I have emphasized the need for this kind of confidence in order to sustain our inquiries in 'Belief, Confidence and the Method of Science,' and in 'On Reading God's Great Poem,' *Semiotica*, 87 (1991): 147–66. The latter paper makes use of David Savan's ideas to argue that Peirce (at some stages in his career) saw scientific observation as a form of religious experience.

27 I have discussed this topic in *Peirce*, ch. 2.

28 This interpretation appears to be defended in Hookway, *Peirce*, 215–16.

29 See n4 to Hookway, 'Belief, Confidence and the Method of Science.'

30 The quotations are all from 1.673.

A Political Dimension of Fixing Belief

DOUGLAS R. ANDERSON

My purpose in this paper is not to unfold a complete Peircean political philosophy. As I shall indicate below, Charles Peirce spent little of his time directly engaged with questions of political philosophy. Rather, I hope to provide a brief sketch of one dimension of Peirce's political thought, construing 'political' here in the broad sense of being concerned with the structure and health of the polis or community. My reason for wanting to do this is that Peirce seems to offer a moment of resistance to the experimentalist and pragmatic political thinking that runs from Jefferson to John Dewey and, most recently, to Richard Rorty. As his various attacks on what he called 'the Gospel of Greed' indicate, Peirce was not an advocate of what seem to many to be the worst demons of American capitalism (6.294).[1] His moment of resistance instead amounted to a subtle nod in the direction of a traditionalism or conservative republicanism that would temper two tendencies to extremes that he foresaw in pragmatic experimentalism: the tendency to over-intellectualize political practice and the tendency to enslave inquiry to practical ends. In his many attempts to outline the fixation of belief, Peirce questioned indirectly both what the proper constitution of a state might be and, more specifically, what role, if any, philosopher-scientists and their community might play in the life and development of the larger, socio-political community.[2] How Peirce understood this role is the focus of what follows. Although what I offer here is largely explicative, I believe that Peirce's moment of traditionalism is an important consideration for the kind of pragmatic experimentalism that calls for constant criticism but occasionally fails to examine its own assumptions and practices in detail.

Although Peirce worked for the U.S. government for thirty years of his life, there is relatively little in his writing that deals with politics in either practical or philosophical ways. In 1894 he wrote that he had 'read and thought more about Aristotle [at least among ancient thinkers] than about any other man'

(MS1604:3). Yet he had only 'skimmed a translation of the Politics' (ibid.). This inattention was extensive in Peirce's reading. Moreover, as Peirce's biographer Joseph Brent notes, despite living through the Civil War, Peirce mentioned it only once in his writing: in a letter to Alexander Bache asking if his work for the Coast Survey exempted him from the war, which it did.[3] Despite this overt neglect of political matters, I agree with Elvira Tarr that there is an undercurrent of social and political thought running through much of Peirce's work.[4] My hope is to bring some of this to the surface as I examine the issues noted above.

I

In *Praxis and Action*, Richard Bernstein rightly claims that 'Peirce was suspicious of the demand that philosophy should become practical in the sense of dealing with current social and political issues.'[5] Indeed, in a review of W.D. Hyde's *Practical Idealism*, Peirce maintained: 'To mingle the two – philosophy and practical wisdom – is to invite vagueness and confusion ...' (N2:161, see also RLT 107). Peirce's reciprocal way of putting it makes it apparent that he not only did not want philosophy confined by practical concerns, but also did not want philosophical thinking substituted for practical wisdom. Nevertheless, in 'The Fixation of Belief' Peirce seemed alive to the needs of both practice and theory, provided they retained their separation.

While 'Fixation' encompassed the fixing of both an individual's belief and that of a community, I shall follow Peirce in emphasizing the latter: 'Unless we make ourselves hermits, we shall necessarily influence each other's opinions; so that the problem becomes how to fix belief, not in the individual merely, but in the community' (5.378).[6] For my purposes it is this social dimension that casts the fixation of belief as a political issue. In asking how a community should govern the processes and contexts of fixing its beliefs, we ask not only about a specific kind of political action, but also about how we might envision the constituency of a healthy community. In responding to his own question concerning the fixing of community belief, Peirce gave his well-known answer: the method of science is the one we ought to follow. It is the only method that is able to deal with the 'social impulse,' precisely because the effects of the impulse are internal to the method. However, in spite of his defence of the method of science, Peirce maintained that he found elements of virtue in each of the other methods: tenacity, authority, and the a priori method. In reading 'Fixation' it is easy to overlook this fact because of the lengthy discussions in which he rejected these other methods as effective routes to truth. Peirce acknowledged, for example, the worst aspects of authority: 'Cruelties always accompany this system; and when it is consistently carried out, they become atrocities of the most horrible kind in the eyes of any rational man' (W3:251). At the same time, however, he argued that the method 'has over and over again worked the most majestic results. The mere structures of stone which it has caused to be put together – in Siam, for example, in Egypt, and in Europe – have many of them a sublimity hardly more than rivaled by the greatest works of Nature' (W3:251). Moreover, the stability authority offers makes it 'the path of peace' (W3:255) whose 'upshot has, on the whole, been success unparalleled' (5.380n1).

Similarly, while tenacity forecloses any possibility of intellectual – or moral – growth, Peirce saw in it some advantage for the individuals who employ it: 'But most of all I admire the method of tenacity for its strength, simplicity, and directness. Men who pursue it are distinguished for their decision of character, which becomes very easy with such a mental rule' (W3:256). Insofar as a community requires marines, stockbrokers, politicians, and the like, it will do well to have some element of tenacious believers in its midst.[7]

Thus, in 'Fixation' we see an initial suggestion of the political need for both theoreticians – philosopher-scientists – and practical persons. These constitute two of the three types of persons that Peirce aligned with his categories: aesthetic persons, practical persons, and scientific persons (see MS304, 1903; MS604, nd). The practical persons 'build up great concerns, they go into politics not as the heeler does, for whining, but in order to wield the forces of state, they undertake reforms of one and another kind' (MS1334:17, 1905). 'The men of the third group,' he added, 'who are comparatively few cannot conceive at all a life for enjoyment and look down upon a life of action. Their purpose is to worship God in the development of ideas and of truth. These are the men of science' (ibid.). The community, as Peirce saw it, thus required two constituencies whose goals were often fundamentally at odds: those who aim at truth through inquiry and those who pursue fixed, proximate, and finite ends through action.[8] The question for Peirce's traditionalism was how they were both to be given a role in the conduct of the community.

Peirce's separation of theory and practice and his seeing a need for both practical persons and philosopher-scientists in the community was, of course, not new. In his first Cambridge Conferences lecture of 1898, Peirce identified himself as an Aristotelian in this connection (RLT 107).[9] Nevertheless, this separation stood in tension with two related and more extreme views of the late nineteenth century, one of which was in line with developments in twentieth century pragmatism. Locating Peirce's 'Fixation' between these two views gives us a better sense of what Peirce had in mind. At one pole was William Kingdon Clifford's attempt, in his 1877 essay 'The Ethics of Belief,' to make practice fully and directly dependent on the method of science. Clifford, with whom Peirce spent some time in 1875, described a view of fixing belief – which like Peirce he understood in roughly Bainian terms – that requires a thorough inquiry prior to any belief and consequent action. If one has *any* living doubt about an idea or action, it is not to be believed or undertaken. Clifford described the story of a ship's owner who allowed his ship to sail with hundreds aboard, despite the fact that there was evidence suggesting he ought to have the ship examined. He achieved a false sense of security and faith in the ship. 'It is admitted,' Clifford said, 'that he did sincerely believe in the soundness of his ship; but the sincerity of his conviction can in no wise help him, because *he had no right to believe on such evidence as was before him.*'[10] There is much in the essay that runs close to 'Fixation,' but Peirce was, I believe, generally in agreement with William James's assessment that 'Clifford's exhortation has ... a thoroughly fantastic sound.'[11] If, as Clifford argued, it 'is wrong always, everywhere, and for every-one, to believe anything upon insufficient evidence,' both individuals and com-munities would find themselves often in states of social paralysis. Clifford wanted to wait for theoretical belief to become lived, practical belief. Peirce, even in 'Fixation,' recognized, at least dimly, the provisional nature of theoreti-cal 'belief' and its consequent insufficiency for practice; this is perhaps why he left room in the community for the other methods. It was not until later, however, that he began to address the ambiguities in 'Fixation' and to develop this point.[12] In 1905 he articulated clearly where he stood in a letter to his brother Herbert: 'With such ideas [motions of the stars], science is in no hurry at all to come to any decision and can wait for the very most superior kind of evidence. But this pro-cedure wouldn't answer at all the needs of practical life – If *action* is to be based on the knowledge sought and if the knowledge is sought while the laborers stand leaning on their shovels, evidently we must take the best guess available now and not wait five centuries to know what those laborers are to do' (L338:113–14).

At the other pole we find the attempt to make theory serve practice. In the twentieth century this position is represented both by Dewey's pragmatism and by some socialist and Marxist thought.[13] Peirce, however, responded initially to Karl Pearson, who, so it seemed to Peirce, demanded that the proper function of philosophy-science was to answer relevant and pressing social questions. In *The Grammar of Science* Pearson maintained that science, as any other 'social institution or form of human activity,' must be justified by showing 'in what way it increases the happiness of mankind or promotes social efficiency.'[14] Peirce probably foresaw in Pearson's general claim the narrower kind of instru-mentalism that was in store for philosophy and science in pragmatism, and he resisted Pearson even more strongly than he did Clifford. In his 1892 review of Pearson's book, he wrote: 'Now, to declare that the sole reason for scientific research is the good society is to encourage those pseudo-scientists to claim, and the general public to admit that they, who deal with applications of knowledge are the true men of science, and that the theoreticians are little better than idlers ... I must confess that I belong to that class of scallawags who purpose, with God's help, to look the truth in the face, whether doing so be conducive to the interests of society or not.'[15] Peirce's concern was twofold: (1) that the immediate concerns of a person or finite community were not ultimate, and (2) that the road to truth need not always follow what were perceived to be the immediate needs of any given society. Practical persons, after all, pursue fixed and finite goals, not the vague and elusive truth after which the philosopher-scientist quests. 'At the very lowest,' Peirce argued, 'a man must prefer the truth to his own interest and well-being and not merely to his bread and butter, and to his own vanity, too, if he is to do much in science' (1.576, see also, 1.45 and L338). For Peirce, the philosopher-scientist must focus on the long run, but, as David Savan claims: 'Where the case before us is unique, where it is a matter of life and death, of vital importance, of immediate practical urgency, we have only the shortest of runs.'[16]

Trying to stand in between the scientizing of practice and the practicalizing of philosophy-science, Peirce after 1877 began to nuance his notion of 'belief' and its methods of fixation. In 'Fixation' it appeared that the 'belief' sought by authoritarians and philosopher-scientists is the same. As Christopher Hookway puts it, describing the doubt-belief theory of inquiry: 'It is clear that this picture is intended to apply to scientific inquiries as well as to common-sense ones.'[17] Peirce's point was that if the quest was for a belief on the way to truth in the long run, then the method of science was the only justifiable method. Peirce leaned heavily in the direction of Clifford's ethics of belief. However, his recognition of the advantages of the other methods hinted at the need to say more about what he meant by 'belief.'

Following Bain, he adopted the notion that belief was that upon which we would be willing to act. Such a conception favours a sense of 'full belief,' the kind with which the practical person most often works (RLT 112, see also 6.538). Yet it became apparent to Peirce that philosopher-scientists, as such, had little of this kind of belief concerning any particular hypothesis they might be entertaining. 'Speaking strictly,' Peirce maintained, '*belief* is out of place in pure theoretical science, which has nothing nearer to it than the establishment of doctrines, and only the provisional establishment of them, at that' (5.60, see also 5.589, 6.3, 7.185, 7.606). If philosophy-science was a caretaker of beliefs on the way to truth, it by and large did not, as Peirce believed, provide the community directly with beliefs upon which it could act; on the contrary, philosophy-science in its highest moments offered provisional beliefs upon which it would be foolish to stake one's life.[18] Communities need practice and practice needs 'full beliefs.' Thus, Peirce had to rethink the issue of fixing community belief as livable, practical belief.

His response can be seen as an expansion of the useful roles he admitted for tenacity, authority, and a priorism. He shifted, drawing on his own earlier thought, to claiming that practical beliefs – and especially the most 'vitally important' ones – were better fixed by instinct than by philosophical-scientific reasoning. And instinctive thought was to be understood broadly, as encompassing both common sense and sentiment together with the cultural tradition that these spawned (1.657, 2.175).[19] In the first of his 1898 Cambridge Conferences Lectures, Peirce went out of his way to make this point together with its corollary: that the philosophical-scientific quest for truth was to be governed by reason – a self-controlled act – not by instinct. '[I]n practical affairs,' he argued, 'in matters of Vital Importance, it is very easy to exaggerate the importance of ratiocination' (RLT 110). The doing of things in the community cannot wait for Thales to climb up out of the well; and even if Thales were at hand it is likely that his mind would be elsewhere – and for Peirce, rightfully so: 'Thus, pure theoretical knowledge, or science, has nothing directly to say concerning practical matters, and nothing even applicable at all to vital crises. Theory is applicable to minor practical affairs; but matters of vital importance must be left to sentiment, that is, to instinct' (RLT 112). In more concrete fashion Peirce elsewhere asked: 'Who could play billiards by analytic mechanics?' (2.3).

On the other side, Peirce still resisted letting theory be directed solely by practical concerns: 'Having thus shown how much less vitally important reason is than instinct, I next desire to point out how exceedingly desirable, not to say indispensable it is, for the successful march of discovery in philosophy and in science generally, that practical utilities, whether low or high, should be *put out of sight* by the investigator ... The point of view of utility is always a narrow point of view' (RLT 113). To follow practice is to destroy the very liberty requisite for the philosopher-scientist's passions, for 'scientific Eros' (RLT 107). This was Peirce's primary quarrel with theology as he understood it. Theology has the practical goal of cleansing the world of impure thought and thus is bent on closing avenues of inquiry; yet it masquerades as a science (6.3). For Peirce, a more general submission of philosophy-science to practical ends could lead only to a more general closure of the avenues of inquiry. Moreover, the kinds of broad tychistic developments that Peirce believed necessary to the growth of thought cannot occur if thinkers are tied to addressing a fixed telos and not to addressing the developmental, and therefore general, telos of truth (6.155–7). Unlike practice, theory, as a speculative endeavour, not only requires reasoning, it *is* reasoning. Philosophy-science not only needs reason but needs to reason about good reasoning – that is, logic – as Peirce broadly construed it: 'unless the metaphysician is a most thorough master of formal logic ... he will inevitably fall into the practice of deciding upon the validity of reasonings in the same manner in which, for example, the practical politician decides as to the weight that ought to be allowed to different considerations ...' (RLT 109). The philosopher-scientist cannot imitate the tenacious, authoritative, or a priori methods of practice and meet with success, precisely because what is sought lies ever beyond the grasp. The testing of philosophical-scientific thinking is not some immediate result or specific event, but the judgment of the infinite community of inquirers constrained by the ever-receding reality of a dynamical object. As Carl Hausman puts it: 'Thus, the   end of inquiry is an ideal, a regulative ideal justifying continued attempts to bring the results of inquiries together for a community of investigators ... the referent of this ideal, when understood from the standpoint of metaphysics, is dynamic.'[20] This process of inquiry requires reasoning and reasoning about reasoning in concerted development.

II

Peirce's separation of practice and theory, of instinct and reasoning, however fraught with difficulties it is, set him apart from the subsequent pragmatic tradition. Schiller, James, and Dewey, though in different ways, had in mind to bring philosophy back to earth. This difference, I believe, involves a political difference concerning the fixing of belief. Peirce's family life and upbringing led to a practical conservatism. As Hilary Putnam points out, 'Peirce was deeply conservative by temperament,' whereas, for example, 'James was a progressive in politics' (RLT 57). Dewey, of course, led the way to early twentieth-century democratic liberalism and experimentalism. Whether or not Peirce's undercurrent of philosophical traditionalism was a result of his conservative temperament, it marks a resistance to pragmatic experimentalism analogous to pragmaticism's resistance to pragmatism. It is a resistance that argues for keeping the speculative work, not just the practical, of philosophy-science within the democratic republic.

Peirce and the pragmatists – Dewey in particular – begin with a common belief: that philosophy-science, whatever its aim, needs to be relatively free from traditional forms of authority in order to carry out its work. Whether one wants to articulate an evolutionary cosmology or make a critical assessment of particular social institutions, there is no way to be effective if authorities such as churches or political parties stand in the way and manipulate one's failure. Dewey, however, seems to argue for a wider freedom, demanding a thoroughgoing experimentalism. Peirce, while he dreamed of wider freedom for the theoretician, believed that political practice required a certain amount of authority to protect and employ a community's tradition – its common-sense beliefs and habits. He was aware that this need of the community entailed some restrictions on the philosopher-scientist's public speech: 'Thus, the greatest intellectual benefactors of mankind have never dared, and dare not now, to utter the whole of their thought; and thus a shade of *prima facie* doubt is cast upon every proposition which is considered essential to the security of the state' (W3:256).[21] There is a hint here of the fallibility of instinctive belief that I shall take up below. Perhaps more importantly, Peirce's admission of the need for some authority, while it constrains the philosopher-scientists, especially concerning matters of practice, does not eliminate their role from the constitution of the community.

The initial agreement between Peirce and pragmatic experimentalism masks, however, a decisive disagreement: that is, their views concerning the status of the political relationship between philosophy-science and practice. If we look at one dimension of Dewey's thought – a very influential dimension – we can get a picture of this disagreement.[22] Pragmatic experimentalism argues that philosophers should pay less attention to the problems of philosophers and focus their intelligence directly on what Dewey called 'the problems of men.' What Peirce feared in general in Pearson's attempt to make inquiry speak solely to the improvement of society showed up as a central tenet of the pragmatism that Peirce himself helped create. As Hookway allows, Peirce was 'anxious to distance himself from William James' promise that pragmatism might serve as a vehicle for the improvement of human welfare ...'[23] In Dewey's work, this tenet took on the look of a political program; in *Reconstruction in Philosophy* Dewey put the point directly:

> Modern philosophic thought has been so preoccupied with these puzzles of epistemology and the disputes between realist and idealist, between phenomenalist and absolutist, that many students are at a loss to know what would be left for philosophy if there were removed both the metaphysical task of distinguishing between the noumenal and phenomenal worlds and the epistemological task of telling how a separate subject can know an independent object. But would not elimination of these traditional problems permit philosophy to devote itself to a more fruitful and more needed task? Would it not encourage philosophy to face the great social and moral defects and troubles from which humanity suffers, to concentrate its attention upon clearing up the causes and exact nature of these evils and upon developing a clear idea of better social possibilities ...?[24]

By outlawing the problems of philosophy because of their unfruitfulness,

Dewey effectively subverts the history of philosophy not just in its content but, as many have noted, in its entire project. Peirce understood pragmatism's submission of philosophy-science to practical demands not as the scientizing of philosophy but as the death of philosophy-science altogether. His shift from 'pragmatism' to 'pragmaticism' in 1903 was not an in-house quarrel but a fundamental disagreement about the nature and function of philosophy-science. In the work of James, Schiller, and Dewey, Peirce foresaw the slippery slope to Rorty's claim that 'the best hope for philosophy is not to practise Philosophy.'[25] In a 1904 draft of a letter to Dewey, he wrote: 'Although I am strongly in favor of your Pragmatistic views, I find the whole volume [Dewey's *Studies in Logical Theory*] penetrated with this spirit of intellectual licentiousness, that does not see that anything is so very false ... I am simply *projecting upon the horizon*, where distance gets magnified indefinitely, the *direction* of your standpoint as viewed from mine' (L123:4–5).

The political situation, as Peirce saw it, is that the subservience of philosophy-science to social needs is yet another, more subtle, form of authority. Indeed, it is a form under which Peirce himself suffered in his work with the Coast Survey.[26] It is an authority over the inquirer urged in the name of reason itself – a reason, Peirce argues, that is 'a sort of half make-believe reasoning which deceives itself in regard to its real character' (1.56). Moreover, this kind of authority has the capacity further to empower traditional authorities, since they often determine what in fact are to be construed as social needs. In his 1901 review of Pearson's *Grammar* he expressed his fear: 'In section 10 we are told that we must not believe a certain purely theoretical proposition because it is "anti-social" to do so, and because to do so "is opposed to the interests of society." '[27] In short, the practically minded come to control inquiry. Unlike the room Peirce allowed for traditional authority in general, room for this version inaugurates the end of philosophy as theoretical and thus of the philosopher-scientist's role, as theoretician, in the constitution of the community and its beliefs. This outcome, of course, enables the actuality of Peirce's greatest philosophical fear: closure of avenues of inquiry. He repeated this fear in a letter to Dewey in April 1905: 'I was somewhat surprised to learn you found so much good in what I said. For your Studies in Logical Theory certainly forbids all such researches as those which I have been absorbed in for the last eighteen years. That is what I liked least in those four papers. First, because it is contrary to a maxim I never infringe "Never permanently bar the road of any true inquiry," ... If it were not for this uncalled for intolerance of your logical theory, I should have no serious objection to it ...' (8.243–4).

The political difference here is, I think, immense. The pragmatic experimentalist's community operates under a supposition of openness that is belied by the loss of philosophy-science and the quest for truth, wholeness, or an architectonic. We are reminded that authority can be accomplished through efficiency or finality; in making philosophy-science's very problems outmoded, pragmatic experimentalism attempts to oust it from the state and to prevent it from playing a role in the development of the community's beliefs. Peirce's own conception of the philosophical-scientific community's role within the larger sociopolitical community involves a much deeper sort of liberalism in which all avenues of inquiry remain open, though in light of an ideal hope of convergence.[28] The best political community, in his eyes, is a democratic republic that keeps the possibility of this deeper liberalism most alive.

III

Peirce's responsive suggestion concerning the politics of fixing belief might be best described as the demand for a slow transaction between instinct and inquiry. At first glance, it might appear that Peirce's separation of theory and practice, of the work of philosopher-scientists and the work of politicians, is complete. But on closer inspection, we see this is not the case. As Maryann Ayim points out, for Peirce 'reason and instinct are continuous.'[29] Peirce, most clearly in his later work, left open two lines of continuity between them.

First, instinct has a route into philosophy-science through abduction or retroduction. Abductive guesses themselves, Peirce argued, hinge on the human instinct for guessing right: 'In regard to instinctive considerations, I have already pointed out that it is a primary hypothesis underlying all abduction that the human mind is akin to the truth in the sense that in a finite number of guesses it will light upon the correct hypothesis' (7.220, see also 6.530, 5.591, 5.604, 6.476). In 'Philosophy and the Conduct of Life' he showed this avenue of continuity: 'The third kind of reasoning [abduction] tries what *il lume naturale*, which lit the footsteps of Galileo, can do. It is really an appeal to instinct. Thus Reason, for all the frills [it] customarily wears, in vital crises, comes down upon its marrow-bones to beg the succour of instinct' (RLT 111). Hookway, returning to the language of 'Fixation,' argues that 'the argument of the later papers advocates something like the a priori method in connection with vital questions.'[30] I agree and would add that this a priori-like moment – the moment of instinct or sentiment – is what keeps theory and practice from an irremediable separation. Peirce then quickly moved to show that such an avenue does not involve a reductive identity. The instinctive element of abduction is quickly converted into the matter of philosophical-scientific inquiry: 'we are driven oftentimes in science to try the suggestions of instinct; but we only *try* them, we compare them with experience, we hold ourselves ready to throw them overboard at a moment's notice from experience' (RLT 112). This line of thought showing a continuity between practice and theory, offered here in the extreme form intended to chide James for his insistence that Peirce lecture on vitally important topics, was developed by Peirce in a somewhat tempered form in his 1905 critical commonsensism. Later, Peirce exemplified it in his 'A Neglected Argument for the Reality of God,' where the notion of a vague God served both as an instinctive full belief functioning as a guide to conduct and also as a hypothesis, and thus a provisional belief, for cosmological inquiry.[31]

The line of continuity running in the other direction has to do with Peirce's awareness that even the provisional 'beliefs' of science always have potential, and occasionally have direct, bearing on conduct – on fixing the beliefs of the community (see, e.g., RLT 106).[32] In liberating inquiry from the narrow constraints of addressing particular social issues, Peirce did not need to reject the claim that the ongoing results of philosophy-science might find their way back to the realm of instinct from which they emerged. Moreover, Peirce seemed to suggest that they may even influence the fixing of belief both constructively and/or critically, though such was not the initial purpose of the philosophical-scientific inquirer. Directly, inquiry aims at knowing; indirectly, however, it may do more. In a 1901 manuscript on the idea of a law of nature, Peirce maintained that there 'is a chain connecting the highest philosophical theory with the humblest arts of life' (HS2:889). In 'Reason's Rules' in 1902 Peirce put it another way: 'If an opinion can eventually go to the determination of a practical belief, it, in so far, becomes itself a practical belief; and every proposition that is not pure metaphysical jargon and chatter must have some possible bearing upon practice' (5.539).[33] Despite the Deweyan sound of this point, it indicates a critical difference between pragmatism and pragmaticism. The meaning of the theoretical belief is in its possible – or 'would be' – effect on practice. The inquiry out of which this meaning arises need not be conducted for practice in any narrow sense; Peirce insisted on this distinction in his move from pragmatism to pragmaticism in a note he affixed in 1906 to a copy of 'How to Make Our Ideas Clear':

> No doubt, Pragmaticism makes thought ultimately *apply* to action exclusively – to *conceived* action. But between that and either saying that it makes thought, in the sense of the purport of symbols, to consist in acts, or saying that the true ultimate purpose of thinking is action, there is much the same difference as there is between saying that the artist-painter's living art is applied to dabbing paint upon canvas, and saying that that art-life consists in dabbing paint, or that its ultimate aim is dabbing paint.' (5.403n3)

Or, as he put it elsewhere: 'it does not follow that because every theoretical belief is, at least indirectly, a practical belief, this is the *whole* meaning of the theoretical belief' (5.539).

Thus, while Peirce maintained the separation of practice and theory, he recognized their continuity as well – a continuity that marked their needs for each other despite, or perhaps because of, their important differences. They exhibited for him a political interdependence. The community, whatever else it is, needs to be a republic including both practice and theory, and therefore persons of practice and persons of theory, each kind allowing the other its special role in the development of community belief. Concerning the fixing of belief in the sociopolitical community, Peirce thus left room for both instinct and inquiry. The upshots of this are several.

First, Peirce openly embraced a functional conservatism in the fixing of belief: 'Sentimentalism implies Conservatism; and it is of the essence of conservatism to refuse to push any practical principle to its extreme limits, – including the principle of conservatism itself' (RLT 111). The political authorities who employ instinctive and common-sense tradition have the weight of this tradition on their side; this requires that changes in full, practical beliefs should not be hastily performed under the guidance of provisional theories.[34] Peirce urged slowness in order to avoid ridiculous and/or dangerous precipitous changes.[35] 'I do not say,' he argued, 'that Philosophical science should not ultimately influence religion and Morality; I only say that it should be allowed to do so only with secular slowness and the most conservative caution' (RLT 108). He therefore resisted the kind of Deweyan or Jeffersonian experimentalism in which experiments might come to lose the contexts that define them as experiments – the kind of environment some of our public school systems have created in recent years.

It is important to note, however, that Peirce's conservatism, in being conservatively applied, left open a kind of middle Deweyan realm in which reason might sometimes directly affect or transform instinct in its guise as a lived tradition.[36] This is a second upshot of Peirce's politics. 'We do not say,' he argued, 'that sentiment is *never* to be influenced by reason, nor that under no circumstances would we advocate radical reforms. We only say that the man who ... would precipitately change his code of morals, at the dictate of a philosophy of ethics, – who would, let us say, hastily practise incest, – is a man whom we should consider *unwise*' (RLT 111). That Peirce had some feel for this middle realm is evidenced in his 1892 essay 'Dmesis,' where he, sounding like a religious Clarence Darrow, questioned the state's right to punish criminals (MS885, *The Open Court*, 29 Sept. 1892).

As Hookway points out, this middle realm is often largely, if not entirely, obscured by Peirce's tenacity in keeping practice and theory at a respectable distance.[37] Nevertheless, Peirce admitted that self-controlled rational inquiry can make a difference in some cases of short-run, non-truth-driven questions of practice. 'In everyday business,' he maintained, 'reasoning is tolerably success-ful; but I am inclined to think it is done as well without the aid of theory as with it' (RLT 109). This, of course, is not enough to satisfy a Deweyan and, from the perspective of pragmatic experimentalism, it seems on the face of it a kind of blindness or political naïvety on Peirce's part. Apart from his occasional forays into social criticism of the kind noted above, he did not seem to develop any thorough account of reason's work as social critic. The closest he came to a sys-tematic approach to the issue was perhaps his critical commonsensism where he admitted the use of imaginative dramatic rehearsals to affect how one would act in certain situations (5.517). Or we might consider the work of practical scien-tists as a scientific analogue to the political middle realm. Nevertheless, if Peirce is short-sighted here, it remains the case that his politics need not dismiss this middle realm altogether; indeed, his synechism would argue for not dis-missing it. His reasons for ignoring it are to be found, as we have seen, in his dual fears of the extremes represented by Clifford and Pearson.[38]

The third, and I believe the most important as Peirce viewed it, upshot of the transaction of instinct and inquiry in fixing belief is that theory, which does not begin with specific social issues, does come back to influence practice. This is an integral part of Peirce's fallibilism which he applied not only to theoretical beliefs but to instinctive ones as well. His conservative conservatism was not meant to harbour a solidification of moral and political beliefs that one knows to be in need of change. In an 1897 letter to James he put the point in a down-to-earth fashion: '"Faith," in the sense that one will adhere consistently to a given line of conduct, is highly necessary in affairs. But if it means you are not going to be alert for indications that the moment has come to change your tactics, I think it ruinous to practice' (L224; RLT 9). 'Instinct,' he argued elsewhere, 'is capable of development and growth, – though by a movement which is slow in the proportion to which it is vital: and this development takes place upon lines which are altogether parallel to those of reasoning' (RLT 121; see also 1.404). The philosopher-scientist's task is to take part in the scientific community's ongoing quest for truth. But since his or her work will have a meaning that could affect conduct, it is possible, given the second line of continuity, that it will come to have some effect on the full beliefs of the sociopolitical commu-nity. 'A theory,' Peirce said, 'directly aims at nothing but knowing. Maybe, if it be sound, it is likely, some day to prove useful' (2.1). The slow transaction maintains the freedom of the philosopher-scientist from special, practical prob-lems that produce 'sham reasoning' (5.57–8) and at the same time gives the philosophic-scientific method a voice in the evolution of community belief. It is this voice of the philosophic-scientific community, as crucial to the fixing of beliefs in the wider community, that Peirce's traditionalism sought to maintain.

IV

In his more cynical moments Peirce was tempted by a narrower, more utopian republicanism in which philosopher-scientists simply took charge of both theory and practice. In 1892, for example, he remarked that a 'modern Pythagorean brotherhood' of 300 men and women who are 'sincerely devoted to pure science' might first make itself 'not only the most exquisitely virtuous society ever on earth, but also, what is far higher in their eyes, the wisest of all the race of men' and then 'subject the rest of mankind to the governance of these chosen best' (HS2:561–2). On many occasions Peirce remarked that those who refused to think for themselves *ought* to be ruled or enslaved. Indeed, as late as 1908 he made the following comment to Lady Welby: 'Being a convinced Pragmaticist in Semeiotic, naturally and necessarily nothing can appear to me sillier than rationalism; and folly in politics cannot go further than English liberalism. The people ought to be enslaved; only the slaveholders ought to practice the virtues that alone can maintain their rule. England will discover too late that it has sapped the foundations of its culture' (PW 78).

Remarks such as these, together with Peirce's apparent acquiescence in his family's anti-abolitionism, give us pause in considering the value of the political dimensions of his work. Nevertheless, the import of his moment of resistance to the pragmatic experimentalist tradition is not so easily dismissed. The traditionalism he offered was a tamer one that required the separate but reciprocally dependent work of instinctively motivated, practising politicians and inquiry-driven philosopher-scientists, who played a crucial though indirect role in the fixing of community belief. Perhaps most importantly, Peirce offered this role as a condition of a deeper liberal spirit – one open to inquiries interested in the long run – in the fixing of community beliefs; any state that exiled philosophy-science or reduced it to an instrument for finite ends would, as Peirce saw it, lose the crucial functioning of this liberal spirit in its endeavour to keep open all avenues of inquiry.[39]

Notes

1 I think that on the whole Peirce's agapasticism, especially after his own suffering in poverty occurred, demanded a more temperate approach of any political or economic structure. Peirce references in the text are to the following editions, and abbreviations are as given at the beginning of this volume: *Collected Papers of Charles Sanders Peirce*, edited by C. Hartshorne, P. Weiss, and A. Burks (Cambridge, Mass.: Belknap Press of Harvard University Press 1931–58); *Writings*

of Charles S. Peirce, edited by M.H. Fisch, E. Moore, and C.W.J. Kloesel et al., 5 vols (Bloomington: Indiana University Press 1982–9); *Reasoning and the Logic of Things*, edited by K.L. Ketner (Cambridge, Mass.: Harvard University Press 1992); Peirce manuscripts from the Houghton Library collection identified in Richard S. Robin *Annotated Catalogue of the Papers of Charles S. Peirce* (Amherst: University of Massachusetts Press 1967); *Historical Perspectives on Peirce's Logic of Science: A History of Science*, 2 vols, edited by Carolyn Eisele (Berlin: Mouton-DeGruyter 1985).

    In addition, reference is made to *Semiotics and Significs: The Correspondence between Charles S. Peirce and Victoria Lady Welby*, edited by C.S. Hardwick (Bloomington: Indiana University Press 1977), identified as PW with page number; and to *Charles Sanders Peirce: Contributions to the Nation*, edited by K.L. Ketner (Lubbock: Texas Tech University Press 1975–87), identified as N with volume and page number.

2 I shall use the term 'philosopher-scientist' throughout for several reasons. First, Peirce's talk of theorizing often included the work of both philosophers and scientists. Second, and perhaps more importantly, while Peirce distinguished philosophers from scientists, he was intent both on showing science that it depended on philosophical assumptions and on showing philosophy that it was in need of a more 'scientific' method. There are problems that arise with this usage, but I do not believe they undermine the central points of the description at hand.

3 Joseph Brent, *Charles Sanders Peirce: A Life* (Bloomington: Indiana University Press 1993), 61. Brent also speculates that Peirce tacitly shared his family's acceptance of slavery.

4 Elvira R. Tarr, 'Roots and Ramifications: Peirce's Social Thought,' in K.L. Ketner, J. Ransdell, C. Eisele, M. Fisch, and C.S. Hardwick, eds, *Proceedings of the C.S. Peirce Bicentennial International Congress* (Lubbock: Texas Tech University Press 1981), 239–46.

5 Richard Bernstein, *Praxis and Action* (Philadelphia: University of Pennsylvania Press 1971), 201.

6 Given Peirce's semiotic-realist approach to both persons and institutions, it is also safe here to draw a Platonic analogy between the soul and the state. Vincent Colapietro puts the point similarly: 'what goes on *within* the life of an individual person and what goes on *between* the generations of an historically extended community are essentially analogous processes.' Colapietro, 'Tradition: First Steps toward a Pragmaticistic Clarification,' forthcoming in a volume from Fordham University Press.

7 Indeed, it was true for Peirce that effective inquiry itself requires elements of tenacity and authority, though not concerning a hypothesis in question.

8 The necessity Peirce suggests here is tied to his categoriology, which argues for a

reciprocal dependence among the categories. The categoriology thus suggests important roles for all three types of persons. My focus here, however, is just on the last two.

9 It is important to note, as many commentators have pointed out, that in the 1898 lectures Peirce purposely overstated the degree to which he thought practice and theory might be separated in reaction to William James's request that Peirce make these lectures deal with 'vitally important topics.' Nevertheless, Peirce stood by the distinction throughout his life.

10 W.K. Clifford, *Lectures and Essays, Volume II* (London: Macmillan and Co. 1879), 178.

11 William, James, *The Will to Believe and Other Essays in Popular Philosophy* (New York: Dover Publications 1956), 19.

12 See Christopher Hookway's 'Belief, Confidence and the Method of Science,' *Transactions of the Charles S. Peirce Society* 29, no. 1 (Winter 1993). Hookway offers here an excellent exposition of the problems facing Peirce in his attempt to separate theory and practice and still maintain a role for scientific method in the fixing of belief. Since my interest is in the political dimension of Peirce's work, I do not address all of these problems in Hookway's direct fashion. Nevertheless, it seems to me that we arrive at pretty nearly the same description of the trajectory of Peirce's thought.

13 I am aware that some Marxists and pragmatists would rather say that they are engaged in eliminating theory altogether. As I shall show below, I believe this is the effect; but it is important to see that one route to this effect is that of making theory serve practice. For a brief comparison between Marx and Peirce, see K.A. Megill's 'Peirce and Marx,' *Transactions of the Charles S. Peirce Society* 3, no. 2 (Fall 1967): 55–65. Megill might not agree to the contrast between Peirce and Marx that I offer here.

14 Karl Pearson, *The Grammar of Science* (London: Walter Scott 1892), 10. In fairness to Pearson, I should point out that his general insistence on the utility of science did not translate into a narrow instrumentalism. However, his nominalism (103) and rejection of logic as a science (39n2) no doubt added to Peirce's suspicion that an instrumentalism was lurking in the grammar.

15 C.S. Peirce, Review in *Popular Science Monthly* 58 (1901): 300.

16 David Savan, 'Decision and Knowledge in Peirce,' *Transactions of the Charles S. Peirce Society* 1, no. 2 (Fall 1965): 48.

17 Hookway, 'Belief,' 2.

18 It is interesting to note that it was by way of this point that Peirce complained to James about Royce's harsh treatment of F.E. Abbot. See L224, CSP-WJ, 11/30/90: 2.

19 For a more detailed account of the importance of sentiment, see Hookway, 'Sentiment and Self-control,' in this volume.

20 Carl R. Hausman, *Charles S. Peirce's Evolutionary Philosophy* (New York: Cambridge University Press 1993), 167.

21 Peirce's point here argues for a more subtle – if not fully Straussian – reading of the history of philosophy. However, apart perhaps from his speculations on the Pythagoreans, Peirce seems not to have taken this route in his own reading of the history of philosophy.

22 In fairness to Dewey, it must be admitted that his account of the philosopher's role is not so narrow as I allow. This is especially evident if we examine *Experience and Nature*. Nevertheless, the narrower conception of Dewey's account of philosophy and metaphysics is one that has had a tremendous impact on both pragmatism and neo-pragmatism; it is for this reason that I employ it here.

23 Hookway, 'Belief,' 3.

24 Dewey, *Reconstruction in Philosophy* (Boston: The Beacon Press 1957 [1920], 124.

25 Rorty, Richard, *Consequences of Pragmatism* (Minneapolis: University of Minnesota Press 1982), xv.

26 See Brent, *Peirce*, 169. More recent examples of this kind of authority can be seen in the National Science Foundation and even the National Endowment for the Humanities processes for funding research. A less formal example has occurred recently in theoretical physics, where students have been told to shy away from pursuing super-string theory on the grounds that it has no empirical foundation and therefore is a career *cul de sac*.

27 Peirce, Review, 300.

28 In a letter to Francis Russell in 1904 Peirce argued his own case: 'I stand for, have always stood for the very freest of free-thinking. If there is anyone who goes beyond me in reprobation of all attempts and any attempt to stifle or discourage free-thought or its proper expression all I can say is that I have never yet met such a person' (L387b, 00287).

29 Maryann Ayim, 'Theory, Practice, and Peircean Pragmatism,' in *Proceedings of the C.S. Peirce Bicentennial International Congress* (Lubbock: Texas Tech University Press 1981), 51.

30 Hookway, 'Belief,' 16.

31 There is of course some nervousness over Peirce's employment of 'God' in this essay. However, some of it might be averted if we recall that Peirce's vague God is best understood in terms of his earlier accounts of agape and the growth of concrete reasonableness and not in the terms of some more specific theological doctrine. Richard Trammell suggests the lines of continuity I have in mind with respect to the God issue: see his 'Religion, Instinct and Reason in the Thought of Charles S. Peirce,' *Transactions of the Charles S. Peirce Society* 8 (Fall 1972): 22.

32 As Hookway rightly points out, Peirce can hold this line of continuity only if he is willing to temper and modify his 'no-belief' thesis concerning the work of

philosopher-scientists. And, as Hookway suggests, this is what Peirce appears to be more directly engaged in doing after 1900. Hookway, 'Belief,' 24–6.

33 Peirce does not, or not fully at least, address the fact that the practicalizing of theoretical 'beliefs' often has a transformative effect on these beliefs. His own 'pragmatism' underwent such a transformation, much to his dismay. His own notion of evolutionism, together with his semiotics, would help to illuminate the nature of such transformations.

34 For an extended pragmaticistic account of the importance of tradition, see Colapietro's 'Tradition.'

35 It is interesting to note that in an 1896 letter to Francis Russell, Peirce identified himself with Russell's self-description as a 'democrat with socialistic tendencies' (L387a, 00257). Yet, this description was qualified immediately by Peirce's resistance to western voters who 'seem to think their business is to have opinions about questions of the utmost difficulty.' Peirce still exercised his conservatism, wanting to allow practical politicians to do their own work according to common sense and tradition.

36 Ayim makes the same point in a more formal way, suggesting the continuity can be addressed 'in postulating a third type of science whose specific task is to interrelate the conclusions and concerns of theoretical and practical sciences' ('Theory,' 51).

37 Hookway, 'Belief,' 23–4.

38 The openness to this middle realm need not undermine Peirce's concerns about these extremes. Clifford's move left the community with no statespersons, and Pearson's left it with *only* the middle realm, with no philosopher-scientists as theoreticians. Peirce's republic attempts to keep the entire spectrum at work in the community, though its focus is in preserving some practical autonomy for the statesperson and some theoretical autonomy for the philosopher-scientist.

39 I am indebted to Vincent Colapietro, Carl Hausman, and Christopher Hookway for providing comments on and criticisms of earlier versions of this paper. They share no blame, however, for its errors.

The First Rule of Reason

SUSAN HAACK

As scarce as truth is, the supply has always been in excess of the demand.
Josh Billings, Affurisms, 1865

What Peirce calls 'the first rule of reason' (FRR) is not, as those familiar with his pioneering work in formal logic might guess, some fundamental logical principle such as the law of identity or non-contradiction; nor, as those better acquainted with his theory of inquiry might hazard, the famous maxim: 'do not block the way of inquiry' – though that is much closer, for Peirce describes this maxim as a direct consequence of the first rule of reason. The key passage runs:

> Upon this first, and in one sense this sole, rule of reason, that in order to learn you must desire to learn, and in so desiring not be satisfied with what you already incline to think, there follows one corollary which itself deserves to be written upon every wall of the city of philosophy:
> Do not block the way of inquiry. (1.135, *c.* 1898)[1]

This paper has four parts: the first traces the connections of the FRR with the many other aspects of Peirce's philosophy into which it ramifies; the second suggests a way to reconcile the FRR with the account of the motivation of inquiry suggested in 'The Fixation of Belief,' with which it is, at least to superficial appearances, in tension; the third begins by distinguishing the FRR from a related tautology, and continues by teasing out stronger and weaker interpretations and arguing that, in a weak but still substantial formulation, the FRR contains an important core of truth; and the last considers the relevance of the FRR, so construed, to the condition of philosophy today.

1 The Role of the FRR in Peirce's Philosophy

'In order to learn, you must desire to learn.' So far as I know, Peirce only once calls this 'the first rule of reason'; and one can only quite rarely identify other formulations of the same idea. The best candidates seem to be: 'in order to reason well ... it is absolutely necessary to possess ... such virtues as intellectual honesty and sincerity and a real love of truth' (2.82, 1902), and: 'the first step towards *finding out* is to acknowledge that you do not satisfactorily know already' (1.13, *c.* 1897).

However, the disposition which the FRR requires of the would-be inquirer (his 'temperament' or 'attitude,' as Peirce says elsewhere) is a theme that recurs again and again throughout Peirce's work. Peirce also writes of 'the desire to find things out' (1.8 and 1.14, *c.* 1897); of 'a craving to know how things really [are]' (1.34, 1869); of 'inquiry into the truth for truth's sake' (1.44, *c.* 1896); of 'a great desire to learn the truth' (1.235, 1902); and of the 'Will to Learn' (5.583, 1898; James's *The Will to Believe*, dedicated to Peirce, was first published in 1897).

One might call this disposition or temperament the 'pure truth-seeking attitude.' Peirce himself often presents it as an observation about, or perhaps a definition of, what it is to be genuinely scientific. For example: 'Science is to mean for us a mode of life whose single animating purpose is to find out the real truth ...' (7.54, nd; cf 1.8, *c.* 1897). But Peirce's references to the pure truth-seeking attitude as characteristic of the scientific inquirer are not properly understood as straightforward factual claims about the temperament of scientists as opposed to businessmen or theologians (to use two of his favourite contrasts). After all, Peirce describes himself as a 'laboratory philosopher' who aspires to make philosophy scientific. 'Scientific inquirer,' as Peirce uses it, is pretty much equivalent to 'genuine, disinterested inquirer.'

But, of course, Peirce chooses to use the phrase 'scientific inquirer' equivalently to 'genuine, disinterested inquirer,' and 'the scientific attitude' as the preferred phrase for 'the pure truth-seeking attitude,' because he believes that scientists, 'laboratory men,' at least usually have the pure truth-seeking attitude, whereas businessmen, teachers, and theologians usually do not. At 7.51 (nd) Peirce concedes that there are a few 'self-seekers' in science – but, he continues, 'they are so few.' It will do no harm, provided Peirce's ameliorative use of 'scientific' is clear, to use 'scientific inquiry,' henceforth, equivalently to 'genuine, disinterested inquiry,' and 'the scientific attitude' interchangeably with 'the pure truth-seeking attitude.' When I wish to refer to the natural sciences, specifically, I shall mark the distinction by writing '*science*.'

The complexities of Peirce's conception of the scientific attitude can be illu-

minated by looking at what he takes to be the characteristic faults of businessmen, practical men, teachers, and theologians, qua inquirers (or qua
'inquirers').

The man of business is unlikely to have the scientific attitude because, for
one thing, he is focused on opportunity, on utility. There are passages which
could convey the impression that Peirce's view is that no study of phenomena
which is, or is potentially, of practical use could count as scientific: '[t]rue science is distinctively the study of useless things' (1.76, c. 1896), for instance.
But in context it is clear that such passages represent Peirce's deliberately provocative way of saying something both more plausible and more interesting:
that what one is doing doesn't qualify as scientific, or as genuine, disinterested
inquiry, unless the possibility or probability of practical applications is irrelevant to one's motivation. A scientific inquirer, Peirce remarks, will be just as
anxious to learn about erbium as about iron, despite the fact that erbium is too
rare to be commercially important[2] – more so, in fact, if the investigation of
erbium will contribute more to knowledge of the periodic table (1.45, c. 1890).
Questions of utility, as Peirce puts it, should be *'put out of sight'* by the scientific investigator (1.640, 1898; cf 1.688, 1898).

The man of business is unlikely to have the scientific attitude for another reason, too, a reason which also applies to the practical man. He is focused on getting things done, on action; and action requires confident belief, certainty that
one has the truth already. Peirce sometimes says that the scientific inquirer
doesn't have beliefs, but only entertains conjectures until they can be tested;
sometimes, however, he says that the scientific inquirer has beliefs, but not full
or confident beliefs, only tentative beliefs which he is prepared to give up. The
passage at 1.635 (1898), which begins with the bold claim that 'what is properly
... called belief ... has no place in science,' but continues, *'[f]ull belief* is
willingness to act upon ... the proposition ... [The] accepted propositions [of sci-
ence] ... are but opinions at most; and the whole list is provisional,' illustrates
the point. Whether one thinks of belief as categorical, and thus of the scientific
inquirer as having, not beliefs, but more or less weak inclinations towards
belief, or whether one thinks of belief as gradational, and thus of the scientific
inquirer as having beliefs, but only in low degree, is not so important. What is
important is that the scientific attitude requires that one not be certain that
one already has the truth; for if one has such certainty, one has no motive to
investigate.

The teacher, like the man of action, is apt to fail to conform to the scientific
attitude, Peirce suggests, because his temperament and task similarly demand
that he have firm, confident beliefs. He must be convinced of what he teaches.

The theologian, according to Peirce, is even less likely to have the scientific attitude than the businessman or the teacher – or than the Christian minister, whom Peirce describes as required to have something of both the businessman's and the teacher's temperaments, his business being to save souls by teaching. The theologian has a temperament even farther removed from the scientific; he is engaged in the very opposite kind of intellectual enterprise, seeking ways to defend a set of propositions his commitment to which is determined in advance. 'Nothing,' Peirce comments, 'can be more unscientific than the attitude of minds who are trying to confirm themselves in early beliefs' (6.3, 1898).

That Peirce wants philosophy to be scientific is well known. Not quite so well known, perhaps, is that he means by this not only that philosophy should use the method of science, experience and reasoning, abductive, deductive, and inductive; not only that philosophical theses are to be construed as abductive hypotheses, but hypotheses testable by reference to features of everyday experience so ubiquitous that they often go unnoticed; but also, and perhaps especially, that philosophy should be undertaken with the scientific attitude, from the motive enjoined by the FRR. In fact, he attributes 'the backward state of metaphysics' to its having been in the hands of theologians, a 'deplorably corrupt' influence (6.3, 1898), which has led to the 'puny, rickety and scrofulous' state (6.6, 1898) of what could and should be a truly scientific study but is in his day in an 'infantile condition' (1.620, 1898).

Under the influence of theologians, according to Peirce, metaphysics has been deplorably corrupted by 'sham reasoning.' Sham reasoning is the presentation of arguments for foregone conclusions which are already immovably believed, which no evidence could induce the sham reasoner to drop. Peirce offers a quasi-historical diagnosis of the origin of sham reasoning. Despite his major contributions to formal logic and the theory of inquiry, he holds that there are significant areas in which reasoning or inquiry is inappropriate. Matters of morality, according to Peirce, belong to the subconscious; they are matters on which it is better to act from instinct than to reason. But people like to think that they regulate their conduct by reason, and so they construct spurious arguments for foregone moral conclusions. '[I]t is no longer the reasoning which determines what the conclusion shall be, but it is the conclusion which determines what the reasoning shall be. This is sham reasoning' (1.57, c. 1896). Sham reasoning, Peirce continues, is 'utterly contrary to the single-mindedness that is requisite in science'; and, of course, to the attitude requisite for scientific philosophy.

'Most philosophers,' Peirce writes, 'set up a pretension of knowing all there is to know – a pretension calculated to disgust anybody who is at home in any real science' (1.128, c. 1905). When Peirce compares the philosophy of his own day with that of the medievals, and when he writes that with Descartes, philosophy 'put off childish things, and began to be a conceited young man' (4.71, 1893), it is a propensity for sham reasoning, a falling away from the scientific attitude, that he has in mind. In respect of 'the *spirit*, which is the most essential thing – the *motive*,' the schoolmen, he remarks, were genuinely scientific philosophers; for they 'devote[d] their whole energies ... in putting [their theories] to tests *bona fide* – not such as [would] merely add a new spangle to the glitter of their proofs' (1.34, 1.33, 1869). It is in this context that he defends the schoolmen against critics who object to the ugliness of their technical jargon, remarking that 'as for that phrase, "studying in a literary spirit," it is impossible to express how nauseating it is to any scientific man,' thus weaving together the thought that the schoolmen have more claim to be scientific philosophers than their modern detractors do, and an idea expressed in his discussion of the ethics of terminology, that scientific inquirers are bound to feel the need for linguistic innovation as they feel the need for new concepts and distinctions (see e.g., 2.219ff, 1903).

A genuine desire to learn, as Peirce points out in the passage that was our starting point, requires that you 'not be satisfied with what you already incline to think.' One aspect of this attitude – avoidance of dogmatism and acknowledgment of one's susceptibility to *error* – is already in focus. But there is also a second aspect, a matter of acknowledging one's inevitable *ignorance*. Though the majority of Peirce's discussions refer to the possibility of error and the dangers of dogmatism, sometimes he makes the second, ignorance-oriented aspect no less, or even more, prominent. At 7.322 (1873) he writes: 'The first condition of learning is to know that we are ignorant. A man begins to inquire and reason ... as soon as he really questions anything ... real inquiry begins when genuine doubt begins.'

The genuine, scientific inquirer 'desires ardently to know the truth' (1.46, *c.* 1896), but there is no guarantee that he will succeed. He looks at the pursuit of truth 'not as the work of one man's life, but as that of generation after generation' (5.589, 1898); 'the idea ... is to pile the ground ... with the carcasses of this generation, and perhaps of others to come after it, until some future generation, by treading on them, can storm the citadel' (6.3, 1898). This is one way in which Peirce connects the scientific attitude with the social character of scientific inquiry.

This comports neatly enough with Peirce's characterization of truth as the opinion which would be agreed were inquiry to continue long enough. But, on the face of it at least, it does not comport so neatly with the account of the motivation of inquiry suggested in one of Peirce's best-known papers, 'The Fixation of Belief.'

2 The FRR and 'The Fixation of Belief'

Peirce's discussions of the temperament required by the scientific inquirer make it apparent that he regards this temperament as relatively unusual. Certainly they convey little of the tenor of Aristotle's dictum, that 'all men by nature desire to know.' But one might wonder whether *anyone* could possess the scientific temperament if the account of the motivation of inquiry suggested in 'The Fixation of Belief' were true. For in that paper Peirce writes:

> The irritation of doubt is the only immediate motive for the struggle to attain belief ... With the doubt ... the struggle begins, and with the cessation of doubt it ends. Hence, the sole object of inquiry is the settlement of opinion. We may fancy that this is not enough for us, and that we seek, not merely an opinion, but a true opinion. But put this fancy to the test, and it proves groundless; for as soon as a firm belief is reached we are entirely satisfied, whether the belief be true or false. (5.375, 1877)

How can this be reconciled with Peirce's claim that the genuine, scientific inquirer is engaged in 'a mode of life whose single animating purpose is to find out the real truth' (7.54, nd)?

The first thing to note is that the apparent conflict – though we happened upon it by contrasting the passage quoted from 'The Fixation of Belief' with passages from elsewhere in Peirce's work – is already present *within* 'The Fixation of Belief.' A few pages after the passage quoted, conceding that the method of tenacity, the method of authority, and the a priori method have certain advantages over the scientific method, Peirce writes: 'A man should consider well of [these advantages]; and then he should consider that, after all, he wishes his opinion to coincide with the fact, and that there is no reason why the results of those three ... methods should do so' (5.387). The explanation we seek is to be found in those passages where, on two much later occasions, Peirce refers back to 'The Fixation of Belief' and restates what he there intended. At 5.564 (*c*. 1906) Peirce describes 'The Fixation of Belief' as 'setting out from the proposition that the agitation of a question ceases when satisfaction is attained with the settlement of belief' and then considering 'how the conception of truth gradually develops from that principle'; the suggestion being that the conception of truth as 'overwhelmingly forced upon the mind in experience as the effect of an independent reality' is the most sophisticated stage of the intellectual development of mankind, which runs from the most primitive, represented by the method of tenacity, through the method of authority, to the a priori method, and finally to the scientific method. And at 6.485 (1908), noting that

'The Fixation of Belief' was written for a popular monthly – hinting that he had oversimplified his real view for this reason – Peirce recalls that he had said that settlement of beliefs, that is, a state of satisfaction, 'is all that Truth, or the aim of inquiry, consists in'; but, he goes on, the first part of the essay had been concerned to show that 'if Truth consists in satisfaction, it cannot be any *actual* satisfaction, but must be the satisfaction which *would* ultimately be found if the inquiry were pushed to its ultimate and indefeasible issue.' (He goes on, by the way, to point out how this distinguishes him from 'Mr Schiller and the pragmatists of today.')[3]

If we interpret 'The Fixation of Belief' along these lines, the appearance of conflict with the FRR turns out to be *mere* appearance. We can read the awkward passage (stressing, 'the irritation of doubt is the only *immediate* motive') in the light of Peirce's comment early in the paper, that '[w]e come to the full possession of our power of drawing inferences, the last of all our faculties' (5.359). On this interpretation, Peirce's position is that the primitive basis of our most sophisticated cognitive activity – scientific inquiry – is a simple homeostatic process, initiated by the disturbance caused when some habit of action is interrupted by recalcitrance on the part of experience, and halted as soon as a new habit is established. But the beliefs thus 'settled' are only *temporarily* fixed; so the most sophisticated cognizers, realizing that, unless a belief is true, though it may be temporarily settled, it cannot be permanently so, and aspiring to *indefeasibly* fixed belief, will always be motivated to further inquiry, never fully satisfied with what they presently incline to believe. The primitive homeostatic basis is thus transmuted – '*aufgehoben*' is the term that irresistibly suggests itself – into the scientific attitude. A scientific doubt, as Peirce puts it, 'never gets completely set to rest until, at last, the very truth about that question gets established' (7.77, nd).

As this last quotation indicates, we must postulate a dual usage, in Peirce, not only of 'fixed' (between 'temporarily fixed' and 'indefeasibly fixed'), but also of 'doubt' (between 'state resulting from interruption of a belief-habit by experience' and 'uncertainty'). The most sophisticated cognizers, seeking fixed beliefs in the stronger sense, are motivated (at the second order, so to speak) by doubt in the weaker sense. This begins to explain why Peirce does not distinguish very carefully between the thesis that the scientific attitude requires acknowledgment of one's susceptibility to error, and the thesis that it requires acknowledgment of one's susceptibility to ignorance.

The interpretation suggested here puts 'The Fixation of Belief' in a new and, I hope, illuminating perspective. But it leaves us with a problem about Peirce's critique of Descartes's Method of Doubt, which relies on the thesis that Descartes's policy of deliberate doubt is impossible *because genuine doubt arises only when an existing belief is interrupted by experience.* In my view, however, though Peirce's criticisms of the constructive phase of Descartes's enterprise are rather successful, his criticisms of the critical phase, and in particular of the Method of Doubt, are in any case thoroughly unsuccessful. Peirce misrepresents Descartes's method, which does not involve deliberate doubt, but deliberate suspension of beliefs found to be objectively dubitable; and 'Critical Common-sensism,' which requires a policy of submitting common-sense beliefs to critical scrutiny and severe test, itself involves something not unlike Descartes's method.[4] This point tends, if anything, to confirm the proposed rereading of 'The Fixation of Belief.'

3 The Interpretation of the FRR

Peirce sometimes writes, as we saw, so as to make it in effect part of the definition of 'science,' as he uses the term, that scientific inquiry is inquiry undertaken with the pure truth-seeking attitude. This involves an element of persuasive stipulation, of course. But that genuine inquiry aims at the truth *is* a tautology, and not in virtue of any stipulation. Thus, *Webster's New Collegiate Dictionary* (1961): 'inquiry: search for truth, information or knowledge; research, investigation.' (There is, however, a lot of pseudo-inquiry about; that is why, when the government instigates an Official Inquiry into this or that, some of us reach for our scare quotes.)

And perhaps there is merit in the thought that 'inquiry aims at the truth' is an *illuminating* tautology; that, rather as the tautology 'every soldier is some mother's child' may serve as an important reminder that soldiers are people, not just cannon fodder, so the tautology 'inquiry aims at the truth' may serve as an important reminder of the dangers of pseudo-inquiry, of bad-faith attempts to find reasons for beliefs which are already evidence-proof, of sham reasoning.

The FRR, however, is clearly intended to go beyond tautology, even illuminating tautology. It is intended as a substantive principle about the pure truth-seeking attitude – a principle which would both explain why utility-driven inquiry is inferior to disinterested inquiry, and tell us what is wrong with sham reasoning.

What exactly is this substantive principle? Peirce's formulation 'that in order to learn you must desire to learn' suggests: that an inquirer's having the pure truth-seeking attitude is a necessary condition of his finding out the truth; his presentation of this as not only the first, 'but in a sense the sole,' rule of reason suggests: that an inquirer's having the pure truth-seeking attitude is not only a necessary but also a sufficient condition of his finding out the truth.

But if this is the intended interpretation, the FRR is false; that an inquirer have the pure truth-seeking attitude is neither necessary nor sufficient for his finding out the truth. It is not sufficient: however ardently an inquirer desires the truth in some department, he may fail to get it if he is intellectually too weak, or using an inappropriate method, or lacking necessary resources or equipment, ... , or, etc. And it is not necessary, either: even a bad-faith pseudo-inquirer may stumble on the truth – for example, seeking to cover up a scandal of allegedly misappropriated funds, the Official Inquiry may discover that the funds were, after all, put to a legitimate use.

However, Peirce himself seems well aware of these considerations. His observations to the effect that the scientific inquirer has to be prepared for the eventuality that he fails, that his will be one of the carcasses over which later generations climb as they storm the fortress of knowledge, imply that the scientific attitude is not sufficient for finding out the truth; as does his remark that *two* qualifications are needed by 'the true man of science': first, 'the dominant passion of his whole soul must be to find out the truth in some department,' but also, second, 'he must have a natural gift for reasoning, for severely critical thought' (7.605, 1903); he must go to work 'by a well-considered method' (1.235, 1902). And the fact that Peirce does not deny that the practical man who investigates only those chemical substances potentially useful as dyestuffs, for example, despite lacking the truly scientific attitude, may nonetheless make genuine discoveries implies that he realizes that the scientific attitude is not necessary for finding out the truth, either.

It is clear from its context that Peirce connects the FRR with the thesis that reasoning is self-corrective – a thesis which he here maintains is true of reasoning of all kinds, not only of induction. This suggests an argument that the desire to learn is, after all, sufficient for finding out the truth, since reasoning, being self-corrective, is bound to arrive at the truth if continued long enough. But this argument has no tendency to show that an inquirer's desiring the truth is sufficient for *his* discovering it; at most it shows that inquirers' desiring the truth is sufficient for the truth to be discovered, if inquiry continues long enough, by some generation of inquirers. So, though it sheds some useful oblique light on Peirce's thesis that logic is rooted in the social principle, this argument is disappointing, yielding at best only a much weakened version of the sufficiency thesis suggested by Peirce's statement of the FRR (and, of course, no support for the necessity thesis).

So if the FRR does gesture towards something true and important about individual inquirers – and I believe it does – more subtlety is needed to identify what that 'something true and important' could be.

It will be, it is clear, something weaker and more hedged than Peirce's bold statement that an inquirer's having the desire to learn is both necessary and suf-

ficient for his learning the truth; something more like his much less bold statement later in the same lecture: 'If you really want to learn the truth, you will, by
however devious a path, be surely led into the way of truth, at last ... Nay, no
matter if you only half desire it, at first ... But the more voraciously truth is
desired at the outset, the shorter by centuries will the road to it be.'[5]

Suppose that A and B are both investigating the chemical properties of some
dyestuff. A has the pure, disinterested truth-seeking attitude, B wouldn't bother
if it weren't for the potential utility of the results of the investigation. But A is
stupid and unimaginative, while B is smart and resourceful – or A is equipped
only with a tea-tray and a few vials, while B has a sophisticated laboratory at
his disposal. It is certainly possible, indeed likely, that B will do better – but,
since this would be beside the essential point, I shall abstract from these com-
plications by assuming, henceforth, that such other things are equal.

Consider, now, the good-faith but utility-driven inquirer, who wants the truth,
but wants only useful truth. I see no reason why, within his limits, he should do
any worse than the disinterested, scientific inquirer. But the limits are significant. It is not just that the utility-driven inquirer will find out about iron, but not
bother with erbium, though that is part of it. More interestingly, his concern for
utility can be expected so to narrow where he looks, what questions he deems
worthy of investigation, that – given the unpredictable interconnectedness of
knowledge – even with respect to the potentially useful matters on which he is
focused, he may fail to pursue lines of investigation which would have proved
fruitful. 'The point of view of utility,' Peirce writes, 'is always a narrow point
of view' (1.641, 1898). He is well aware, also, that we simply can't identify, in
advance, what inquiries will prove useful; the theme of the passage (1.75–6,
c. 1896) where he says that '[t]rue science is distinctively the study of useless
things' – a theme that puts that remark in a very different light – is how badly
people tend to misjudge the potential usefulness of this or that avenue of
inquiry. Contemporaries of Kepler, Peirce observes, deplored the study of
'geometry,' including the beginnings of the differential calculus, 'because they
said it was UTTERLY USELESS.' And yet 'Kepler's discovery rendered Newton possible, and Newton rendered modern physics possible, with the steam
engine, electricity, and all the other sources of the stupendous fortunes of our
age.' Another characteristic comment, that 'oftentimes it is precisely the least
expected truth which is turned up under the ploughshare of research' (1.138, c.
1899), points in the same direction. The defect of utility-driven inquiry is a kind
of tunnel vision which may be self-defeating even from a strictly utilitarian perspective.

A fuller understanding would require us to distinguish – as Peirce generally
does not – two ways of looking at an inquirer's success or failure: (a) narrowly,

as a matter of his discovering or failing to discover the truth with respect to some specific question; or (b) broadly, as a matter of his discovering or failing to discover substantial, significant truths with respect to some area of inquiry. (Peirce's tendency to downplay this distinction is no doubt connected both with his sometimes writing indifferently of acknowledgment of error and acknowledgment of ignorance as required by scientific inquiry, and with his definition of the truth of a proposition as its belonging to the hypothetical ultimate opinion.) The argument of the previous paragraph is now seen implicitly to involve two phases: the first, and more direct, pointing out that the utility-driven inquirer is bound to be less successful than the scientific inquirer in the broad sense; and the second, and less direct, appealing to the unpredictable interconnectedness of knowledge, showing that the utility-driven inquirer is likely, as a consequence, to be at a disadvantage with respect to success in the narrow sense as well.

Consider, now, the bad-faith pseudo-inquirer who has some immovably held preconceived belief for which he is trying to make a case. If the preconceived belief happens to be true, things are not so bad; he may find good evidence and arguments. Even so, however, he will try to suppress or explain away evidence that appears unfavourable to his thesis. And even if he succeeds in marshalling genuine evidence for a true thesis, this success will be more by luck than by judgment. If, on the other hand, the preconceived belief is false, the likeliest upshot is that his evidence will be selected in a partial way and that his arguments will be elaborately misleading. It is not impossible that he will turn up some evidence that points to the truth of the matter, but if he does he will either suppress it or try to explain it away.

It is also instructive to consider another deviation from the (pure) truth-seeking attitude, which Peirce does not discuss explicitly, but of which his observations about the corrupting effect of 'vanity' (1.34, 1869) indicate he is aware. This is the inquirer (or 'inquirer') whose primary concern is the promotion of his own reputation. Like the sham reasoner, such an 'inquirer' is not truth-oriented even in the narrow sense in which the utility-driven inquirer, who wants truths, but only useful truths, is. He is indifferent to the truth-value (though not to the publicity-value) of the propositions for which he seeks to make a case. Peirce comes closest to an overt discussion of this, as I shall call it, 'fake reasoning,' in this biting comment on a contemporary of his: 'real power ... is not *born* in a man; it has to be worked out; and the first condition is that the man's soul should be filled with the desire to make out the truth ...; but —— is full of himself, and it stands immovably in the way of a thorough devotion to truth. He ought not to try to combine two aims so disparate and incompatible.'[6]

By choosing the term 'fake reasoning,' I hinted at a point which certainly needs making explicit. Scientific inquiry is motivated purely by the desire for the truth. Utility-driven inquiry is also truth-directed, but in a restricted, impure, interested way. But neither sham reasoning nor fake reasoning qualifies even in a restricted way as aiming at the truth – both aim, rather, at making a case for some predetermined proposition or propositions. Neither, therefore, is really a form of *inquiry* at all. Hence Peirce's 'sham' and my 'fake.' 'Scientific inquiry' or 'genuine, disinterested inquiry,' then, contrasts both with 'utility-driven, interested inquiry' and with 'pseudo-inquiry.'[7]

The arguments about the defects of sham reasoning apply, *mutatis mutandis*, to fake reasoning. And fake reasoning, even more than sham reasoning, is an important source of what Locke called 'affected obscurity.'[8] Someone whose prime motivation is to enhance his reputation, finding that a good way to do this is to exploit the common presumption that what is obscure must be deep, will be motivated to present the banal or the meaningless under cover of pretentious obscurity. This danger is especially severe in philosophy. The prevalence of fake reasoning is, probably, a major part of the explanation of why too much philosophical writing is, as Peirce wrote of 'ontological metaphysics' (the bad, unscientific kind), 'meaningless gibberish' (5.423, 1902).

Now consider the scientific inquirer, who desires the truth in some department, whatever the colour of that truth, and who is indifferent to whether it is useful or not, or whether it enhances his reputation or not. His work will be marked by *persistence* – since he really wants the truth, he won't give up until he has pursued all the relevant avenues of investigation he can think of; by *breadth* – since he is indifferent to the utility of his results, he will pursue the investigation where it leads rather than ignoring questions that lead off into apparently useless theoretical puzzles; and by *candour* – since he wants the truth to be got more than he wants it to be himself who gets the truth, he will not only make his work freely available to other inquirers, but will also present what he has done, to himself as well as others, without attempting to make it seem as if he has achieved more than he has.

This description offers support for a striking claim of Peirce's: that the genuine inquirer, even if he doesn't (as he may not) get the truth, will at least *make better, more fruitful mistakes*. 'It is far better to ... follow perfectly untrammeled a scientific method, *predetermined* in advance of knowing to what it will lead. If that course be honestly and scrupulously carried out, the results reached, even if they be not altogether true, ... can not but be highly serviceable for the ultimate discovery of truth' (1.644, 1898). The scientific inquirer, though he may reach conclusions which are false, will not deliberately avoid, ignore, or block avenues of inquiry likely to prove hostile to some foregone conclusion; and he will not cover his tracks as the sham or fake reasoner is motivated to do. He will be ready – indeed anxious – to acknowledge where his evidence seems to him weakest, his argument shakiest, his articulation vaguest. And (here I am thinking of philosophical inquiry especially) he will shun the affected obscurity with which a fake reasoner may try to impress others.

These reflections are highly congruent with Peirce's description of the co-operative character of scientific inquiry: of inquirers' 'unreserved discussion with one another,' of 'each being fully informed about the work of his neighbour, and availing himself of that neighbour's work'; which is how 'in storming the stronghold of truth one mounts upon the shoulders of another who has to ordinary apprehension failed, but has in truth succeeded by virtue ... of his failure' (7.51, nd).

But isn't all this, you may be asking, hopelessly idealistic? Well, I certainly grant that thus far I have presented the issues in unrealistically black-and-white terms, and that subtler shading is highly desirable. My distinction of four types – the scientific inquirer, the utility-driven inquirer, the sham inquirer, and the fake inquirer – needs to be qualified by an acknowledgment that people's motivation is virtually always mixed. My imputation of simple dishonesty in the sham and the fake reasoner needs to be qualified by an acknowledgment of the ubiquity of various kinds and degrees of self-deception. And my arguments for the superiority of scientific inquiry need to be moderated by a recognition that the desire for fame, or money, or for the betterment of society or one's family, or for the furtherance of some religious or political cause, can all be very powerfully motivating, and may prompt very energetic and sustained intellectual effort.

To the extent that their work is subject to the informed and honest scrutiny of other workers in the field, or even of other sham or fake reasoners with different axes to grind, the potential damage done by sham and fake inquirers may be mitigated, and the contributions they may make despite their dubious motivation may be put to good use. And to the extent that it is the case that fame and fortune in intellectual fields are achieved by those, and only those, who make successful efforts towards discovering the truth, we could expect a fair simulacrum of scientific inquiry to be achieved by persons who are not pure truth-seekers, but whose less admirable, but powerful, motives can be harnessed to the service of truth.

4 The Relevance of the FRR to Philosophy Today

But now here comes the tough part (not the most difficult, but the least palatable). Philosophy today, in my view, is not only not in the most desirable condition of scientific inquiry; it falls well short even of the passable simulacrum of scientific inquiry for which the previous paragraph suggests one might less idealistically hope.

Perhaps some will be tempted to smugness. After all, it might be said, philosophy today is not dominated by theologians; in fact, it is much closer to *science* than it used to be. 'Laboratory philosophy' has superseded 'seminary philosophy,' the pollyannish might continue, and metaphysics has overcome its previous 'infantile condition.' I think such optimism would be just about completely misplaced – that it would latch onto the letter of Peirce's remarks about making philosophy scientific while completely missing their spirit, the spirit of the FRR.

Theologically oriented philosophy is still to be found, for example, in the 'Reformed epistemology' of some Calvinist philosophers.[9] But perhaps philosophy *is* closer to *science* than it used to be, in two ways: with respect to its content, and with respect to its organization. There is a *rapprochement* of philosophy with the *sciences*, notably, for instance, of epistemology with psychology, biology, and artificial intelligence; and this may be indicative of the waning popularity of the idea of philosophy as an a priori, autonomous discipline. Such naturalism, you might think, is Peircean in spirit. It is much less so, I believe, than it superficially appears; for a closer look reveals a marked tendency for these appeals to the *sciences* to displace or distort, even sometimes to denigrate the legitimacy of, the epistemological issues ostensibly being addressed '*scientifically*.' 'Naturalism,' in late twentieth-century epistemology, includes: (i) the extension of the term 'epistemology' to include natural-*scientific* studies of human cognition; (ii) the claim that some, or even all, traditional epistemological problems can be handed over to the natural *sciences* of cognition to be resolved; (iii) the thesis that results in the natural *sciences* of cognition have shown the traditional epistemological questions to be misconceived; (iv) acknowledgment of the contributory relevance of *scientific* studies of cognition to such traditional epistemological issues as the nature of perception or the meta-justification of induction.[10] Of these, the first is harmless but uninteresting; the second and third represent more or less gross forms of scientism; and only the fourth has any true affinity with Peirce's conception of the continuity of philosophy and *science*.[11]

The rise of the kind of scientism I have been, by implication, deploring may be explicable in part by reference to the second factor mentioned earlier. The prestige of the *sciences* is such as to prompt deference on the part of philosophers as well as the lay public (though also such as to prompt a kind of resentment which from time to time shows tendencies to transmute justified criticisms of abuses of *science* into more or less gross forms of irrationalism). When *science* commands prestige and money, and philosophy, in its own right, neither, is it any wonder that we find philosophers claiming that they can resolve the old problems of epistemology by appeal to cognitive psychology, or dissolve them by reference to connectionist neurophysiology? But the point I want to stress here concerns the sociology of knowledge: *scientific* work has become very expensive, and, in consequence, *science* has become, *inter alia*, big business. And because of the prestige of the *sciences*, other disciplines have tended to mimic their organisation and, like them, to adapt to a business ethos.

Perhaps the escalating cost of *scientific* research is inevitable. Peirce, indeed, argued that, though in the early days it was possible to do important *scientific* research with 'a few test-tubes and phials on a tea-tray' (7.144, 1879), as *science* proceeds it will inevitably get more and more expensive to get new truths. It is clear, however, that this argument does not extrapolate to philosophy, not even to scientific philosophy as Peirce conceives it. For what, according to Peirce, is bound to make *scientific* research increasingly expensive is the need for ever more sophisticated means to get access to ever more recherché observations; whereas the observations relevant to philosophy, according to Peirce, are precisely *not* recherché, but so commonplace that the difficulty is to become distinctly aware of them. But for quite adventitious reasons philosophy has got more like *science* in its organization – to such an extent that the whole apparatus of philosophical research projects, funding applications, and so forth and so on, is now so ordinary that we scarcely notice how extraordinary it is.

As *science* has become big business, *scientists* have had to become, *inter alia*, businessmen; and this has made it harder for *scientists* to sustain the scientific attitude. At the same time, many university administrators have become enamoured of a business management ethos which values 'entrepreneurial skills,' that is, the ability to obtain large sums of money to undertake large research projects, above originality or depth, and which encourages a conception of 'efficiency' more appropriate to a manufacturing plant than to the pursuit of truth. And as philosophy has adjusted itself more and more to the forms, the manner, of contemporary research in the *sciences*, it has become even harder for philosophers than for *scientists* to sustain the scientific attitude.

I hope this hasn't given the impression that I think scientism the bane of contemporary philosophy. The *real* bane is sham and fake reasoning. This has been encouraged by philosophy's mimicking the organization of contemporary *science*, but it comes in many forms besides the scientistic; certainly those who advocate doing philosophy 'in a literary spirit' are no less given to sham and fake reasoning than those of a scientistic bent. I don't mean to suggest that no serious intellectual work is getting done; I do mean to say that pseudo-inquiry is commonplace. Occasionally, indeed, sham or fake reasoning seems to be openly professed. Here are some examples from my collection:

A return [to psychologistic conceptions of epistemology] is especially timely now, when cognitive psychology has renewed prestige ...

This is a good time to be naturalizing epistemology ... Technological developments in research in the neurosciences ... have been spectacular ... [T]he advent of cheap computing makes it possible to simulate neural networks ... Truth, whatever that is, definitely takes the hindmost.

[I] commend an antiessentialism and antilogocentrism on the ground of its harmony with the practices and aims of a democratic society ...

The right way of reading these slogans ['common humanity,' 'natural rights'] lets one think of philosophy as *in the service* of democratic politics ...

Feminist academics are the intellectual arm of the women's movement. If we're not, we've betrayed our trust.[12]

Perhaps Peirce would not have been altogether surprised. He was well aware that the scientific attitude is not robust enough for complacency. Though 'science is, upon the whole, at present in a very healthy condition,' he wrote in 1901, '[i]t would not remain so if the motives of scientific men were lowered.' The worst threat, he continued, is that there are too many 'whose chief interest in science is as a means of gaining money' (8.142). Another shrewd observation is also apropos. This remark has, perhaps, been thought of simply as an expression of Peirce's professional disappointment; it may indeed be that, but it is also an important comment on the dangers of professionalization: 'Wherever there is a large class of academic professors who are provided with good incomes and looked up to as gentlemen, scientific inquiry will languish,' and, Peirce goes on, if bureaucrats take control, 'the situation will be still worse' (1.51, *c.* 1896).

The scientific temperament is not commonplace, but relatively rare. And it is fragile.[13] In part, this fragility is inevitable; for any serious intellectual work demands a substantial investment of time and energy, and it is human nature to want to cling to the ideas or theories in which one has made such an investment. In other words, the personal investment involved *already* creates a pull away from the scientific attitude, a tendency to resist the force of unfavourable evidence. But the environment in which intellectual work is done may be more or less supportive of, or more or less hostile to, the intellectual integrity demanded by the scientific attitude.[14] And in some ways the environment of philosophy today is markedly hostile to the pure truth-seeking attitude, markedly encouraging to sham and fake reasoning.

An environment of 'professionalism' in which reputation and money depend on one's ability to get one's ideas heard and talked about is – as Peirce's comment on Paul Carus makes it clear he realized – an encouragement to sham and fake reasoning. Combine this with – what Peirce could not have anticipated – an explosion of publications and meetings, a mind-numbing clamour in which championship of a simple, startling idea, even, or perhaps especially, a startlingly false or an impressively obscure idea, cleverly promoted, is a good route to reputation and money, and you have an environment markedly hostile to honest intellectual work. When, today, I read Peirce's observation that 'it is infinitely better that men devoid of genuine scientific curiosity should not barricade the road of science with empty books and embarrassing assumptions' (1.645, 1898), my reaction is: *Oh dear!* – isn't yours?

The grants-and-research-projects apparatus and the conceptions of productivity and efficiency it fosters discourage candid acknowledgment that it is part of the meaning of 'research' that you don't know how things will turn out, and constitute a standing temptation to exaggeration, half-truth, and outright dishonesty about how much has been achieved. To get the grant, you have to fill out the application explaining what it is that your work is going to achieve, which had better sound as important, novel, and exciting as possible; and if you want ever to get another, you had better not report, in due course, that it turned out that your line of investigation reached a dead end. In principle, of course, it is possible that an inquirer's private estimation of the worth of his work should be uncontaminated by this; in practice, and equally 'of course,' this is seldom entirely achieved.

The grants-and-research-projects apparatus and the conceptions of productivity and efficiency it fosters also significantly affect what kinds of work get done;[15] it is surely at least partly responsible for the fashion for such 'vitally important topics' as medical, professional, and business ethics, for instance, and for the popularity of interdisciplinary work, especially work which allies philosophy with other, more prestigious, disciplines such as cognitive psychology, artificial intelligence, or connectionist neurophysiology. The point I want to press here focuses on the second kind of example, and it presupposes the conclusion of the previous paragraph. This is that the set-up is such as to encourage 'inquirers' who endorse a certain kind of conclusion, for example, that epistemological questions unresolved for thousands of years can be swiftly resolved by cognitive psychology, or as swiftly dissolved by connectionist neurophysiology; rather than encouraging undistorted investigation of the truth of the matter, even if the truth of the matter turns out to be (as, in these instances, I think it is) that the epistemological relevance of these disciplines, though real enough, is undramatic and indirect.

Ideally, there ought to be a paragraph about here which offers some explanation of the ubiquity of politically motivated sham and fake reasoning in philosophy today (especially in view of the fact that their overtly political character is a noteworthy feature of several of the professions of sham or fake reasoning I quoted earlier). Perhaps part of the explanation is that, when government bodies become major supporters of research projects in the humanities, their desire not to appear unsympathetic to the interests of certain groups, women, for example, may distort the process of deciding what work is most worthy of support in a way which, once again, encourages a certain type of conclusion, such as that women are capable of revolutionary insights into the theory of knowledge or the philosophy of *science* not available, or not easily available, to men; rather than encouraging undistorted investigation of the truth of the matter, even if the truth of the matter happens to be (as, in this instance, I think it is) that epistemological questions are *hard*, very hard, for any philosopher, of either sex. Well – in a sketchy way, and despite my distaste for the task, maybe I have written that paragraph after all![16]

Here is Peirce on what will happen if sham reasoning is commonplace: 'men come to look upon reasoning as mainly decorative ... The result ... is, of course, a rapid deterioration of intellectual vigor ...' (1.58, *c.* 1896). And, he continues: 'man loses his conception of truth and of reasoning. If he sees one man assert what another denies, he will, if he is concerned, choose his side and set to work by all means in his power to silence his adversaries. The truth for him is that for which he fights.' (1.59, *c.* 1896).

There are signs in philosophy today of just such consequences as Peirce anticipated. For example, Rorty tells us that 'true' just means 'what you can defend against all comers,' and that truth is 'entirely a matter of solidarity'; that 'rationality' just means 'respect for the opinions of those around one' – or, if it doesn't, that it should; that those who ('solemnly') describe themselves as seeking the truth are 'old-fashioned prigs.' (Rorty says 'lovably old-fashioned prigs,' but I for one am not charmed.)[17] Stich tells us that it is mere epistemic chauvinism, parochial and narrow-minded, to care whether one's beliefs are true; that the task of the epistemologist should be to 'improve' people's cognitive processing so as to help them believe whatever it is, true or false, such that their believing it will conduce to what they value.[18] (What a grotesque irony that these egregious falsehoods should be described by their perpetrators as 'pragmatism'!)[19]

Peirce understood what serious intellectual work is, as these vulgar pragmatists, apparently, do not; and his 'first rule of reason' tells us something important about what serious intellectual work requires. Indeed, the more solemnly old-fashioned it sounds to say, as Peirce did, that 'a scientific man must be single-minded and sincere with himself. Otherwise, his love of truth will melt away, at once' (1.49, *c.* 1896), the more important it is that it *be* said.

Notes

I would like to recall the help and encouragement of the late David Stove, whose astringent and witty letters sustained me during the writing of this paper. He had the scientific attitude.

The paper was first read at the conference on 'New Topics in the Philosophy of Charles Peirce' held in Toronto in October 1992. It has since been read to the philosophy departments of the University of South Florida, Tampa; the University of New Mexico; Washington State University, Pullman; McGill University; and the University of Łódź. I am grateful for the many helpful comments made on these occasions.

1 This comes from Lecture Four, entitled 'The First Rule of Logic,' of Peirce's Cambridge Conferences Lectures of 1898, parts of which appear in various places in the *Collected Papers*, and all of which are published in Kenneth Laine Ketner and Hilary Putnam, eds, *Reasoning and the Logic of Things* (Cambridge, Mass., and London: Harvard University Press 1992).
2 'Erbium: a metallic element, one of the rare-earth metals that occurs with yttrium' – *Webster's New Collegiate Dictionary* (1961). (The word was coined, apparently, in 1843.)
3 And, one might add, from some self-styled pragmatists of today; see section 4 below.
4 Cf Susan Haack, 'Descartes, Peirce and the Cognitive Community,' *The Monist* 65, no. 2 (Apr. 1982): 156–81, reprinted in Eugene Freeman, ed., *The Relevance of Charles Peirce* (La Salle, Ill.: Monist Library of Philosophy, Open Court 1983), 238–63.
5 Peirce, 'The First Rule of Logic,' in Ketner and Putnam, eds, *Reasoning and the Logic of Things*, 170.
6 C.S. Peirce, in Carolyn Eisele, ed., *The New Elements of Mathematics*, 4 vols (The Hague: Mouton 1976), 4:977.
7 The fake reasoner's indifference to the truth-value of the propositions he advances is precisely the attitude Frankfurt takes to be characteristic of the bullshitter. See Harry Frankfurt, 'On Bullshit,' in *The Importance of What We Care About* (Cambridge: Cambridge University Press 1989), 117–33.
8 John Locke, *An Essay Concerning Human Understanding*, 1690, III.x.6ff.
9 See, for example, the essays in Alvin Plantinga and Nicholas Wolterstorff, eds, *Faith and Rationality* (Notre Dame, Ind., and London: University of Notre Dame

Press 1983). The following passage, from a paper by George Marsden, is worthy of note in the context of Peirce's thesis of the inevitability of sham reasoning in theology-driven philosophy: '[S]in creates a widespread abnormality. Trust in God which ought to be a spontaneous act providing us with intuitive first principles of knowledge is lacking in most people. Christians should not be embarrassed to say frankly that this is the issue. If one trusts in God, one will view some evidence differently than a person who basically denies God' (257). I also note the occurrence in recent issues of *Jobs for Philosophers* of several advertisements which specify commitment to one or another kind of religious doctrine as a requisite for a position.

10 For amplification, see chapter 6, 'Naturalism Disambiguated,' of Susan Haack, *Evidence and Inquiry: Towards Reconstruction in Epistemology* (Oxford: Blackwell 1993).

11 Cf 5.521, *c.* 1905, where Peirce argues that it is inappropriate to expect *science* to solve philosophical questions.

12 Alvin Goldman, 'Epistemics: The Regulative Theory of Cognition,' *Journal of Philosophy* 75, no. 10 (1978): 523 (Goldman goes on, I should add, to advert, less alarmingly, to the fact that cognitive psychology promises to improve our understanding of cognitive processing); Patricia Smith Churchland, 'Epistemology in the Age of Neuroscience,' *Journal of Philosophy*, 75, no. 10 (1987): 546–7 and 549 (the last sentence quoted, I should say, comes from a later paragraph than the rest, a paragraph about evolutionary epistemology; but taking it out of context is not misleading, for it *is* Churchland's view that the idea that truth is the goal of inquiry needs to be overthrown 'in the age of neuroscience'); Richard Rorty, *Essays on Heidegger and Others* (Cambridge: Cambridge University Press 1991), 135; Richard Rorty, *Contingency, Irony and Solidarity* (Cambridge: Cambridge University Press 1989), 196; Alison Jaggar, *Ms*, Oct. 1985, 38.

13 As Frankfurt reminded us in his Presidential Address to the Eastern APA, 1991, A.E. Housman describes the love of truth as 'the faintest of all human passions' (*M. Manilii, Atronomicon I* [London 1903, xliii]; see Harry Frankfurt, 'The Faintest Passion,' *Proceedings and Addresses of the American Philosophical Association* 66, no. 3 [1992]: 5–16).

14 In the painful task of working out the arguments of the rest of this paper I have been helped by Michael Polanyi's shrewd ruminations on the organization of *science* (especially 'The Republic of Science,' in Marjorie Grene, ed., *Knowing and Being* [Chicago: University of Chicago Press 1969], 49–62) and by David Stove's candid appraisal of the condition of the Faculty of Arts at the University of Sydney ('A Farewell to Arts,' *Quadrant* [May 1986]: 8–11). Since writing the paper I have read, with appreciation, Michael Dummett's candid account of the effects of inappropriate conceptions of efficiency on the condition of graduate work in philosophy at Oxford

(*Frege: Philosophy of Mathematics* [Cambridge, Mass.: Harvard University Press 1991], viii–x).

15 I can testify that at Warwick the argument was heard that the department should specialize in contemporary French and German philosophy, 'because we can get Euro-money to do that'; I don't know whether the anticipated funds were in fact obtained.

16 Cf Susan Haack, 'Epistemological Reflections of an Old Feminist,' *Reason Papers* 18 (Fall 1993): 31–43, reprinted, slightly modified, under the title, 'Knowledge and Propaganda: Reflections of an Old Feminist,' in *Partisan Review* (Fall 1993): 556–64, for arguments that 'feminist epistemology' is misconceived.

17 Richard Rorty, *Philosophy and the Mirror of Nature* (Princeton: Princeton University Press 1979), 38; *Objectivity, Relativism and Truth* (Cambridge: Cambridge University Press 1991), 32 and 37; *Essays on Heidegger and Others*, 86.

18 Stephen P. Stich, *The Fragmentation of Reason* (Cambridge, Mass., and London: Bradford Books, MIT Press 1990), ch. 5.

19 Cf ch. 9, 'Vulgar Pragmatism: An Unedifying Prospect,' in Haack, *Evidence and Inquiry*, for detailed discussion of Rorty's and Stich's critiques of epistemology, and of their claim to be descendants of the tradition of classical pragmatism. See also Susan Haack, 'Philosophy/philosophy, an Untenable Dualism,' *Transactions of the Charles S. Peirce Society*, 30, no.3 (Summer 1993): 411–26, for a detailed critique of Rorty's interpretation of Peirce; and '"We Pragmatists ..."; Peirce and Rorty in Conversation,' a dialogue between Peirce and Rorty compiled from their own words, forthcoming in *Partisan Review*.

The Dynamical Object and the Deliberative Subject

VINCENT M. COLAPIETRO

Introduction: *Deliberate* Critical Appraisal

Near the conclusion of *An Introduction to C.S. Peirce's Full System of Semeiotic,* David Savan suggests that: 'The most important turning point in the history of a sign or a set of signs is the point at which deliberate critical appraisal of the norms themselves begins' (1987–8, 63).[1] It is one thing to rely upon signs in our interpretations of utterances or in our explanations of phenomena; it is quite another to do so in a self-conscious, self-critical, and self-controlled way. In short, reliance upon signs does not entail consciousness (much less criticism or control) of them: though we cannot think without signs (see, e.g., 5.250–3), we need not in most situations think about them. It may even be that, in many ordinary circumstances, our reliance upon signs is of such a character as to entail *un*consciousness of them (cf Langer 1942; Deely 1990). However that may be, the degree and respects in which our cognitive undertakings, our sustained exertions, and our emotional responses depend upon signs are the focal concerns of those who have taken what might be called the semiotic turn.[2] Yet, as the text from Professor Savan's *Introduction* makes clear, mere attention to the extent and ways we rely upon signs is not adequate. *Critical* assessment of our semiotic practices, extending to the norms and even ideals governing these practices, is required. In characterizing critical assessment as deliberate, there is the recognition that we do not have to wait for difficulties actually to occur but can – indeed, should – anticipate them as best we can: 'If you have reason to expect trouble, it may be better to look for it than to have it catch you unawares' (Haack 1983, 249). In a sense, deliberation is the process of looking for trouble!

But why do so? History forcefully attests that we are driven towards such critical assessment of our semiotic practices by our very engagement in them. Animated by our inherited purposes and procedures, we are forced to ask, time and again, Do we adequately know what we are doing? (e.g., Do these laws ensure justice for all the relevant parties? or, Does this method facilitate discovery of a responsibly held belief?). Philosophers characteristically suppose that we are equipped – or can become equipped – to undertake such an assessment. The scope and character of critical assessment, especially when conceived as a *radical* critique of our semiotic practices,[3] are none the less highly controversial topics. Think here of the disputes surrounding the various accounts of literary interpretation or the rival theories of scientific inquiry. These accounts and theories frequently take on a life of their own, operating at a distance from first-hand participation in the norm-governed practice supposedly being illuminated in these accounts or theories.

One way to describe my aim in this paper is this: to prepare the ground for considering, from several different angles, the hypothesis that critical assessment is the more or less natural extension of the deliberative process as this is sustained and even revised by what might be called the implicated participant (cf Taylor 1989). Though modestly conceived (for I aim here only to prepare the ground for considering a hypothesis), the endeavour is none the less worthwhile. The value of such an inquiry resides, however, not in establishing compelling conclusions but in offering fruitful suggestions for (a) how to interpret Peirce's project and (b) how to appreciate the distinctive contribution which this original philosopher might make to several crucial debates in contemporary philosophy.

By the implicated participant, I mean the deliberative subject insofar as s/he is implicated in some evolved and evolving practice (i.e., some open-ended, norm-governed process). And, by the deliberative subject, I mean (at least) the human organism which, as the result of being subjected to a complex array of critical appraisals, has acquired the capacity to appraise its own endeavours (including its own motives [1.585]). Deliberate critical appraisal is rooted in the ongoing efforts of implicated participants to orient themselves in a progressively comprehensive, flexible, and nuanced way to the world of their experience. This orientation towards the world is linked to what might be called an interiorization of the self (the process in which the interiority of the self is explored and even enlarged and enhanced [Colapietro 1989, 115–16]): The aesthetic ideal, 'by modifying the rules of self-control[,] modifies action, and so experience – both the man's own and that of others, and this centrifugal movement thus rebounds in a new centripetal movement, and so on ...' (5.402n3). The drive towards outward, public activities and encounters generates a drive towards inward, personal deliberations and musements (6.458ff); in turn, these deliberations and musements propel the self outward. In this to-and-fro, a twofold possibility is itself generated: the arena in which the implicated self is destined to act might become wider and deeper; the powers of the self might become more far-reaching and deep-rooted.

If critical assessment is seen as a task undertaken not by a transcendental but by an implicated subject, certain seemingly intractable problems dissolve (above all, the problem of undecidability regarding the norms and criteria of critical evaluation [again, cf Taylor 1989]). The vantage point of the disengaged spectator needs to be replaced by that of the implicated participant.[4] As a result, objectivity will come to be seen as (in large measure) a demand that *we* make upon ourselves and agency as a form of responsibility which we assume for ourselves. For all that, the demand for objectivity is no irresponsible wish (e.g., a longing for pure presence) or tyrannical impulse (e.g., a desire for absolute closure); nor is the assumption of agency a subjective delusion.

Deliberate critical appraisal is a process of deliberation undertaken by a necessarily implicated agent and directed towards potentially accessible realities. In the course of such appraisal, we come to realize not only that deliberation is the root of our autonomy ('deliberate conduct is self-controlled conduct' [5.442]), but also that 'control may itself be controlled, criticism itself subjected to criticism' (ibid.). Futhermore, we come to sense that 'ideally there is no obvious definite limit to the sequence.' But the pragmatic maxim was formulated by Peirce in part to ensure that such indeliminable reflection be something more than idle speculation, for this maxim insists that the signs on which such reflection depends be translated into directives for how to comport ourselves in the world.[5] So, too, as a central part of his mature defence of critical commonsensism, he explained the way in which the commonsensist can without contradiction undertake a thoroughgoing criticism of 'first principles' (5.505ff).[6] Such a criticism is, according to the hypothesis being entertained in my paper, an extension of the more narrowly circumscribed deliberations of implicated participants. This is, indeed, a defining feature of Peircean commonsensism. Finally, such a criticism is made possible by hypostatic abstraction, the semiotic process by which the signs with which an operation is performed are themselves made the objects to which other operations are directed. Hence, deliberate critical appraisal, as a process encompassing a thoroughgoing criticism of first principles, needs to be regarded as a phenomenon (cf 5.419) explicable only in light of (at least) Peirce's pragmatism, commonsensism, and semiotics.

Viewed against the background of evolution,[7] this process grows out of the blind, frantic gropings of immediately imperilled organisms and grows towards the explicit, nuanced self-consciousness of historically informed inquirers. In the section devoted to 'Situating the Deliberative Subject,' we will examine how Peirce conceived this growth. Viewed from the perspective of one involved in deliberation, the process is felt to be engendered by doubts, either actual, unanticipated or feigned, deliberate doubts. In the section concerned with 'Delineating the Deliberative Process,' we will consider, from the viewpoint of the agent, the process of deliberation. But before either of these discussions is undertaken, a two-stage treatment of what deliberative critical appraisal above all encompasses should help bring our main topic into sharp focus.

Accessible Objects and Modifiable Subjects: A First Formulation

Above we noted that critical assessment of our semiotic practices is a frequent (if not fated) consequence of engaging in such practices. This general point applies with particular force to the theory of signs itself. On the one hand, the signs we use to articulate the theory of signs are themselves destined to become *objects* of criticism, if they are not such objects at the very outset of inquiry (see, e.g., 8.343). On the other hand, these same conceptions – insofar as they simply make possible and, beyond this, strongly encourage self-criticism – are *instruments* of criticism.[8]

Moreover, in the development of many semiotic systems (e.g., various social sciences), we can observe a drive towards reflexivity, towards conceiving those systems in terms drawn from themselves (even though these terms were originally crafted for purposes other than self-explication). Hence, we find psychoanalytic accounts of psychoanalysis, historical perspectives on history, and sociological theories of sociology. The drive towards reflexivity (apparently inherent in some semiotic practices) should not, however, be construed as necessarily a drive towards insularity, towards couching the system of signs in terms which protect it from external criticism (cf Descombes 1986). While it must be admitted that this drive has historically served in more than a few cases to insulate a practice or system from criticism, the drive towards reflexivity in itself does not entail the avoidance of appraisal (including outside appraisal). Quite the contrary can – indeed, should – be true concerning, at least, semiotics. A truly developed theory of signs will be, at once, one in which this account of signs is itself explained in terms of the signs of this account *and* also one thrust towards confronting both other discursive practices and the actual disclosures of our lived experience. Such a theory must possess the resources to explain its own status, character, and function(s).[9] So, too, it must exhibit the drive to expose itself to its others (most notably, to the dynamic objects indicated[10] by its own theoretical assertions and to those other discourses bearing upon the nature, varieties, and uses of signs).

In 'Sign, Structure, and Play in the Discourse of the Human Sciences,' Jacques Derrida suggests that there are 'two interpretations of interpretation, of structure, of sign, of play' (1978, 292). This suggestion exhibits the very drive towards reflexivity noted just above; it also provides an opportunity to bring titular concerns into sharper focus.

What, then, are according to Derrida the two interpretations of interpretation? Upon one construal, the process of interpretation is animated by the dream of disclosing, fully and finally, the truth about that which it is proffered: it dreams of deciphering a truth or an origin which, in the end, escapes the play of signifiers (i.e., which attains the status of a transcendental signified). Accordingly, such an approach 'lives the necessity of interpretation as an exile,' as one which not only has been cast out from its proper sphere but also struggles to return to this sphere. The other interpretation of interpretation 'is no longer turned toward the origin'; it 'affirms play and tries to pass beyond man and humanism, the name of man being the name of that being who ... has dreamt of full presence, the reassuring foundation, the origin and the end of play' (ibid.). For anyone awakening from this epochal dream of full presence and reassuring foundations, neither the interpreted text nor the interpreting subject can be conceived apart from the play of signifiers (1981, 28). For such a person, the text can no more be granted the status of *arché* than the interpreter can be granted that of agent.[11]

From a Peircean perspective, there is something deeply right, but also something deeply misguided, about the way Derrida conceives these rival construals of the interpretive process. The text (understood here in a very broad sense to mean the set of signs in and through which meaning is conveyed, even if only to be deferred) is not so much an originating as a constraining reality, one which moreover has the character of a *re*source (a locus to which we can go, time and again). This shift in emphasis helps us to avoid being deflected *from* the crucial issue (the constraining pressure exerted by the dynamic object *within* an ongoing process) *to* an illusory problem (the recovery, in an absolutely pristine form, of the object as the *arché* of interpretation or inquiry) (cf 8.12). So, too, any being in any way identifiable (by humans, at least) as an agent is not a transcendental subjectivity capable of either exercising absolute self-determination or attaining complete self-presence; rather such a being is, *qua* agent, itself a sign, something at once essentially incomplete and largely inaccessible to itself. As a sign, the agent is not only essentially incomplete or open-ended, but also semiotically determined[12] or sign-directed. Even so, acknowledging the semiotic character of personal agency does not necessitate denying the agential status of the 'man-sign.' Hence, an uncompromisingly semiotic interpretation of either the interpreted object or the interpreting subject does not entail rendering thoroughly problematic all claims to objectivity or (on the other side) all ascriptions of agency. The strenuous insistence upon the possibility of objectivity[13] and upon the inescapability of agency marks, perhaps more than anything else, the Peircean interpretation of our interpretive practices. Objectivity is, in its most rudimentary sense (a sense suggested by the etymology of the word: a being which throws itself in our way), what naturally and communally implicated agents are compelled to acknowledge; it is, in a more exalted sense, what such agents are resolved to approximate, principally by means of deliberately assessing the evidence in support of their claims. Part of this assessment is critical attention to the (potentially) distorting influence of unrecognized biases.

Objectivity and agency, in their distinctively human forms, are unrecognizable apart from 'the play of signifiers' or (to use Peirce's own terms here) the evolution of interpretants, precisely because they are unrealizable apart from this process. In this context, objectivity is above all else an ideal of interpretation or inquiry: it is what interpreters or inquirers aim at. As such, it is self-imposed. In its turn, the agent is ineluctably a participant in a community. As such, s/he is other-directed, though (to stress the point just made) in a self-sustained manner. In sum, then, objectivity is a demand we, as interpreters or inquirers, make upon ourselves; agency is, in its own way, also a demand we make upon ourselves, for at its core is the resolve to hold ourselves acccountable for not only our actual exertions but also our critical sensibility itself (i.e., our ideals no less than our actions).

Thus, as Professor Savan observes, thought comes of age and a discipline is likely to come into being when a set of signs evolves to the point at which the users of these signs undertake 'a deliberate critical appraisal of the norms' governing these signs (1987–8, 63). Such moments are (to repeat) the most important turning points in the evolution of a semiotic system. As far as the theory of signs itself is concerned, this evolution is fostered by several crucial distinctions. There is, first, the distinction between the *immediate* object (the object as a given sign represents or presents it) and the *dynamical* object ('the really efficient but not immediately present Object') (8.343; see Savan 1987–8, 24–40). There is also the distinction which Peirce draws among the immediate, the dynamic(al), and the 'normal' interpretant.[14] But the very notion of the 'normal' interpretant (the properly 'semiotic effect which *would be* produced by the sign if it could finally and fully satisfy the norm by which it is intended to be judged' [Savan 1987–8, 52]) is obviously an explicitly normative one; for this reason Professor Savan suggests that the 'name *Normal* might better have been *Normative*' (62). This better captures Peirce's intention of identifying the type of interpretant which provides 'a norm or standard by which particular stages (Dynamical Interpretants) of an [ongoing] historical process may be judged.' The notion of the dynamical object is also normative, although perhaps only implicitly so; for it designates what has the capacity to exert a disrupting influence and, by virtue of that capacity, what *would* perform the role of a rectifying force – if the sign were being misinterpreted.

Parallel to Peirce's explicit notion of the dynamical object, there is an implicit notion of what might be called the deliberative subject.[15] By virtue of such conceptions as the dynamical object, the 'normal' (or normative) interpretant, and the deliberative subject, one can secure a fallibilistic outlook and, in turn, one can from the vantage provided by this very outlook enhance the critical resources of semiotic inquiry. The fallibilistic underpinnings of Peirce's semiotics no less than the semiotic articulation of his fallibilism thereby come into view.

In 'Issues of Pragmaticism' (1905), Peirce contends, after confessing that he 'was a pure Kantist [or thoroughgoing Kantian] until he was forced by successive steps into Pragmaticism,' that the Kantian 'has only to abjure from the bottom of his heart the proposition that a thing-in-itself can, however indirectly, be conceived' (5.452). Upon renouncing any commitment to this proposition, s/he must then 'correct the details of Kant's doctrine accordingly'; once s/he has done so, the outlook of such a rectified Kantian will turn out to be that of critical commonsensist (ibid.). From the perspective of such commonsensism, the thing-in-itself is transformed into the dynamical object (the object as it is in itself, quite apart from how it is represented by some individual or group). From this same perspective, the self-in-itself conceived as a transcendent, autonomous subject (i.e., as an empirically inaccessible and absolutely free self) is seen as nothing more than a version of the *cogito*; accordingly,[16] this conception needs to be replaced by a vision of a situated, deliberative agent whose autonomy resides not in the dispassionate exercise of a purely formal capacity but in the passionate participation in a historically evolving process (Polanyi 1958; Burrell 1968).

Agents are free by virtue of deliberation in a twofold sense (punning here on the word 'virtue'). They are free (1) as a result of the virtues engendered by and requisite for the deliberative process and (2) as a result of the enlarged perspective afforded by authentic deliberation (5.339n1), that is, deliberation which avoids degenerating into rationalization (finding bad reasons for what we impulsively desire). But *both* the object as an efficacious reality and the subject as a deliberative agent are indispensable notions for critical commonsensism. It is unclear whether Peirce actually did arrive at these conceptions via a radical modification of his early Kantian commitments. However Peirce might have been led to these notions, their importance for an appreciation of his mature philosophical position cannot be exaggerated, even though it has been largely overlooked.

While Peirce's concept of the dynamical object has been itself the object of critical attention,[17] his vision of the deliberative subject has been all but ignored.

Some critics have even gone so far as to claim that Peirce's alleged failure here is not an incidental omission, but a fated outcome. In effect, these critics are asserting that the absence in Peirce's writings of even a minimal sketch of personal agency (most relevantly for our purposes, an individual agent capable of undertaking self-controlled inquiry) is the inevitable consequence of specific views to which Peirce was deeply committed. Manley Thompson makes this point in one way (1953, 267), Richard Bernstein in another (see, e.g., 1971, 198). It is even possible to construe Jürgen Habermas's early critique of Peirce's pragmatic account of human inquiry as principally related to the question of the subject, for he charges in *Knowledge and Human Interests* that (like positivism) Peirce's pragmatism depicts inquiry as being exclusively rooted in a specific interest, a knowledge-constitutive interest, to be sure, but only one such interest – namely, technical control of natural processes. The other two interests with which Habermas was concerned in this work, mutual understanding and human emancipation, are granted virtually no status within Peirce's theory of inquiry, even though this theory depicts human investigation as essentially a communal process. Like positivism, pragmatism allows its preoccupation with technical control to eclipse any consideration of mutual understanding (let alone of human emancipation); hence, Habermas turns from Peirce to Dilthey, from an allegedly instrumentalist to an explicitly hermeneutic construal of inquiry. What is most pertinent to our exploration is Habermas's charge: in order for Peirce to account for the process of inquiry (a process which, on Peirce's own presuppositions, involves an ongoing dialogue among irreducibly distinct investigators), he must go beyond the limits of his pragmatism.

Habermas, Thompson, and Bernstein exaggerate the inadequacies of Peirce's approach to the self (Colapietro 1989, 65ff). It is easy to understand how such informed and sympathetic students of Peirce's writings could misjudge the strength of his position and, indeed, the very character of his shortcomings (conceiving the undoubted omission of any developed theory of human subjectivity as an inevitable rather than an incidental outcome); for Peirce himself did in fact fail to provide anything approximating a detailed and extended treatment of his views on this topic. In addition, what he did say is often perplexing and not obviously consistent.

Even so, there cannot be any question that Peirce stressed the importance of not only a modifiable subjectivity but also a character determinable (to no slight degree) by deliberation. This much can be gathered from his contention in 'What Pragmatism Is' (1905) that

Among the things which the reader, as a rational person, does not doubt, is that he not merely has habits, but also can exert a measure of self-control over his future actions; which means, however, *not* that he can impart to them any arbitrarily assignable character, but, on the contrary, that a process of self-preparation will tend to impart to action (when the occasion for it shall arise), one fixed character, which is indicated and perhaps roughly measured by the absence (or slightness) of the feeling of self-reproach, which subsequent reflection will induce. Now, this subsequent reflection is part of the self-preparation for action on the next occasion. (5.418)

The process of such self-preparation, in which our feelings of self-reproach play a critical role, is nothing other than deliberation.

The possibility that such a process will be sustained or even arise in the first place depends, above all else, on the two factors indicated in the title of the present section. The notion of a determinate yet modifiable subjectivity is, in a sense, parallel to that of an independent yet accessible reality. The hypothesis which distinguishes truly scientific (or objective) inquiry from other ways of fixing belief is that things are, in principle, distinguishable from our represent-ations of them (cf Ransdell 1979 [1986]). The things to which our representa-tions refer have a status and tenure apart from these representations. But the necessity of drawing this distinction is, in some measure, forced upon us (or forcefully suggested to us) by the *experience* of doubt (the fear that our expecta-tions, even our unconscious ones, may be thwarted); it is also, to some degree, maintained by the deliberate resolve of the responsible inquirer. Hence, this crucial distinction is neither forced upon us wholly *ab extra* nor simply self-legislated. Herein we catch a glimpse of Peirce the critical commonsensist; for here he stresses, on the one hand, a commonsensical distinction (one rooted in the universal experience of virtually every human being of sound mind), but on the other the Kantian emphasis itself upon the self-legislative role of human reason even in its theoretical employment.

The 'external permanency' affirmed by Peirce near the conclusion of 'The Fixation of Belief' (1877) is transformed, in time, into the constraining pres-ence of the dynamical object. The autonomous agency implicit in the doubt-belief theory of inquiry is incorporated eventually in an explicit (though largely undeveloped) way in Peirce's reformulation of his own doctrine of pragmatism. Both notions (like that of deliberate critical appraisal itself) are points at which three of Peirce's most important philosophical achievements – semiotics, prag-maticism, and commonsensism – intersect. The notion of the dynamical object receives a highly nuanced and technical elaboration, while that of deliberative agency assumes a central (even if not as elaborated) significance at this vital intersection. But the two main points can be put simply and commonsensically, which is just as it should be. Things are not necessarily the way we depict them;

put another way, we ourselves are not necessarily disposed towards them in such a way as to fulfil our own desires or to facilitate our own motives. In brief, the possibility of error is omnipresent.

Securing a Fallibilistic Outlook: A Further Elaboration

Let us explore this topic of error more deeply. Indeed, one way to conceive of Peirce's theory of signs is as an elaborate, detailed, and yet uncompromising attempt to secure a fallibilistic outlook. This theory (like his doctrine of categories) is *essentially* a heuristic framework, one actually conceived in some of its most important details in light of fallibilism. So, let us consider in some detail what this hypothesis means.

A primary datum, or inescapable fact, of human existence is that we make mistakes, ranging from the trivial to the tragic. Despite our best efforts and our greatest precautions, we are seemingly unable to avoid error. For our purposes, these observations need to be linked to our efforts as sign-users. If our interpretations of signs were completely flawless and, thus, completely fluid, it is almost certainly true that our awareness of signs would be minimal or less – non-existent. In making a mistake, what we take to be the thing itself manifests itself as an unreliable or misleading appearance: there is actually an *experience* of diremption, of something forcing upon our attention that it is otherwise than we imagined or supposed. It is as unreliable or untrustworthy appearances that signs as such are initially recognized. The actual experience of having been mistaken and the abiding sense of his own fallibility are deeply inscribed in Peirce's theory of signs. While other sets of signs reach a decisive stage in their ongoing development simply when they evolve to the point of deliberate critical appraisal of their procedures, norms, and ideals, the theory of signs only truly takes a decisive turn towards theoretical maturity when it evolves to the point of conceiving itself as a general organon of critical appraisal. But in conceiving itself in this way, semiotics in effect pays homage to its origin, for such an organon can be nothing less than an attempt to come to terms (as fully and finely as possible) with the omnipresent possibility of human error. So, our actual experience of being mistaken not only generates our practical awareness of signs as such but also (in conjunction with our abiding sense of fallibility) informs our theoretical accounts of signs in general, at least if these accounts are Peircean in inspiration. Let us explore this point a little more deeply.

From a Peircean perspective, critical appraisal depends above all on several commonsensical assumptions. Before identifying what are arguably the most important of these assumptions, however, let us discuss in some detail what 'deliberate critical appraisal' means in this context. And let me begin this discussion with an example. The mere use of a sign is often, if not always, governed by a set of norms which have themselves evolved in the service of a constellation of ideals. When a child who is first learning a language uses a word appropriately, s/he is exhibiting competency at the most minimal level – proper usage. There are, of course, higher levels of semiotic competency. For our purposes, let me identify two such levels. Without suggesting the possibility of drawing sharp lines of demarcation among these three levels of semiotic competency, let me suggest none the less that three such levels can be more or less clearly distinguished. Appropriate designations might be (1) proper usage, (2) critically informed usage (including deliberately 'improper' usages), and (3) critically appraised usage. By a critically informed usage, I mean one informed by a more or less explicit awareness of the norms actually embedded in some semiotic practice or institution (e.g., a natural language). In a sense, such a usage is uncritical, for it merely accepts these norms as given: a person at this level of competency does not subject the actual norms themselves to critical appraisal. In other words, there is no effective distinction drawn between *de facto* and *de jure* norms; that these *just are* the norms of this practice is taken to be sufficient justification for their authoritative status. And, by a critically appraised usage, I mean one informed by a more or less systematic appraisal of the the actual norms and ideals embedded in a practice or institution.

A thorny issue concerns just how such critical appraisal is possible. One response to this difficulty is to move in the direction of a resolute historicism; another and indeed counter tendency is to move in the direction of some form of transcendental justification. Richard Rorty exemplifies the former tendency, while Jürgen Habermas illustrates the latter. Such historicism in effect collapses the distinction between critically informed and critically appraised practice, but ordinarily with an important proviso: the actually evolved norms ought not to be taken as absolutely fixed. It is at least possible to 'appraise' in a variety of ways some of the norms actually in place, not the least effective of ways being ridiculing or simply ignoring some norm. While all we have are historically contingent guidelines and norms, these are historically mutable: we are no more imprisoned in our historical ethos than we are in our incarnate existence. To suppose that being situated either in this particular ethos or this particular body is a kind of imprisonment betrays what is, at bottom, an infantile longing – to be everywhere and everyone at once.

In contrast to these views, thinkers inclined towards some form of transcendental justification insist upon a formal defence of any actual norm(s). For them, the appeal to actual norms and principles, especially if these are admitted to be only historically contingent, simply does not count as an adequate justification. Nothing short of an appeal to universal (i.e., transhistorical), necessary principles will satisfy transcendental philosophers such as Habermas.

Peirce was an advocate of neither a historicist nor a transcendental approach to the issue of systematic critical appraisal. He combined an uncompromising historicist sensibility with an insistent transcendental impulse (in response to Rorty's frequently repeated quip, Peirce would likely say that he is scratching because there *is* an itch and this itch is symptomatic of something real!). In this context, the given is a normative practice – or set of such practices – in which we, qua deliberative agents, are always already implicated. Such a practice is not something we occupy or inhabit in any simple or static manner; it entails what might be called an implicated occupancy. An example of such occupancy would be the way one 'inhabits' one's own body, for such occupancy implicates inhabiting an environment. In other words, it entails being thrust (as it were) beyond and outside of oneself. Also, part of such occupancy is the vagueness of boundaries; while for most purposes it is possible to distinguish the embodied self from its enveloping conditions, it is occasionally impossible to draw any sharp or certain distinction between organic and environmental factors and forces. The distinction between inner and outer is irreducibly vague, though for many (if not most) purposes it can be rendered precise enough. The relevance of these observations and suggestions to our topic might be summed up by noting: (1) to participate in a practice is always in some measure and manner to be implicated in context(s) other than that defined by the practice itself, that is, to be thrust beyond the confines established by the presuppositions and commitments of the practice itself (to engage in speaking this language ordinarily arises in and – far more important – ineluctably drives towards non-linguistic involvements); and, thus, (2) to participate in a practice should never be conceived in terms of simple location, such that being *inside* this practice precludes the possibility of being in any others. There is no insular inside to any human practice. All human engagements ensure what is neither a theoretical illusion nor necessarily a pathological condition – the fact that human actors are always beside themselves: they are never indivisible units occupying simple locations. The human self is never completely one with itself; nor is it ever entirely other than its apparent others (how often we resemble our enemies, those hated others against whom we are disposed to thrust our entire being!).

From a distinctively Peircean viewpoint, then, deliberate critical appraisal is at once a historically embedded and formally critical process. It is undertaken by practitioners in the service of the very practices to which they are committed. To participate in such a practice, especially if it has evolved to the point where critical appraisal in some form is a constitutive feature of itself, is to be thrust, willy-nilly, into an ongoing historical process defined (in part) by a developmental teleology. Thus, while there is no transhistorical perspective from which to appraise the actually evolved and continuously evolving norms of our historical practices, there are resources within these very practices by which our inherited outlook, our particular ethos, might be effectively transcended and even transformed.

For Peirce, critical appraisal in this sense depends on various assumptions, not the least of which are: (1) we must distinguish between our representations of reality and reality itself; and (2) we can help what we think and, to a less but still significant degree, what we believe. In Immanuel Kant's transcendental idealism (the system by which Peirce was initiated into philosophy), these commonsensical distinctions are elevated into theoretical dualisms, namely, the dualism between appearances and things-in-themselves as well as that between the determined empirical ego and the autonomous self-in-itself. From other philosophical viewpoints, these distinctions are effectively collapsed; for example, phenomenalism is rooted in the resolute refusal to distinguish appearance and reality (put positively, it is rooted in the thoroughgoing insistence on identifying phenomena as the only conceivable realities), whereas determinism refuses to recognize a transcendent, autonomous subject in addition to the experiential, necessitated self. In opposition to such reductivist approaches, Peirce insists on these distinctions, but (in contrast to the Kantian dualisms) he refuses to elevate these distinctions into dualisms. Stated more precisely, he does not so much insist on just these distinctions as on the two following ones: the distinction between the actual, habit-bound self and the real, ideal-espousing self; and that between appearances and realities, understanding the latter term as equivalent with cognizables.

For Peirce, the point of drawing these distinctions is, first and foremost, heuristic: it is to guide and simply to goad inquiry. Apart from supposing that there is an other at which my signs aim and by which they might be constrained (cf Hausman), Peirce supposes that critical appraisal becomes impossible. Apart from supposing that I can think and even believe otherwise than I actually do, Peirce supposes, again, that critical appraisal is precluded. The conditions securing the possibility of critical appraisal turn out to coincide with at least several of the most fundamental distinctions in Peircean semiotics. This is not accidental, for his general theory of signs is closely linked to his project of formulating a normative theory of inquiry (if they are not in the end one and the same [Savan; Fisch; Kent]). In other words, his doctrines of signs and of fallibilism are intimately related, so much so that we might say, on the one hand, that signs are anything upon which we might *mistakenly* rely (cf Eco 1976, 7) and, on the other hand, that making a mistake is the semiotic phenomenon *par excellence* (i.e., it is that which calls for an explanation and, as it turns out, requires an explanation in terms of signs). Not only the self but also the sign is discovered as part of an attempt to render error intelligible.

How, indeed, are errors possible? Because *I* have taken things to be one way when I could and, beyond this, should have taken them to be some other way; also because the way things appear, in a given context, might turn out to be unreliable for the realization of some more or less definite purpose. Accordingly, there is a need to recognize a continuous subject (an enduring 'I') who can recognize itself as such; there is also a need to recognize a constraining object which has the capacity to frustrate our exertions and, thereby, to vitiate our expectations. The continuity of the self is such that it establishes the possibility of conflict; the constraining presence of the dynamical object is such that, on those occasions when this presence thwarts our efforts and confounds our expectations, it announces the necessity for mediation.

Situating the Deliberative Subject

Embedded in some of the most crucial details of Peirce's theory of signs (indeed, at those very points where his semiotics, pragmaticism, and commonsensism converge), then, is a strenuous fallibilism. As he forcefully insisted, 'the first step toward *finding out* is to acknowledge you do not satisfactorily know already'; accordingly, 'no blight can so surely arrest all intellectual growth as the blight of cocksureness' (1.13). But a vague or general sense of the paucity (1.116–20), unsatisfactoriness, and narrowness of our knowledge is not sufficient; a nuanced array of concepts, the very use of which propels the inquirer towards confrontation with the objections of other inquirers and the exertions of dynamical objects, is required. In fact, Peirce offers more than this: he sketches nothing less than a sweeping vision of deliberative subjects as emergent agents. In seeing such subjects in this light, we will need to situate them in the context in which Peirce himself was led to locate such subjects – namely, cosmic evolution. Deliberative subjects emerge out of a cosmic process; moreover, it is only in reference to this process (especially as illuminated by the categories) that the personal agency of beings like ourselves can be adequately comprehended. Apart from this frame of reference, we can offer at best only a trivial and trivializing account of ourselves.

Our autonomy is located not in 'the smallest bits of our conduct' (say, the conscious resolution of ourselves to execute a specific deed) but in the ongoing formation of our characters (4.611). All supremacy of mind, including sovereignty over our own selves, 'is of the nature of Form' (ibid.). But the sense of Form intended here (the form of Form, as it were) needs to be clearly understood. As a pragmaticist, Peirce stresses that he 'does not make Forms to be the only realities in the world, any more than he makes the reasonable purport of a word [or other symbol] to be the only kind of meaning there is' (5.434). (Herein he supposes that his pragmaticist orientation differs significantly from Hegel's absolute idealism. See, e.g., 5.436.) But Peirce does count Forms among the realities ingredient in (or constitutive of) the cosmos. They are real. In terms of its abstract definition, the attribution of reality to the forms means that they are conceived as possessing 'that mode of being by virtue of which the real thing [here, the Form itself] is as it is, irrespective of what any mind or any definite collection of minds may represent it to be' (5.565). In terms of its pragmatic clarification, this attribution means that the forms have the status and efficacy to initiate and to terminate inquiry (though not – for us at least – to terminate this process in an absolutely final way). Thus, they are (contra nominalism) not figments whose being is that of 'airy nothings' (6.455), might-be's whose barely 'audible' claim to being is that they *might be* given a 'local habitation' or actual instantiation, if only in the musings of some mind (ibid.). Nor should the forms be conceived as existents or actualities, *entia* whose mode of being is that of brute actuality or oppositional insistency. Such brute actualities are preclusive presences whose loudly assertive claim to being is that they have effectively crowded out rival possibilities from some theatre of reactions and, in addition, have pitted themselves against rival actualities in this same theatre. Positively, the forms are best conceived as habits, that is, as more or less general forms of activity (including receptivity).

Peirce proclaims that the pragmatic orientation enables us to discern 'some fundamental truths that other philosophers have seen but through a mist, and most of them not at all' (6.485). Prominent among these truths is the 'acknowledgment that there are, in the Pragmatistical sense, Real habits (which Really would produce effects, under circumstances that may not happen to get actualized, and are thus Real generals)' (ibid.). Thus, 'the *will be's,* the actually *is's,* and the *have beens* are not the sum of the reals. There are besides *would be's* and *can be's* [or might-be's] that are real' (8.216).

The most general of habits is the one Peirce ascribes to the original chaos out of which he imagines the actual universe to have evolved and even now to be evolving – namely, the slightest imaginable tendency, the most precariously present disposition, to take dispositions. This tendency or disposition is one which Peirce called the law of mind, presumably because the capacity to acquire new habits and (as a condition for the acquisition of new habits) the capacity to shed old habits are complementary aspects of a single disposition, this disposition being most manifest in those living creatures whose exertions unmistakably exhibit a mindful character. These creatures are able to mind matters in at least a threefold sense: they can be troubled by, attentive to, or caring of, things (cf Dewey 1934 [1987]). Only organisms which can be variously vexed, flexibly attentive, and discriminately caring are beings to which we can with any measure of confidence attribute mind. But it is just such organisms which manifest to a remarkable degree the capacity to acquire new habits and to shed old ones. Indeed, this disposition or (more precisely) the plasticity and instability required for this disposition to be present are what most deeply underlie the possibility of mindfulness: 'Uncertain tendencies, unstable states of equilibrium are,' in Peirce's own words, 'conditions *sine qua non* for the manifestation of Mind' (7.381). Such tendencies and such states are ineliminable features of the organic constitution of any embodied agent whose habits are not rigidly fixed, whose dispositions are not completely determined (as are those habits or dispositions known as instincts). The absence of fixed habits entails the presence of uncertain tendencies.

The initial movements towards acquiring novel habits are just these uncertain tendencies, including blind gropings and conflicting impulses. The 'normal' outcome is, of course, the taking root of the novel habit itself. What is most manifest in organisms like ourselves provided Peirce with a hint for how to explain the cosmos itself, insofar as it is explicable (Peirce 1898 [1992], 242ff). But, in turn, these uncertain tendencies themselves can (and, for Peirce, must) be considered in light of 'the circumambient All' (6.429).

Our uncertain tendencies (exertions by which our deliberative reflections are prompted) need to be seen against the vast and wild backdrop of cosmic evolution, a process originating in and periodically renewed by cataclysmic explosions. They also need to be seen against the more immediate background of our actual situation (a distinctive biological niche significantly, if not radically, transformed by a multifaceted cultural inheritance).

Our deliberations are generated and structured by oscillations. These oscillations provide us with a clue for how to solve the riddle of the sphinx (how to form a guess at the riddle of the universe). But they do so only because they themselves partake of the very character of the universe itself.

The means by which the self attains sovereignty over itself are not exclusively 'of the nature of Form' (4.611). Brute exertions, including strenuous inhibitions (e.g., holding one's tongue or withholding one's assent), play an important role here. So, too, do the openings for self-determination provided by mere glimpses, often frustratingly fleeting, of what might be. The tyranny of the actual is undermined by our dreams of the possible.

But, even though brute exertions and imagined possibilities are indispensable for attaining self-sovereignty, we attain mastery over ourselves primarily in and through our reliance on the forms requisite for deliberation. At the most rudimentary level, these forms are the largely tacit procedures and habitudes that, in their sum total, make up our *logica utens*. At the most refined level, these forms are deliberately cultivated ideals. After noting that pragmaticism takes the purport of a symbol to consist in a conditional proposition concerning conceivable conduct, Peirce calls attention to an extremely important implication of this construal: 'a *sufficiently deliberate consideration* of that purport ought to be regulated by an ethical principle, which [in turn] by further self-criticism may be made to accord with an esthetical ideal' (5.535).

For Peirce, self-controlled conduct *is* deliberate conduct, our exertions insofar as they bear the stamp of our deliberations. Such conduct is only rarely the result of an *immediately* prior act of deliberation and not the product of a contemporaneous deliberation: 'the power of self-control is certainly not a power over what one is doing at the very instant the operation of self-control is commenced' (8.320). Neither in the actual performance of a deed nor in the immediately antecedent moments to such a performance is there adequate room for a sufficiently deliberate consideration of what ought to be done. Of course, it might seem obvious to us what we ought to do in a particular circumstance, but (alas) it also might turn out that our confident response to the exigencies of the actual case was, in the light of later deliberation, a regretted deed.

It might be helpful to relate Peirce's sweeping vision of cosmic evolution and the emergent status of deliberative agents within this encompassing process to Charles Taylor's recent exploration in *Sources of the Self.* Here Taylor follows 'the theme of self-control through the vicissitudes of our Western tradition' (1989, 174). What he finds is 'a very profound transmutation' at the heart of which is a shift 'from the hegemony of reason as a vision of cosmic order *to* the notion of a punctual disengaged subject exercising instrumental control' (ibid.; emphasis added). In the classical outlook, logos is essentially linked to – in fact, discoverably embodied in – the cosmos itself. In the modern outlook, reason is the capacity of a subject whose relationship to its own body, let alone an order beyond itself or its body, is radically contingent; it is related, first and foremost, to a subject whose dignity and despair reside in its capacity to disengage from any actual entanglement, including its embeddedness in the natural world and its inheritances from human history. The shift from the earlier to the later world-view was, at bottom, a shift from seeing ourselves as located in a cosmos to seeing ourselves as defined in and through our relationship to ourselves.

Peirce's own vision of the cosmos is, at once, one in which his emphasis on emergent order (the continuous growth of concrete reasonableness) recalls the objectivist thrust of the classical outlook, yet one in which his stress on the ongoing task of self-interpretation anticipates the hermeneutic, narrative, and (albeit tentatively) religious thrust of Taylor's own suggestive proposal. But, unlike the cosmic order envisioned by classical philosophers, this is truly an emergent order (the degree and even the forms of order are emerging in a process shot through with contingency). The view that there is an overarching order (concrete reasonableness) and that this is discoverable in some measure by human beings (i.e., rational agents) links Peirce with these philosophers and distances him from such thinkers as Nietzsche and Sartre. Yet, whatever order is evolving out of chaos, it is such that it 'comes indexed to a personal vision, or refracted through a particular sensibility' (Taylor 1989, 491). While it might be in some respects an impersonal order, it cannot be a mechanistic one; nor can it be anything but a semiotic order (the universe 'is perfused with signs, if it is not composed exclusively of signs' [5.448n1]). But, the other side of this is Peirce's claim that signs are 'the only things with which a human being can, without derogation, consent to have any transaction' (6.344). From a Nietzschean perspective, this can only appear as a desperate – perhaps, pathetic – attempt to cling tenaciously to a discredited outlook, an attempt betraying the courage to come to terms with cosmic solitude. But the refusal of such contemporaries of ours as Taylor and Alasdair MacIntyre to grant Nietzsche the last word suggests that the sort of position which was staked out by Peirce is more worthy of a hearing than even many Peirceans are disposed to imagine. In any case, his position is one which breaks with the classical vision of an 'ontic logos' (an order of intelligibility and value inscribed, once and for all, in the very nature of things [Taylor 1989, 189, 254, 257]), yet also is suspicious of thinkers who celebrate their own hardiness in confronting cosmic solitude. The classical vision seems to imply too cosy a home, the Nietzschean too sullen an attitude towards having been thrown out of such a home. Nietzsche is the shadow cast by Plato. Perhaps Peirce is the prism through which is refracted not only the truth inherent in the classical understanding of logos (see, e.g., 1.615) but also the challenge generated by an uncompromising commitment to evolution. The guess of this physicist at the riddle of the universe (1.7) is part and parcel of his attempt to achieve a sufficiently deliberate understanding of his own cosmic situation; that is, it *is* the guess of a physicist, but then it is even more.

Since our autonomy is located not in 'the smallest bits of our conduct' (our individual deeds or, even less so, the conscious intentions often animating such deeds) but rather in the ongoing formation of our characters, and since deliberation is the most crucial factor in this fateful process, we need to look at how Peirce envisaged this process.

Delineating the Deliberative Process

The oscillations which reverberate throughout nature assume, in the unique circumstances of organic life (especially mammalian life), a distinctive form.

While all things in and through their characteristic modes of interaction manifest habits, organisms exhibit the capacity to alter their habits. The oscillations – the random reactions, the blind gropings, and the tentative accommodations – often leave their mark on the malleable constitution of natural substances (1.414). Material bodies are, in a certain respect, the oldest dogs in the universe: they simply can't be taught any (or, at most, very many)[18] new tricks! They are beings hidebound with habits. In contrast, living beings are more or less malleable; and rational beings are self-modifiable. Whenever we actually reason (i.e., whenever we do something more than manipulate symbols in abstraction from any conceivable practical circumstance), we have (in however implicit and inchoate a way) 'a sense of taking a habit, or disposition to respond to a given stimulus in a given kind of way' (5.440). A 'sense of learning' (1.377) – a consciousness of being in some manner and measure altered – characterizes reasoning in its proper sense. 'But the secret of rational consciousness is not so much to be sought in the study of this one peculiar nucleolus, as in the review of the process of self-control in its entirety' (5.440). Peirce delineates the stages of this process as follows:

> of course there are inhibitions and coordinations that entirely escape consciousness [but which, none the less, are part of the economy of self-control]; There are, in the next place, modes of self-control which seem quite instinctive. Next, there is a kind of self-control which results from training. Next, a man can be his own training-master and thus control his self-control. When this point is reached much or all the training may be conducted in imagination [cf 5.440]. When a man trains himself, thus controlling control, he must have some moral rule in view, however special and irrational it may be [e.g., 'Only do what benefits me at this moment']. But next he may undertake to improve this rule; that is, to exercise a control over his control of control. To do this he must have in view something higher than an irrational rule. He must have some sort of moral principle. This, in turn, may be controlled by reference to an esthetic of what is fine [admirable, or adorable in itself] (5.533).

Peirce did not suppose that he enumerated here all of the grades of self-control, musing even that '[p]erhaps their number is indefinite' (ibid.). But a survey of the process of self-control in its entirety would do well to focus its attention on these levels.

For our purposes, two points especially deserve to be stressed. There is, first, the role of the imagination in the process of deliberation (once again, see 5.440). Indeed, Peirce goes so far as to suggest that 'the whole business of ratiocination, and all that makes us intellectual beings, is performed in imagination' (6.286). Second, the process which Peirce is delineating ought to be construed not as one primarily involving a logical or formal derivation but as one concerning most of all a personal and (he would say) spiritual transformation. Part of this second point is that the process is just that – a process: it takes time, in fact, nothing less than a lifetime (but even this turns out not to be adequate, for 'in all his life long no son of Adam has ever fully manifested what there was in him' [1.615]). It is an ongoing process of cultivation (the horticultural metaphor being one to which Peirce was drawn [see, e.g., 1.521 and 6.289]).[19] Ideals and ideas have, for Peirce, a life of their own (e.g., 1.219). Our task is to cultivate ourselves and these in such a way as to facilitate the growth of both; indeed, the flourishing of ourselves is inextricably tied to the flourishing of the ideas and ideals which have taken root in our characters. Peirce was, of course, aware that this could only sound mad in the ears of the mechanist (cf MS290, 58; quoted in Colapietro 1989, 113; cf 5.499). But that ideas or signs 'have life, generative life,' he took to be 'a matter of experiential fact' (1.219). What prevents us from seeing this fact is a metaphysical prejudice (though one more often than not unrecognized for what it is – a metaphysical position). For Peirce, *this* prejudice was the epitome of madness.

Deliberation is a process of cultivation. The best image for the deliberative subject is that of the gardener who cherishes her flowers (6.289). Part of the significance of insisting upon signs having a life of their own is that it acts as a check on our tendency to absolutize ourselves, in this context, to take ourselves as the ultimate source of both intelligibility and significance. Like plants, signs have an inherent dynamic over which we might assume responsibility, but for the very presence of which we have no title.

The actual circumstances of human existence, ranging from our everyday engagements to our most extraordinary undertakings, demand that fallible agents be, in some measure, deliberative subjects. But, as the wilful ignorance and self-deceptive strategies of such agents make clear, 'deliberation' is more often than not a process of rationalization (of finding bad reasons for what we impulsively desire or irrationally want). In sum, we do not attend to our garden with sufficient care, often pulling up the flowers and leaving the weeds!

Conclusion

At the third (or pragmatic) level of clarity, signs are the forms by which we are able to assume responsibility for the course and the upshot of our thinking. The complex signs indicative of the deliberative subject no less than of the dynamic object are, in the context of semiotics itself, such forms *par excellence*. They are both integral parts of this general theory (the deliberative subject no less than the dynamical object), if only it is considered in its full scope.

Not only does David Savan's *Introduction to C.S. Peirce's Full System of Semeiotic* remain, to date, the most illuminating interpretant of that full system, but the character of this gentle, thoughtful man was, especially for those who knew him personally rather than exclusively through his writings, an exemplar of the deliberative subject. In these writings and in his conversations, he was always painstakingly, yet imaginatively, engaged in confronting both the forceful objections of others[20] and the otherness of the dynamical object. Since this object was so often either the sign in its myriad forms or Peirce in his full complexity, investigators of signs and students of Peirce are especially indebted to Professor Savan for his deliberate critical appraisals of these phenomena and these texts.

Notes

1 Questions concerning the manner and, indeed, the very possibility of such appraisal are difficult yet important. It is my belief that we can find in Peirce's writings a relatively novel approach to these questions, one which steers a course between the ahistoric formalisms of a transcendental approach and the inevitable reductionism of (at least, a strong) historicist approach. The ideals, norms, and procedures by which critical appraisals are animated and guided are essentially historical: they have not descended from another world but have emerged within the tangled course of human history. But they provide the resources to transcend the confining contingencies of any actual epoch. We are no more prisoners of a particular time and place than we are surveyors of all time and eternity: we are no more forced to equate the right way with our way than we are able to attain a God's-eye view.

2 To speak in this context of 'our cognitive undertakings, our sustained exertions, and our emotional responses' is intended to recall the triad of thinking, acting, and feeling which Peirce himself in effect deconstructs in an attempt to show that any actual state of human consciousness includes a cognitive, an exertive, and a qualitative aspect (see, e.g., 1.375ff). Hence, to speak of a cognitive undertaking is to refer to a state in which the cognitive aspect is predominant, though one in which the other two aspects are also present (to however slight a degree). Professor Savan's own study, 'Peirce's Semiotic Theory of Emotion,' throws much-needed light on this and other related topics.

3 The use of 'radical' (*radix*, 'root') here is deliberate, though it is not intended to suggest that the sort of assessment which I have in mind is extreme; rather, it is intended to convey that anyone undertaking such an appraisal is trying to get to the root of the matter. In my judgment, the biological metaphor implicit herein is much better than the architectural metaphor implicit in the term 'foundation.'

4 Such a view was originally suggested to me by John Dewey's *Reconstruction in Philosophy* and Michael Polanyi's *Personal Knowledge,* and has been recently confirmed by Charles Taylor's *Sources of the Self* and Seyla Benhabib's *Situating the Self.* But, in this context, it perhaps merits emphasis that I am taking these authors to provide resources for assisting me in either making explicit what is implicit in Peirce's own writings or supplementing Peirce in a manner consistent with his own thought.

5 An extremely important text in which Peirce makes not only this point but also explicitly links his distinctive form of pragmatism with the normative sciences of ethics and aesthetics can be found in a manuscript published in the *Collected Papers* under the title 'Pragmaticism and Critical Common-Sensism': 'since pragmaticism makes the purport [of a concept] to consist in a conditional proposition concerning conduct, *a sufficiently deliberate consideration* of that purport will reflect that the conditional conduct ought to be regulated by an ethical principle, which by further-self-criticism may be made to accord with an esthetical ideal' (5.535; emphasis added). An equally important text is this: 'If conduct is to be thoroughly deliberate, the ideal must be a habit of feeling which has grown up under the influence of a course of self-criticisms and of hetero-criticisms; and the theory of the deliberate formation of such habits is what ought to be meant by esthetics [rather than silly reflections on the sources and forms of sensual pleasure!]' (1.574).

6 For a complete account of how Peirce offers a *via media* between transcendental and historicist approaches to the question of justification (especially justification of the ultimate norms and ideals to which we appeal), it would be necessary to explore in depth 5.505ff. In these pages, Peirce tries to respond to this challenge: 'Criticism and Common-sense are so immiscible that to plunge into either is to lose all touch with the other. The Criticist believes in criticizing first principles, while the Common-sensist thinks such criticism is all nonsense [or, at best, pointless]. So I can find no meaning in your straddling phrase ['critical commonsensism']' (5.505). It is significant that the penultimate conclusion of his involved response is that the *Ding an sich* 'can neither be indicated nor found' (5.525), his ultimate conclusion being that: 'The kind of Common-sensism which thus criticizes the Critical Philosophy and [at the same time] recognizes its own affiliation to Kant has surely a claim to call itself Critical Common-sensism' (5.525). Central to the argument of my own paper is that Peirce's notion of the dynamical object is the commonsensical (and, for that matter, the pragmaticist) rendering of the Kantian conception of the thing-in-itself: this notion is an attempt to capture the truth in a conception which, as it was actually formulated by Kant, is nonsensical (however, see Thompson 1983; also Westphal 1968).

For an excellent account of how Peirce, in his capacity as a commonsensist, can undertake a thoroughgoing criticism of first principles, see Haack 1983 (especially pp 248–54). She relates this to the Cartesian project of universal doubt rather than the Kantian project of critical philosophy.

7 For illuminating treatments of Peirce's 'thoroughgoing evolutionism' (6.14), see: Joseph Esposito's *Evolutionary Metaphysics* (Athens, Ohio: Ohio University Press 1980), Sandra Rosenthal's *Speculative Pragmatism* (Amherst: University of Massachusetts Press 1986), and Carl Hausman's *Charles Peirce's Evolutionary Philosophy* (Cambridge: Cambridge University Press 1993).

8 Animated by somewhat different objectives and rooted in another research tradition, Julia Kristeva none the less notes that: 'At every instant of its production, semiotics thinks (of) its object, its instrument and the relation between them.' In the process of 'thinking (of) itself,' semiotics is 'an open form of research, a constant critique that turns back on itself and offers its own autocritique.'

9 Insofar as semiotics attains the status of a formal system, it is not certain whether it can be *both* consistent and complete, for Godel's theorem or a relevant variation of it might be applicable to such a system. Even so, the demand of performative consistency and that of formal comprehensive need to be taken by the investigator of signs with the utmost seriousness.

10 This term is intended here to indicate or point to the indexical function which is necessarily an ingredient in any meaningful theoretical utterance. As Peirce notes, 'a symbol, in itself, is a mere dream; it does not show what it is talking about. It needs to be connected with its object. For that purpose, an *index* is indispensable' (4.56; cf Goudge 1965; Savan 1987–8, 25–6; 36–9).

11 One place in which we can clearly see the explicit effacement of the interpreter as a personal agent is in an interview in which Derrida asserts that: 'I am not a pluralist and I would not say that every interpretation is equal, but *I* do not select. The interpretations select themselves' (1980, 21; cf Smith 1988, 47). In addition, he claims that: 'I would not say that some interpretations are truer than others. I would say that some are more powerful than others. The hierarchy is between forces and not between true and false' (21). This leads him to suggest that: 'Meaning is determined by a system of forces which is not personal. It does not depend on the subjective identity but on the field of different forces ... No one is free to read as he or she wants' (22).

12 For what determination means in this context, see *Writings of Charles S. Peirce*, ed. M.H. Fisch, G. Moore, and C.J.W. Kloesel et al. (Bloomington: Indiana University Press 1984), 2:155–8; also Joseph Ransdell's 'Semiotic Causation: A Partial Explication' in *Proceedings* and T.L. Short's 'Life among the Legisigns' (1982 [1986]: 108–9).

13 For helpful discussions of this and related topics, see Eugene Freeman's 'Charles Peirce and Objectivity in Philosophy,' Susan Haack's 'Descartes, Peirce and the

Cognitive Community,' T.L. Short's 'Peirce and the Incommensurability of Theories,' and Joseph Ransdell's 'Semiotic Objectivity.'

14 Peirce offers several distinct classifications of the interpretants of a sign (see Savan 1987–8, 48ff). How these classifications are to be coordinated with one another is an extremely vexed question. It is fortunate that, for our purposes, this question need not be resolved. The classification of interpretants as immediate, dynamic, and 'normal' suffices (in abstraction from other classifications) to make the main point here. It is likely that the other classification(s) might serve as well.

15 It is only appropriate to point out that my use of 'object' and 'subject' violates Peirce's own ethics of terminology! In a letter to Victoria Lady Welby, he explained that, according to his own ethics of terminology: 'I use the term "object" in the sense in which objectum was first made a substantive early in the XIIIth century; and when I use the word without adding "*of*" what I am speaking of the object, I mean anything that comes before thought or the mind in any usual sense ... I will add, while I am about it, that I do not make any contrast between Subject and Object, far less talk about "subjective and objective" in any of the varieties of German senses, which I think have led to a lot of bad philosophy, but I use "subject" as the correlative of "predicate," and speak only of the "subjects" of those signs which have a part which separately indicates what the object of the sign is' (Hardwick 1908 [1977], 69). What in part justifies my 'violation' is that my usage is itself informed by Peirce's own observation that: 'The case of philosophy is very peculiar in that it has positive need of popular words in [their] popular senses – not as its own language (as it has too usually used those words) but as objects of its study' (2.223). But the prohibition which Peirce defends here (that of using, as appropriate terms in philosophical discourse itself, popular words in their popular senses) is not one which it would even be possible to follow.

16 This follows only if Peirce thoroughly rejects the Cartesian conception of human subjectivity. That he does is rather well known; for discussions of how and why he does, see Haack's 'Descartes, Peirce and the Cognitive Community' and my own book, *Peirce's Approach to the Self*.

17 Carl Hausman, in particular, has made the dynamical object a focal concern of his investigations into Peirce; but he does not allow his strong emphasis upon recognizing the constraining pressure exerted by dynamical objects to eclipse recognition of either the creativity characteristic of human inquiry or the alterability exhibited by reals themselves. The very title of his recent book, *Charles S. Peirce's Evolutionary Philosophy*, captures this nuanced approach; and, in this and other writings, Hausman proves himself to be faithful to Peirce.

18 It should be recalled that Peirce used 'habit' in a very broad sense to denote 'a specialization, original or acquired, of the nature of a man, or an animal, or a vine, or a crystallizable chemical substance, or anything else, that he or it will behave, or

always tend to behave, in a way describable in general terms upon every occasion ... that may present itself of a generally describable character' (5.538). So conceived, habits are by no means either a mental (5.492) or even a biological phenomenon: 'Empirically, we find that some plants take habits. The stream of water that wears a bed for itself is forming a habit' (ibid.).

19 Another significant example of what is, in a way, a horticultural metaphor (moreover, an example which is directly related to the topic of deliberation) can be found in 5.546. Here Peirce asserts that 'a judgment is something that *ripens* in the mind.' He immediately goes on to suggest that 'there is a vernacular phrase which betrays a feature of the ripe judgment, the phrase "I says to myself, says I."' Hence, it does not seem illicit for me to suggest that such a judgment is the fruit (!) of deliberation, the process in which the self is struggling to hold itself more fully and finely accountable for its deeds.

20 A good illustration of this is the exchange between Professor Savan and Thomas Goudge; another is that between him and T.L. Short.

References

Benhabib, Seyla. 1992 *Situating the Self*. New York: Routledge.

Bernstein, Richard J. 1971. *Praxis and Action*. Philadelphia: University of Pennsylvania Press.

Brent, Joseph. 1993. *Charles Sanders Peirce: A Life*. Bloomington: Indiana University Press.

Burrell, David. 1968. 'Knowing as a Passionate Quest: C.S. Peirce.' In *American Philosophy and the Future*, edited by Michael Novak, 107–37. New York: Charles Scribner's Sons.

Colapietro, Vincent M. 1989. *Peirce's Approach to the Self*. Albany, N.Y.: State University of New York Press.

Deely, John. 1990. *Basics of Semiotics*. Bloomington: Indiana University Press.

Derrida, Jacques. 1978. 'Sign, Structure, and Play in the Human Sciences.' In his *Writing and Difference*, translated by Alan Bass. Chicago: University of Chicago Press.

– 1980. 'Interview' in *Literary Review* (London), no. 14.

– 1981. *Positions*. Translated by Alan Bass. Chicago: University of Chicago Press.

Descombes, Vincent. 1986. *Objects of All Sorts: A Philosophical Grammar*. Translated by Lorna Scott-Fox and Jeremy Harding. Baltimore: Johns Hopkins University Press.

Dewey, John. 1934. *Art as Experience*. New York: Putnam.

Esposito, Joseph. 1980. *Evolutionary Metaphysics*. Athens, Ohio: Ohio University Press.

Fisch, Max H. 1986. *Peirce, Semiotic, and Pragmatism*. Edited by Kenneth Laine Ketner and Christian J.W. Kloesel. Bloomington: Indiana University Press.

Freeman, Eugene. 1983. 'C.S. Peirce and Objectivity on Philosophy.' In *The Relevance of Charles Peirce*, edited by Eugene Freeman, 59–79. La Salle, Ill.: Monist Library of Philosophy.

Goudge, Thomas. 1965. 'Peirce's Index.' *Transactions of the Charles S. Peirce Society* 1:52–70.

Haack, Susan. 1983. 'Descartes, Peirce and the Cognitive Community.' In *The Relevance of Charles Peirce*, 238–63. See Freeman for full citation.

Habermas, Jürgen. 1971. *Knowledge and Human Interests*. Translated by Jeremy Shapiro. Boston: Beacon Press. Translation of *Erkenntnis und Interesse*. Frankfurt: Suhrkamp Verlag 1968.

Hardwick, Charles S. 1977. *Semiotic and Significs: The Correspondence between Charles S. Peirce and Victoria Lady Welby*. Bloomington: Indiana University Press.

Hausman, Carl. 1993. *Charles S. Peirce's Evolutionary Philosophy*. Cambridge: Cambridge University Press.

Kent, Beverley. 1987. *Charles S. Peirce: Logic and the Classification of the Sciences*. Kingston and Montreal: McGill-Queen's University Press.

Kristeva, Julia. 1969. *Recherches pour une semanalyse*. Paris: Seuil.

Langer, Susanne. 1942. *Philosophy in a New Key*. New York: Mentor.

Peirce, C.S. 1898. (1992) *Reasoning and the Logic of Things*. Edited by Kenneth Laine Ketner. Cambridge, Mass.: Harvard University Press.

– 1931–58. *Collected Papers of Charles Sanders Peirce*. 8 vols. Edited by C. Hartshorne, P. Weiss, and A. Burks. Cambridge, Mass.: Belknap Press of Harvard University Press.

Polanyi, Michael. 1958. *Personal Knowledge*. London: Routledge and Kegan Paul.

Ransdell, Joseph. 1979. 'Semiotic Objectivity.' *Semiotica* 26, nos. 3/4: 261–88. Reprinted in *Frontiers in Semiotics*, edited by John Deely, et al. Bloomington: Indiana University Press 1986. All references in this paper are to *Frontiers*.

– 1981. 'Semiotic Causation: A Partial Explication.' In K. Ketner et al., *Proceedings of the C.S. Peirce Bicentennial International Congress*, 201–6. Lubbock: Texas Tech University Press.

Rosenthal, Sandra. 1986. *Speculative Pragmatism*. Amherst: University of Massachusetts Press.

Savan, David. 1981a. 'Peirce's Semiotic Theory of Emotion.' In K. Ketner et al., *Proceedings of the C.S. Peirce Bicentennial International Congress*, 319–33. Lubbock: Texas Tech University Press.

– 1981b. 'The Unity of Peirce's Thought.' In *Pragmatism and Purpose: Essays Presented to Thomas A. Goudge*, edited by J.G. Slater, L.W. Sumner, and F. Wilson, 3–14. Toronto: University of Toronto Press.

– 1986. 'Response to T.L. Short.' *Transactions* 22 no. 2: 125–43.

– 1987–8. *An Introduction to C.S. Peirce's Full System of Semeiotic*. Toronto: Monograph Series of Toronto Semiotic Circle, no. 1.

Short, T.L. 1982. 'Life among the Legisigns.' *Transactions* 18 no. 4 (Fall): 285–310. Reprinted in *Frontiers in Semiotics*. 105–19. See Ransdell 1979 for full citation. All references in this paper are to *Frontiers*.

– 1983. 'Peirce and the Incommensurability of Theories.' In *The Relevance of Charles Peirce*, 119–31. See Freeman for full citation.

– 1986. 'What They Said in Amsterdam: Peirce's Semiotic Today.' *Semiotica* 40, nos 1/2:103–28.

– 1988. 'The Growth of Symbols.' *Cruzeiro Semiotico* no. 8 (Jan.): 81–87.

Smith, Paul. 1988. *Discerning the Subject*. Minneapolis: University of Minnesota Press.

Taylor, Charles. 1989. *Sources of the Self*. Cambridge, Mass: Harvard University Press.

Thompson, Manley. 1953. *The Pragmatic Philosophy of C.S. Peirce*. Chicago: University of Chicago Press.

– 1983 'Things in Themselves.' *Proceedings and Addresses of the American Philosophical Association* 57, no. 1 (Sept.): 33–48.

Westphal, Merold. 1968 'In Defense of the Thing in Itself.' *Kant-studien* 59, no. 1: 118–41.

Hypostatic Abstraction in Self-Consciousness

T.L. SHORT

Peirce held that we have no direct knowledge of ourselves (or, as he said, of 'the inner world') but know ourselves only by 'hypothetical reasoning from our knowledge of external facts' (5.265).[1] It is not immediately obvious that inferring the 'inner' from the 'outer' is possible. From where would a concept of the inner come if we never observe it directly but know it only by inference from something else that, by conception, is quite different? This question is made no easier by Peirce's famous dictum: 'The elements of every concept enter into logical thought at the gate of perception and make their exit at the gate of purposive action; and whatever cannot show its passport at both those two gates is to be arrested as unauthorized by reason' (5.212). If all perception is of the outer, and all elements of any concept must be from perception, then it is only by elements drawn from perception of the outer that we may conceive of the inner. The aim of this essay is to examine the way in which concepts of selves, oneself, thoughts, feelings, and powers of thought and decision are formed. My conclusions are drawn as an explication of Peirce's philosophy, but I also think they are true.

I

It is necessary to make some preliminary observations about Peirce's conception of concepts and concept-formation. For such a purpose, one can hardly avoid turning to one of Peirce's most famous statements – that of the pragmatic maxim, in 1878:

> Consider what effects, that might conceivably have practical bearings, we conceive the object of our conception to have. Then, our conception of these effects is the whole of our conception of the object. (5.402)

This, however, poses several difficulties. The maxim states that our concept of any object, that is, of anything and not just of physical objects, involves concepts of effects, of practical bearings, and of the original object itself (which must be conceived of in conceiving of the effects *it* has). But as all of these are also objects of conception, we are thrown into an infinite regress. And if a concept of the object (as having certain effects) is part of our concept of the object, then we also find ourselves in a nasty little circle. Finally, if to this maxim we add the thesis that we know the inner only by inference from the outer, then it appears that we have contradicted ourselves. For this maxim makes the conception of any object, including therefore outer objects, to depend on a concept of oneself and one's habits of action, as is implied by the words, 'practical bearings': 'To develop its meaning, we have, therefore, simply to determine what habits it produces ... there is no distinction of meaning so fine as to consist in anything but a possible difference in practice' (5.400). And if we cannot conceive of outer objects without conceiving of their bearing on our own habits of action, then we cannot conceive of the outer without conceiving of the inner; in which case the inner cannot be inferred, *ab initio*, from the outer.

However, all of these difficulties arise from ignoring the point of Peirce's maxim. It is, he said, 'the rule for attaining the third grade of clearness of apprehension.' That is, it is not an account of what must be in one's mind who possesses a certain concept, but of what must be in one's mind who raises that concept to this highest grade of clearness. That grade of clearness is the result of reflecting, in accordance with the rule given, on concepts already possessed – necessarily, at lower grades of clearness. At the lowest grade of clearness, an idea 'will be recognized wherever it is met with' (5.389), by which, I take it, Peirce meant that one can identify the objects that that idea applies to. It does not mean that he can explain that idea to anyone else. That would be a second grade of clearness ('distinctness'), at which one can define the idea in terms that are themselves understood at the first grade of clearness (5.390, 392). But even the designation of such ideas as 'clear' suggests a lower level still, at which we may possess unclear ideas. (Indeed, what's new? If it were not for the prevalence of confused and obscure ideas, those paid to be 'philosophers' would be out of business; lest this dread result occur, the latter produce a goodly number of unclear ideas of their own.)

The first two morals I wish to draw from this are (a) that concept-formation takes place through several gradations, from less to greater clarity, and (b) that this is a bootstrap operation. Moral (a) means that we *must* begin with ideas that are less clear, before we can possess them in a form that is more clear. Moral (b) means that we *can* use ideas that are *less* clear to make other ideas *more* clear.

It is a mistake to assume that an explication can be no clearer than the ideas used in it. If the latter are clear enough to perform the function assigned to them in that explication, then that suffices. Why does this seem so counter-intuitive? Perhaps it is because we tend to think of explication as a kind of definition, *à la* G.E. Moore. In that case, of course, the parts must be less problematic than the whole, if the whole is to succeed. But Peirce's maxim points in a different direction altogether, towards a type of explication that will grow with a growth in factual information and, hence, towards an explication in which there are elements that refer as well as elements that describe. The differentiation of linguistic role within an explication accounts for why the whole can be more clear than its parts. For reference can succeed even with quite unclear – even with mistaken! – conceptions. Take, for example, the concept of temperature.

A person who can distinguish a hot from a cold stove has some idea of temperature, but not so clear a one as he who can explain the difference between heat and temperature and show you how to measure degrees of temperature. But would we have arrived at the latter idea without having begun with the former? And when heat was first distinguished from temperature, by Joseph Black in 1760, it was in terms – 'quantity of heat' versus 'intensity of heat' – that were themselves more suggestive than exact. Even this advance would not have been possible had means not been devised – as much as 168 years earlier, by Galileo – for measuring what was still very confusedly conceived. When Fahrenheit introduced the mercury thermometer and established standard scales, from about 1715 to 1724, that was still several decades before Black's work and, hence, before anyone could study how mercury conducts heat (which Henry Cavendish did in 1783). Thus, the mercury thermometer resulted in a clearer conception of temperature even though its own operation was poorly understood. And it had to have been developed first, before those investigations that distinguished heat from temperature became possible, since it is what made them possible. Finally, the concept of a molecule was necessarily as crude as any mechanical concept can be, when it was used, in the nineteenth century, to further clarify the concepts of heat and temperature (in the kinetic theory).

Thus, the infinite regress seemingly implied by Peirce's maxim is avoided by the fact that the ideas used to bring a given idea to the third grade of clearness may themselves be of a lower grade. So also the apparent circle: there is no problem with the use of an idea at a lower grade of clearness in the explication that raises that very same idea to a higher grade. To repeat: it is a mistake to assume that the whole explication can be no clearer than its parts, if the parts are clear enough to perform the function assigned them in that explication. Finally, the concept of the inner can be derived from concepts of outer things *before* the latter have been raised even to the second grade of clearness. Thus, concepts of the inner, at a low grade of clearness, are available to be used in raising concepts of outer things to the third grade of clearness.

Lessons of the same sort apply equally to the *first* formation of a concept, that is, at its level of greatest obscurity: it, too, does not come from nothing but, rather, presupposes an amount of preconceptual experience and preconceptual skill in dealing with things and persons. Part of this preconceptual experience and skill is linguistic. The child must babble, then begin to reproduce articulate sounds; it must also respond in certain determinate ways to others' production of articulate sounds, much as a dog might run to the door when his master says, 'Let's go for a walk, Fido.' Nor does it matter much where we draw the line between the conceptual and the preconceptual. You can say that the dog has a concept of going for a walk, if you like. Certainly the dog has acquired a habit of action associated with certain sounds, and behaves differently when on the walk than when not on it. But, of course, he cannot talk about it nor, therefore, use words to think to himself about it. Nor can the young child do this who has not yet learned to say 'walk' while tugging an adult doorward. However, the direction from the preconceptual to the conceptual is clear, just as the direction towards greater clarity is clear: it is towards increased linguistic skill.

And that is the third moral I want to draw from the foregoing: (c) language use is the key to our concept of the conceptual. Certainly it was so for Peirce. But with that moral come two more: (d) language use does not count when it is self-contained but only when it mediates between sensation and action. To know what concept a word expresses, you must understand how certain uses of that word would influence conduct. And: (e) this pragmatic theory of meaning does not reduce meaning to anything less general, such as actions, sensations, or Kantian schemata. In a well-known 1906 gloss on his 1878 pragmatic maxim, Peirce said that 'pragmaticism' makes the 'purport' of thinking to '[lie] in conditional resolutions to act' (5.402n3). Thus, when, in 1903, Peirce spoke of 'the elements of every concept' and said that they enter at the gate of perception, he could not have meant that concepts are composed of the lingering contents of sensation, as Locke and other British empiricists claimed. Earlier in the same lecture of 1903, Peirce explained that it is perceptual *judgments* that provide the materials of thought and that these judgments, which are the first or uncontrolled judgments we form in response to any particular sensory stimulus, always 'contain general elements, so that universal propositions are deducible from them' (5.181). Those general elements are concepts, explicable in terms of universally quantified, conditional rules. Peirce, in that same gloss of 1906, insisted that in his maxim he employed 'five times over ... derivatives of *concipere*' precisely in order to 'avoid all danger of being understood as attempting to explain a concept ... by anything but concepts.' Thus, if concepts of the inner are to be formed from perception of the outer, it is, more precisely, from concepts of the outer that they are to be formed.

Our task, then, is set. (1) The mark of possessing a concept of one's self is linguistic: the full and proper use of the word 'I' and other terms for selves and their indoor furniture. ('It has already been pointed out by Kant that the late use of the very common word 'I' with children indicates an imperfect self-consciousness in them ...' [5.227].) (2) We are to trace the development of these linguistic skills from the experiences and skills that precede them. And (3) we are to explicate the meaning of the words thus newly employed in terms of concepts that refer to outdoor furniture. Does this commit Peirce to a behaviourist theory of mind? I shall argue the contrary thesis.

II

Most of what Peirce said directly about self-awareness is familiar to those who have studied his philosophy. These are the salient points. First: 'We become aware of ourself in becoming aware of the not-self' (1.324). The reference here is to the immediate sense of effort and resistance, not yet to a concept of self and other. Second: the concept of self is formed negatively: 'Thus, he becomes aware of ignorance, and it is necessary to suppose a *self* in which this ignorance can inhere' (5.233). 'In short, *error* appears, and it can be explained only by supposing a *self* which is fallible' (5.234). 'Ignorance and error are all that distinguish our private selves from the absolute ego of pure apperception' (5.235). Third: in this concept of self, a knowledge not only of material others but also of other persons is implicated. This is clear from the way in which Peirce developed the point in the essay from which we have just been quoting – as follows.

The child, Peirce remarked, observes his own body as an object of peculiar interest and notes similarities of this object to certain others (5.229, 231), and this manifestly before he acquires self-consciousness (5.227–8, 230); he also learns some words of a language and learns to associate the production of those sounds with lips like those he can touch in his own face (still without conceiving of it as 'own') (5.232). His grasp of the language proceeds to the point, still before self-consciousness, where he can understand what others say about the things around them, 'So much so, that testimony is even a stronger mark of fact than *the facts themselves*, or rather than what must now be thought of as *appearances* themselves ... So testimony gives the first dawning of self-consciousness' (5.233). If it is *testimony* that gives the first dawning of self-consciousness – the testimony of others that contradicts one's own thoughts – then to conceive of oneself is to conceive of one who is distinct from, but in communion with, those other selves who see the world differently. Peirce does not explicitly draw the latter conclusion, but it is implicit in the account just summarized.

Let us come to the same conclusion another way. The distinction between appearance and reality arises at the same time as the distinction between self and world. Appearance is the world from the limited perspective of oneself at a given moment; reality is the world defined by the testimony of oneself and others over time. Therefore, the two preceding distinctions imply a third: that between self and other selves.

If a child begins to learn a language before acquiring self-consciousness, then that alone shows that self-consciousness does not precede consciousness of other selves. For part of learning a language is learning to which things to address words and from which to expect words – those things become 'whos' and 'whoms.' Even the first stuttering stages of speaking a language place one in a community of speakers. And, thus, when one attains self-consciousness, it is as a member of that community. This would be so in any case, but is especially so given the role Peirce assigns to that community – the power of its testimony to define reality and to impress a child with a sense of his own ignorance and error – in producing self-consciousness.

All of this is not yet enough to justify Peirce's further conclusion that society constitutes or determines the self. There is a logical gap between determining consciousness of the self and determining the self one becomes conscious of. But let me remind you of how far Peirce went in stating the latter view: 'Nor must any synechist say, "I am altogether myself, and not at all you." If you embrace synechism, you must abjure this metaphysics of wickedness. In the first place, your neighbors are, in a measure, yourself, and in far greater measure than, without deep studies in psychology, you would believe. Really, the selfhood you like to attribute to yourself is, for the most part, the vulgarest delusion of vanity' (7.571). We shall return to this point much later.

Let us draw one final implication of the foregoing. If each of us conceives of himself as one among others, it is as one speaker among other speakers. Persons interact in a variety of ways, but not all of these make them persons. She that nurtured Romulus and Remus was not thereby a person. The things that become 'whos' and 'whoms' are those who speak to us and to whom we speak. We think of persons (in the first dawning of self-consciousness, and also thereafter) as those who possess the power of speech or other linguistic expression – the power, namely, to testify to one another about the material world, to command, to obey, and to articulate feelings. Thus, the social component of self-consciousness is also a linguistic component. As we noted earlier, one does not possess a concept without having the ability to express it; but in the case of the concept of persons, whether oneself or others, that power is also part of the concept's *content*. Whatever else it involves, the conception of a person includes that entity's having certain powers of linguistic expression.

Peirce changed his mind about several matters of fundamental importance, but not, so far as I know, about any of the preceding. The passages quoted above have been taken from a variety of periods: 1868, 1903, 1892.

III

Peirce said that we must suppose a self as that in which ignorance inheres and which is fallible. The types of ignorance and error that testimony can correct are propositional. Thus, to conceive of oneself in this way, one must first discriminate (in practice, not conceptually) strings of words that are propositional in form. This is possible only because we have learned to speak, however incompletely and imperfectly, before having to form a concept of persons or selves. The contents of the conceptions of ignorance and error are thus derived from speech.

So far, this sounds Searlean, and, to a significant degree, John Searle's account of the concept of the mind as modelled on speech is indeed Peircean. However, there is a crucial difference. For we need also to notice the *form* of the conception each derives from speech. The form of that concept in Peirce's explication of it is that which he elsewhere discussed under the rubric 'hypostatic abstraction.' The use of this form means that the linguistic 'model' is not applied directly, indeed, is not really a model at all. Rather, the self is defined *indirectly* by its *presumed relation to* speech; and from this nothing follows immediately, even in the form of model or metaphor, about the intrinsic character of that self.

To see what this entails, let us dwell for a moment on Peirce's account of abstraction.[2] Hypostatic differs from precisive abstraction: the latter consists in selecting one feature from a complex of features or a concrete object, as when we say of something that it *is large*, while the former makes this feature into an object of reference, as when we speak of something's *largeness* (4.322, 2.364). Hypostatic abstraction is thus identical with abstraction as Quine and some others use the term: it is the transition from first- to second-order predicate logic. By introducing appropriate operators binding the variables of a general description to form a singular term, we can designate classes, attributes, and relations; from uses of 'is the father of' we can abstract the class, fathers, the attribute, fatherhood, and so on.

Peirce remarked that hypostatic abstraction 'may be called the principal engine of mathematical thought' (2.364, see also 4.234 and 5.534). 'It is by abstraction that a mathematician conceives the particle as occupying a point.

The place is now made a subject of thought ... When the mathematician regards an operation as itself the subject of operations, he is using abstraction ...' (NEM 4:11). With respect to its use in mathematics, Peirce made two points about hypostatic abstraction, that it 'is a necessary inference whose conclusion refers to a subject not referred to in the premiss' and that 'the new individual is spoken of as an *ens rationis*; that is, its being consists in some other fact' (4.463). 'For what is an abstraction but an object whose being consists in facts about other things?' (NEM4:11). For example, the existence of the class $\hat{x}Px$ consists in there being at least one individual, a, such that either Pa or ~Pa. Hence, the inference from $\forall x(Px \rightarrow Qx)$ to $\hat{x}Px \subseteq \hat{x}Qx$ is logically necessary. For while the conclusion introduces two entities not referred to in the premiss, the being of those entities consists in facts presupposed in the premiss.

It does not follow that every fact about an *ens rationis* is inferable from facts about other things. Second-order predicate logic is not reducible to first-order predicate logic; mathematics could not be done without referring to classes or to other abstract entities. The cardinal number of the set 'frogs in my room' is not deducible from any facts about those frogs themselves. However, the question of mathematical existence, thus raised, is not germane to our present topic.

Not everything introduced into discourse by hypostatic abstraction is an *ens rationis*. Even when speaking of mathematics, Peirce's favourite example of hypostatic abstraction was Molière's burlesque of scholasticism: when asked why opium puts people to sleep, the scholastic response is that it has a dormitive virtue. Peirce commented that even in this, 'the operation of hypostatic abstraction is not quite utterly futile. For it does say that there is *some* peculiarity in the opium to which sleep must be due' (5.534). If it is not futile to mention this entity, it must be because it is thought of as something beyond the fact that people who take opium tend to fall asleep: it must be supposed to be some reality that explains that phenomenon. This, if it exists, cannot be a mere *ens rationis* but must be something that actually acts on the human nervous system.

The reason postulating a dormitive virtue is a hypostatic abstraction is that the virtue is identified exclusively in terms of a fact that makes no reference to it, namely, the fact that people who take opium tend to fall asleep. It is, thus, abstracted from that fact. The abstraction is hypostatic because it posits an entity.

However, since the postulated virtue is not thought to *consist in* the fact from which it is abstracted, it is not an *ens rationis*. And neither is the inference to it logically necessary. Rather, that inference could be deductively valid only with the additional, logically contingent premiss that the regularity in question has an explanation and that part of that explanation is to be found in opium. Absent that assumption, the inference is not deductive but is an extreme case of what

Peirce called 'abduction': it introduces a hypothesis on the ground that, if true, it would explain the stated fact.

Such phrases as 'that which' serve to distinguish the entity postulated from the fact from which it is abstracted. Opium's dormitive virtue is *that* in opium *which*, when ingested, causes drowsiness. The very indirectness of its characterization makes this posited entity more a question than an answer. Its importance is not in explaining anything but in giving a direction or focus to inquiry: let us examine opium to see what in it causes sleep. We want to know what the dormitive virtue is 'in itself,' that is, apart from the phenomenon it is supposed to explain. (The problem with scholasticism is not in positing 'virtues,' but in thinking that that alone is explanatory, without having to go on to identify the materials and mechanisms in which those virtues or powers consist. However, I do not believe that all powers can be reduced to mechanisms, but, rather, the other way about: mechanisms and materials must ultimately be understood in terms of their powers, that is, powers – dispositional properties, forces, and fields – having certain spatio-temporal loci. Such powers are introduced by hypostatic abstractions not further explicable; but we cannot know in advance of trying to explain them which those are.) In general, as I argued in an earlier paper, in empirical science, hypostatic abstraction posits an entity defined by its assumed physical relation to a known phenomenon.[3]

If the self is first posited as that in which ignorance inheres and which commits errors, then it is introduced by hypostatic abstraction from certain publicly accessible speech acts. It is not identified with speech, but it is defined in terms of it, as *that which* did not say X or as *that which*, alas, did say Y. Of course, a full understanding of speech would in some respect reverse this relationship. But, before they learn that words are governed by social conventions and express concepts, and that sentences have to be understood in terms of the presumed intentions of competent speakers, children already in some deficient manner understand and employ some sentences. And that is enough for them to bootstrap into self-consciousness.

Or almost enough. Peirce skimps on the details in this matter, which in any case are better left to empirical investigation. Even a little such investigation (Peirce was not a parent) would reveal that, as is typical of him, he overemphasized the intellectual. Before children learn to use the word 'I,' they employ 'me' and their own given names (or some lisped version thereof). Furthermore, they use these terms not to express awareness of factual error but to make demands: 'Me! me! me!' or 'Johnny wants Mama!' Those terms are thus already available when a name is needed for the locus of intellectual failure. Proper use of the word 'I' comes later, and it reveals the child's grasp of the fact that it is but one among many selves, equivalent in selfhood, each of whom refers to itself by the word 'I.' But the main points remain: that self-awareness is initiated by an abductive inference from publicly accessible phenomena; that this inference is a hypostatic abstraction; hence, that the new entity it introduces is defined indirectly in terms of its effects, vulnerabilities, and so on; and that the latter are in significant part linguistic.

IV

It is still not clear that the inner can be inferred from the outer. Two problems are evident. First, how does one acquire the idea of an inner being (which is not even the idea of being inside an organism)? Indeed, what is that idea? Second, is the sort of inference Peirce indicated really from 'our knowledge of external facts'? Above, I weasled by talking of 'publicly accessible phenomena.' Speech is publicly accessible, but is it really externally perceivable? The child who discovers ignorance and error is responding not just to articulated sounds but to those sounds as interpreted and understood. The child has interpreted them by the rules he has learned. And is it correct to identify *interpreted* sounds with 'external facts'? To be sure, being sounds, such speech is not 'internal.' Rather, it seems a kind of hybrid.

Peirce is simply wrong that the inner is inferred from the outer. It would be more accurate to say that the private is inferred from the public or the inner from the hybrid. Such an inference is possible only to one who is, before self-consciousness, already engaged with other people in conversation, in the rule-informed production and decoding of sentences. Those sentences are not physical things or events, because they are taken with the meaning that human minds give them. Yet they are public, not private, because that meaning is shared by all those belonging to the same linguistic community.

But this is evident in the account that Peirce himself gives of dawning self-consciousness – in the same article in which he also announced that the inner must be inferred by hypothetical reasoning from external facts! Therefore, we have reason to suppose that the latter words were not intended to be taken at face value. They were the dramatic opening of a discussion more subtle than themselves. They announced, in effect, that the Cartesian doctrine of mind and body was about to be turned upside down; and that is what Peirce proceeded to do. For the fact that the inner is inferred not from the outer but from interpreted speech still leaves the outer the point of entry to the inner world. Let us see why.

A child's acquired competence in the language is manifest in the regularity of his purely physical behaviour: he utters the right sounds on enough occasions and reacts in the right way to enough of the words he hears. What *we* count as 'right' depends on the linguistic rules that *we* know, but the sounds and actions thus judged are observed in the same way any physical event is and without any prior supposition that the child knows those same rules or, indeed, any rules. And the child has learned these rules from observing similarly sparse regularities in our verbal behaviour. The child catches on quickly because, let us agree, there are linguistic universals hard-wired in his brain. Nevertheless, in either case – either in language acquisition or in identifying linguistic competence – it is uninterpreted regularities that provide the information needed. Thus, even if interpreted speech is not exactly 'external fact,' this poses no threat to the doctrine that, in the end, all that is 'inner' has to be explicated in terms of rules or habits that govern external actions: 'we have an occult nature of which and of its contents we can only judge by the conduct that it determines ...' (5.440).

This solution to the second problem gives us a handle on the first. For now we are thinking of the inner in terms of acquired rules or habits that govern humans' outer behaviour. Hence, the entities posited by hypostatic abstraction from speech acts – entities supposed responsible for those acts, and revealed in them – are *ipso facto* 'inner.' No other notion of something distinct from external fact is required. The inner, whatever it is, if it is at all, is that which, though not directly perceived, is supposed to account for certain features of observable behaviour, especially verbal behaviour.

This is not yet a view of the mind clearly distinct from behaviourism. For the behaviourist, too, is willing to venture beyond descriptions of external behaviour to the organism's habits, dispositions, and so on, that account for regularities in behaviour, and to explicate mentalistic talk as referring, really, to those dispositions. The one possible difference depends on behaviourism's continued alliance with operationalism or one of nominalism's other modern progeny. For while the latter identify a disposition with an observed regularity, Peirce took dispositions to be 'real generals' – 'would-be's' or laws irreducible to the regularities they explain. However, an analysis of self-consciousness as an act of hypostatic abstraction is committed, initially, not even to so much as an identification of the posited entity with a disposition or set of dispositions. So far as this analysis has as yet been pushed in the present essay, we are free to regard the postulated entities (by definition, 'inner') as *entia rationis*, as realities, or as fictions; and if as realities, then perhaps as dispositions and perhaps as something else.

It is because, on our analysis, the concept of the self or of the 'inner' is formed by hypostatic abstraction that it (1) is formed wholly from concepts of the outer, physical world and, yet, (2) does *not* reduce the mental to the physical, or even require that we 'model' the mental on anything physical or even on that hybrid phenomenon, speech. The peculiar power of hypostatic abstraction lies in the indirectness by which it identifies what it posits, leaving the latter open to the widest possible range of subsequent interpretation.[4]

V

Why should the supposed determinants of human behaviour, or some of them, be distinguished as 'inner,' in contradistinction to the instincts and acquired habits that govern the behaviour of the lower animals and to our own automatic reflexes, breathing, and beating hearts (not to mention the insides of clocks and the dispositional properties of substances)? This is a question to which behaviourism can give no or only a trivial answer.

An anti-behaviourist answer might invoke the fact of our being conscious. According to Peirce, however, consciousness is not unique to humans or even to animals. Rather than attempting to explain this troublesome condition, he makes consciousness, in its most basic or rudimentary form, a pervasive and fundamental feature of the world (Leibniz and Whitehead employed similar strategies). It is feeling or firstness: 'Viewing a thing from the outside, considering its relations of action and reaction with other things, it appears as matter. Viewing it from the inside, looking at its immediate character as feeling, it appears as consciousness' (6.268); 'nothing but feeling is exclusively mental' (5.492); 'The whole content of consciousness is made up of qualities of feeling ... To be conscious is nothing else than to feel' (1.317–18).

Any number of passages may be found that seem to contradict this view. As those passages quoted here are all of 1892 or later, it is possible that Peirce changed his mind; certainly the formulations quoted depend upon his later 'phaneroscopy' or phenomenological categories. But I think a deeper and more accurate, if not complete, explanation of Peirce's variations of statement is that there are, on his view, degrees or grades of consciousness, and that sometimes when he was writing about a higher grade of consciousness he used the word exclusively in reference to that grade. (Similar remarks apply to Peirce's use of the words 'mind' and 'mental.') In 1902, he wrote that 'the synechist will not believe that some things are conscious and some unconscious, unless by consciousness be meant a certain grade of feeling. He will rather ask what are the circumstances that raise this grade ...' (6.174; see also the extensive discussion of these grades, c. 1900, in 7.539–52).

The circumstances that raise the grade of consciousness are not hard to find. Think of the irritability of protoplasm versus the sensations and reactions conditioned by physiological organization. Nearly all of the extremely complex mechanisms and processes of the eye and visual cortex are beyond our consciousness and control, but they result in the exquisitely detailed images of normal vision. Not only in vision, but also in hearing and in kinaesthetic and locomotor experience, diverse sensations are organized into spatio-temporal complexes, often including a differentiation of foreground and background and an intensification of certain feelings that thus constitute a focus of attention.

Peirce claimed that consciousness 'exercises a real function in self-control' (5.493). This begins with the irritability of protoplasm, but self-control is graded much as consciousness is graded, and the two advance in grade together. The infinite detail, far, near, and wide, available to humans in vision permits an enormous variety and flexibility of response. It permits large-scale actions that are minutely precise and constantly readjusted as they are being performed. Planning is made possible by the vision of things at a distance and of the intervening space, cluttered as it is with obstacles and opportunities.

One might say, after all, that it *is* consciousness that distinguishes human life – if what is meant by this is not consciousness *per se* but the grade of consciousness. Peirce, however, spoke more often of that which parallels consciousness, namely, self-control. 'The brutes,' he said, 'are certainly capable of more than one grade of control; but it seems to me that our superiority to them is more due to our greater number of grades of self-control than it is to our versatility' (5.533).

By 'self-control,' Peirce intended both 'logical' self-control, or the control of thought over thinking, and 'ethical' self-control, or the control of thought over behaviour (5.533). These two, he said, follow 'precisely the same complicated course,' which he described as proceeding from 'inhibitions and coordinations that escape consciousness,' through instinct and training, to being one's own 'training-master,' that is, to altering one's habits of action in light of other rules. The latter may be subjected to revision in light of still more general rules, and the most general rules may be 'controlled by reference to an esthetic ideal of what is fine' (5.533). (What makes the ideal 'esthetic' is that it is not recommended to us by any rule, but is simply found attractive in itself, and thus provides a standpoint from which to criticize the most basic rules: see 1.611–13.)

Many types of animal learn from experience; that is, they alter those modes of their behaviour that have failed. Thus, dogs, seeking approval or fearing punishment, become house-broken. Becoming one's own training-master requires one to survey his habits, much as the master surveys his dog's behaviour, and to compare them to an ideal or to intermediate principles. How is such a survey and comparison possible? What grade of consciousness does that degree of self-control require? The answer brings us back again to the role of language in human life. The acquired capacity to signal our needs or circumstances to others becomes, as well, a capacity to represent them to ourselves. And one representation can be put beside another and compared. The visual and auditory discrimination and ability to remember that we share with advanced species of the lower animals enable us to examine and compare those diagrams and strings of words by which we represent the world to ourselves.

Just as physiology organizes complex sensations and focuses attention, the manipulation of words and other signs concentrates feeling, bringing diverse facts into conspicuous order. Words better than telescopes bring the distant near and permit the juxtaposition of items not found together in fact. Thus semeiotic activity builds on relatively high grades of consciousness and produces higher grades still. Rather, it *is* a higher grade of consciousness.

In becoming one's own training-master, however, there is a peculiarly self-referential use of language, a step taken beyond the use of language to represent the world, one's body, and one's actions. Peirce wrote: 'All thinking is by signs; and the brutes use signs. But they perhaps rarely think of them as signs ... Brutes use language and they seem to exercise some little control over it. But they certainly do not carry this control to anything like the same grade that we do ... One extremely important grade of thinking about thought ... is performed when something, that one has thought about any subject, is itself made a subject of thought' (5.534). But to make what one has thought (or represented) about something into a subject of thought (or object represented) is, of course, an act of hypostatic abstraction. And, indeed, in this same paragraph, Peirce proceeds immediately to his favourite example from Molière and to a discussion of the role of hypostatic abstraction in mathematics. In another place he comments,

> That wonderful operation of hypostatic abstraction by which we seem to create *entia rationis* that are, nevertheless, sometimes real, furnishes us the means of turning predicates from being signs that we think or think *through*, into being subjects thought of. We thus think of the thought-sign itself, making it the object of another thought-sign. Thereupon, we can repeat the operation of hypostatic abstraction, and from these second intentions derive third intentions. (4.549)

In this case, the entities introduced by hypostatic abstraction are not selves but, rather, thoughts, whether attributed to selves or not.

At the highest levels of self-control, however, it becomes necessary to bring diverse thoughts, sensations, emotions, decisions, resolutions, actions, and bodily parts into an integrated whole, spanning past and future, connecting decision to decision in a single plan, and making many plans into a single life.[5] This is achieved by attributing these various entities to a single underlying entity – the self that is introduced by hypostatic abstraction as *that which* thinks those thoughts, suffers those emotions, makes those decisions, commits those actions, forms and breaks those habits, and possesses that body and its parts.

The diagrams through which we explore alternative courses of action and their predictable consequences (see 1.529), and thereby gain control over the principles of our own conduct, include, conspicuously, a sign – often the word 'I' – designating this supposed entity.

The highest grades of self-control and consciousness therefore entail self-consciousness. As we have here analysed self-consciousness, it is not an immediate awareness of oneself; instead, it is an act of hypostatic abstraction in which a self is posited in relation to other entities, including those, like thoughts, that are themselves posited in abstractions made from behaviour, largely verbal behaviour. The self one is conscious of is, thus, not one's body and its actions, or is not these alone. Self-consciousness, to express it another way, is the representation by a human organism of a posited 'self' to which it represents itself as 'belonging.'

The fact that one's self is posited in an act of abstraction does not mean that one is *not* conscious of oneself. For abstraction, hypostatic or not, is itself a mode of consciousness. Furthermore, precisely because this abstraction unifies and concentrates the many feelings that make up the human organism's consciousness, that organism will be more directly, not to mention more intensely, aware of the supposed self to which it belongs than any others can be. Once the idea of the self has been established, the human seems to feel himself in all the parts of his body, in all his actions, and so on. Particular feelings will be identified as one's thoughts, emotions, and decisions.

These feelings are immediate, but the identification of them is not. In every case, one is interpreting them in light of an idea introduced on the basis of overt behaviour and abstracted from that behaviour. Feelings are immediate but do not by themselves constitute knowledge, not even knowledge of themselves. In addition, there are those unsettling moments in which we discover that in some respects others know us better than we know ourselves, and these experiences prove that the self is not known immediately by anyone.

The reason we describe the self and its furniture as uniquely 'inner' is, first, that they are not conceived of, known, or felt as physiological mechanisms or even as dispositions revealed in behavioural regularities. Instead, they are introduced by hypostatic abstractions in which they are not identified with anything at all; they are defined or identified indirectly, by their presumed relation to other things, and ultimately to overt behaviour. And, second, after those ideas have been applied to congeries of feelings, in the interpretation or conceptualization of them, then the entities they represent, no longer contentless, are felt directly, but only by that individual. It is as if the individual can look within and cannot, even if he would, share that view with anyone else. This way of talking is clearly metaphorical. And we could dismiss the experience it represents as a familiar but insignificant illusion, except for one thing: the mode of consciousness described in this metaphorical language of 'inwardness' is essential to all that makes human life distinctive and to all that gives it its unique dignity. Inwardness, or self-consciousness, is essential to the highest grades of self-control, on which human creativity and moral responsibility depend and which we have named 'freedom.'

VI

Whether the self one is thus conscious of is real is, of course, another question. I am beset by many figments and illusions, and perhaps I number among them. We have denied that the illusion, if that is what it is, is insignificant, but it may be an illusion none the less.

Peirce himself wrote with a consistent suggestiveness, perhaps elusiveness, on the topic. For example, in his long *Monist* paper of 1892, 'The Law of Mind,' he developed an idea of personality that is closely connected with if not identical to his idea of the self or person. 'Personality,' he said, 'so far as it is apprehended in a moment, is immediate self-consciousness' (6.155). Obviously, the idea of immediate self-consciousness needs to be squared with the rest of Peirce's doctrine; I suggest that he here referred to the feelings that are organized under the idea of one's self and that are immediate though not, in themselves, cognitive. Despite the immediacy with which one feels one's self or one's personality, it is, Peirce said, 'not a thing to be apprehended in an instant. It has to be lived in time; nor can any finite time embrace it in all its fullness.' The reason is that the personality is a 'coordination or connection of ideas' and, as such, a 'general idea.' Indeed, this, Peirce suggested, explains why the phenomenon of multiple personalities is possible. Each personality is a different way of organizing the human organism's behaviour, hence, of forming its system of thought and feeling. Most of us have but one such system, however incoherent and swiftly changing it may be, but some switch back and forth between entirely different systems and are not always, as one says, 'the same person.'

A personality is a coordination that is constantly evolving: 'the word coordination implies ... a teleological harmony of ideas, and in the case of personality this ... is a developmental teleology' (6.156). Apparently, Peirce had in mind the fact that we do not simply carry out fixed purposes but adopt new purposes as time goes on: 'Were the ends of a person already explicit, there would be no room for development, for growth, for life; and consequently there would be no personality' (6.157). The language used here implies that there is a gradual discovery of one's true purpose, not at first 'explicit,' and that one's personality is the consequence of choices made within this ambit of partial understanding and partial ignorance. A purpose proven impossible or, in light of another purpose, too costly to achieve, is dropped or modified; a purpose achieved that then disappoints is replaced by another that might be more satisfying. One thus seeks a harmony of purposes – a 'teleological harmony' – and, moreover, a harmony or system that will not disappoint, that will not result in unexpected frustration, boredom, regret, remorse, disgust. The course of experience by which we gradually discover new purposes, refine old ones, and bring them together under larger ideas is the same as that we have already seen described as self-control at its highest grades, wherein the most fundamental rules are tested against an 'esthetic ideal of what is fine' and these ideals themselves are modified as we gain a clearer vision of what is admirable in itself.

It follows from this that the self is not a single, simple, stable entity, but is constantly in the process of being formed. Nor is it coextensive with a single human body. On the one hand, 'a person is not absolutely an individual. His thoughts are what he is "saying to himself," that is, is saying to that other self that is just coming into life in the flow of time' (5.421). On the other hand, 'the man's circle of society ... is a sort of loosely compacted person' (5.421). For it, too, includes shared feelings and an evolving purpose. These last remarks were published in 1905. In another paper of 1892, 'Man's Glassy Essence,' Peirce wrote: 'All that is necessary, upon this theory, to the existence of a person is that the feelings out of which he is constructed should be in close enough connection to influence one another ... [I]f this be the case, there should be something like personal consciousness in bodies of men who are in intimate and intensely sympathetic communion' (6.270). The phrase 'esprit de corps' that Peirce uses a little later in the same paragraph, is so familiar an expression of this idea that one might easily fail to realize all that it implies.

These remarks give our analysis of self-consciousness a startlingly different complexion. The idea of the self introduced by hypostatic abstraction, at first peculiarly empty because of its indirect definition, gains positive content by being applied to the interpretation of feelings; these feelings then become the immediate content of self-consciousness. At the same time, however, the reality of the self is *not* thereby assured! To the contrary, one's existence as a person is seen to be highly uncertain and problematic – not philosophically, but practically. For that existence depends on there being success in the coordination of that human's feelings and actions, subordinate to a system of purposes that is itself coherent and stable.

Now we approach what may be the greatest of paradoxes. Language plays three, entirely different, roles in self-consciousness. First, all conception is linguistic in form: the criterion of an individual's having a concept of anything, including himself, is his correct use of certain words. Second, the content of the concept of selfhood is derived, directly or indirectly, from speech acts: we think of selves as those beings that can express themselves in words or as those beings that can think, and thinking we think of as that which can be expressed in words. But, third, we now discover that certain uses of words actually create and sustain the self: there would be no self if it were not for the linguistic legerdemain known as hypostatic abstraction. This, by positing a self, brings diverse feelings, habits, and actions into a single, organized whole, and this unification actually constitutes the self that is posited. In dramatic contrast to other cases, this case of hypostatic abstraction is a critical step in the creation of that which it posits. To the extent that a teleological harmony is not achieved, the self this act posits fails to be made real.

Cogito ergo sum is almost right: not that thinking that I think reveals a substantial self but that it creates an insubstantial one – one that is in process of becoming substantial. Being of 'two minds' about too many issues or about issues that are too fundamental, suffering from conflicting purposes, or being weak and irresolute in action – these constitute fissures within or a breakdown of the ego, or reveal that this human never did achieve full selfhood, responsibility, and freedom. Nor can thinking alone achieve selfhood. (The belief that it can is the characteristic error of philosophers, from which Peirce, for one, suffered.) When resolution, Hamlet-like, is sicklied o'er by the pale cast of thinking to no effect, then the self so desperately denoted is illusory.

Since the language a person learns from others is that in which he conceives of himself and thereby creates himself, it follows that each of us is intrinsically social in nature. There is no self-consciousness and, hence, no personality or ego apart from past actual relation and future potential relation to other persons. To these others one is bound by a common language, shared feelings, and joint purposes. That is why Peirce, in the passage from 7.571 that we quoted much earlier, said that 'your neighbors are, in a measure, yourself.' This suffices to ground an ethic of the Kantian type: to the extent that we place our own interests above those of others, we subvert our own personalities and diminish our personal existence. To become thoroughly immoral is not to exist as selves at all, at which point even immorality is impossible to us and we are no more than amoral beasts.

It follows, in addition, that the man considered in social and political theory is not natural man but artificial man: the creature, the creation, of a civilization. Different forms of society will produce different forms of individual, some less free and responsible than others. The several-thousand-year development of our civilization has resulted in a system of artifices and in an unnatural discipline that has proven to yield the maximum known degree of personal responsibility, individual creativity, and human freedom. The failure to maintain those artifices and that discipline risks destroying individual freedom and the society that depends upon its exercise. But one must be cautious in drawing bold conclusions from these premises. We have almost no knowledge of how specific social reforms would alter human personality: to date, all utopian schemes have failed. And the social nature of the self by no means implies that one's community is of a transcendent value, eclipsing that of the individual and making his sacrifice to state purposes permissible. To the contrary, the tendency of the present argument is towards the conclusion that the free and responsible individual, the human self, with its anguished burden of self-consciousness, is the highest good, justifying the social forms that produce it.

We come at last, then, to the question whether this self is real. The theory we have drawn from Peirce's writings is a great deal like one of those entertained yet rejected in Plato's *Phaedo* – the one that Simmias suggested, that the self is no more than a harmony of parts, like a well-tuned lyre. One cannot dismiss such a self as unreal, since every entity of any degree of complexity whatsoever is itself real only insofar as its parts are organized by and subordinated to some law. If these laws or habits of action are not real, then nothing is real. The reality of the human personality is manifest in the differences it makes: in the forms of behaviour that would not occur were there no self-consciousness. As this behaviour is transforming the face of the globe and is beginning to penetrate outer space, it has to be admitted to be among the most consequential realities we know. And this despite our individual failures to achieve the full unity of personality and degree of freedom open to us.

Yet Simmias noted that such a self will not outlast the parts it harmonizes. Did Plato express his own estimate of the harmonic theory when he allowed Simmias to say this uncontradicted? Consider that the deepest connection between Plato and Peirce is their shared teleology and that Peirce made it quite plain that selfhood depends upon subordinating feeling, thought, action, and habit to purposes neither given nor arbitrarily chosen but, through painful experience, discovered. Such a purpose, if it exists at all, exists independently of human thought.[6] Its reality lies in its power to select among fortuitous variations, shaping processes towards its own actualization. Such is a purpose embodied in teleological coordinations that endure. Its reality is, then, the reality of the selves it makes possible, even though each self contracts that purpose in a different way, adapting it to the particular conditions in which it finds itself, and interpreting it incompletely and inaccurately. But such purposes do not perish. As early as 1867, when Peirce was twenty-eight years old, he said:

Each man has his own peculiar character. It enters into all that he does. It is his consciousness and ... enters into all his cognition ... his way of regarding things; not a philosophy of the head alone – but one that pervades the whole man. This idiosyncracy is the idea of the man; and if this idea is true he lives forever ... (7.595)

Notes

1 Peirce references in the text are to the following editions: *Collected Papers of Charles Sanders Peirce*, 8 vols, edited by C. Hartshorne, P. Weiss, and A. Burks (Cambridge, Mass.: Belknap Press of Harvard University Press 1931–58); *The New Elements of Mathematics of Charles S. Peirce*, 4 vols, edited by Carolyn Eisele (The Hague: Mouton 1976). Abbreviations are as given at the beginning of this volume.
2 The following account of hypostatic abstraction is condensed from the first two sections of my article 'Hypostatic Abstraction in Empirical Science,' *Grazer Philosophische Studien* 32 (1988): 51–68.
3 Ibid., *passim*. The point I tried to make there is that, in its use in empirical science, this feature of hypostatic abstraction provides a solution to the problems posed by the incommensurability of theories.
4 Vincent Colapietro, in his ground-breaking book, *Peirce's Approach to the Self: A Semiotic Perspective on Human Subjectivity* (Albany: State University of New York Press 1989), urged that Peirce's negative characterization of the self should not be taken to exclude the possibility of a positive characterization. I think that is correct and, indeed, that this possibility is accounted for by the fact that the self, when characterized negatively, is also posited abstractly. For thus it is not characterized directly at all, and the self's intrinsic nature, like a blank, remains to be filled in, if at all, by something else. In fact, Colapietro developed Peirce's positive theory of the self without any difficulty and came to much the same view as that presented here. I am unable to say to what extent my conclusions have been influenced by Colapietro, but it would be no embarrassment if the influence were great.
5 For an extensive, penetrating, and nuanced account of Peirce's theory of emotion, of emotion's distinction from and relation to feeling, and of emotion's role in the coordination of effort, see David Savan, 'Peirce's Semiotic Theory of Emotion,' in K.L. Ketner et al., eds, *Proceedings of the C.S. Peirce Bicentennial International Congress* (Lubbock: Texas Tech University Press 1981).
6 It may seem foolish to espouse a theory that depends crucially on teleology – that outmoded and obscurantist doctrine! However, in another paper I have defended teleology not merely as being consistent with modern science but as implicated in some of its most secure theories and in some of its recent developments: T.L. Short, 'Teleology in Nature,' *American Philosophical Quarterly* 20, no. 4 (1983): 311–20.

David Savan:
In Memoriam

CALVIN G. NORMORE

David Savan played many public roles. He was a devoted friend of graduate students, and for several years administered a bursary fund to which he himself contributed heavily (and very quietly). He was a devoted teacher. He was very active in defence of political prisoners. But he was very deeply, perhaps most deeply, a philosopher.

Although he thought widely in philosophy and published on figures from Plato to Dewey, two philosophers occupied him most fully – Spinoza and Peirce. There is much which unites these two, but one thing seems to me of signal importance in explaining David Savan's interest in them. They were both, far more than they realized perhaps, the heirs of Stoicism.

David Savan was much interested in Stoicism, though as far as I know he published only one short note on the subject (in the *Encyclopedic Dictionary of Semiotics* in 1986), and the aspect of Stoicism which most interested him was the Stoic theory of signs. Of some interest here is that Stoicism did not distinguish sharply between belief and desire but thought them different ways of regarding the same cognitive state. This raised a series of puzzles about the relations among beliefs, emotions, and linguistic expressions which fascinated

Savan. It is no accident that his enduring articles on Spinoza concern Spinoza's theory of language and his account of the emotions.

But it is as an interpreter of Peirce (he was president of the Peirce Society in 1969–70) that Savan did what may well prove to be his most important philosophical work; and it is his interpretation of Peirce which was most fully and most fruitfully organized by his fascination with the interplay of belief, emotion, and linguistic expression. Savan saw Peirce not primarily as a metaphysician or epistemologist but as a semiotician. In the introduction to his own *Introduction to C.S. Peirce's Full System of Semeiotic*, his fullest study of Peirce's philosophy, he quotes Peirce as saying that 'it has never been in my power to study anything ... except as a study of semeiotic,' and characterizes it as 'a profoundly just self-appraisal.' The quotation is from Peirce's correspondence with Lady Welby, and it is that correspondence which seems to me to have centred Savan's reading of Peirce.

Savan saw Peirce first and foremost as a semiotician. That Peirce is part of the argument of his paper 'The Unity of Peirce's Thought,' which he wrote for a Festschrift for his colleague and fellow Peirce scholar Thomas Goudge. Moreover, Savan saw Peirce's categories as emerging out of his semiotics. This does not mean that he read Peirce as an idealist. On the contrary, he argued against what he called 'semiotic idealism' both as a philosophical position and as a reading of Peirce. He thought Peirce to be very clear, and rightly clear, about there being a dimension of experience which was prior to any interpretation. This insight, Savan thought, lay at the core of the Peircean category of secondness.

Savan had a worked out and novel account of Peirce's categories. For example, firstness he thought of as rather like 'Wittgensteinian logical space' (he even calls it quality space). It is 'the possibility of abstraction of isolation which is best exemplified by quality.' That the account is presented in semiotic terms is characteristic of Savan's approach to Peirce's metaphysics, an approach informed throughout by the thought that the Peircean categories both undergirded and emerged out of semiotics.

Savan was a superb and a superbly clear expositor of Peirce's semiotics, but he was not by any means an uncritical one. He thought, for example, that Peirce had pretty hopelessly confused the notion of a qualisign (very closely related to the concept of a sample); and that although Peirce saw clearly that there were no criteria of identity for qualities, he none the less was led by this confusion to think that qualisigns were very different from what he called legisigns; and so led to adopt a much more essentialist account of qualities than his own theory would support. It was again characteristic of Savan's approach that he kept clearly in mind both the letter of the text he was studying and the philosophical value of the argument it expressed. Though a powerful and persuasive scholar, Savan never forgot that scholarship was in the service of philosophy.

The book you hold in your hands grew out of a conference which David Savan helped plan but which he did not live to attend. Though it ranges widely over the whole enormous field of Peirce's thought, like Savan's own work it is centred on the logical and semantic issues which he had urged us to regard as central to that thought.

So as we work on the Peirce whom David Savan loved, let us remember him in the way most appropriate to a philosopher, by informing our own work with his.

Contributors

Douglas R. Anderson is an associate professor of philosophy at the Pennsylvania State University. His primary philosophical interests are the history of American philosophy, aesthetics, and the relationship of history and idealism. He is the author of two books on the work of Charles Peirce.

Robert W. Burch has taught at Rice University, the University of Southampton, and Queens College, City University of New York. He is currently a professor at Texas A&M University. He specializes in American philosophy and the history and philosophy of logic.

Vincent M. Colapietro is a professor of philosophy at Fordham University. He is the author of *Peirce's Approach to the Self* (State University of New York Press 1989) and *Glossary of Semiotics* (Paragon House 1993). His scholarly interests include American pragmatism, the general theory of signs, and contemporary approaches to subjectivity. His work in these and other areas has appeared in such journals as *The Journal of Philosophy, The Monist, The Journal of Speculative Philosophy, International Philosophical Quarterly*, and the *Southern Journal of Philosophy*. He is presently co-editing with Thomas Olshewsky a collection of essays, entitled *Peirce's Doctrine of Signs: Theory, Application, and Connections* (Mouton-De-Gruyter); and he has recently been named by Fordham University Press the editor of a newly launched American Philosophy Series.

Paul Forster is a professor at the University of Ottawa. His interests are in pragmatism (past or present), philosophy of language, and twentieth-century critiques of metaphysics. He has published several articles on Peirce.

Susan Haack (MA, BPhil, Oxford; PhD, Cambridge), formerly professor of philosophy at the University of Warwick, U.K., is now professor of philosophy at the University of Miami. She is the author of *Deviant Logic, Philosophy of Logics* (both Cambridge University Press), and, most recently, of *Evidence and Inquiry: Towards Reconstruction in Epistemology* (Blackwell 1993), as well as of numerous articles on the philosophy of logic and language, epistemology and metaphysics, and pragmatism. She was president of the Charles Peirce Society in 1994.

Carl R. Hausman is emeritus professor of philosophy and fellow of the Institute for the Arts and Humanistic Studies, Pennsylvania State University. He was chair of the Department of Philosophy at Penn State and has been president of the Charles S. Peirce Society. His publications include articles and a book on Peirce – *Charles S. Peirce's Evolutionary Philosophy* (Cambridge University Press 1993) – and articles and books on creativity and metaphor – *A Discourse on Novelty and Creation* (State University of New York Press 1984) and *Metaphor and Art* (Cambridge University Press 1989).

Jaakko Hintikka was born in 1929 and received his education mostly in Finland. In 1956–9 he was Junior Fellow at Harvard University, and later held professional appointments at the University of Helsinki, Stanford University, Academy of Finland, and Florida State University. Since 1990 he has been professor of philosophy at Boston University. Hintikka has published twenty-five books and about 300 scholarly articles on philosophical and mathematical logic, language theory, epistemology, philosophy of science, and history of philosophy (on Aristotle, Descartes, Leibniz, Kant, Peirce, Husserl, and Wittgenstein).

Christopher Hookway is professor of philosophy at the University of Sheffield, England. His publications include *Peirce* (1985) and a number of papers on Peirce's philosophy as well as work in the philosophy of language and epistemology, including *Quine: Language Experience and Reality* (1988) and *Scepticism* (1990).

Isaac Levi is John Dewey Professor of Philosophy at Columbia University, a member of the American Academy of Arts and Sciences and holds an honorary doctorate from the University of Lund. He is the author of *Gambling with Truth, The Enterprise of Knowledge, Hard Choices, The Fixation of Belief and Its Undoing* and many articles, some of which are anthologized in *Decisions and Revisions*. He has been preoccupied with offering a positive account of how means are adjusted to ends in cognitive decision making and other efforts to justify changing one's mind.

Calvin Normore teaches philosophy at the University of Toronto and the University of California, Los Angeles. Born in Newfoundland, he was educated at McGill and the University of Toronto and has taught at York, Princeton, Columbia, U.C. Irvine, and the Ohio State University. Most of his research is in medieval and early modern philosophy and in the history of logic. His interests, however, are much wider than that.

Helmut Pape teaches philosophy at the University of Hannover, Germany, and lives, for a part of the year, in southern France. Together with Günter Wohlfart, he founded in 1989 the Académie du Midi – Institut for Philosophy whose symposia are held in southern France. He has published extensively, especially on Peirce. Among the sixteen books which he has edited, translated (from English to German), or authored are books by H.N. Castañeda, Saul Kripke, Nicholas Rescher, a book on visual ontology, and the world's longest monograph on Peirce's semiotics. His five volumes of translations of Peirce into German include a three-volume edition of Peirce's semiotical writings (in collaboration with C.J.W. Kloesel).

Richard S. Robin is professor of philosophy at Mount Holyoke College. He is author of the *Annotated Catalogue of the Papers of Charles S. Peirce* and most recently has co-edited and co-authored *From Time and Chance to Consciousness: Studies in the Metaphysics of Charles Peirce*. Currently he is co-editor of the *Transactions of the Charles S. Peirce Society.*

Sandra B. Rosenthal is professor of philosophy at Loyola University, New Orleans. In addition to more than 125 articles on pragmatism and on the relation between pragmatism and continental philosophy, she has authored or co-authored seven books in these areas, among the most recent being *Speculative Pragmatism* and *Charles Peirce's Pragmatic Pluralism*. She is on the editorial boards of several journals and book series, and is past president of the Charles Peirce Society, the Society for the Advancement of American Philosophy, the Southern Society for Philosophy and Psychology, and the Southwest Philosophical Society; president-elect of the Metaphysical Society of America; and a past member of the executive council of the American Philosophical Association, Eastern Division.

T.L. Short taught philosophy at Kenyon College and has edited a journal for the National Association of Scholars, of which he is a vice-president. His research interests are in the philosophy of science and Peirce's philosophy. He has written on the problem of incommensurabilty, in defence of both realism and teleology, on Peirce's theory of signs, and on the bearing of the theory on the philosophy of mind; but, being of a choleric disposition, he has also addressed problems currently affecting higher education.

Jay Zeman is at the University of Florida; he is a long-time student of Peirce, pragmatism, and symbolic logic. He is interested in connections between pragmatism and Gestalt therapy, and is currently widening his horizons by studying counselling.